Church and State
in Early Modern England,
1509–1640

Church and State in Early Modern England, 1509–1640

Leo F. Solt

New York Oxford
OXFORD UNIVERSITY PRESS
1990

Oxford University Press

Oxford   New York   Toronto
Delhi   Bombay   Calcutta   Madras   Karachi
Petaling Jaya   Singapore   Hong Kong   Tokyo
Nairobi   Dar es Salaam   Cape Town
Melbourne   Auckland

and associated companies in
Berlin   Ibadan

Library of Congress Cataloging-in-Publication Data
Solt, Leo F. (Leo Frank), 1921–
Church and state in early modern England, 1509–1640 / Leo F. Solt.
p. cm.   Bibliography: p.   Includes index.
ISBN 0-19-505979-4
1. Church and state—England—History—16th century.   2. Church
and state—England—History—17th century.   3. England—Church
history—16th century.   4. England—Church history—17th century.
I. Title.
BR377.S64   1990
322′.1′0942—dc20   89-15999   CIP

2 4 6 8 9 7 5 3 1

Printed in the United States of America
on acid-free paper

For Catherine Anne
and Susan Jane

Preface

In several ways this is a most propitious time to send this volume off to press. For one thing, I have been able to use many studies, too numerous to mention but all reflected in the footnotes, which have substantiated and filled out my views of events from what they were when I first began this study many years ago. Perhaps more important than the many new and significant secondary sources that I have been able to use is the change in historical writing that has taken place during this interval. The analytical exploration of such themes, for example, as the rise of the gentry or the role of Court versus Country, have not provided us with the magic keys to unlock the mysteries of, say, the English Civil Wars (to use a fairly neutral term). A greater sympathy than hithertofore has surfaced for a selective rather than an all-inclusive narration of events. And there is also greater recognition that religion helped to shape these events. The dangers of such an approach, which I have tried to avoid, range from trying to match the massive detail of Samuel R. Gardiner to succumbing to what Richard B. Schlatter once called "the new religiosity of our time."

Although the study of church and state could be gauged in a fairly restrictive sense, I have chosen to interpret the relationship very broadly. "State" means not only the Crown and its advisers as well as Parliament and its members, but also local magistrates, common law judges, and lawyers. "Church" means all organized religion, including Catholics and Protestants—the term "Protestant" designed to embrace conforming Anglicans, whether Foxeans or Laudians, as well as all shades of Puritans, both within the Church and outside of it, whether moderates, radicals, semi-Separatists, or Separatists. Unlike the "Church" today, which has become increasingly involved in the political, economic, and social issues that in the sixteenth and seventeenth centuries were generally regarded as almost the exclusive jurisdiction of the "state," certain aspects of the Church's chief concerns in the Tudor and earlier Stuart period determined the potential areas of conflict. These areas included forms of church worship, types of ecclesiastical organization, the variations of protestant theology, and, above all, the pervasive concept of

the royal supremacy. Indeed, I have sometimes thought that this book might
be more accurately entitled "Religion and Politics in Early Modern England,
1509–1640," but that degree of comprehensiveness would have required a
volume nearly twice as long.

I have tried to give not only the main contours of the relationship of
church and state, but also my own interpretations of these momentous events.
These interpretations, both in particularity and generality, appear in chapter
and section summaries which, I hope, build a meaningful structural framework for the whole period. Each chapter contains from eight to eleven
sections, each of which amounts to a short topical chapter—a unit sufficient
unto itself. Yet, the sections in each chapter have a chronological and the-
matic unity, which justifies the chapters' length and makes the chapters
appear to be major divisions of the book.

Much of the story may be familiar to some readers, but not since Gilbert W. Child's *Church and State under the Tudors* (1890) and H. M. Gwatkin's *Church and State in England to the Death of Queen Anne* (1917) has
anyone tried to synthesize the current scholarship on the subject in quite the
same way. Claire Cross' book, *Church and People, 1450–1660* (1976) comes
the closest, but her emphasis is different from mine, as her subtitle *The
Triumph of the Laity in the English Church* indicates. Enough important
results have appeared since Child's book appeared nearly a century ago, and
since Gwatkin's book appeared seventy years ago, to make a fresh attempt to
write about this fascinating topic worthwhile.

A brief glance at the footnotes and the selective bibliography will indicate
that I have drawn heavily from both primary and secondary sources. The
primary sources include much of the printed documentation available as well
as a very limited use of manuscript sources. The printed materials include the
writings of secular and religious figures of major and minor significance and
the proceedings of councils, parliaments, courts, conferences, and churches,
among much else. The secondary-source bibliography is select in that it
contains only about one-fourth to one-third of the articles and books I have
consulted at one time or another in preparation for this study. The attempt to
synthesize the evidence of the primary sources with the findings of the
secondary sources has proved to be the most challenging and, ultimately, the
most rewarding aspect of drafting this study.

In the course of writing this work, I have incurred a number of debts to
other laborers in the vineyard. Stanford Lehmberg of the University of
Minnesota read an earlier version of chapter one; Winthrop Hudson of the
Colgate-Rochester Divinity School, chapter two; Leland Carlson of the Huntington Library and Roger B. Manning of Cleveland State University, chapter
three; Maurice Lee of Rutgers University, chapter four; and my colleague,
Paul Lucas, chapter five. Martin Havran of the University of Virginia and
Martin Ridge of the Huntington Library, my former colleague at Indiana
University, gave me critical readings of the entire manuscript. I am indebted
to all of these scholars for their helpful suggestions as well as to a number of
former graduate students who have read portions of the manuscript at one

time or another. I have especially benefitted from the suggestions of Sheila Cooper, my former student and colleague during my tenure as dean of the Graduate School at Indiana University, who commented extensively on all chapters. I am also grateful for the research support I have received from Indiana University during two sabbatical leaves, from two summers of research at the Huntington Library and one summer at the Folger Library, and from a year's fellowship in Britain from the Simon J. Guggenheim Foundation. Finally, my wife Mary Ellen has been very supportive throughout all stages of the research and writing.

Bloomington, Indiana   L. F. S.
August 1989

Contents

Church and State
in Early Modern England,
1509–1640

1

The Henrician Schism

Despite the efforts of Rome to set up a papal hierocracy in England during the early middle ages, the Crown had gained a great deal of control over the English Church during the later middle ages. Evidence of that control is abundant by the beginning of the sixteenth century. For example, nominees of the king filled the bishoprics and minor benefices most of the time. Moreover, very few appeals could go from English courts to the papal curia without the king's permission. But in one important area Henry VIII did not control the Church: appeals to Rome in matrimonial cases. When Henry decided to divorce Catherine of Aragon and to wed Anne Boleyn, he and his ministers formulated a theory of royal supremacy based upon an "imperial" concept of immunity from all papal control. After forcing the English clergy into submission, Henry and the Reformation Parliament, under the guidance of Thomas Cromwell, passed legislation which permitted Henry, now Supreme Head of the Church, to take over those remaining areas of Church jurisdiction that had eluded him and his predecessors. In the process, Henry not only appointed Cromwell as Vicegerent of the Church in order to bring about some religious reform, but also dissolved the monasteries, together with Parliament's aid. In addition, the King approved some formularies of belief in the 1540s, notably the Six Articles Act and the King's Book, which echoed his earlier conservative theological sentiments. To what degree had Henry changed church-state relationships after 1509, when he came to the throne, or in 1529, when the Reformation Parliament first met? Was Henry's program essentially a minor break with Rome, or was it a major religious revolution? In either case, just what did the royal supremacy, which Henry had formally assumed with the title of Supreme Head of the Church, specifically mean?

The Medieval Background

The harmony that existed between church and state when Henry VIII came to the throne contrasted sharply with the border warfare that had characterized their relationship in the twelfth and thirteenth centuries. To be sure, a few skirmishes took place in the reign of Henry VII, but they were by no means of the same magnitude as those between Henry I and Archbishop Anselm over lay investitures, between Henry II and Archbishop Becket over benefit of clergy, or between John and Pope Innocent III over the appointment of an archbishop. The Church had won several of those earlier battles on the boundary line between church and state, and the popes and archbishops regarded these victories as a crucial part of their war of liberation against the intrusions of the state into the realm of religious affairs, sometimes called caesaropapism. Until the investiture controversy, English monarchs made no claims in the realm of spiritual affairs, but all through the middle ages they had consistently argued that many aspects of ecclesiastical affairs fell within their natural boundaries. They claimed that procedures concerning taxation, appointment, appeals, and punishment of the clergy fell under their hegemony. The Church, after all, controlled about one-third of the land of England, and its leading officeholders, especially the bishops, were often important civil servants of the Crown.

Inspired by the success of the independence movement, Pope Innocent III, under the banner of the plentitude of pontificial power, *plenitudo potestatis*, boldly extended the Church's claims into what the state had regarded as part of the temporal realm. Through a papal hierocracy, the pope hoped to make the interests of the state subservient to those of the Church. John, forced to pledge homage and fealty to Innocent, surrendered all of England as a papal fief to Rome. But the papacy, like the Crown, had limited goals. Neither wanted total conquest. The pope never attempted to govern England as he did the papal states in Italy, nor did the pope's papalocaesarism in the reign of John's son, Henry III, amount to anything much more than papal legates acting in response to advice from the king's secular counselors. In the fourteenth and fifteenth centuries, an aggressive English monarchy threw off the hollow claims of the papal hierocracy, and the Church, weakened by the Babylonian Captivity and the papal schism, relinquished all of that domain it had previously liberated, and more.

Taxation was one area of contention between church and state. Ever since Anglo-Saxon times, English monarchs had sent the Rome-Scot (later known as Peter's Pence)—a tax of a penny on each hearth—to Rome to provide for an English school in Rome, but the tax later became fixed at just under £200 annually. With Edward II's reign, the papal court also collected annates or first fruits (the first year's income from newly appointed archbishops and bishops). But in 1414 Parliament limited annates to the "customary level" because the papal power to transfer bishops from one see to another had greatly increased papal revenue. In addition, an annual tribute of a thousand marks had been paid to the papacy since the reign of John; but in 1366, when Edward III and Parliament repudiated the papal claim to feudal overlordship, payment of the annual tribute ceased. After the thirteenth century, the clergy paid annually a papal tax of a tenth of their annual income; but Edward II, jealous of this flight of English gold, regularly retrieved more than

90 percent of it. When Pope Boniface VIII issued his famous bull, *Clericis Laicos* (1296), forbidding the clergy to pay taxes to temporal rulers without papal permission, the province of Canterbury clergy, in convocation assembled, refused a royal tax request. When Edward I outlawed the clergy by placing them outside his civil jurisdiction, Archbishop Robert Winchelsea advised individual clergymen to act according to their consciences. The clerics capitulated; the king had his tax, and the pope modified his bull to provide for royal taxation, but only in cases of "perilous necessity." Although some of the lost papal revenue was made up from the granting of dispensations and other special privileges, England was no longer called the "milch-cow" of the papacy.[1]

The appointment of archbishops and bishops was the most important battleground between the church and state. The Anglo-Saxon concept of theocratic monarchy, in which the king possessed some priestly power, revived briefly during the investiture controversy in the reigns of William Rufus and Henry I. The anonymous York Tractates (1100) claimed that the king possessed a superior sacerdotal power in selecting the bishops of the Church. But Henry I, at the insistence of Pope Gregory VII and Archbishop Anselm, surrendered the priestly right of the Crown to invest the bishops with the seals of their office. Although Henry thereby gave up lay investiture, and with it the last remnants of theocratic monarchy in England, he continued to nominate all bishops by a letter missive even though the cathedral monks required a formal election, called by a royal writ, *congé d'élire*. In addition, he demanded homage and fealty from all bishops in exchange for their temporalities (clerical income from landed properties).[2]

The most dramatic challenge to the royal powers of clerical appointment arose in John's reign. Neither John's nominee for archbishop of Canterbury nor the man elected by the monks at Canterbury was acceptable to Pope Innocent III, whose choice was Stephen Langton. When John refused Langton entry into England, the pope stopped all ecclesiastical functions in the realm with an interdict, excommunicated John, and threatened to depose him with an invasion from France. By capitulating to Rome, John became the vassal of Innocent III, thereby shrewdly avoiding an invasion from King Philip Augustus in a war with France that was going badly for England. John's ecclesiastical charter of 1214, as well as the first chapter of Magna Charta in 1215, provided for the free election of all bishops and abbots by the churches and monasteries. He no longer issued the letter missive nor denied the *congé d'élire*, which had to be obtained from him. With only a few exceptions over the next century, neither the papacy nor the Crown attempted to interfere with free canonical elections to major benefices.

In the early fourteenth century, the papacy, which Frenchmen would dominate for the next hundred years, began to provide bishops on a scale unknown to the thirteenth century. By the middle years of the fourteenth century, however, the king nominated bishops to the pope after a cathedral election of the royal nominee, but papal bulls of provision and consecration were necessary before consecration of the bishops could take place. If the cathedral chapter differed with the king over the nominee, the pope usually sided with the Crown; and, in the last analysis, the king could exercise his regalian right to revoke the temporalities of the see. As a result, the king usually was able to raise any able counselor to whatever vacant bishopric he wished. In 1345 Pope Clement VI remarked, "If the king of England were to petition for his ass to be made a bishop, we could not say him Nay." [3]

Second only in importance to the struggle over the appointments of bishops was the contest over the appointments to minor benefices of the Church. Of particular interest to the pope were the dignities and prebends of many cathedral chapters and collegiate churches, which consisted of the offices of dean, precentor, chancellor, treasurer, archdeacons, and canons. Whenever any of these offices became vacant, the local bishop usually possessed the advowson—the right to fill the vacancy with a person of his own choice. The Crown, too, became involved in the appointment of individuals to the minor benefices, because English kings traditionally had claimed the advowson when a bishopric was vacant. The absentee holders of these minor benefices were often Italians that the papacy appointed in the thirteenth century to provide income for its expanding bureaucracy. When Innocent IV wished to present his nephew to a canonry at Lincoln in 1253, the bishop, Robert Grosseteste, proclaimed, "With all filial respect and obedience I will not obey, I resist, I rebel." Sometimes the pope would excommunicate those who resisted him or, in the case of bishops, transfer them to other sees.[4]

During the Hundred Years War (1338–1453), the strongest opposition to papal provisions, especially against absentee Frenchmen, came from laymen in Parliament. Parliament passed two statutes of Provisors (1351, 1390) which stated that if patrons, as in the appointment to minor benefices, or electors, as in the election of bishops, did not fill a church office because of a papal provision or appointment, then the king, as "patron paramount," should fill the vacancy. The king now could pose as the champion of the Church against the papacy—"we must protect you against yourselves." In a futile gesture, Pope Boniface IX annulled the statutes.

The Concordat of 1398 between Boniface IX and Richard II reaffirmed the procedures already established for bishoprics, and they achieved a working compromise for the minor benefices—roughly two appointments for the king to one for the pope. Evidence indicates that papal provisioning to minor benefices, particularly of aliens, subsequently declined. In the third decade of the fifteenth century, Pope Martin V brought pressure upon Archbishop Henry Chichele to secure the repeal of those "execrable" statutes of Provisors, but Henry VI impounded a papal bull to deprive the reluctant archbishop of his legatine powers. "It is not the pope," Martin V concluded, "but the king of England who governs the church in his dominion." [5]

The conflict between church and state over papal provisions sometimes resulted in appeals from English civil courts to the papal curia in Rome. Royal restrictions on appeals to Rome dated from the days of William the Conqueror. Appeals to Rome over advowsons first became important in the reign of Henry II. The advowsons for England's roughly 9,000 parish churches usually belonged to the clergy as might be expected, but a large number, unlike the minor benefices, also belonged to lay patrons. According to clause one of the Constitutions of Clarendon (1164)—a document which, according to Henry II, restored the "ancient customs" of the realm in ecclesiastical matters—only the civil courts should settle disputes over patronage between laymen, or between laymen and clergy. After all, the civil courts generally viewed the advowson as a piece of real property.

To enforce this advowson clause as well as give substance to related jurisdictional disputes between the civil and ecclesiastical courts, which had been separate since William the Conqueror's day, the Crown issued writs of prohibition. The writs of prohibition had the effect of limiting jurisdiction of the ecclesiastical courts, but these courts also handled many other matters. These other matters included mortuary and testamentary cases; cases dealing with heresy, perjury, defamation, and tithes; some cases of sexual misconduct such as incest, adultery, and fornication; all cases involving clerical felonies, including murder, robbery, and rape, which, because of "benefit of clergy," did not call for the death penalty; and, finally, cases of marriage and divorce, which became so important to Henry VIII. For these ecclesiastical matters, clause eight of the Constitutions of Clarendon stated that appeals beyond the archbishop's court required the consent of the king, but this clause dropped out at the reconciliation of Avranches in 1172. In 1279, Archbishop John Pecham, with strong support from Pope Nicholas V, attacked writs of prohibition as an infringement upon the independence of the Church; but when he posted Magna Charta as a symbol of that independence, he later rescinded it.

The popes of the fourteenth century never seriously challenged advowsons for parish churches, where many laymen were also patrons; but when royal courts upset the papal provisions to minor benefices, where the bishops were patrons, appeals to Rome increased. The Crown and Parliament responded by using the advowson clause of the Constitutions of Clarendon as the basis for the statutes of Praemunire (1353, 1365, 1393). Upon pain of outlawry, these statutes prevented the appeal of disputed advowsons to Rome as well as the entry into England of any instruments of papal authority for the transfer of bishops and for sentences of excommunication. The most important of the statutes of Praemunire, the loosely-worded statute of 1393, did not bring forth any action from the papacy as the statutes of Provisors had done. Nor did it become much more than a dead letter, except in the case of Cardinal Henry Beaufort, who wanted to recover "the pristine liberty of the Church" in the fifteenth century. Still in all, appeals to Rome tended to decline as papal provisions also declined.[6]

John Wycliffe, the greatest English heretic of the age, was also the greatest critic of papal supremacy. As a forerunner of the Reformation, Wycliffe relied heavily on the authority of the Bible, urged its accessibility to laymen through an English translation, rejected the doctrines of transubstantiation and clerical celibacy, and conceptualized a church of the predestined elect. Together with such men as Marsiglio of Padua and William of Ockham, Wycliffe severely criticized the papal hierocracy as set forth by Boniface VIII in his famous bull *Unam Sanctam* (1302). Pope Boniface had stated that obedience to Rome in both spiritual and temporal affairs—the celebrated theory of the two swords—was a prerequisite for eternal salvation. Wycliffe argued that the temporal power or dominion of the king was superior to the spiritual power or dominion of the pope.[7]

Here was a theory of sovereignty made to order for the English monarchy; it was also one that was close to the claims of Richard II for monarchy by divine right. However, Richard's successor, Henry IV, at the urging of Archbishop Thomas Arundel, introduced legislation into Parliament against Wycliffe's followers, the Lollards. The statute, *De Haeretico Comburendo* (1401), provided that the sheriff would burn unlicensed preachers who refused to abjure their heretical views when brought before the ecclesiastical courts. And a new heresy statute in 1414 provided for indictment in civil courts, trial in ecclesiastical courts, and punishment in civil courts. This was close to the same procedure as that set forth in clause three of the Constitutions of Clarendon, which Henry II had failed to get Archbishop Thomas Becket to accept in the case of clergymen who claimed benefit of clergy. Having once opposed the state for meting out the death penalty where the infringements of the law—felonies—were indisputably of a temporal nature, the Church now condoned the state's award of the death penalty in matters where the infringements of the law—heresies—were indisputably of a spiritual nature. The Lollards, who questioned the spiritual authority of the pope, became the victims of a law which allowed the monarch to punish for spiritual causes.

At the beginning of the sixteenth century, church and state in England had come to an understanding that the Crown's authority in religious affairs was limited. The Crown did not try to interfere in spiritual matters. The Church's supremacy in matters of theology, liturgy, and the cure of souls was essentially unchallenged. Consequently, there was a universal Church, and the pope was the head of that Church. When the Lollard heresy appeared in the fourteenth century, the Crown and Parliament readily assisted the Church in applying sanctions rather than defining doctrine. Still, in doing so, they became partners in a kind of punishment which hitherto had not been within their jurisdiction.

In ecclesiastical affairs, however, the situation was quite different. Although the king permitted some revenue to flow from England to Rome, it no longer amounted to what it had been in earlier centuries. The king could not make appointments directly to Church offices, except those for which he held the advowson, but he was usually able to get his candidates into the bishoprics and minor benefices in spite of papal provisioning. Despite the fact that the convocations of the clergy, both at Canterbury and York, technically could assemble without royal permission and make their own canon laws without the king's assent, a royal writ almost invariably summoned them, and they acted in accordance with instructions from royal commissioners.

Although English synods or convocations enacted Roman canon law—papal ordinances and resolutions of general councils—English ecclesiastical courts neither enacted nor carried out some parts of it, and they sometimes expressed their opposition through petitions for papal dispensations. A number of areas of jurisdiction in the Church courts remained untouchable to the king, but he was able to curtail their power through the use of writs of prohibition. The king did not attempt to prevent all appeals from English courts to the papal curia, but he succeeded in diminishing the number of disputes over advowsons. Although kings sold licenses allowing laymen to give land to the Church, the Statute of Mortmain (1279) prevented such gifts as a means of building up clerical endowments because they permanently withdrew land from the secular community. The Crown would not allow any large degree of Church independence, whether by archbishops or popes, in areas that it regarded as its own legitimate concern.

Unquestionably, there had been a steady growth in the power of the state over the Church since the twelfth and thirteenth centuries—so much so that the statutes of Provisors asserted the existence of "The Holy Church of England" as one of several national churches within the universal Church.[8] Furthermore, the Crown exercised a control over papal policy in some of the most crucial aspects of the realm of ecclesiastical affairs. Symbolic of this increased royal control over the Church in the later middle ages was the location of the official residence of the archbishop of Canterbury. As the papacy's official residence, whether at Rome or Avignon, was dependent upon the policies of the French monarchy, that of England's leading archbishop was located, not at Canterbury—the seat of the largest province—but at Lambeth Palace, just across the Thames from Westminster, the center of civil government.[9]

The Ascendancy of Wolsey

When Henry VIII came to the throne in 1509, England enjoyed, among the countries of Europe, a very special relation to the papacy. Unlike most of the continental countries, it generally respected the spiritual leadership of the Italian popes without serious questioning despite the control that the Crown increasingly exercised over the ecclesiastical concerns of the Church. England also possessed a very strong tradition which allowed the episcopal bench a forceful role in the affairs of government. Among the various bishops who had held secular office under Henry's father, perhaps the most eminent was the archbishop of Canterbury, William Warham, who served as lord chancellor. Yet, despite these indications of a positive relationship between church and state, a shrewd observer would have noted some signs of potential distress. Lollardy, which had gone underground during the early fifteenth century, began to re-emerge, especially in the north. And Christian humanism, which in the earlier years of the reign of Henry VII had made a significant appearance with Thomas Linacre, William Grocyn, and John Colet, would soon contribute to England its two finest exponents of Church reform,

Desiderius Erasmus and Thomas More. Other menaces to the stability of church-state relationships were the Hunne and Standish affairs.

Anticlericalism sparked the first dramatic confrontation between church and state in the reign of Henry VIII. The bishop of London, Richard Fitzjames, ordered the arrest of Richard Hunne, a well-to-do London merchant, for heresy in December, 1514. A search of Hunne's house had revealed a Lollard Bible. While awaiting trial in the prison of the bishop, the Lollard's Tower, Dr. William Horsey, the bishop's chancellor, found Hunne dead from hanging. The bishop's court, alleging that Hunne had taken his own life because of a guilty conscience over his heresy, speedily declared him to have been a contumacious heretic and delivered his body to the civil authorities for burning in accordance with the statute of 1401. Hunne's friends declared that his heresy had consisted of refusing to surrender the bearing sheet of his deceased infant son as a mortuary fee three years earlier, of bringing a slander suit against a rector's assistant for not holding an evensong service while he was present, and of having invoked the statute of Praemunire in the court of King's Bench in order to stop the Church from collecting the mortuary fee. A coroner's jury, ignoring the finding of heresy in the bishop's court, found Hunne's jailors and Horsey guilty of murder by strangulation. The public seemed to believe that Hunne "was made a heretic for suing a Praemunire," and Bishop Fitzjames observed that anticlerical Londoners would condemn any cleric "though he were as innocent as Abel." Thomas More, who believed Hunne was a Lollard holding John Wycliffe's beliefs, thought that Hunne was not only a heretic but also a suicide. The threatened trial of Dr. Horsey and the jailors in a secular court raised the question of benefit of clergy.[10]

Recent parliamentary legislation had dealt with the subject of benefit of clergy, and the renewal of discussion on this topic, both in and out of Parliament, brought the active intervention of the king into the affairs of the Church. Since the reign of Henry II, the privilege of benefit of clergy had been extended to such minor Church officers as doorkeepers, readers, jailors, subdeacons, and, finally, to practically anyone who could read. Parliament had passed an act in 1489 ordering all clergymen—except those in major orders—convicted of a felony to be branded on the thumb so that the privilege could not be claimed again. A temporary act in 1512 had restricted benefit of clergy only to those in major orders (bishops, priests, and deacons), thereby reducing substantially the number of people who, under the act of Henry VII, had been allowed to claim it. In the midst of the furor over the Hunne affair, Richard Kidderminster, abbot of Winchcombe, denounced the act of 1512 as an infringement upon the liberties of the Church—"Touch not mine annointed." Only a few months before, Pope Leo X, in rhetoric reminiscent of Innocent III, had declared that no law, human or divine, could claim authority over the clergy.

At a disputation with Kidderminister before the king, Dr. Henry Standish, Warden of the Grey Friars, argued that no papal decree could give immunity to clergymen in minor orders. Summoned to appear before the

Canterbury Convocation of the Clergy for heresy, Standish appealed to the king. In the presence of a large assembly of church and state officials gathered at Blackfriars, the king's judges declared that the members of the convocation had made themselves liable to a *praemunire* for having appealed to a foreign jurisdiction. Moreover, the judges insisted that the passage of legislation in Parliament did not require the presence of bishops and mitered abbots, who held seats in the House of Lords as well as in the upper chambers of the two convocations of the clergy.

At a later session at Baynard's Castle, Thomas Wolsey, who was rising rapidly in the service of both church and state, suggested that the question of benefit of clergy be referred to Rome for a decision because "in the opinion of the clergy the convening of ecclesiastics before temporal judges was directly contrary to the laws of God." Henry VIII removed any doubt about his own views by declaring, "We are, by the sufferance of God, King of England, and the Kings of England in times past never had any superior but God; know, therefore, that we will maintain the rights of the Crown in this matter like our progenitors."[11] These phrases did not give warning of the schism to come; they should not be taken to mean much more than a flamboyant statement of what had been the royal position, *vis à vis* the Church, at the beginning of the Tudor era. Horsey, although not brought to trial, was fined and forced to leave London; Standish became bishop of St. Asaph three years later; no referral went to Rome; and Wolsey made a partial submission on behalf of the Church. But Parliament did not renew the act of 1512. The whole episode, however, set a precedent. A church court could not move against an individual who appealed to a parliamentary statute that impinged upon canon law. Significantly, the Church failed to take any action to reform itself.

Henry VIII's support of the ecclesiastical position of Henry Standish conformed with the views of late medieval English monarchs; the same was true of his criticism of Martin Luther. Luther, like Wycliffe more than a century earlier, differed greatly with the Crown over theological matters. In fact, Wycliffe and Luther held much ground in common, but the Englishman did not share the German reformer's great emphasis upon the doctrine of justification by faith. Luther believed that man's salvation was beyond his own will, and dependent only upon the will of God. Henry VIII did not take issue with Luther, as did Erasmus of Rotterdam, by proclaiming the freedom of the human will so that man's rational faculties could bring about his salvation. But the king did believe that Luther was giving too much credit to faith and too little to the sacraments.

At the suggestion of Cardinal Wolsey, Henry chose to respond to Luther by shaping into its final form a work entitled, *Assertio Septem Sacramentorum* (1521), dedicated to Pope Leo X. In addition to its defense of the seven sacraments, including, ironically, statements about the indissolubility of marriage, the *Assertio* included a chapter, perhaps from an earlier manuscript of Henry's, on papal authority. In it Henry referred to the pope as the "Chief Priest and Supreme Judge upon earth."[12] While Henry worked on this part,

Sir Thomas More warned him against raising the pope's authority too high. "I think it best, therefore," said More, "that that place be amended and his authority more slenderly touched." But Henry would have none of his friend's advice. "We are so much bounden unto the See of Rome," the king replied in words that he was to contradict within a few years, "that we cannot do too much honor unto it." When More reminded Henry of the restrictions placed upon papal authority by the statute of Praemunire, the king replied: "Whatsoever impediment be to the contrary, we will set forth that authority to the uttermost. For we received from that See our crown imperial."[13] Both Innocent III and Boniface VIII would have been delighted at this unusual statement of pontifical power by an English king. Leo X, especially pleased, dubbed Henry "Defender of the Faith." When considering the true relationship of church and state at this time, one must have even greater reservations about this large exaggeration of papal power in Henry's response to Luther, primarily for external consumption, than to the small exaggeration of royal power in the Standish case, primarily for internal consumption.

The long career of Thomas Wolsey in the service of the king is a good indication that Henry was not really interested in putting into practice the pontifical power which he had raised so high in the *Assertio*. Like the great ecclesiastical statesmen of preceding reigns, Henry Beaufort and John Morton, Wolsey held some prestigious posts in both church and state. Created archbishop of York and cardinal, Wolsey became Henry's lord chancellor as well, the highest post in the civil government. At the request of Henry in 1518, Leo X appointed Wolsey as legate *a latere*. Thus he was empowered to speak as a special envoy from Rome, a place, incidentally, where Wolsey had never been. Wolsey's own attempts to become pope in the 1520s ended in failure. He spent the bulk of his energies as a diplomat, far less concerned with following a pro-papal policy than with the royal quest, albeit fruitless, for peace in Europe. As legate in England, he surmounted the otherwise superior ecclesiastical jurisdiction of the archbishop of Canterbury, William Warham; deprived ecclesiastical patrons of the use of advowsons by means of papal bulls; made appointments to Church benefices by using papal provisions; suppressed some monasteries with the consent of the pope; and, as papal legate and lord chancellor, eased some of the friction between the royal and ecclesiastical courts over writs of prohibition and bulls of excommunication.

But Wolsey did not try to bring papal hierocracy to England by his combination of religious and temporal authority. In ecclesiastical as well as foreign affairs he served the king, not the pope. Yet, he did not enhance the royal supremacy at the expense of the Church in ecclesiastical matters, even though he gave the clergy some hard knocks. Nor did he lay the groundwork for the break with Rome, except through the antipapal attitude that his actions engendered. The supreme test of Wolsey's legatine power, and indeed of his continued favor with the king, came when Henry VIII asked him in 1527 to persuade the pope to give Henry a divorce from his queen, Catherine of Aragon.

The King's Great Matter

The question of the validity of the king's marriage initiated the Crown's supreme crisis with the papacy. Although the chronology is difficult to establish, Henry became infatuated in the mid-1520s with Anne Boleyn, a lady-in-waiting at court who refused to become his mistress. At about the same time he lost interest in Queen Catherine, realizing, among other things, that she had not and most likely would not provide the desired male heir to the throne. In fact, the King became convinced that he had been living in sin for fifteen years or so.

Henry found solace in the biblical injunction of Leviticus 20:21, which stated that if a man shall take his brother's wife, they shall be childless. And Henry had taken his brother's widow. Also, though the queen had borne a healthy daughter (Mary) amid several miscarriages, stillbirths, and infants who had died shortly after birth, no son survived to carry on the Tudor dynasty. Nonetheless, Catherine's supporters could easily cite a biblical verse, Deuteronomy 25:5, that seemed appropriate to the situation: "When brethren dwell together, and one of them dieth without children, the wife of the deceased shall not marry to another; but his brother shall take her, and raise up seed for his brother." The most commonly accepted reconciliation of the two Biblical passages—taken from St. Augustine, reinforced by Pope Innocent III, and held by Thomas More—was to forbid a marriage between a man and his brother's wife, as provided in Leviticus, except where the brother had died childless, as provided in Deuteronomy. Henry's case as determined by biblical precedent was extremely weak.

Technically speaking, Henry did not seek a divorce. He wanted an annulment of a 1503 dispensation from Pope Julius II, which had allowed the young king to marry his brother's widow. The preamble to that dispensation stated that his brother Arthur's marriage with Catherine had "perhaps" been consummated. The main text, however, based upon divine law, proceeded to remove Catherine and Henry from any impediment of affinity, which could only have arisen from consummation of the marriage to Arthur. The dispensation said nothing about any impediment of public honesty between either of the parties and the other's relatives which could have been created by the church-made marriage contract. As long as Henry claimed that Arthur and Catherine had consummated their marriage, it was very difficult to challenge the pope's annulment action, except by seeming to challenge the very papal power of dispensation itself.[14]

If, however, Henry had taken the clue from the preamble that the marriage had "perhaps" not been consummated, then he could have made the argument that there had not been any impediment of affinity for Julius to remove. And without any impediment of affinity, canon law would have necessitated a specific statement dispensing for the impediment of public honesty. Since Julius II had not done this, Henry could have argued that his marriage to Catherine was invalid. This line of argument would have allowed

Henry to challenge the papal interpretation of the facts, as presented by the English government in 1503, rather than the principle of papal power.

And what were the facts about the consummation of the marriage between Catherine and Arthur? There was, as might be expected, some partly remembered boudoir gossip and adolescent bravado suggesting that Arthur and Catherine, both aged fourteen, had consummated their marriage. Catherine's father, King Ferdinand of Spain, thought that it had been consummated, but Catherine's dying mother, Queen Isabella, did not. It was at the latter's insistence, as well as that of King Henry VII, that the word "perhaps" had been inserted into the preamble of the papal bull. Before the divorce proceedings began, Henry VIII had confessed several times to Catherine's virginity at the time of his marriage, but after the divorce proceedings had begun the king told the imperial ambassador, Eustace Chapuys, that he had only been jesting on those occasions. Catherine never wavered in asserting her virginity when she came to Henry's marriage bed, and never more so than at the legatine court held at Blackfriars in the summer of 1529. On that occasion, in the presence of a silent king, she spoke as follows:

> When you had me at the first, I take God to be my judge, I was a true maid without touch of man, and whether it be true or no I put it to your conscience. If there be any just cause by the law that you can allege against me, either of dishonesty or any other impediment, to banish and put me from you, I am well content to depart, to my great shame and dishonor. And if there be none, then here I most lowly beseech you let me remain in my former estate and to receive justice at your princely hands.

Two months after the adjournment of the legatine court, Henry told Catherine at dinner one evening that he was content with "the fact that you were not known by the prince my brother and that he had nothing to do with you." But, he added, "you are not my wife for all that since the bill did not dispense" the impediment of public honesty.[15]

As if Henry did not have enough canonical problems with Catherine, his situation was further complicated by canonical problems with Anne Boleyn. Henry previously had taken Anne's sister, Mary Boleyn, as his mistress, thereby raising again an impediment of affinity. In addition, Anne's having an earlier clandestine fiancé, perhaps even a clandestine husband, raised again the possibility of an impediment of public honesty. But first the matrimonial problems with Catherine had to be solved.[16]

Papal vacillation and royal frustration characterized the early negotiations over the divorce. While Wolsey questioned Henry in a collusive court action at Westminster about why he had lived in sin for some eighteen years—an action whose outcome in any event Rome would have had to review—the troops of Emperor Charles V, king of Spain and the nephew of Catherine, had captured Pope Clement VII and sacked the Eternal City. When this news arrived in England in early June, 1527, Wolsey adjourned his court at Westminster. He hoped that Clement's humiliation had increased Henry's chances with the pope. Wolsey left for France in the summer of 1527 with a bold plan to become the papal vicegerent, but a lack of cooperation from the Italian cardinals, plus the pope's release, thwarted Wolsey's efforts for temporary control of the papacy. In the autumn of 1527, a royal envoy, William Knight, obtained a dispensation from the pope for Henry to marry Anne, but only if the marriage with Catherine should be declared invalid—a proviso indicative of the great pressure that Charles exerted upon Clement in behalf of his aunt.

After months of haggling, the king's secretary, Stephen Gardiner, succeeded in getting the pope to grant a general commission so that the case could be heard by Cardinal Wolsey and Cardinal Lorenzo Campeggio, absentee bishop of Salisbury and protector of England at the papal curia. The general commission did not decree, as the king had hoped, that the cardinals should rule in Henry's favor. Thus, Wolsey had Gardiner obtain a secret decretal commission, which would have permitted such a ruling, but the decretal commission did not state whether the decision rendered would be final. The success of French arms, which had allowed the pope to move in Henry's direction, turned to defeat before the Spanish armies of Charles V, and so the pope ordered Campeggio, while still enroute to England from Italy, to procrastinate so that no verdict at all would be given. The gout-ridden Campeggio delayed opening proceedings by urging Catherine to enter a nunnery, which she would not consent to do, and the pope urged the king to marry Anne, thereby committing bigamy. Such a proposal was only a ruse by the pope to permit him to escape responsibility and to avoid rendering a decision.

In early March, 1529, the queen appealed to Clement to have her case tried in Rome instead of England. Meanwhile, the aforementioned legatine court at long last assembled at Blackfriars in late May, and Catherine begged Henry not to cast her aside. The queen cited Rome as the only true arbiter of her case, but the court then declared her contumacious. The proceedings lagged until July 23 when Campeggio, true to the pope's command, adjourned the court in accordance with the summer recess of the papal court. Wolsey learned the day before that Clement had revoked the case to Rome. "By the Mass!" exclaimed the duke of Suffolk, "now I see that the old said saw is true, that there was never legate nor cardinal that did good in England."[17]

Henry did not have to look far to find a scapegoat for the fiasco. After a brief sojourn at York, Wolsey, summoned before the Court of King's Bench for having used his legatine power in defiance of the medieval statutes of Provisors and Praemunire, died on his way from York to Westminster to attend the court. On his deathbed he opined, "If I had served God as diligently as I have done the king, he would not have given me over in my grey hairs."[18]

There seems to be very little doubt from all of the evidence that Catherine was still a virgin when she married Henry VIII. But even though Henry persisted in publicly maintaining that she was not, the papal bull had covered that contingency. The contingency had been met by the insertion of the word "perhaps" before the word "consummated" into the papal bull, thereby making possible the removal of the impediment of affinity from the marriage of Catherine and Arthur. What appears to have been crucial later was the realization of the earlier omission in the papal bull of the removal of any impediment of public honesty between Catherine and Henry. Catherine's advocates argued that according to canonical law, going back to the Fourth Lateran Council during the reign of Pope Innocent III, the bull had implicitly removed the impediment of public honesty whenever any impediment of affinity was removed. Therefore, Catherine's second marriage was valid. Henry's advocates, however, seized upon the papal omission of the impediment of public honesty as a sure indication that the papal permission for Henry to marry Catherine was flawed. Therefore, Henry's marriage was invalid. As a church-imposed impediment, public honesty, unlike the divine law on the impediment of affinity, could easily be removed by the pope. Unfortunately for Henry, Cardinal Wolsey, who was not convinced of the validity of the public honesty argument, had a crisis of conscience over the king's contention that Catherine was not a virgin, and Pope Clement VII was not able to accept the public honesty argument.

The Subjugation of the Clergy

With the fall of Wolsey, Henry assumed more direct control over his strained relations with the papacy. It is usually said that an obscure Cambridge don, Thomas Cranmer, in the late summer of 1529 suggested that Henry seek the opinions of the universities of Europe regarding his divorce. Whatever the source of the idea, Henry hoped to use the findings, which included favorable judgments from eight universities—including Paris and Bologna—when Catherine's appeal came before the Rota, the papal court in Rome. Throughout the spring and early summer of 1530, Henry continued to believe, as he had done ever since the inception of the idea of a divorce, that the pope had the final jurisdiction, but by August he had executed a dramatic about-face.

Sometime during the summer of 1530, Henry learned of a compilation of texts and precedents known as the *Collectanea Statis Copiosa*. Probably compiled by Edward Foxe, the king's almoner, the compilation may have been given to Henry by Thomas Cromwell, a former secretary to Wolsey. Citing ancient authority, the *Collectanea* claimed the independence of the English Church and its immunity from papal control as well as the right of kings to rule their churches as priestly monarchs. For instance, Henry referred to clause eight of the Constitutions of Clarendon—a clause, incidentally, abandoned by Henry II—for the prevention of appeals beyond the archbishop's court without the consent of the king. In doing so, he claimed both a national and a personal immunity from the pope's jurisdiction for the first time. The king's agents in Rome demanded that the pope allow the English clergy—the bishops of Canterbury, London, and Lincoln, or the southern convocation of the clergy—to make the decision. The pope, however, merely cited the medieval precedent of Henry II, whose own matrimonial case had been decided at Rome. Either not yet fully convinced of the new arguments promised by the radicals such as Foxe and Cromwell, or still under the influence of conservatives such as Stephen Gardiner, secretary-to-be, and Thomas More, the new lord chancellor, Henry once again turned to the universities for support.[19]

Meanwhile, in September, 1530, he instructed his agents in Rome to tell the pope that he believed himself to be "not only prince and king, but set on such a pinnacle of dignity that we know no superior on earth." Just as during the Hunne and Standish affairs, Henry claimed to have no earthly superior. This time, however, he also seemed to be claiming an "authority imperial," as he described it to his agents, in Rome, which would not put him "under the pope in any other matter than heresy." In October the king asked leading members of the English laity and clergy if he should bypass Rome and permit the archbishop of Canterbury to make the decision. They answered no. The second set of findings from the universities showed that only two supported the king. The Universities of Paris and Orleans agreed that his case should be decided in England rather than Rome, but they felt it should be decided by papal judge-delegates rather than the English clergy. Although he had gone a long way toward declaring his theoretical independence from the pope, in practice Henry had made no advance over the legatine court of Campeggio and Wolsey.[20]

Having failed to get the divorce he wanted by threats to Rome, and having coveted the Church's wealth ever since the granting of a clerical subsidy in 1523, Henry decided to bully the clergy into submission. In the summer of 1530, proceedings were initiated in the Court of King's Bench against fifteen clerics and one lay proctor from the Court of Arches for having submitted themselves to Cardinal Wolsey in his capacity as papal legate *a latere*. Eight of the fifteen clerics were bishops, of whom six had had their differences with Wolsey, and of whom four—including Henry Standish of St. Asaph and John Fisher of Rochester—were among Queen Catherine's strongest advocates. Four of the fifteen clerics were abbots, of whom three supported Henry's divorce. Before these cases were prosecuted, Henry charged all the clergy with "'illegal' exercising of spiritual jurisdiction" in the Church courts. In exchange for a statutory "general and gracious pardon," the clergy was to grant the king, whom the royal charge parenthetically called the "protector and highest head" of the English Church and clergy, a clerical subsidy of £100,000—the same amount as in 1523. Henry's political objectives included both the divorce and financial supply.[21]

Taken by surprise at these demands, the Canterbury Convocation drafted a petition stating the terms under which they were prepared to grant a subsidy: confirmation of the independence of the clergy as guaranteed by chapter one of Magna Charta, and a definition of praemunire which would preclude future prosecution for the "'illegal' exercising of spiritual jurisdiction." Henry responded to the convocation's terms by demanding that the convocation recognize him as "sole protector and supreme head" of the English Church and clergy. Moreover, the king also demanded that the Canterbury Convocation recognize that the cure of souls was "committed" to the king. Rather than interpret this ambiguous statement to mean that the king had the pastoral power of a priest, and therefore could take the pope's place as the radical councilors wished, the convocation with a few grammatical changes stated that the clergy exercised the cure of souls by the king's authority, as the conservative councillors wished. Convocation agreed to Archbishop Warham's proposal to accept the king's new title with the equally ambiguous phrase, "as far as the law of Christ allowed." After all of the sparring, only the £100,000 subsidy and a "free pardon" were incorporated into the parliamentary statute for Pardon of the Clergy. Ambassador Chapuys took the Pardon of the Clergy to mean that Henry was now "pope in England," but the king told the papal nuncio that he had no intention of setting up a "*nouvelle papalité* in England."[22]

After the York province of convocation ratified the new title and contributed nearly £20,000, Bishop Cuthbert Tunstall of Durham wrote to the king that the phrase "supreme head" should be modified by the words "*in temporalibus*," a temporal supremacy which did not include the teaching of doctrine, administration of the sacraments, or the government of the Church. What Bishop Tunstall probably had in mind was that degree of control over the Church that the Crown already enjoyed at the beginning of the Tudor period. In his reply to Tunstall, Henry accepted the bishop's distinction between temporal and spiritual affairs, but he insisted that the clergy's spiritual affairs were restricted to what was, in effect, the cure of souls. In addition, Henry asserted that the license and consent for elections of bishops and abbots, the control of all clerical property, the delegation of jurisdiction to the clerical courts, and the punishment of the clergy were all part of the royal supremacy. Although Henry had retreated from his earlier claims to make the ecclesiastical courts totally dependent on the Crown, a defeat for the radicals, he had, in fact, enlarged the claims of the royal supremacy in ecclesiastical affairs.[23]

Further extension of royal supremacy in ecclesiastical affairs is contained in an undated collection of proposals for future parliamentary legislation. This remarkable document, in which the lawyer Christopher St. German was involved, was probably completed in 1530 and worked up in 1531 for Parliament. Its proposals, in addition to those dealing with social reform, called for the establishment of "a great standing council" of bishops and laymen in order to take a close look at many aspects of ecclesiastical jurisdiction. The "council" was to determine whether a vernacular translation of the New Testament should be authorized, to investigate initially all cases of heresy and to turn over only the "hard cases" to the bishops for trial, to reform canon law and custom either by parliamentary statute where appropriate or by the Crown's negotiation with the clergy, and to enforce a more rigorous observance of the liturgy at the parish level. Also, Parliament was to reform or abolish certain abuses such as payment of fees for burial service and masses for the dead, as well as the racketeering that sometimes appeared at pilgrimage centers and shrines. Although the "great standing council" was never created, the document does show how some members of the government were trying to combat the growing hostility of the laity toward the clergy with detailed legislative plans at a stage fairly early in the life of the Reformation Parliament.[24]

Apart from the Standish affair, Henry had not displayed a strong anticlerical spirit up to this point in his reign. Henry reacted favorably, however, to a scurrilous attack upon the clergy by Simon Fish in *A Supplication for the Beggars*. Lord Chancellor More had placed this book on his list of banned heretical works—a list far more suggestive of the *Index* of the forthcoming European Counter-Reformation than the Christian humanist emphasis on education with which More has usually been associated. In his *Supplication of Beggars*, Fish wrote of the clergy: And what do all of these "sturdy, idle, holy thieves" wish to do? "Nothing but translate all rule, power, lordship, authority, obedience, and dignity from your grace unto them[selves]." To the strong anticlericalism of the House of Commons, Henry now joined his own. He desired to subdue the clergy so that the decision regarding his divorce— whether it be made in England by an English archbishop or convocation— would be favorable to the Crown.[25]

The result of this alliance was a House of Commons petition (1532) known as the Supplication Against the Ordinaries. The ordinaries, as clerical judges in the ecclesiastical courts, had been under heavy criticism ever since Hunne's case, and the Commons particularly abhorred the procedures in heresy cases, which increasingly involved its gentry members. An early version of the Supplication may have appeared in the first session of the Reformation Parliament in 1529 that passed acts regulating mortuary and testamentary fees, restraining pluralism and nonresidency, and punishing felons by thumb-branding those who sought the privilege of sanctuary in churches for the traditional forty-day period. An early version of the Supplication may have appeared in the second session of the Reformation Parliament in 1531 when that body again discussed complaints against the clergy.

Whenever the preliminary versions of the Supplication first appeared in the Commons, Thomas Cromwell corrected them. Cromwell also helped to draft the final version of the Supplication during the third session of the Reformation Parliament (1532), after he had become a privy councillor and was shaping Henry's policy. The Supplication condemned specific heresy procedures in the ecclesiastical courts, which were anathema to the Commons: citing subjects without "probable cause" at the suggestion of "undiscreet persons" to answer "many subtle questions and interrogatories" by which they might be "trapped" and, subsequently, sent to prison without bail. But the Supplication also reiterated Henry's view that the ordinaries should continue their authority to punish "the detestable crime of heresy." The first paragraph, however, interested the king the most; it charged Convocation with having made canon laws, some of which even concerned the Crown's "liberty and prerogative royal," without the king's consent. Gardiner, newly-created bishop of Winchester by papal provision, helped to draft the clergy's lengthy reply. That rebuttal insisted that because of its divine origin the legislative power of the convocation of the clergy was independent of the Crown.[26]

In May the king sent the Canterbury Convocation three new demands: convocation, like Parliament, was not to meet unless the Crown agreed; all future canons were to receive the king's consent; and all past canons were to be reviewed by a thirty-two member commission of clergy and laymen—a close approach to the "great standing council" proposed in 1530–1531. When Convocation refused these demands, Henry told the Speaker and twelve members of the House of Commons:

> Well-beloved subjects, we thought that the clergy of our realm had been our subjects wholly, but now we have well perceived that they be but half our subjects, yea, and scarce our subjects; for all the prelates at their consecration make an oath to the Pope, clean contrary to the oath that they make to us, so that they seem to be his subjects, and not ours. The copy of both the oaths I deliver here to you, requiring you to invent some orders, that we be not thus deluded of our spiritual subjects.[27]

Pressure by leading lay supporters of the king upon the members of Convocation, especially Archbishop Warham, and the draft of a parliamentary bill threatening drastic treatment of clerics, brought about the complete Submission of the Clergy (both convocations) to the king's demands. Archbishop Warham, who had been cited on a praemunire charge for consecrating Henry Standish as bishop in 1518, planned a stand of defiance similar to that of Thomas Becket against Henry II. But in the final showdown, the eighty-four-year-old metropolitan was unable to defend the concept of a double sovereignty and a divided clerical allegiance. Bishop Gardiner resigned as secretary, and Thomas More, albeit a layman, gave up the lord chancellorship. It was a victory of the radicals over the conservatives. No matter what the outcome of the controversy between the king and the pope would be regarding the divorce, the English clergy had become totally subordinate to the Crown in ecclesiastical matters. It was this Submission of the Clergy, as we shall see, that set the stage for the final break with Rome.[28]

The death of Archbishop Warham on August 23, 1532, precipitated a series of events which gave Cromwell the opportunity to carry out his imperialist solution to Henry's problems with the papacy. The prospect of a new archbishop of Canterbury who could grant Henry his divorce from Catherine probably influenced Anne Boleyn to surrender to the king after waiting about seven years. A gift to Anne of lands and the title of Marquis of Pembroke on September 1 may well have sealed the bargain. In mid-November Cranmer received word that he was designated for the Canterbury archbishopric. By mid-December Anne was pregnant, and Henry secretly married her on January 25, 1533. Since the baby had to be born legitimate, Henry had only a few months to obtain his divorce. But the pope had to issue the necessary bulls of provision and consecration for Cranmer.

The fourth session of the Reformation Parliament had already taken precautionary measures with the Act in Conditional Restraint of Annates. That statute, in addition to giving the king considerable leverage in his pressure on the papacy by letting him decide when the first fruits of newly appointed bishops should be withheld from Rome, also provided that archbishops were to be "consecrated and invested" by two other bishops. This means of consecration was not used in Cranmer's case, however, since his appointment was rapidly approved by Rome and supported by Cardinal Campeggio. This conciliatory move by the papacy may have prompted Henry to tell Ambassador Chapuys on March 31 that he would reconsider his moves toward schism if Clement would "do his pleasure in this affair." [29]

Still, the Crown worried that Catherine might appeal to Rome the divorce decision the new archbishop would make in favor of the king. Cromwell had considered that possibility before Anne ever became pregnant. Initially he planned to draft a parliamentary bill preventing an appeal to Rome against a divorce settled in England by Convocation and by Parliament. His later idea, incorporated into a statute, was far more comprehensive, abolishing not only appeals to Rome in a divorce action but appeals in other cases as well.

Two days before the passage of the Act in Restraint of Appeals in early April, Henry's earlier efforts to bring about the Submission of the Clergy were rewarded in the Canterbury Convocation, followed shortly by the York Convocation. Both convocations voted that the papacy had possessed no power to grant a dispensation to a man when a wife's previous marriage to his deceased brother had been consummated, and that in Catherine's marriage with Arthur this consummation had been proved. On May 10 Cranmer, having taken his oath to the king after his oath to the pope, opened a special divorce court at Dunstable, which Catherine refused to attend. Within two weeks Cranmer declared Henry's marriage to Anne valid, but, on July 11, as might be expected, the pope rendered exactly the opposite decision. In addition, the pope excommunicated both Henry and Cranmer, suspended in the case of the king. At long last the king had achieved the divorce he had wanted, but in the process he had opened up the larger issue of the papal connection and taken an important step toward severing it.

For years scholars have contended that Henry's divorce was the occasion but not the cause of an English Reformation. As a Protestant argument against a Catholic interpretation that Henry alone was responsible, this was a useful corrective. After all, a grass-roots movement for reform of the Church developed after the Hunne case, in part from a revived Lollardy and from the incipient efforts of Lutheran reformers such as those, for example, who gathered at the White Horse Tavern in Cambridge in the 1520s. It is quite likely that some further extensions of royal supremacy over ecclesiastical affairs and, eventually, some spiritual affairs, would have happened even if Pope Clement VII had complied with Henry's wishes or if, inconceivably, the king had renounced his quest for a divorce. The result might well have been a concordat between Henry VIII and Clement VII sometime in the 1530s.[30]

Yet much of the anticlericalism in the late 1520s and early 1530s within and outside Parliament—which built upon earlier manifestations—received its central thrust from an external force, namely, Clement's failure to comply with Henry's desire to get a divorce. It is difficult to believe, for example, that Henry's anticlerical manifestations in 1529 would have been as wholehearted had he not wished to use the issue for his own personal ends; or, for that matter, that he would have formulated an imperial theory as early as 1530 had he not desired to find a royal jurisdiction superseding that of the papacy for his matrimonial problems. Without the divorce proceedings, the break with Rome would have been unlikely, at least at this time. In that sense the divorce was a cause, indeed the necessary precipitant, of the Henrician Schism, and anticlericalism was more a consequence than it was a cause of that schism.[31]

The Royal Supremacy

With Cromwell firmly in control of the king's policies, the Act in Restraint of Appeals was the single most important piece of legislation passed by the Reformation Parliament. It set forth the theoretical outlines of the Henrician Schism. The preamble stated that "divers sundry old authentic histories and chronicles" (shades of the *Collectanea!*) declared "this realm of England is an empire," free from all interference from any foreign princes, including the "see of Rome." The phrase, "see of Rome," rather than the "See Apostolic" as in earlier drafts of the Act of Appeals, demeaned the pope by reducing his title to merely the bishop of Rome. The concept of "empire," as a contracting jurisdiction for the pope and an expanding jurisdiction for the king in ecclesiastical affairs, was not new, since it was closely related to the "imperial authority" that Henry's agents had professed to the pope as early as 1530. At that time Henry had admitted that he was still under the pope in matters of heresy, and in 1533 the final version of the Act of Appeals did not prohibit appeals in heresy cases. Henry seemingly still believed that heresy was part of the pope's jurisdiction, but Cromwell finally deleted Henry's customary desire, which had appeared off-and-on in the earlier drafts, to assert his true Catholic faith.[32]

In a passage reminiscent of the views of the Byzantine Emperor Justinian, the preamble also stated that the body politic of this "empire," which is governed by "one supreme head and king," was made up of the "spiritualty" (the English Church) and the "temporalty" (the English state). No attempt was made to define the jurisdictional borderline between the "spiritualty" and the "temporalty" or, indeed, between Convocation and Parliament, as Henry had done with Bishop Tunstall in 1531. A passage, however, stating that English kings, as vicars of God, had once made laws in both spiritual and temporal matters, did not appear in the final version of the Act. Another attempt to draw upon the precedents of the past appeared in the final version of the preamble: Henry's noble progenitors—Edward I, Edward III, Richard II, and Henry IV—had found it necessary to have laws passed against the bishop of Rome in order to protect the "imperial crown" of the realm. This was a far cry from Henry's statement in the anti-Lutheran *Assertio* that the English monarch received the "crown imperial" from the Holy See.[33]

The laws protecting the "imperial crown" were, of course, the statutes of Provisors and Praemunire, which prohibited appeals arising from the papal provisioning of ecclesiastical benefices. These medieval statutes, however, did not prohibit other appeals, which "appertaineth to the spiritual jurisdiction," and, therefore, had traditionally gone to Rome. Since these spiritual appeals, which related to testaments, matrimony, divorce, tithes, oblations, and obventions, had given the king "inquietation, vexation, troubles, cost and charges," the main body of the Act of Appeals prohibited them. All of these spiritual appeals now came under the jurisdiction of the king's spiritual and temporal courts.

The main text does not indicate which of the royal courts would get what cases, but the preamble stated that the spiritual jurisdiction would include "any cause of the law divine" or of "spiritual learning." This statement suggests that the Church courts were to keep those areas of jurisdiction that they had possessed since the Middle Ages but without citations, interdictions, or excommunications issued from Rome. Furthermore, the bishop of Rome was not to interfere with the jurisdiction of the English clergy in sacraments, divine services, "and all other things within the said realm and dominions" that "catholic and Christian men ought to do." All ecclesiastical appeals affecting the king in the future, excluding Catherine's earlier appeal to Rome, would move from the archdeacon's court to the bishop's court or from the bishop's court to the archiepiscopal court, and from the archiepiscopal court to the Upper House of Convocation. Despite the very broad powers claimed in the preamble of the Act, the enacting clauses limited the jurisdiction of the English church courts to those specific areas no longer to be appealed to Rome.

The first of two parliamentary sessions of 1534—the fifth of the Reformation Parliament—widened the breach with Rome by passing three additional pieces of important antipapal legislation: the Act for the Submission of the Clergy, the Act in Absolute Restraint of Annates, and the Dispensations Act.

The Act for the Submission of the Clergy embodied the agreement of both convocations in 1532 that the king should consent to all future canons and a thirty-two member commission of clergy and laymen should review all past canons. In a section that members of the Long Parliament were to cite in 1640 as invalidating the Laudian canons of that year, it also provided that "no canons . . . shall be made or put in execution within this realm by authority of the convocation of the clergy which shall be contrariant or repugnant to the King's prerogative royal, or the customs, laws or statutes of this realm." Sometimes called the Second Act in Restraint of Appeals, this statute enlarged the jurisdiction of its namesake by prohibiting all appeals whatsoever to "the Bishop of Rome." The Church suffered a blow *vis à vis* the state, also, when the High Court of Delegates, a commission of the king's Court of Chancery, replaced the archiepiscopal court in its short-lived role as the highest ecclesiastical court of appeal.

The Act in Absolute Restraint of Annates prohibited further payment of annates to Rome. The statute also revived the procedure for selecting bishops which had preceded the free elections of the thirteenth century and papal provisions in the fourteenth and fifteenth centuries. Once again a *congé d'élire* would call for a cathedral election with the king's choice for bishop indicated by a letter missive. The complete exclusion of the papal bulls of provision and consecration strengthened the long-accepted practice of the king getting whomever he wanted on the episcopal bench. The act also meant that the bishops would no longer have to take the oath to the papacy which Henry had asked a few members of the Commons to try to abolish during the Submission of the Clergy in 1532. Within a few months the Suffragan Bishops Act would permit some bishops to nominate two candidates for the post of suffragan bishop in certain designated towns within their dioceses, the final choice resting with the king.

The Dispensations Act, also drafted by Cromwell, was a mixture of diverse antipapal actions. Its preamble continued the "empire" theme of the Act in Restraint of Appeals by stating that the pope had usurped all "causes which he called spiritual" to the "great derogation of your imperial crown and authority royal." The preamble also proclaimed that England recognizes "no superior under God, but only your Grace," and, most important of all, it referred to the king as "the supreme head of the Church of England," without any such restrictive clause as that added by Canterbury Convocation in 1531. The main body of the statute incorporated a statement, very similar to the one which Cromwell had deleted in the final draft of the Act in Restraint of Appeals: in no sense was there any intention of deviating from "Christs Church in any things concerning the very articles of the Catholic faith of Christendom." The main ideas of the enacting clauses of the statute were to cut off all monetary payments to Rome, including the ancient tribute known as Peter's Pence, as well as to permit the archbishop of Canterbury rather than the pope to issue licenses and dispensations of the canon law not contrary to the law of God. A short clause gave the king the right of visitation to those monasteries that had been exempt from the jurisdiction of the archbishop of Canterbury. The last provision of the statute provided the king with the option to annul the entire statute, perhaps with the idea, as in the Act in Conditional Restraint of Annates, of exerting some pressure upon the pope in the hope that he might still give way. But that was not to be possible, since the pope had already made his decision.

Just one week before all of these acts were signed by Henry on March 30, Pope Clement finally decided to uphold the validity of Henry's marriage to Catherine. Clement had resisted the advances of his suitor for almost as long as Anne Boleyn presumably had resisted hers. Only an act of God could prevent a schism.

Within a few months Parliament formally established royal supremacy over the English Church. That supremacy had been forecast in the grudging surrender of the clergy with the saving proviso of 1531, had been implicitly stated in the short phrase "supreme head" in the preamble of the Act of Appeals, and had been explicitly stated, without the proviso, in the preamble of the Act of Dispensations. The Act of Supremacy, passed during the second parliamentary session of 1534—the sixth of the Reformation Parliament— now set forth that royal supremacy. The preamble of this brief statute declared that the king "is and ought to be the supreme head of the Church of England," yet for "corroboration and confirmation" of this fact the main body of the statute stated that he should be so accepted as "the only supreme head in earth of the Church of England, called *Anglicana Ecclesia.*" In short, Parliament gave only formal recognition to what the king claimed was already in existence.

The statute enlarged upon the king's spiritual jurisdiction by giving him full power

> to visit, repress, redress, reform, order, correct, restrain, and amend all such errors, heresies, abuses, offences, contempts, and enormities, whatsoever they be, which by any manner spiritual authority or jurisdiction ought or may lawfully be reformed, repressed, ordered, redressed, corrected, restrained, or amended, most to the pleasure of Almighty God.

Although the Act of Appeals had conceded to the pope the right to hear appeals in matters of heresy, the Act of Supremacy gave the king the right to repress heresy. This was the opening wedge into an area of spiritual jurisdiction where no English sovereign had ever trespassed. Ambassador Chapuys found Henry "was at once king, emperor (and if I recollect right) Pope also in his dominions." Actually, Henry had not claimed that much.[34]

Henry did not claim what the canon lawyers called the *potestas ordinis*— the sacerdotal power of a priest to deal with the man's inner spiritual relationship with God. The king, wrote St. German, "has no authority to minister any of the sacraments, nor to do anything whereof our lord gave power only to his apostles and disciples."[35] Henry had claimed in 1531 that the cure of souls had been "committed" to him, but he did not preach sermons from the pulpit, celebrate the mass, perform marriages, ordain priests, or administer the last rites. He neither claimed the right to dispense with penances and vows nor to excommunicate from the Church. Although he did appoint bishops, he did not consecrate them.[36]

Henry did claim what the canon lawyers called the *potestas jurisdictionis*, or the power of ecclesiastical administration. This jurisdictional power, as Henry interpreted it, included the appointment of bishops, regulation of the Church courts, approval of canon law, taxation of the clergy, visitation and discipline of the clergy (including the monasteries), and the seizure and administration of ecclesiastical property. Some of this jurisdictional power over ecclesiastical affairs already belonged to the Crown when Henry came to the throne, and the Crown appropriated the rest of it after 1529. The *potestas jurisdictionis* also included, curiously, the power to define the true doctrine. The Dispensations Act stated no intention of deviating from the "articles of the Catholic faith"; nevertheless, the king subsequently became involved, both in Parliament and out, in drawing up declarations of faith. The king's interest in formulating theological documents was an extension of his spiritual supremacy.

While the king and Parliament fixed the limit of royal supremacy over the Church, pamphleteers provided an ideological justification for the supremacy by seeking the respectability of the past. They argued that the papacy had usurped the spiritual supremacy, as suggested in the preamble of the Dispensations Act, from the early Christian emperors who exercised both spiritual and temporal powers over their empires. For example, the Emperor Constantine had presided over the first Christian Council at Nicea; and the Emperor Justinian, according to Bishop Gardiner, had made "laws on the holy trinity, on the Catholic faith, on bishops, clerks, heretics, and other such like." They also found support for these caesaropapist views in the writings of the medieval imperialist, Marsiglio of Padua, whose *Defensor Pacis* was translated into English in 1535, partly at the behest of Cromwell. The chief appeal of Marsiglio was his argument that the clergy had no jurisdiction over the spiritual affairs of this world except whatever the state gave them. Skillful editing had dropped all those passages of the *Defensor Pacis* that had dealt with the people's right to depose a tyrannical ruler, thereby allowing for the enunciation of a doctrine of nonresistance to the state.

The pamphleteers disagreed, however, over which body in England—the king-in-Council or the king-in-Parliament—actually controlled the spiritual supremacy, now that the tyranny of the bishop of Rome had been overthrown. Some, like St. German, said that the power of the state, limited by natural law and common law, was vested in the statutory laws of the king-in-Parliament. Furthermore, he argued, when common law is at variance with canon law, the decisions of the common law courts should stand against decisions of the ecclesiastical courts. Others, such as Bishop Gardiner and William Tyndale, appealed to a higher law than man—a divine right—which was far more a theory of Church government than of state government. Bishop Gardiner, who had switched from an opposition to allegiance to the Crown, wrote in his *De Vera Obedientia* (1536) that the "king representeth as it were the image of God upon earth," and he must be obeyed, "yea, though he were an infidel."[37] Tyndale, a reformer and—with Cromwell's support—an early English translator of the Bible, wrote in his *Obedience of a Christian Man* (1528)—another book on More's prohibited list—that "the King is, in this world, without law; and may at his lust do right or wrong, and shall give accounts but to God only."[38] Yet Tyndale, departing from Luther and from Gardiner, noted that if the prince commands something contrary to God's word, he must be passively disobeyed but not actively resisted. The doctrine of passive disobedience in Tyndale seriously qualified the divine right position, but he did not extend this disobedience to the point of tyrannicide advocated by a handful of Protestants like John Knox a quarter of a century later.

The legislation of the Reformation Parliament also reflected the disagreement among the pamphleteers over which institution—the king-in-Council or the king-in-Parliament—should control the royal supremacy. Some, but not all, of the declaratory preambles of that legislation can be associated with the power of the king-in-Council, and some, but not all, of the enacting clauses can be associated with the power of the king-in-Parliament. The declaratory preambles of the statutes of Appeals, Dispensations, Supremacy, and Six Articles (1539) accepted the royal supremacy as already existent from ancient times, and set forth, in accordance with Henry's views, a personal supremacy derived from God. The enacting clauses of the statutes of Annates, Appeals, Dispensations, and Submission of the Clergy authorized specific designs to carry out royal supremacy, and sometimes, as in the Six Articles Act, even provided penalties for their violation. These enacting clauses enlarged the king's control over the Church, in accordance with Cromwell's views, by the authority of the king-in-Parliament.[39]

But there is some conflicting evidence. The declaratory preamble of the Dispensations Act posited that the king-in-Parliament had the power to dispense with all of the statutory laws in the realm, and the preamble of the Six Articles Act stated that both Convocation and Parliament, "after a great and long, deliberate, and advised disputation and consultation," had consented to the Six Articles. Nor did the enacting clauses of the Supremacy Act create royal supremacy on the same basis of parliamentary authority as the enacting clauses of the other statutes had done; instead, the enacting clauses of the Supremacy Act merely called for the acceptance—corroboration and confirmation—of royal supremacy that the preamble had already declared to be in existence. The evidence, then, from the declaratory preambles and the enacting clauses is somewhat contradictory regarding the authority of the king-in-Council versus that of the king-in-Parliament.

Some additional evidence about the grounding of the king's ecclesiastical authority in Parliament or in the Crown itself, however, emerged in the method used for regulation of the convocation of the clergy and the alteration of articles of faith. A draft bill of 1532, which would have given Parliament control over the convocations, was never enacted. Two years later, however, the statute for the Submission of the Clergy had given the king, not Parliament, the authority to appoint a thirty-two member commission to review the canons of the convocations. In addition, the statute for the Advancement of True Religion (1543) gave the king power to alter any clause in the Six Articles (1539) without parliamentary consent, a feature that greatly enhanced royal supremacy. The conflict between the two theories of sovereignty over the Church persisted throughout the Tudor period. But Henry, like Elizabeth after 1563, treated the Church as if it were under a personal and absolute supremacy by the Crown-in-Council rather than a limited supremacy by the Crown-in-Parliament.

The Henrician Martyrs

The opposition to the break with Rome proved surprisingly small, since there were only two prominent subjects of the Crown, apart from Catherine (now Princess Dowager) and a few Carthusian monks, who would not bow to Henry's will: John Fisher, the immovable member of the episcopal bench, and Sir Thomas More, the former lord chancellor. While serving as lord chancellor (1529–1532), More did not actively oppose Henry's efforts to get a divorce from Catherine, even though he did not favor it, but he had enjoyed the support of the king because they shared a common desire to persecute heretics. In the eight years before More, when Cardinal Wolsey was lord chancellor (1521–1529), not one heretic had been burned; in More's two and a half years as lord chancellor, six were burned under the statute of 1414, including the Lutheran, Thomas Bilney, whom More may falsely have charged with recanting his heresy just before he was burned. More, who engaged weekly in self-flagellation until his hairshirt dripped with blood, was a more zealous prosecutor than Wolsey. Not only was More instrumental in the burning of heretics once the Church had delivered them to the secular arm of the state, he also wrote several books against them. His *Dialogue Concerning Heresies* (1529) attacked the Lutheran translator of the Bible, William Tyndale; his *Supplication of Souls* (1529) answered that outspoken critic of the clergy, Simon Fish; and several of his books, written after his retirement as lord chancellor, raged against the aging common lawyer, Christopher St. German. Both Tyndale and St. German had strongly supported royal supremacy, and Fish's anticlericalism also pleased Henry.[40]

By the summer of 1533, both Fisher and More had met Elizabeth Barton, the Nun of Kent, whose visions revealed that the king would die within a month after he married Anne Boleyn. In fact, this nun from Canterbury told Henry to his face of the imminent disaster. Fisher, who apparently believed her, realized that the prophetess might be of political use, whereas More was much more cautious, especially when recounting his meeting with her in two letters to Cromwell later. The Nun of Kent and her associates were convicted of high treason and executed at Paul's Cross. Fisher and More were accused of misprision of treason—specifically, of failing to inform the magistrate of Barton's treason. The names of both men were included in the parliamentary bill of attainder, which found them guilty and sentenced them to life imprisonment. Fisher denied any desire to commit misprision of treason, stating that, after all, the Nun of Kent to his knowledge had made her dire prophecy only to the king in person. In a letter to Henry and Cromwell, More disassociated himself from "the wicked woman of Canterbury" and begged to have his name deleted from the bill of attainder. In another letter only to Cromwell, he indicated that he had never done anything to hinder Henry's marriage to Anne, whom he called "this noble woman really anointed Queen,"[41] nor to hinder Henry's wishes regarding papal supremacy, which he said he had never particularly favored until Henry had published his book, the *Assertio*. After his abject submission to Henry and Cromwell, More's name was deleted from the bill of attainder, and Fisher, who was sentenced to life imprisonment, was pardoned by the king.

A little over a month after More had written his letter of submission to Cromwell in the spring of 1534, Fisher and More refused to take an oath required in principle (but not stated with a specific wording) by the Succession Act (1534). The Succession Act had settled the future of the Tudor dynasty upon the heirs of Henry and "his beloved lawful wife Queen Anne." More, although willing to accept Elizabeth's succession to the throne, refused the oath, which, he told his wife, was "not agreeable with the statute," because it put his soul in jeopardy of perpetual damnation. Fisher and More were imprisoned in the Tower of London for misprision of treason.

It is possible that the oath More was asked to take was not the one formally adopted by Parliament the following November, requiring subscription only to the Succession Act itself with its mildly antipapal preamble, but, instead, a much broader one, taken by all members of Parliament the previous April. The April parliamentary oath included a clause requiring subscription to "all other acts and statutes made in the present Parliament," statutes such as Appeals and Dispensations with their preambles declaring royal supremacy.[42] More rightly saw that the government wanted to use the oath of succession, even if it was just the November parliamentary oath, with its required denial of obedience to any "foreign authority, prince or potentate," as an implicit expression of support for royal supremacy.

After the passage in November, 1534 of the Supremacy Act declaring Henry the supreme head of the Church of England, as well as after a new Treasons Act, stating that anyone who deprived the king of any of his titles was guilty of high treason, Cromwell, Cranmer, and others interrogated both Fisher and More in the Tower about royal supremacy. Cromwell asked Fisher whether he accepted the king's divorce from Catherine, his marriage to Anne, and royal supremacy. Fisher asked to be excused from replying on grounds that it might incriminate him. Cromwell asked More the same question about royal supremacy, and More, when pressed, said that the question was unfair because it was like a double-edged sword: *if*, and it was only an *if*, he did not believe Henry to be the supreme head of the Church, then by giving an affirmative answer he would perjure his soul, and *if* he refused to give an affirmative answer, he would endanger his life. But Cromwell observed that More had forced people suspected of heresy to answer whether or not they believed the pope was head of the Church, so why should he not have to answer as well? More replied that when he was lord chancellor *every* country in Europe believed in papal supremacy, whereas now England was the *only* country in Europe which did not.[43]

In May, 1535, when the new pope, Paul III, gave Bishop Fisher a cardinal's hat, an enraged Henry decided to bring More and Fisher to trial for high treason under the new Treason Act (1534). Fisher admitted that he had deprived the king of one of his titles (namely supreme head), which the treasons statute specifically prohibited, but he argued that he was not guilty of high treason because he had not "maliciously" denied royal supremacy, which the act specifically required. Together with three Carthusian monks whom Cromwell tried to assist, Fisher was found guilty, but, unlike the monks who were hanged, drawn, and quartered at Tyburn, Fisher was beheaded on Tower Hill.

More was much more cautious at his trial, stating at one point that his silence about royal supremacy must be interpreted as consent. But the court sought a definite answer from him, as definite as those he as lord chancellor had sought from heretics. The testimony of Sir Robert Rich, to which More (though denying Rich's veracity) did not give his own explanation, may have proved to be the former lord chancellor's undoing. Rich, who was soon to become attorney general for Wales, testified that More had told him in the Tower as truth what More had only hypothesized to Cromwell in response to the secretary's doubled-edged sword question. Despite the fact that More, too, was not guilty of acting "maliciously," a jury found him guilty of high treason.[44]

Addressing the court after its decision, More stated that the particular realm of England, "being but one member and small part of the Church, might not make a particular law dischargeable with the general law of Christ's holy Catholic Church." Contrary to the views of St. German, and despite the precedent of the Standish case, More told the court, "I am not bounden, my Lord, to conform my conscience to the Council of one realm against the General Council of Christendom." It was the Catholic Church for which More died. He never committed himself to any notion of papal sovereignty, whether absolute or limited, believing firmly that any limitations upon that sovereignty should come from the Church and not from any Crown. More was executed in July, 1535, thereby prompting Henry's second excommunication (also suspended). Catherine of Aragon died in January, 1536, the same year in which the seventh and final session of the Reformation Parliament passed a statute extinguishing all papal authority in England. None of the Henrician martyrs became champions of liberty of conscience, and religious conformity became a test of political loyalty through the use of the oath of supremacy—an oath eventually required of all newly appointed religious and civil officeholders (1536).[45]

The Dissolution of the Monasteries

In order to implement his supremacy over the Church, Henry appointed Cromwell as his vicar-general and vicegerent for ecclesiastical affairs in January, 1535. The broad powers delegated to the vicegerency, somewhat similar to the papal legateship held earlier by Cardinal Wolsey, gave a layman other than the king virtually all of the jurisdiction over the Church courts and the Church hierarchy. Specifically, the vicegerent's powers included the right to conduct visitations, punish the clergy, collect revenue during clerical vacancies, hold and preside over convocations, select bishops and preside over their election, and issue injunctions. A symbol of these vast powers was a parliamentary statute in 1539 granting Cromwell a seat in the House of Lords, where he sat above the archbishop of Canterbury at the right side of the throne. Although the details of Cromwell's vicegerency remain somewhat obscure, a special seal and a special vicegerential court, probably headed by William Petre, existed from October, 1535 to February, 1540.

The vicegerential court replaced the papal court in relation to the archiepiscopal or provincial courts, which, in turn, received a new organization. Cases of probate of property from more than one diocese went to the Prerogative Courts of Canterbury and York; some cases of appeal went to the Courts of Audience of Canterbury and York; and cases of first instance as well as appeals from diocesan courts went to the Court of the Arches (Canterbury) and the Court of Chancery (York). Cromwell probably planned to reform these provincial courts and the subordinate diocesan and archidiaconal courts, but while considering several plans for court reform, the government suspended the Court of the Arches and the Prerogative Court of Canterbury. The government did not accept the scheme of Richard Pollard, one of Cromwell's servants with legal experience, to merge the ecclesiastical courts with the civil courts. Nor did it accept a less drastic proposal contained in an undated memorandum, probably by Petre, indicating certain areas of jurisdiction that might be removed from the ecclesiastical courts: tithes, defamation and perjury suits, and the probate of testaments involving money. In January, 1536, Cromwell appointed Petre as his deputy in relation to the probate of testaments and the administration of estates. Also, the king inhibited jurisdiction on testamentary matters, by far the largest percentage of all kinds of suits, at all levels of the ecclesiastical courts.

Another important feature of Cromwell's vicegerency was the temporary inhibition placed upon all bishops in September, 1535, preventing them from exercising any of the powers that had been delegated to the vicegerent. A royal letter to Archbishop Cranmer prohibited the bishops from holding visitations on the grounds of an impending royal visit of the monasteries and all of the churches in the realm. It quickly became apparent that the office of the vicegerency could not handle all of the ecclesiastical matters formerly handled by the bishops, so the bishops recovered most of their traditional powers. The bishops did not regain the right of visitation until 1536, and by that time the vicegerent's visitations of the monasteries had done their damage.[46]

The chief purpose of the vicegerent's visitations seems to have been to increase the revenue of the Crown through the suppression of the monasteries. Long before Cromwell became vicegerent, however, a number of steps had weakened the religious houses which, except for a few, had ceased to be a living spiritual ideal—no longer fervent and disciplined. In the preceding century, the Crown had suppressed a handful of monasteries, including the alien priories. Cromwell had assisted Wolsey as papal legate in the suppression of about thirty monasteries in order to obtain funds for educational purposes, especially the Cardinal's College at Oxford. And the Dispensations Act had brought those religious houses, which were directly dependent upon Rome and not upon the English bishops, under the control of the Crown.

The passage of the Act for First Fruits and Tenths late in 1534 had already revealed the financial rapacity of the Crown. That statute had annexed annates or the first year's income, plus an annual tenth of the net income, of all ecclesiastical benefices to the Crown. In order to make an appraisal of the Church's total wealth, the act also provided for the appointment in each diocese of ecclesiastical commissioners under Cromwell's direction who would file returns not only of the accounts of the ecclesiastical benefices but also of such institutions as colleges, hospitals, and, above all, the monasteries. The result was a detailed survey called the *Valor Ecclesiasticus*. First fruits and tenths paid to the Crown averaged over £45,000 between 1535 and 1547, about ten times the yearly average paid to Rome between 1485 and 1534.[47] Still, Cromwell, despite some plans to nationalize the entire English Church, left most of the income of ecclesiastical benefices intact, including the sees. No such generous fate, however, was in store for the monasteries where the net annual income, the *Valor Ecclesiasticus* found, was just under £140,000 annually, about triple the Crown's annual income from its own landed estates.[48]

Having determined the vast extent of wealth that the monasteries possessed, Cromwell proceeded with vicegerential visitations, which ultimately resulted in the death of English monasticism. In most respects the visitations followed the pattern of those undertaken by medieval bishops except that the Henrician visitors—laymen such as Petre—sometimes conducted them with greater speed. What the visitors reported seems to have been what they were looking for—"manifest sin, vicious, carnal, and abominable living," as stated in the 1536 Act for the Dissolution of the Lesser Monasteries. By this statute Parliament dissolved more than 300 religious houses—all with an income of less than £200 a year. Cromwell created a special Court of Augmentations to handle the annual revenue from the former monastic lands, which reached more than a quarter of a million pounds by the 1540s. Very little of this money found its way into hospitals or education for the poor, as specified in the act, but five Regius professorships in Greek, Hebrew, Theology, Civil Law, and Medicine were established at both Oxford and Cambridge, and cathedral grammar schools received sizable endowments.[49]

Soon the larger monastic houses surrendered to the government, as a result of either threat or promise from Cromwell. In 1539, Parliament formally recognized the capitulation of these larger houses and vested their property, as well as that of all the remaining houses yet to be surrendered, in the hands of the Crown. Between 1537 and 1540, some 158 monasteries and thirty nunneries were dissolved. While the friars were turned out unpensioned, and the nuns were only very poorly pensioned, most of the monks received a meager five to six pounds per annum. Although the abbots and priors received handsome pensions, they lost their seats in the House of Lords. As a result, the traditional ecclesiastical majority in that body was reduced to a minority. Thereafter, the Lords spoke primarily with a secular voice.

Within a few months after the visitation and seizure of the lesser monasteries, a series of uprisings, called the Pilgrimage of Grace, occurred in

Lincolnshire, the East Riding of Yorkshire, and the northwestern counties of Cumberland and Westmoreland. Economic conditions such as the bad harvest of 1535 and the disappointing one of 1536, helped cause the outbreaks in the northwest, but religious grievances proved of greater significance in Lincolnshire and eastern Yorkshire, areas which contained a large number of monasteries. Robert Aske, the leader of the eastern Yorkshire uprisings, said that the Dissolution of the Monasteries and the fear of heresy alone would have been sufficient to cause the revolt because they appealed to all groups in society, whereas the social grievances, such as enclosures, affected only different classes. Aske, however, admitted that most of the Pilgrims opposed the Dissolution because they feared that the siphoning off of monastic rents and first fruits and tenths would create poverty in the north. In Lincolnshire and eastern Yorkshire, the religious grievances included both a concern about a new declaration of faith called the Ten Articles and a fear that the parish church organization, indeed parish church property, lay in jeopardy.[50]

Although the Dissolution of the Monasteries emerged as an issue in the discussions of the rebels, the real leaders of the rebellion—Robert Constable and two members of the lesser nobility, Thomas Darcy and John Hussey—interested themselves in something else. All three of these plotters, whom the greater northern aristocrats did not join, not only communicated with the Imperial ambassador, Chapuys, but also strongly opposed Anne Boleyn, heresy, and Thomas Cromwell. These plotters, who constituted the remains of the Aragonese faction at court, wanted to put Princess Mary on the throne, eliminate the Ten Articles and other supposedly heretical actions, and get rid of Cromwell, especially because of his reforming ideas. The Pilgrimage of Grace, hardly a spontaneous uprising, thus resulted in part from a disgruntled court faction's calculated effort to move its opposition from the council chamber to the battlefields of the north.[51]

The question of royal supremacy received varying degrees of support from the rebels. The Lincolnshire rebels mentioned it only once, and then with a grudging acceptance, whereas in Yorkshire a small group headed by Aske, not necessarily representative of all of the Pilgrims, mentioned it indirectly near the end and directly near the beginning of the Pontefract Articles (December, 1536). Article twenty-one asked for the repeal of the Treason Act of 1534, under which some 300 people had been prosecuted for words against the royal supremacy, and article two asked that the royal supremacy "touching *cura animarum*" should be held by the pope. Aske's purpose in article two seems to have been to prevent any further extension of royal supremacy to a cure of souls, a position which the Yorkshire Protestant, Sir Francis Bigod, also took.

Bigod, however, rejected the papal supremacy altogether. Just before he raised his own revolt in January, 1537, which (like Aske's) the Crown crushed, he wrote a treatise stating his views on church and state. In the treatise now lost, Bigod apparently argued that clerics such as the archbishop of Canterbury, not laymen such as the king, should be the supreme head of the English Church. Bigod was more concerned with Henry's current, and possibly new, abuses of the royal supremacy than he was with bringing back the old papal supremacy.[52]

In some ways the long-term social consequences of the Dissolution, while more difficult to assess, are more significant than the Pilgrimage of Grace itself. In sixty years, beginning with the Dissolution, over a quarter of the land of England passed via the monasteries, chantries, and episcopal lands from the Church into the hands of laymen. A few families of considerable wealth benefited from the sale of the monastic lands seized by the Crown but, for the most part, the Dissolution benefited a group of men with small or moderate fortunes who secured small estates or supplemented existing ones. By extending their property, these landed gentry acquired a vested interest in the Dissolution. As a result, they would have strongly opposed any attempt at a large scale restitution of these lands. Some of these gentry, such as the Russell family, acquired a permanent stake in Protestantism, but others, like the Arundels, remained zealous Catholics. Later, Mary Tudor could not fully reestablish Roman Catholicism because she lacked the support of these Protestant and Catholic gentry for a restitution of monastic land.

Another far-reaching consequence of the Dissolution was the rendering into lay hands of the presentation of clergymen to churches of which the monasteries had possessed the advowson. The transference of monastic ad-vowsons to lay patrons meant that it would be increasingly difficult for the Crown to maintain an ecclesiastical and doctrinal uniformity. In short, while the king actually won control over the entire Church at the national level, he lost an opportunity for control over some of the churches at the local level.

The Declarations of Faith

The Ten Articles of 1536, which created some religious grievances in the north during the Pilgrimage of Grace, was the first of several declarations of faith promulgated during the Henrician supremacy. Confirmed by a joint session of both convocations, which Cromwell chaired and the king attended, the Ten Articles, as a Protestant formulary, reflected to some extent a Lutheran influence from the Wittenberg Articles (1536). Both sets of articles were similar, first, because of the noncontroversial material upon which they agreed—the three historic creeds (Apostolic, Nicean, and Athanasian); and second, because of their common omissions—they mention only three sacraments (baptism, penance, and the Eucharist). Both sets of articles taught the doctrine of the real presence of Jesus Christ in the Eucharist, that is, the body and blood of Christ being substantially or corporally present in the bread and wine. Neither made mention of it in the form known as consubstantiation (the bread and wine coexisting with Christ's body and blood) or in the form known as transubstantiation (the bread and wine changing into Christ's body and blood).

Yet among the similarities there are important differences over controversial issues. While both sets of articles defend baptism against the errors of Anabaptism, the Ten Articles adopted auricular confession in the sacrament of penance. While both sets of articles denied that private masses could deliver souls from purgatory, the Ten Articles admitted a purgatory and enjoined prayers for the dead there. On the question of justification by faith alone, the Wittenberg Articles unmistakably influenced the Ten Articles, but the latter also upheld the role of good works in man's salvation. The Ten Articles enjoined all of the clergy having the cure of souls to explain the meaning of the Articles to the people in accordance with a provision in Henry's first set of royal injunctions (1536) drawn up by the vicegerent. The injunctions, the result of Cromwell's visitations of both the regular and secular clergy, again asserted Henry's role as supreme head of the Church of England to whom all Englishmen "owe most loyalty and obedience, fore and above all other powers and potentates in earth."[53]

The same kind of statement about royal supremacy appeared in the second declaration of faith to come out of the Henrician supremacy. *The Godly and Pious Institution of A Christian Man*, properly called the Bishops' Book, represented a compromise among the bishops. Half the episcopal bench were conservative bishops, such as Gardiner and Tunstall—overwhelmingly secular or worldly clergy with a very strong interest in the law—and about half were reforming bishops, such as Cranmer and Hugh Latimer—about equally divided between regular clergy (in a religious order) and secular clergy but nearly all of whom had taken divinity degrees.[54] The Bishops' Book, first printed in 1537 for a three-year period, stated, "without the . . . power and license of your majesty," which had not been given, "we knowledge and confess that we have none authority."[55] The Bishops' Book was less Lutheran than its predecessor because the four sacraments, omitted from the Ten Articles, reappeared. While the Book only indirectly referred to predestination, it did state that the elect could not fall finally from grace.

A few months after the printing of the Bishops' Book, when the birth of his son, Edward, and the death of his third wife, Jane Seymour, no longer occupied his attention, Henry examined the Bishops' Book at his leisure. His lengthy comments to Cranmer did not simply reflect his Catholic orthodoxy. Henry rejected the strong statement of the Lutheran doctrine of justification by faith alone and affirmed a semi-Pelagian doctrine of good works, but his comments regarding some of the sacraments departed considerably from the views he had set forth in his *Assertio* in 1521. It is somewhat surprising, after what he had been through, that Henry wished to elevate the sacrament of marriage to the lofty position that the Bishops' Book gave to the sacraments of baptism, penance, and the Eucharist.

Henry's strongest criticism focused upon the Bishops' Book's assertions about the sacrament of "holy orders" or ordination.[56] The Bishops' Book stated that Christ and his apostles not only gave to kings and princes their "civil power and governance" (*potestas gladii*) but also that Christ and his apostles granted to "certain other ministers or officers" of the "church militant" their priestly powers (*potestas ordinis*). Among these priestly powers was the ordination of bishops and priests through the imposition of hands, but not, of course, the selection of particular persons for these ecclesiastical positions. In the case of bishops, the Crown nominated them as specified in the Act in Absolute Restraint of Annates, and, in the case of priests, patrons presented them. One implication of the distinction between the *potestas gladii* and the *potestas ordinis* was that kings should have nothing to do with the latter. In fact, the Bishops' Book specifically stated that "we may not think that it doth appertain unto the office of kings and princes to preach and teach, to administer the sacraments, to absolve, to excommunicate, and such others things belonging to the office and administration of bishops and priests."[57] But Henry seems to have been disturbed about the complete independence of the clergy in priestly matters. He wrote in the margin of the Bishops' Book that all priestly powers should be in accordance with "the laws of every region." This revision suggests the king's desire to bring the *potestas ordinis* under the regulation of the king-in-Parliament.

Whereas the Bishops' Book distinguished between essentials and ceremonies, Henry's second set of royal injunctions (1538), issued like the first set by Cromwell as vicegerent, distinguished between those ceremonies that were not necessary for salvation and those that should be proscribed altogether as superstitious. The latter included the burning of candles and tapers to images, the kissing of relics, and the making of pilgrimages. The immediate consequence of this last prohibition was the destruction in September, 1538 of Becket's shrine at Canterbury, which had attracted pilgrims long before and after those immortalized by Chaucer. Outraged by such pillage, Pope Paul III drew up a papal bull deposing Henry from his throne, but the king's kinsman, Cardinal Reginald Pole, like so many other sons of the Catholic Church in the past, could not execute it. Henry in turn denounced Becket as a rebel who had fled to France "to procure the abrogation of wholesome laws."

Henry's second set of injunctions, unlike the first set, possessed a distinctively Erasmian influence, especially in connection with the Bible. The new injunctions provided for the preaching of sermons at least once every three months, the payment of tithes in accordance with the law, the keeping of parish registers in parish chests in order to record all christenings, weddings, and burials, and the placing of an English Bible in every church.[58] For this purpose, Miles Coverdale produced the Great Bible (1539), the culmination of several earlier translations by Tyndale, John Rogers, and himself. The clergy were to exhort everyone to read it, as well as to recite the Ten Articles and the Pater Noster, as essential steps for achieving salvation. While the clergy were "to avoid all contention and altercation therein," and "to refer the explication of obscure places to men of higher judgment in Scripture," the Great Bible soon became a source of common disputation. An act of Parliament in 1543 for the Advancement of the True Religion, in addition to censoring religious books, restricted Bible-reading only to male members of the nobility and gentry and to merchant householders; but two years later,

Henry complained to his last Parliament that "the word of God, is disputed, rhymed, sung, and jangled in every alehouse and tavern, contrary to the true meaning and doctrine of the same."[59]

In the months after the adoption of the second set of injunctions, Henry sent some Lutheran theologians home, undertook diplomatic negotiations with the Lutheran-allied duchy of Cleves—resulting in his marriage to the duke's elder sister Anne (no Lutheran herself), and presided over the heresy trial of John Lambert, whom he condemned as a sacramentary for denying the real presence. Moreover, Henry issued a harsh proclamation, which instituted a stricter censorship, regulated the importation, sale, and publication of Bibles, prevented discussion of the Eucharist, retained many "popish" ceremonies, forebade clerical marriage, expelled all Anabaptists and sacramentaries from the land, and stated that Thomas Becket was "a rebel and traitor to his prince." The proclamation marked a significant retreat from the positions of the second injunctions and a return to religious conservatism.[60]

The proclamation, which represented Henry's traditional religious predilections, foreshadowed the introduction, in effect, of a bill of uniformity in Parliament. The duke of Norfolk and Bishop Tunstall took the lead in the House of Lords, and Bishop Tunstall led this conservative approach in the concurrent "Synod and Convocation of all the Archbishops, Bishops, and other learned men of the clergy." The crystallizing event occurred when conservative, anti-Cromwellian councillors revealed to Henry the doctrinal dissension in England's port of Calais. In Calais the English lord deputy, Arthur Plantagenet (Lord Lisle), sought advice from Cromwell on eucharistic policy. In Cromwell's absence and despite the opposition of Cranmer and other reforming bishops, Norfolk and Tunstall provided the formula for the Act for Abolishing Diversities of Opinion (1539), which both convocation and Parliament accepted. More commonly called the Six Articles Act, the statute, which Cranmer opposed at first but later supported, was the third major declaration of faith during Henry's reign. It affirmed communion in one kind for the laity, celibacy of the priesthood, the permanence of vows of chastity, the benefit of private masses, auricular confession, and transubstantiation. Here was a formidable array of Catholic orthodoxy that prompted John Husee to write to Lord Lisle: "I think men will not be so liberal of preaching as they hath been time past."[61]

This new statute, sometimes called the "whip with six strings," also doubled as the second heresy act of the reign. Henry's first heresy act (1534), which responded to the complaints of the parliamentary gentry in the Supplication against the Ordinaries, had repealed the act of Henry IV (1401) but had upheld the act of Henry V (1414), thereby making it possible to bring indictments for heresy only through the civil courts. The act of 1534, however, had continued the fifteenth-century procedure where, after indictment, the Church tried the accused and the state punished any convicted person who refused to abjure the heresy or relapsed after abjuration. The Six Articles Act gave both the ecclesiastical courts and the common law courts (plus new quarterly commissions made up of clergy and laity) the right to bring indictments for heresy. But more significantly, the Six Articles Act gave to the common law courts for the first time the right actually to try heresy cases as if they were regular felony cases. When a statute of 1543 stated that *all* indictments under the Six Articles Act should be made only "by the oath of twelve men before commissioners authorized," nearly the whole judicial process for handling the 1539 heresies, including sentences of death at the stake for denial of transubstantiation and death by hanging for second offences against the other five articles, moved from the hands of the Church into the hands of the state.

In late July, 1640, the conservatives convinced Henry that Cromwell was a sacramentary—someone who did not believe in the real presence. Although the vicegerent had been careful not to say very much publicly about religion that might hurt himself, throughout the 1530s he seems to have become more and more Protestant in theological doctrine. So the king allowed Cromwell to be executed by an act of attainder for treason and heresy. It is not easy to believe that the king could have so easily put to death the remarkable minister who had served him so well in fashioning many of the pieces of legislation that had brought about the schism with Rome, in bringing about the dissolution of the monasteries, and in attempting to reform the institutional structure of both Church and state. But the conservative reaction of the late thirties, spearheaded by the king himself and manifested in the Six Articles Act, brought down the minister who had dominated court politics from 1532 to 1540. Unlike Wolsey, who had attributed his downfall to his failure to serve his God as diligently as his king, Cromwell attributed his downfall to his failure to obey his king's "most gracious grave Councils."[62]

Two days after Cromwell's execution, three Lutherans including Robert Barnes, who denied the ambiguous charge of Anabaptism, died at the stake for heresy, and three Catholic priests died on the gallows as traitors for denying the royal supremacy. The simultaneous execution of the three Protestants and the three Catholics prompted a shrewd observation from the French ambassador: "It is no easy thing to keep a people in revolt against the Holy See and the authority of the Church, and yet free from the infection of the new doctrines, or, on the other hand, if they remain orthodox, to prevent them from looking with attachment to the Papacy."[63]

A commission of bishops and theologians met in 1540 in order to reconcile the Bishops' Book with the king's *post-facto* comments as well as the Catholic orthodoxy set forth in the Six Articles Act. The mood of the commissioners reflected the depression of the reforming bishops over the king's divorce from Anne of Cleves and of the rejoicing of the conservative bishops over the king's infatuation with Catherine Howard, who became Henry's fifth wife. Seventeen Interrogatories, including six on the sacrament of ordination, were posed to the commission, and some of the replies, including those of Cranmer, indicate the Commission's concern over possible royal usurpation of the *potestas ordinis*.[64]

The tone of Cranmer's reply on ordination surfaced in his statement that the consecration of the clergy by bishops was unnecessary since election or appointment, in effect the royal choice, would suffice. Henry's responses to other theologians on ordination questions indicated that he, too, possessed some reservations about consecration. Specifically, the King asked why the consecration of the clergy should be only in the hands of bishops. Cranmer, in fact, was willing to go even further, indicating that willingness when he answered two hypothetical questions on ordination. Cranmer's first hypothetical question was whether an unconsecrated "prince Christian-learned," who had conquered a country of infidels with only "temporal-learned" men, should preach the Word of God and "make and constitute" priests. The other hypothetical question asked whether a king, whose bishops and priests were all dead, should "make" bishops and priests to handle the sacraments. To both of these questions Cranmer replied that God's law did not forbid it. In special cases, then, involving emergency situations, Cranmer gave the Crown the power to "make" priests.

In his reply to another question on ordination, Cranmer broadened the discussion to the cure of souls. Cranmer stated that God had "committed" to all Christian princes the "ministration of things political and civil" and "the administration of God's word for the cure of souls," but he quickly added that princes "must have sundry ministers unto them, to supply that which is appointed to their several offices." In this instance Cranmer was not claiming that the king had the direct cure of souls himself. Indeed, it is possible that the archbishop's statement approximated Henry's view at the time of the Pardon of the Clergy, when the king had claimed that the cure of souls had been committed to royal authority. Nevertheless, these extensions of royal supremacy by Henry and Cranmer show how close they were getting to a royal claim to the *potestas ordinis*.

The fourth and last major declaration of faith in Henry's reign, *The Necessary Doctrine and Erudition for Any Christian Man* (1543), treated the subject matter, the replies, and the responses of the Seventeen Interrogatories. Although the conservative bishops, especially Gardiner, revised the Bishops' Book in order to produce *The Necessary Doctrine*, the new formulary was properly called the King's Book, since Henry added the preface and some further revisions. Both convocations, united together, and Parliament gave the King's Book their blessing, the latter in the parliamentary statute for the Advancement of True Religion (1543). The statute stated that any "articles of the faith" (referring to the Ten Articles and the Bishops' Book), which were contrary to the doctrine set forth since 1540 (referring to the Six Articles Act) or the doctrine to be set forth by Henry (referring to the King's book) should be abolished. In the King's Book man's justification is not achieved by faith alone; the Book sets forth both free will and good works—the latter modified, however, from the Catholic concept. Cranmer's theology, to say nothing of the archbishop himself, seemed irretrievably lost. The king had, in fact, just saved Cranmer from a plot by the Council to remove him for heresy.

The discussion of the sacrament of ordination in the King's Book, as in the Bishops' Book and the Seventeen Interrogatories, examined the limitations of royal supremacy. The King's Book categorically stated that the sacrament of "orders is a gift or grace of ministration in Christ's church, given of God to Christian men, by the consecration and imposition of the bishop's hands upon them.[65] That sentence destroyed the notion, as suggested in the Seventeen Interrogatories, that consecration should be omitted or placed in the hands of the king. On the other hand, the distinction in the Bishops' Book between the *potestas gladii* and the *potestas ordinis*, which implicitly excluded the Crown from priestly powers, dropped out of the King's Book. In addition, the statement in the Bishops' Book which explicitly denied to the king the cure of souls, including the *potestas ordinis*, also dropped out of the King's Book. Despite the difference on ordination between the Seventeen Interrogatories and the King's Book, these eliminations might have helped Henry had he claimed to exercise a cure of souls with priestly powers himself, but he never did.

The King's Book did not give Henry the *potestas ordinis* when it stated that kings and princes had the power "to defend the faith of Christ and his religion, to conserve and maintain the true doctrine of Christ, and all such as be true preachers and setters forth thereof, and to abolish abuses, heresies, and idolatries, and to punish with corporal pains such as of malice be the occasion of the same." For canon lawyers still regarded the foregoing tasks as part of the *potestas jurisdictionis*. So also was the substance of the passage included in the King's Book, which Henry had written into the margin of the Bishops' Book in a slightly different phraseology, stating that priests and bishops should execute their office with "such limitations as the ordinances and laws of every Christian realm do permit and suffer." These manifestations of the *potestas jurisdictionis* by the king and the king-in-Parliament further extended the royal supremacy into the spiritual realm.[66]

During the crucial years of the early 1530s, when the king wrested the independence of the English Church from the authority of the pope, Henry had not wanted to handle matters of heresy, change doctrine, or, with one unlikely exception during the Surrender of the Clergy in 1531, personally claim a cure of souls. After the Act of Supremacy, however, the king became deeply involved in all three of these aspects of the Church's spiritual life. Medieval English kings like Henry V had only argued with heretics; Henry VIII, however, conducted a heresy trial himself, even though he did not claim to excommunicate anyone from the Church. Although Henry recognized the pope's supremacy in matters of heresy as late as 1534, within five years he and Parliament had defined heresy anew. Medieval English kings had neither written lengthy books on the sacraments of the Church nor issued formularies of theological belief. Henry accomplished the latter with a group of declarations in the late 1530s and early 1540s. Although Henry maintained throughout his life the essential theological conservatism of the *Assertio* with respect to four of the sacraments, especially the doctrine of transubstantiation in the Eucharist, he did substantially depart in the King's Book from the *Assertio* with respect to the other three sacraments: confirmation, extreme unction, and, especially, ordination. And although the Ten Articles and the Bishops'

Book expressed Lutheran doctrine, the king and Parliament replaced them with declarations of faith, namely the Six Articles Act and the King's Book, which largely bore out Henry's intention, expressed as late as 1534, not to deviate from the main articles of the Catholic faith.

Medieval English kings had not attempted to exercise priestly powers after Henry I abandoned lay investiture of the bishops; Henry VIII and Archbishop Cranmer, however, came very close to, but not within the domain of, the Anglo-Saxon concept of theocratic monarchy. Henry's statements regarding the cure of souls never claimed that the king personally possessed the *potestas ordinis*, and Henry never attempted to exercise priestly powers. But the Kings' Book indicated that the king-in-Parliament should have a regulatory control over priestly powers that had been traditionally exercised by the convocations and the ecclesiastical courts. With a few exceptions, then, Henry clung to the *status quo* in substantive matters of heresy, theology, and the cure of souls, giving some truth to the argument that in spiritual matters alone the Henrician schism resulted merely in "Catholicism without the pope." However, Henry's interference with the heretical, theological, and sacerdotal aspects of the Church established procedural precedents that could be used as the basis for future reform.

The reign of Henry VIII enlarged upon existing precedents of royal control over the papacy to bring about the termination of the papal connection. It interrupted exchange between England and Rome at both ends. In the cases of papal revenue and appeals, Henry withheld something from Rome. The medieval monarchy limited papal revenue, but Henry's monarchy stopped the remaining amounts—including those from Peter's Pence, first fruits, and tenths. The statute of Praemunire, though seldom enforced, had prohibited appeals to Rome over advowsons, but the Act for the Submission of the Clergy prohibited all of the remaining kinds of appeals including those over marriage and divorce. In the cases of papal provisions and canon law, Henry rejected something from Rome. Late medieval bishops, nominated by the Crown and automatically elected by the cathedral chapters, nearly always received papal bulls of provision and consecration, but the Act in Absolute Restraint of Annates completely eliminated these papal bulls. Medieval kings did not challenge Roman canon law, such as papal ordinances and resolutions of general councils, as well as the dispensations for which English synods or convocations—indeed English kings—had petitioned the pope in order to depart from this canon law. But under Henry a thirty-two member commission reviewed all past canon laws, both English and Roman.

In the process of extruding Rome from England and withdrawing England from Rome, it was necessary to allocate administratively each one of the former papal powers either to the Crown or to the English hierarchy. First fruits and tenths went to a new royal court of that name; all appeals terminated with the archiepiscopal courts except in matters concerning the king, which were always decided in a royal court; the king appointed the bishops although they handled their own consecration; and Crown-appointed lay and clerical commissioners now reviewed the canon law although the archbishop of Canterbury handled dispensations of that law. Thus the Crown and the Church divided papal privileges about evenly.

The Crown's ecclesiastical gains from the papacy, however, were not as momentous as they seemed at first glance. For instance, the royal income from first fruits and tenths represented only about one-third of what the Crown already received from the Church; or, the royal appointments to bishoprics amounted to little more than what the Crown had been doing for decades anyway; or, despite the royal prohibition of the study of the Roman canon law, the king's failure to appoint the lay and clerical commission meant that Roman canon law continued in effect in the ecclesiastical courts except, according to a Henrician statute, where it conflicted with the law of God and the king. Yet, these ecclesiastical changes were more than a mere consolidation of victories already won against pre-Henrician popes. After all, it was now possible for the king to get a dispensation of his marriage or to prevent an appeal of his divorce without any assistance or interference from Rome. But perhaps most important of all was the psychological impact of the new title on all groups in society; the king was now the formal head of the Church of England and the pope was not!

Henry VIII also enlarged upon medieval precedents of royal control over the Church as he proceeded to implement his concept of the supreme headship. Many of the changes that Henry's reign made had little or nothing to do with the extinction of papal power, since they represented matters traditionally controlled by the English regular and secular clergy. These included Church convocations, courts, and monasteries as well as the privileges of sanctuary and benefit of clergy. Either the king or the archbishop (usually the former) summoned medieval convocations of the clergy, and their actions required no ratification, but, under Henry's act for the Submission of the Clergy, only the king summoned them, and all future canons required the royal consent. Medieval Church courts exclusively had tried heresy cases, but under Henry the civil courts tried them as felonies. By 1540 the king and Parliament nearly destroyed the medieval privilege of ecclesiastical sanctuary, substituting eight cities of refuge, each of which could protect only twenty persons at a time under strict supervision, mostly for debt. Later Henrician statutes further limited the medieval privilege of benefit of clergy by excluding escaped prisoners, servants who robbed masters, and those found guilty or who stood mute to charges of specified felonies. Wolsey had extended the bishops' medieval visitations of the monasteries and the Crown's medieval suppression of a few monasteries, but by the late 1530s the Crown had visited, suppressed, and seized the wealth of all the monasteries.[67]

The consequences of the seizure of the monasteries and their wealth are of such great importance in assessing the Henrician relationship of church and state that by almost any standard of measurement it is very tempting, especially when one adds the new aspects of the royal supremacy derived from the papacy, to label them a religious revolution. The temptation grows when one adds the powers assumed by Cromwell as vicegerent: the visitation and discipline of the secular clergy in lieu of visitation by bishops, the issuance of royal injunctions for Church reform in lieu of papal ordinances, and the issuance of royal writs of prohibition in lieu of some clerical and administrative functions. Nevertheless, even if one includes the powers of the vicegerency, which largely disappeared with Cromwell's death, the basic ecclesiastical structures of the Church and of the Church courts still stood as they had for centuries. Cromwell's plans for the reform of the latter, as well as his plan for the nationalization of the lands and income of the Church—similar to what had happened to the monasteries—came to naught. Still, Cromwell, like Henry, had set some of the revolutionary precedents that another Cromwell would help to transform into a religious revolution of the mid-seventeenth century. In the mid-seventeenth century revolution, however, the Church hierarchy, its courts, its lands, its doctrine, and its liturgy were all to be abolished.

2

The Anglican Reformation

The term "Anglican Reformation" applies best to those two periods in the mid-sixteenth century which cover the six years of King Edward VI (1547–1553) and the first five years of Queen Elizabeth I (1558–1563). They are the periods when Archbishop Cranmer, Parliament, and Convocation created, and Elizabeth, Parliament, and Convocation selected, those important Protestant reforms, especially in worship and belief, which form the historic base of the Anglican Church essentially as we know it today. In the decade before Edward's six years, Henry VIII had reformed the Church minimally, and in the four decades after Elizabeth's first five years, the queen resisted practically all suggestions for change. Sandwiched in between the reigns of his two younger children was the Catholic restoration of Henry's eldest, Queen Mary I (1553–1558). Ironically, Mary's own burning of heretics, reminiscent of the Spanish Inquisition, and the subsequent emigration of English men and women to the continent, provided the stuff of Protestant martyrology for centuries and exposed a new generation of laymen and clerics to the Protestant experiments of the Rhineland. With so much instability—so many shifts in direction—in the sixteen years from 1547–1563, the three children of Henry VIII produced a series of dramatic changes in the Church which can be rivaled only by those of the mid-seventeenth century.

The Last Years of Henry VIII

Some scholars have stated that towards the end of his reign Henry VIII had a significant change of heart in favor of Protestant theology and liturgy which made the triumph of Protestantism inevitable after his death. Supporters of this view note that the king's sixth and last wife, Catherine Parr, sympathized with Protestant views; that Protestant tutors educated the king's young son and heir, Edward; that Protestants dominated the regency council appointed by Henry for Edward; and that Archbishop Cranmer heard Henry tell the French ambassador that both France and England should change the mass into a communion service and should try to get Emperor Charles V to do the same. But these points are far from being the complete story.

Henry became so concerned about his wife's Protestant views that he signed a bill of articles, drawn up by Bishop Gardiner, accusing Catherine of heresy and treason. The king, however, as with Cranmer in 1543, did not allow the lord chancellor, Thomas Wriothesley, to make the arrest after Catherine pleaded that she had not meant to instruct the supreme head. Both of Edward's tutors, John Cheke and Richard Cox, later became Protestant reformers under Edward and Protestant exiles under Mary, but under Henry VIII Cheke enjoyed a reputation as one of the foremost scholars in the humanist tradition of Erasmus, and Cox had served as one of the authors of the King's Book.

A sympathy toward Protestantism did not primarily determine Henry's selection and omission of members of the regency council who were to exercise majority rule until Edward was eighteen years of age. The uncles of the young heir to the throne, Edward Seymour (Earl of Hertford) and John Dudley (Viscount Lisle), who were pro-French in diplomacy as well as successful military campaigners against the Scots, received appointments to the regency council whereas Bishop Gardiner, who was pro-imperial in diplomacy and out of favor at court because of his transfer of episcopal lands, did not. Both Hertford and Lisle wore their Protestantism lightly, perhaps by necessity, whereas Bishop Tunstall and Lord Chancellor Wriothesley, also appointed to the regency council, were well-known religious conservatives. The nomination of several Protestants to the regency council, and the inclusion of Archbishop Cranmer as well, enabled Henry to protect his Church settlement from a return to papal Catholicism after his death.

Henry's statement to the French ambassador regarding a communion service should also be seen in the context of diplomacy as well as of religion. In the French war of the mid-1540s, the English had captured Boulogne, and King Francis I had recognized Henry as supreme head, but Charles V's successes against the German Protestant states brought about a rapprochement between England and France in 1546. As with the Ten Articles in 1536, Henry did not hesitate to use religion as an instrument of foreign policy. However, it is quite possible that Henry genuinely considered some changes in the mass for religious reasons. He had, after all, asked Cranmer and two other bishops in 1544 to examine all mass books with the idea of making some liturgical changes, and the following year Parliament transferred select chantries—those listed in the *Valor Ecclesiasticus*—to the Crown. The liturgical changes, such as the elimination of "creeping to the cross" on Good Friday, were only of a minor nature, and Henry's own will provided money for masses for his soul. In view of the foregoing evidence, it seems most unlikely that Henry was on the verge of initiating the thorough-going theological and liturgical reforms that were such an important part of the Anglican Reformation in the reigns of Edward and Elizabeth. Within forty-eight hours of Henry's death, the earl of Hertford, who was a moderate and tolerant Protestant reformer, was appointed lord protector on the basis of letters patent (said Ambassador Chapuys) issued by the late king.[1]

The Edwardian Transition

Six months after the nine-year-old Edward VI ascended the throne of England in February, 1547, Archbishop Cranmer issued a set of royal injunctions. Much of the material in these Edwardian injunctions had already appeared in both sets of the Henrician injunctions: the removal of images and shrines, for example. Some of the Edwardian injunctions elaborated upon the Erasmian features of the Henrician injunctions of 1538. These included the injunction which required the clergy to provide each church with a copy of an English Bible and an English translation of Erasmus' *Paraphrases* of it. Other Edwardian injunctions required the use of the Litany of 1544, the *Primer* of 1545, and the *Book of Homilies* of 1547, three religious works that had been drawn up under the archbishop's supervision during the last few years of Henry's reign.

The Litany was a liturgical responsive prayer sung in English for processions, but the injunctions required the faithful to sing it while kneeling and not in procession around the church. The *Primer* incorporated the Litany, but the rest of it, including a 1541 rendering of the Creed, the Lord's Prayer, and the Ten Commandments in English, was fairly traditional.[2] The *Book of Homilies* contained official sermons in English on various subjects, any one of which the injunctions required to be read in each church on Sunday. One of the homilies attributed to Cranmer, "Obedience," took much the same position as Tyndale had put forward a few years earlier. The high power and authority of kings must be obeyed "although they be wicked and wrong doers." If kings commanded anything contrary to the law of God, however, men must obey God rather than man. Yet in such an event "we may not in any wise withstand violently, or rebel against rulers, or make any insurrection, sedition, or tumults, either by force of arms (or otherwise). . . . But we must in such case, patiently suffer all wrongs, and injuries."[3]

The *Book of Homilies* also occasioned Cranmer's introduction of some Protestant doctrine to both clergy and laity, doctrine contrary to the Catholic views expressed in the King's Book. His homilies on justification, which set forth a qualified version of the Lutheran doctrine that only faith justifies the sinner, especially distressed Bishop Stephen Gardiner. Here was the ironic spectacle of a man who, as one of the staunchest advocates of obedience to the royal supremacy under Henry, decided not to stand idly by while Cranmer used that same supremacy to undermine Gardiner's own theology. It was a choice which the archbishop himself would experience under reverse circumstances with Queen Mary's attempt to return England to Roman Catholicism. Gardiner, like Cranmer later, took his stand on behalf of his religious convictions.

At first, Gardiner argued that during Edward's minority the supreme headship was in abeyance, thus rendering any religious changes invalid. A Henrician act of 1536, empowering Edward upon reaching his twenty-fourth year to annul whatever had been done before he attained his majority, lent considerable plausibility to this position. But Gardiner and all the bishops had tacitly recognized Edward's supreme headship at the very beginning of the reign, when the earl of Hertford had required them to accept new episcopal commissions just like any other Crown servant. And in fact, the earl of Hertford (now duke of Somerset and lord protector) had suspended all episcopal authority until a royal visitation could test a bishop's compliance with the new injunctions.

Later, Gardiner declared that the religious doctrines of the *Homilies*, which the convocations had not adopted, were in violation of the religious doctrines of the Six Articles Act (1539) and of the King's Book (1543), which both Convocation and Parliament had approved. Any reading of the *Homilies*, therefore, contradicted what had been established by law, and to order people to violate the law, Gardiner contended in a dubious conclusion, was to make them liable to the penalties of the statute of Praemunire, as in the case of Cardinal Wolsey in 1529. Gardiner's refusal to enforce the reading of the *Homilies* in his diocese, except with parliamentary approval and even then an approval which would be effective only after fifteen years, did not prevent the Privy Council from sending him to the Fleet prison. Bishop Bonner of London suffered the same fate, but his release came after two months. Eventually, in 1551, Gardiner lost the bishopric of Winchester, and the Crown confiscated many of the see's lands, a practice which became more widespread because of the financial gain.

The imprisonment of Gardiner did not reflect the warming air of religious change that Parliament claimed had suffused Protector Somerset's regime, especially after the first session of Edward's first Parliament abrogated what some of the members may have regarded as Henry VIII's chilling legislation. The preamble to the Edwardian Act of Repeal, initiated by Parliament rather than the protector, set the political climate: "as in tempest or winter one course and garment is convenient, in calm or warm weather a more liberal race or lighter garment both may and ought to be followed and used." The statute's repeal of the heresy laws and, to a much lesser extent, its modification of the treason legislation marked a reversal of policy from the last year of Henry VIII. Swept away was the surviving heresy legislation from the medieval period (including the 1414 act of Henry V), the heresy legislation of Henry VIII (including the Six Articles Acts of 1539 and 1543), the King's Book, and the penalties imposed by Henry in 1543 on printing, selling, or possessing the Bible in English. The common law courts now handled all matters of heresy, but the burning of heretics still continued, as the cases of two Anabaptists, Joan Bocher and George van Parris, indicate.[4] The Edwardian Act of Repeal, like the Treasons Act of 1534 which it replaced, still made it high treason to write, print, or commit any overt act against the supreme head, but words, speeches, or sermons against the supreme head were to be high treason only on the third offense. Neither More nor Fisher would have been executed under these provisions.

Not surprisingly, some Protestants expressed much "unseemly" criticism of the mass. The body of Christ, for example, was denounced as, among other things, a "Jack-in-the-Box" or a "Round-Robin," and the words of consecration, *hoc est corpus meum* [this is my body], as "Hocus-pocus." Somerset issued proclamations against any disputes over the Eucharist and against all forms of private innovation on it. Parliament responded more constructively with a statute providing penalties for revilers against the Eucharist and requiring communion in both kinds—both the bread and the wine—for the laity. This legislation, which was implemented through a directory called *The Order of the Communion* (1548), was an important step in transforming the mass (with stone altars) into a communion service (with wooden tables).

Edward's first Parliament did not loosen the authority of the Crown over the bishops. If anything, it tightened its Marsilian control over the bishops in still another statute by setting forth a procedure, provided as an alternative in the 1534 Act in Absolute Restraint of Annates, to eliminate the formality of episcopal elections. An outright royal appointment through letters patent replaced the royal *congé d'élire* and accompanying letter missive. Either way it meant a royal selection with no free elections. The preamble of this Edwardian statute declared in general that "all authority of Jurisdiction, Spiritual and Temporal, is derived and deducted from the King's Majesty, as supreme head," and, more particularly, that the "Courts Ecclesiastical . . . be kept by no other power, or authority, either foreign or within the Realm," except by the king. An enacting clause, however, citing the authority of the king-in-Parliament, gave to the archbishops, bishops, or others having authority such as a dean—shades of the Henrician vicegerent—the implementation of all processes in the ecclesiastical courts in the name of the king. Here was the last instance of the tension, present in some Henrician legislation, between the power of the king-in-Council in the declaratory preambles and the power of the king-in-Parliament in the enacting clauses.

One of the most important pieces of legislation passed in the opening session of Edward's first Parliament was the statute relating to the chantries. The chantries, founded by merchants and gentry in the fourteenth and fifteenth centuries, were endowments in real estate to support unbeneficed priests who, while not having the cure of souls, could hold private masses for the souls of deceased individuals in order to decrease their time in purgatory. The Six Articles Act found private masses agreeable with God's law, but the King's Book deemed it improper to limit these intercessory masses for the dead to particular individuals, adding that people should abstain from the "name of purgatory." [5]

The new legislation exceeded the Henrician statute of 1545. That statute had dissolved only select chantries in order to raise revenue for Henry's wars. The 1545 act had not reflected any significant doctrinal change on the part of the king. In fact, Henry's last will and testament, revised only a month before his death, had provided for the full panoply of intercessory masses in behalf of his soul. The emphasis on the future destiny of the dead in the Edwardian injunctions and the antipurgatorial doctrine of the *Homilies*, however, suggested some further changes for the chantries. [6]

The Edwardian Act of 1547 specifically provided that certain chantries (including those sustained by corporations, guilds, and fraternities), colleges (excluding those at Oxford and Cambridge), and free chapels, along with their possessions, should be turned over to the Crown because, as the preamble stated, "superstitions and errors in Christian religion hath been brought into the minds and estimation of men . . . by devising and phantasing vain opinions of purgatory." Altogether, the act dissolved almost 3,000 chantries, colleges, and free chapels, valued at nearly £650,000, in order to erect grammar schools, to augment the universities, and to make "better provision for the poor and needy." Certain chantry foundations already were grammar schools, and these were refounded as Edward VI grammar schools. But the government built neither new grammar schools nor almshouses, and it only slightly increased the previous level of support, small as it was (about eleven percent of the total endowment), for these charitable institutions.[7] The dissolutions of both the chantries and the monasteries provided small pensions for the displaced priests and monks as well as substantial increments to the Court of Augmentations. The chantries, however, when compared with the monasteries, possessed only about one-fourth of the capital investment, and their dissolution was not followed by a major uprising against the Crown. In addition, chantries were more widely distributed geographically than the monasteries, so the impact of their dissolution was more widely dispersed among the English people.[8]

Because the liturgy of the Church was in a state of flux, Cranmer, in collaboration with other divines, drafted the first Book of Common Prayer in the English language. The Prayer Book of 1549 was more of a liturgical work than a formulary of religious doctrine such as the Ten Articles, the Bishop's Book, or the King's Book. As a liturgical work, it drew heavily upon the Great Bible of Tyndale and Coverdale, the Catholic rite according to the Use of Sarum, and the Lutheran Church Orders. It also incorporated the Litany and included in the vernacular the words of administration from *The Order of the Communion*. The title the Prayer Book gave to the Eucharist—"The Supper of the Lord and the Holy Communion Commonly Called the Mass"—reflected the mixture of old and new.

As a formulary of religious doctrine, the new Prayer Book dealt with theological aspects of the Eucharist. Cranmer's own eucharistic thought seems to have followed three imprecise stages: transubstantiation, the real presence, and the true presence.[9] The archbishop seriously began to question the Catholic doctrine of transubstantiation about the time of Lambert's trial in 1538. His commonplace books during the next few years show that extracts from Zwingli's views of the Eucharist as a memorial were effectively answered by Luther's doctrine of the real presence. Cranmer began to give up the doctrine of the real presence in 1546, partially under the influence of Bishop Ridley's concept of a spiritual or true presence, which had received affirmation in *The Order of the Communion*. Three months later, however, the archbishop published an English translation of a Lutheran catechism, but he sought to remove the real presence of Lutheranism, thereby making it possible for an interpretation along the lines of a true presence.

In the early part of the debate over the new Prayer Book in the House of Lords in December, Cranmer, perhaps under the influence of the Polish reformer, John à Lasco, spoke of the bread and wine as merely "figurative" elements—strongly implying the "Real Absence" of Zwingli. By the end of the debate, however, he echoed the opinions of Bishop Ridley. The words of consecration in the new Prayer Book, which stated that the body and blood of Christ "may be unto us," differed from the words "may be made unto us," in the old Use of Sarum. Despite this omission of the word "made," which permitted the denial of transubstantiation but was compatible with either a real presence or a true presence, the conservative Bishop Gardiner endorsed the new Prayer Book, claiming that it implied a belief in transubstantiation. Whatever ambiguity churchmen perceived in the new Prayer Book may well have reflected Cranmer's own views of the Eucharist, which had slowly changed over the immediately preceding months and years.

The second session of Edward's first Parliament and the Canterbury Convocation authorized the new Prayer Book in early 1549 through an Act of Uniformity. The Act, so named because it prescribed a uniform liturgy in English to be followed by all the churches throughout the kingdom except those at the universities of Oxford and Cambridge, gave no heed to old Latin rites and local usages. The state could levy only moderately graduated penalties against the clergy for violations of the Act, and no penalties could be levied against laymen who did not attend the authorized services.

Despite general compliance with the Act throughout most of the country, armed rebellion broke out in Devonshire in June and spread to much of the West Country. The leaders of the Western Rebellion contended that they acted primarily as a result of the religious changes authorized by Edward's first Parliament, including the new Prayer Book. The rebels' conservative manifesto called for the restoration of the Six Articles, private masses for souls in purgatory, the Latin mass with communion in one kind (and that only at Easter), and some of the ancient ceremonies, including the use of images, ashes, and palms. The manifesto also called for the withdrawal of the Great Bible from use, since the clergy then would no longer be able to confound heretics with it, as well as the withdrawal of the new liturgy, since, as a "Christmas game" in a foreign language (namely English), only a few Cornish men could understand it.[10] It also demanded that half of the expropriated chantry and abbey lands be used to create two new abbeys in each county. The manifesto did not, surprisingly, call for a celibate clergy, although Parliament's second session approved marriage of the clergy; the demand for a restoration of the Six Articles, however, clearly implied celibacy. The quelling of the rebellion gave the government an opportunity to enforce the ideas set forth in the homily of "Obedience." Four West Country men were hanged in January, 1550. Agrarian discontent, particularly enclosures, inspired the other unsuccessful rebellion during the summer of 1549—Kett's Rebellion in East Anglia—which, however, had a religious dimension. Most of Kett's religious demands were pro-Protestant yet anticlerical, one of which focused upon clergymen who used litigation to increase their tithes.

Indeed, the second parliamentary session enacted a bill, dealing with tithes, that would adversely affect the financial resources of the Church for many years to come. Henceforth, predial tithes (a tenth part in kind of corn or of hay or of an increase in livestock) and personal tithes (a tenth part of the profit of merchants and craftsmen) would be collected according to the custom of the preceding forty years. Thus the Church lost those tithes that were not customary. The statute also provided that all day laborers would henceforth be exempt from the payment of tithes, and new land brought into cultivation would be exempt for seven years. If anyone not exempted should not pay the personal tithes, the ordinary of the diocese could call the offending party before him for examination, but the ordinary could no longer require that party to take an oath to tell the truth. Finally, should a clergyman charge someone with nonpayment of tithes in the ecclesiastical courts, where the only punishment was excommunication, the defendant could obtain a prohibition against the ecclesiastical suit from a common law court upon presentation of a "suggestion" for libel. To be sure, if the common law court did not later accept the "suggestion," there would be a double penalty. But the high cost of such litigation for clergymen, and the sympathies of the common law courts for laymen, put the clergy at a decided disadvantage.[11]

The interaction between church and state under Protector Somerset shows a surprising amount of continuity amid some change. A number of early Edwardian reforms extended or modified Henrician actions. These included Parliament's approval for the royal appointment of bishops without the formality of episcopal elections, the parliamentary dissolution of the chantries, and the destruction of images in a renewed set of royal injunctions. In addition, some things formulated in Henry's reign did not receive implementation until the rule of Somerset. These included the Litany, the *Primer*, and the *Homilies*—all incorporated into the Edwardian Injunctions. The Litany and *Primer*, however, did not represent a marked change from the earlier practices of Henry's reign, nor did the homily on "Obedience," since it set forth the Henrician views of Tyndale. Cranmer's homilies on justification by faith reaffirmed Lutheran doctrine as stated in the Bishop's Book, but, of course, Henry had rejected that belief in the King's Book. During Somerset's protectorship, Parliament did repeal the medieval heresy laws and Henry's Six Articles Act. Although these repeals removed the major obstacles to theological reform, no steps were immediately taken to implement them. Such, however, was not the case with liturgical reform, because Parliament adopted communion in both kinds and because the clergy adopted *The Order of the Communion*, both important deviations from the Six Articles Act. However, despite the substantive inclusion of several of these changes in the First Prayer Book, it retained many of the old liturgical practices from Henry's day. The declaratory preamble of the statute for the appointment of bishops kept the phrasing that suggested the Henrician personal supremacy, but, for the most part, the religious legislation under Somerset, including the First Act of Uniformity, laid stress upon the authority of the king-in-Parliament.

The Cranmerian Reforms

When Somerset fell from power, John Dudley (earl of Warwick and soon to be duke of Northumberland), a more vigorous Protestant, quickened the pace of Protestant reform in the Church. The views of several of the Swiss Reformers who had recently come to England sustained the increased tempo. Men of Calvinist and Zwinglian persuasion, these immigrants included à Lasco, Valerand Poullain, Peter Martyr, and Martin Bucer. Cranmer hoped to bring all of the Swiss Reformers into an ecumenical council which would be the Protestant answer to the Catholic Council of Trent. With the aid of the Swiss Reformers, Cranmer and the reforming bishops were able to produce the four important documents that represented the high tide of the Anglican Reformation: the Ordinal, the Second Book of Common Prayer, the Forty-Two Articles, and a revision of the canon law. After Northumberland became president of the Council, some new faces appeared on the episcopal bench. The Henrician conservative bishops such as Gardiner, Tunstall, and Bonner lost their sees, and reformers such as Nicholas Ridley, John Ponet, Miles Coverdale, and John Hooper assumed bishoprics or were transferred from other sees. Hooper, who received an appointment as bishop of Gloucester in April, 1550, refused to comply with some of the provisions of the Ordinal, which the third session of Parliament authorized sight unseen.

The Ordinal, drawn up by a commission presided over by Cranmer and aided by recommendations from Bucer, retained the ecclesiastical structure of the Church based upon bishops, priests, and deacons. It deprived the priest of his old power to offer Christ's body as a propitiatory sacrifice, and it set forth the manner—a prayer and the imposition of hands—for making and consecrating the clergy. Hooper took exception to two things in the new Ordinal: the existing vestments of the clergy, which he regarded as the hallmark of a priest, and the swearing of the customary oath to the Crown at the time of consecration "by God, all Saints and the holy Evangelists," which he regarded as blasphemy.[12] Cranmer also regarded the form of the oath as sacrosanct. Nevertheless, the Council under Northumberland decided to appoint Hooper without his wearing the prescribed vestments and swearing by the "Saints" and "Evangelists." Hooper's nonconformity and disobedience bothered Cranmer, as it would in the Black Rubric controversy.

Criticism of the First Book of Common Prayer came not only from those who felt that it had carried the liturgy too far in the direction of the Reformed faith, but also from those new holders of influential English university professorships, Bucer and Martyr, who felt that it had not gone far enough in removing the vestiges of Roman Catholicism. While the major influences in the First Prayer Book, apart from the Eucharist, had been Roman Catholic and Lutheran, the major influences in the revised or Second Prayer Book, drafted by Cranmer and others with the aid of criticisms by Martyr and Bucer, were Reformed. For example, the word "mass" does not appear in the Book. Communion tables, located in the body of the church (the ends facing east and west with the minister standing on the north side), replaced altars, unmentioned by name since they were regarded as places of sacrifice. Followers of Archbishop Laud challenged these details nearly a century later. The Prayer Book forbade the medieval sacerdotal vestments of the clergy, namely the alb, chasuble, and stole (leaving only the surplice), and it also forbade the cope for the bishops (leaving only the rochet). These proscriptions became the subject of controversy once again under Elizabeth.

As for the Eucharist, Cranmer had set forth his final position in his lengthy *Defense* of the First Prayer Book in 1550 and an *Answer* to Bishop Gardiner in 1551. In these works he further developed the view of a true or spiritual presence in the Lord's Supper through faith given by the Holy Spirit. He joined both Calvin and Zwingli in holding that the body of Christ was actually in heaven—what Luther scornfully called some celestial "swallow's nest"—but he rejected Calvin's view of a substantial participation in the body and blood of Christ as well as Zwingli's figurative commemoration with the bread and wine as empty symbols. Cranmer's doctrine of the Lord's Supper stands between the participation of Calvin and the memorialism of Zwingli.[13]

Some aspects of both memorialism or "remembrance" and participation or "feeding" appear in the subjective words of administration for the Lord's Supper contained in the Second Prayer Book: "Take and eat this in remembrance that Christ died for thee and feed on him in thy heart by faith with thanksgiving. Drink this in remembrance that Christ's blood was shed for thee and be thankful." Although Cranmer's own views did not receive an explicit formulation in these words of administration, the use of the word "this" in two instances implies that the communicants were to take something more than just the figurative bread and wine of the "real absence" and something less than the literal body and blood of the real presence.

The use of the revised or Second Prayer Book, like the Ordinal of 1550, was prescribed by the authority of the fourth session of Parliament (1552), but, unlike the First Prayer Book, it was apparently not submitted to the Canterbury Convocation of the Clergy. The preamble to the Second Act of Uniformity did not pay tribute to or mention the role of the archbishop in the formulation of the Second Prayer Book, as the First Act of Uniformity had done with the First Prayer Book. An enacting clause of the 1552 measure did provide that every lay person within the realm would attend his or her parish church diligently and faithfully every Sunday and holy day. If anyone failed to attend church, the ecclesiastical authorities should mete out heavy penalties.

After the act was passed, but in the interim before it became operative, John Knox, the Scottish reformer, and Bishop Hooper wanted the Privy Council to add a rubric to the yet-to-be-released Prayer Book for the receiving of communion in a standing rather than a kneeling position. Despite the intervention of Northumberland, Cranmer refused to make any change since he said that that issue had already been carefully considered. The result was a compromise implemented first by an Order of Council and then by a royal proclamation: the issuance of the Black Rubric—black because it was not printed in red ink as other rubrics were in this edition. The Black Rubric retained kneeling but specifically stated, as Cranmer would have agreed, that it did not amount to an adoration of the elements in and of themselves, that is, to a belief in the real presence, because Christ's body was in heaven. Once again, the Council and the king seemed to be a bit more radical than the archbishop.[14]

Henry VIII had proposed the reform of the ecclesiastical law by a thirty-two member commission (half laymen and half clergy) as early as the Submission of the Clergy in 1532. Despite legislation in 1534, 1536, and 1544 calling for such action, and despite a set of Henrician canons drawn up (*circa* 1535) in order to depapalize English canon law, the third session of Edward's first Parliament in 1550 made a fresh start. The Commons defeated a bill to give the bishops and ordinaries the power to enforce Church discipline by excommunication and imprisonment; but the Lords passed a bill setting up the thirty-two member commission once again, even though ten of eleven bishops, including Cranmer, voted against it, probably because they thought it was just another attempt to delay action. Not until 1552 did the new commission, including Cranmer and Martyr, block out the main lines of the document that John Foxe in 1571 would call the *Reformatio Legum Ecclesiasticarum.*[15]*1*

The *Reformatio*, which was not just a later version of the aforementioned Henrician canons, gave the bishops the power to punish immorality, something which they had sought in the Commons' bill of 1550. If ecclesiastical censure failed, the bishops should resort to excommunication and imprisonment in extreme cases. Heretics, such as Anabaptists, should be excommunicated, but only if they proved obstinate could they be turned over to the state for punishment. Divorce could be granted for adultery, ill-treatment, and desertion, a change that would not have helped Henry VIII with Catherine of Aragon.

The influence of the Swiss Reformers appeared in the *Reformatio*'s proposal for synods at the diocesan and provincial levels that laymen, as well as clergy, would attend. Even at the congregational level, laymen known as "seniores" or elders were to work with the minister in implementing church discipline. In short, here was a form of what came to be known as the presbyterian system adapted for use by episcopal church government. It had been practiced in Zurich in the 1520s, developed theoretically by Bucer in Strassburg in the 1530s, and practiced at the local level in à Lasco's London Church of the Strangers in the late 1540s.[16]

When Northumberland abruptly rejected the *Refomatio* because the commission had exceeded its charge, the Anglican hierarchy missed a splendid opportunity to bring itself into collegiality with the lay people it was designed to serve. The next extensive Church reform of the canon law would come in 1604, but by then it would be too late to assert this collegiality. Puritanism had already preempted the cause of canon law reform, and the ecclesiastical politics of confrontation had become the order of the day.

The culmination of Cranmer's spiritual pilgrimage was the eclectic formulary known as the Forty-Two Articles (1553). Prepared by a commission and revised by Cranmer, this new declaration of faith endorsed such Cranmerian achievements as the *Book of Homilies*, the Ordinal, and the Second Book of Common Prayer. At one extreme, some of its articles attacked the traditional views of Roman Catholics: transubstantiation, a sacrificial mass, purgatory, clerical celibacy, and papal supremacy. At the opposite extreme, other articles attacked the radical views of the continental Anabaptists: denial of original sin, dispensing with moral law, lay preaching, communal property, forswearing of oaths, blasphemy, soul-sleeping, millenarianism, and universal salvation. Indeed, in 1552 the Privy Council urged the archbishop to repress an Anabaptist sect, probably the Family of Love, which had been founded in Holland by Hendrick Niclaes with certain pantheistic and antinomian views.[17]

Still others of the Forty-Two Articles dealt with specific points of the liturgy and theology. On liturgy, article twenty-nine restated Cranmer's views of the Lord's Supper but largely in negative rather than positive terms: because the body of Christ is in heaven, faithful men should not believe in the real presence of Christ's flesh and blood in the Eucharist. On theology, some articles, based upon the Thirteen Articles of 1538, which had reflected Henry's rapprochement with the German Lutherans, set forth the Lutheran doctrine of justification by faith alone as well as the admonition that men do not have the power of free will to do works acceptable unto God. Article seventeen set forth the Lutheran doctrine of "Predestination to life" for those whom God had chosen before the creation of the world for everlasting salvation. Although it could be argued that article seventeeen included by implication the Calvinist doctrine of double predestination—that those not chosen by God would suffer everlasting damnation—it did not assert the rigid Calvinist doctrine that the elect cannot finally and totally fall from grace. The doctrine of single predestination, which also appeared in the Geneva Catechism, was also stressed in Bishop Ponet's Short Catechism appended to the published version of the Forty-Two Articles.

And finally, several articles dealt with the civil magistrate. Article thirty-six baldly stated that the king of England "is Supreme head in earth, next under Christ, of the Church of England" but without any mention of the distinction between the *potestas ordinis* or the *potestas jurisdictionis* as in the Henrician formularies. It also stated that "the civil magistrate is ordained and allowed of God," but this time, unlike the homily on "Obedience," it asserted that he must be obeyed not only for fear of punishment "but also for conscience sake." In addition, article thirty-six condoned civil laws that gave the magistrate the right to levy capital punishment for "heinous and grievous" offenses as well as to bear arms and to fight in wars. The Forty-Two Articles were referred to the royal chaplains, including Knox. Convocation sanctioned them without debate, but Edward's second and last Parliament never saw them. Instead, Northumberland and the Council promulgated them. Within a few months, however, Edward, the young Josiah, died at the age of fifteen, and the most creative period in the history of the Anglican Church had come to an end.[18]

The interaction between church and state under Northumberland shows a significant amount of change amid some continuity. A number of late Edwardian liturgical, doctrinal, and disciplinary innovations, which were initiated under the aegis of Cranmer and the reforming bishops, had not been envisioned either by the Henrician Church or by the state. The major innovations included a Reformed system of Church discipline, a comprehensive statement of Reformed doctrine, and a revised manual of Reformed liturgy. On the other hand, when Northumberland and the Privy Council rejected the *Reformatio*, with its quasi-presbyterian system of church discipline, Parliament reaffirmed the traditional hierarchy of the Church by approving a revised Ordinal. Neither the Privy Council nor Parliament interested themselves in changes in any form of church organization which might have departed from that in force in Henry's day.

When Protector Northumberland and the Privy Council approved the Forty-Two Articles, Parliament no longer acted as a participant in authorizing theology, even traditional theology, as it had done earlier in ratifying the King's Book and in providing penalties for offenses against the Six Articles Act. In doctrinal matters, then, the Crown had gained at the expense of Parliament since Henry's day. When Parliament authorized the Second Prayer Book in a statute that did not contain any of the Henrician preambles declaring a personal supremacy, the Council subsequently added the Black Rubric, which Cranmer opposed on procedural rather than substantive grounds. In liturgical matters, Parliament could claim the more important share of this major breakthrough for the state.

Although Parliament's loss in theological control offset somewhat its gain in liturgical control over the Church, one trend does emerge. For the most part, in the religious areas under discussion, the Henrician government and Parliaments opted for tradition, and Northumberland's government and Parliament opted for innovation. This difference between the two regimes may well have occurred because the impetus for change under Edward, and particularly Northumberland, stemmed largely from the Church rather than the state, as under Henry. In the succeeding century, the only strong rivals to Cranmer's documentary achievements under Edward were the theological, liturgical, and disciplinary counterparts produced by the Westminster Assembly for approval by the Long Parliament during the 1640s. At both times—during the Anglican Reformation and the Westminster Assembly—the reformers in the Church were attempting to bring about creative religious change. One of the major differences, of course, is that the Anglican changes, except for a brief interval under Mary, were to last for centuries, whereas the Puritan changes were not to last beyond the Caroline Restoration.

The Marian Restoration

After Northumberland's abortive attempt to place the sixteen-year-old Protestant Lady Jane Grey on the throne in place of the thirty-six-year-old

Catholic Princess Mary—an attempt which failed largely because of the loyalty of the gentry and others in heavily Protestant East Anglia—Mary slowly began to reverse the religious trends that had taken place during the reign of her half-brother. Initially, the queen used the title "Supreme Head," having received a special dispensation for its use from the pope; later she abandoned it in favor of "Defender of the Faith, etc.," which suited her very well. Ironically, she found it necessary to continue to use the authority of the royal supremacy. For example, Mary employed that authority to deprive Edwardian bishops—Ridley, Hooper, Coverdale, and Ponet—and to restore Henrician bishops—Bonner, Tunstall, and Gardiner—the last to be her chief minister. And she imprisoned Cranmer for having supported Lady Jane Grey, but she allowed Martyr, à Lasco, Poullain, and Knox (Bucer having died in 1551) to leave the country.

For Catherine of Aragon's pious and loyal daughter, who had been forced as a teenager to make a humiliating surrender to her father's demands—to acknowledge the royal supremacy, to renounce the papacy, and to admit her own illegitimacy—the royal proclamation of August, 1553 seemed to be quite moderate in tone. In it she stated that she could not "hide that religion which God and the world knoweth she hath ever professed from her infancy hitherto," and which she "would be glad the same were of all her subjects quietly and charitably embraced." But she would not compel any of her subjects to do so, she added, until such time as "common consent" could be taken by Parliament. These statements are very similar to those made by another Roman Catholic sovereign, James II, when he acceded to the throne.[19]

Mary, like Sir Thomas More, did not recognize the validity of acts of Parliament when they were contrary to the law of God, as she at least perceived it. But Bishop Gardiner, who had been a strong defender in Henry's reign of the royal supremacy (by the king alone), persuaded her to seek the parliamentary concurrence which Gardiner had demanded in Edward's reign. The result strengthened Parliament's authority in religious matters under Mary as had been the case, except for theology, under Edward. Mary's first Parliament removed the stigma of her illegitimacy by setting aside that part of Henry's Act of Succession of 1536 which had bastardized her. More significantly for affairs of church and state, Parliament also repealed nine statutes of Edward's reign, including those dealing with communion in both kinds, the selection of bishops by letters patent only, the marriage of priests, and the adoption of the two Prayer Books. All religious services were to revert to those employed in the last year of the reign of Henry VIII. But Mary's first Parliament showed its independence by refusing to rescind the royal supremacy for the papal supremacy.[20]

Mary issued a set of royal injunctions for the Church in March, 1554, just as her father and half-brother had done, under the authority of royal supremacy. The Marian injunctions eliminated several of those Protestant reforms that her first Parliament had not repealed, and implemented one Catholic practice, namely, the celibacy of the clergy, that had been restored. The injunctions erroneously seemed to assume that Northumberland had accepted the *Reformatio Legum Ecclesiasticarum* since Mary ordered the enforcement of all canon laws of Henry's reign not contrary to statute law. The revival of all church processions, either spoken or sung in Latin, directly repudiated the Litany. Repudiation also befell *The Order of the Communion* with the re-institution of the old ceremonies and with schoolmasters teaching schoolboys how to respond to the priest at mass. Homilies for the instruction of the parishioners continued, but the provision for a uniform doctrine ruled out the inclusion of the sermons by Cranmer on justification by faith. Still, attendance at this instruction by sermons was compulsory, just as it had been in both of Edward's Acts of Uniformity. Any priest ordained by the Edwardian Ordinal, the injunctions stated, had not been truly ordained, and the episcopal oath to the Crown, some parts of which Hooper had opposed at the time of his ordination, dropped out. The bishops or officers of the Church, while performing their official acts, no longer could use a phrase to which they had long since become accustomed—"sanctioned by royal authority."

Several injunctions carried out the celibacy of the clergy, and it was on this clear-cut issue, rather than the differences about eucharistic doctrine, that Mary's government chose to take its stand *vis à vis* the English clergy. Those married priests who had taken vows of chastity before their marriages had to get divorces and lost their livings, but the remaining clergy had the option of either staying married but becoming laymen or giving up their wives and changing ecclesiastical benefices. Altogether some 2,000 priests lost their livings.

Mary's second or "addled" Parliament (April–May, 1554), which was far more important for the legislation it did not pass than for that it did, provided a connecting link on religious matters between the moderate steps of Mary's first Parliament and the drastic changes made in her third Parliament about six months later. On the positive side for Mary, Parliament consented to the forthcoming marriage between the queen and the twenty-seven-year-old Prince Philip of Spain. The prospect of that marriage, not any bill of Protestant religious demands, had provoked Wyatt's uprising in Kent a few months before.[21] Once again, as in Henry's day, some Englishmen began to identify the Catholic cause with foreign intervention in English spiritual and temporal affairs.

On the negative side for Mary, Parliament was far less cooperative on bills regarding heresy and abbey lands. Mary believed that heresy and treason were inextricably combined, so the Catholic clerics under Bishop Gardiner (now lord chancellor) drew up a parliamentary bill to revive the *De Haeretico Comburendo* statute of 1401 and the Six Articles Act of 1539. The proposed bill passed the Commons, but the Catholic laity under William Paget defeated it in the Lords. Paget's supporters, alarmed by Gardiner's proposal in the Council to suppress Mary's title of "Supreme Head," became convinced that the complementary restoration of the papal supremacy would mean the restoration of the monastic lands and, though less catastrophic, the restoration of a clerical majority in the House of Lords. Gardiner, anticipating this fear of sequestration, introduced another parliamentary bill, stating "that neither the Bishop of Rome nor any other spiritual person shall Convent any person for Abbey lands." This conciliatory measure, which passed the Commons, also came to naught, after the Lord's defeat of the heresy bill.[22] Lay Catholic economic and political interests were in this Parliament stronger than religious cohesion. The frontier between church and state in the spring of 1554, except for the deep intrusions made by the king-in-Parliament against the positions once held by the great monasteries and the chantries, stood in just about the same place as it had in 1536: *after* the legislation of the Reformation Parliament but *before* the Henrician injunctions or formularies.

The blueprint revealed in the Council and Parliament, indicates, however, that Mary did not intend to stop there. During the summer of 1554, two things contributed to the restoration of papal supremacy in Mary's third Parliament. First, Philip and Mary were married, thus making it unnecessary any longer for Charles V to prevent Cardinal Reginald Pole, who had opposed the marriage, from returning to England as papal legate *a latere* after more than twenty years in exile. Second, Pope Julius III agreed to give up any rights to hear appeals regarding monastic property, thus making it possible to allay the fears of sequestration which had stopped negotiation over papal supremacy in Mary's second Parliament.

Mary's third Parliament, much more compliant to royal wishes than the first two, brought England back into the papal fold with Mary's Second Act of Repeal (1554). In the preamble the Lords and Commons declared themselves "very sorry and repentant of the schism and disobedience committed in this realm . . . against the said See Apostolic" and sought absolution so that "we may as children repentant be received into the bosom and unity of Christ's Church." In the enacting clauses Parliament repealed all of the antipapal legislation passed since 1529: Conditional Annates, Appeals, Submission of the Clergy, Absolute Annates, Dispensations, Suffragan Bishops, Supremacy, Extinguishing Papal Authority, and the treason sections of the Edwardian Act of Repeal. Untouched was most of the anticlerical legislation: mortuary and right of sanctuary, benefit of clergy, and, temporarily, the First Fruits and Tenths Act of 1534. It was a matter of concern to the queen that she still received first fruits and tenths since, in her judgment, they rightfully belonged to the Church. All persons who had lawfully gained possession of Church lands and property, however, whether it was the transfer of episcopal lands, the dissolution of the monasteries, or the suppression of the chantries, were allowed to keep them free from Church censure. This major concession of the Second Act of Repeal did not restrict Mary from giving back those Church lands still in the possession of the Crown. Accordingly, she restored several monastic houses, and she turned over Westminster Abbey to John Feckenham and a band of Benedictine monks.

Cardinal Pole and the queen also made some minor concessions in the Second Act of Repeal. The use of the title "Supreme Head" under Henry and Edward, while not regarded as having been lawful, was to be valid on all papers on which it had been used, and its omission on papers under Mary, while the Act of Supremacy had been in effect, was not to make them less valid. All papal bulls, dispensations, and privileges obtained from Rome since 1529 were to be put into execution, providing that they did not contain anything prejudicial to the royal authority of the realm. And finally, the statement that the pope should have such authority as he had in 1529 should not diminish any of the prerogatives of the "imperial Crown" as of that date.

The Protestant Martyrs

The same Marian Parliament that ended the Henrician Schism also revived the medieval (but not the Henrician) heresy legislation that Henry VIII and Edward had stricken from the statute books. Within a month a special commission, presided over by Bishop Gardiner, had tried, condemned, and burned at the stake the first Protestant martyrs of Mary's reign. John Rogers, a married priest associated with Tyndale's Bible, was burned at Smithfield, and a little later John Hooper, the former bishop, suffered a particularly excruciating death at his old diocese in Gloucester because the customary bag of gunpowder around his neck failed to explode before the flames enveloped him. Here was the formal beginning of the Marian persecution of heretics.

Who was responsible? Mary's advisers played their parts, especially Cardinal Pole, but Gardiner soon became disillusioned with the process, and Philip was not yet the advocate of the wholesale burnings he later carried out in the Netherlands. Whether because of long-cherished revenge, the fear of future rebellions, depression resulting from a false pregnancy, or some other motivation, Mary—"Bloody Mary" as she became known—must bear the primary responsibility for the nearly 300 persons who perished at the stake from 1555–1558, as well as those who died in prison. This figure was almost four times the number burned during the much longer reign of Henry VIII and about three times the number burned from 1401 to 1529.

The martyrs represented all social classes except for the nobility, but most came from the lower, and hence less educated, orders of society living largely in the southeastern counties. Some held Anabaptist views and might have been burned in Henry's reign. Others, such as the martyrs burned at Oxford, held Protestant views that had been the official position of the Edwardian Church just two years before. Among the Oxford martyrs were the former bishops, Latimer and Ridley. Latimer reputedly uttered those prophetic words at the stake, which presumably have inspired later Protestant martyrs: "Be of good comfort, Master Ridley, and play the man. We shall this day light such a candle by God's grace in England, as I trust shall never be put out."[23]

In September, 1555, the archbishop of Canterbury was brought to trial at Oxford for heresy even though he had already been convicted of treason in the civil courts for his role in the Lady Jane Grey affair two years before. A papal commission confronted Cranmer with sixteen charges, most of which dealt with his views on the Eucharist and papal authority. Cranmer again denied the real presence and said he would "never consent to the bishop of Rome . . . for I have made an oath to the king, and I must obey the king by

God's laws."[24] Cranmer had experienced no difficulty under Henry VIII and Edward VI with his own doctrine of obedience to the sovereign because the Crown and the archbishop generally agreed on theological and liturgical matters as well as on royal supremacy itself. But under Mary, Cranmer suffered because his Protestant views varied greatly from the queen's Catholicism and because the restored papal supremacy had extinguished the royal supremacy. In mid-October, Cranmer witnessed the burnings of Latimer and Ridley. In mid-December, the papal consistory decided that the sixteen charges against him had been proven and the archbishop should be turned over to the civil authorities for punishment. Not long after, he found himself unable to answer to the governor of his prison why, given his belief that the Crown should regulate the Church, he should continue to resist the queen.[25]

Out of Cranmer's psychological crisis came the first of six recantations of his Protestant faith, each more abject than the last. It may be that he recalled his own admonition to Sir Thomas More some twenty years before. "You know for a certainty, and a thing without doubt," Cranmer had said to More, "that you be bounden to obey your sovereign lord your King and therefore are ye bounden to leave of the doubt of your unsure conscience in refusing the oath, and take the sure way in obeying of your prince, and swear it."[26] But the archbishop's logic had not prevailed with the lord chancellor, nor did it prevail with the archbishop himself. By recanting at the stake all of his previous recantations, even by plunging the hand that had signed the earlier recantations into the fire first, Cranmer, like More, disobeyed his sovereign, followed the voice of his own conscience, and met martyrdom, though each man died for a different concept of religious supremacy.

What caused this final dramatic change? One can only speculate on Cranmer's innermost thoughts. It may have been the archbishop's final realization that his recantations would not save his life, especially since Mary had taken the unusual step, which defied the traditional practice followed in the case of Edward's tutor, Sir John Cheke, of not allowing a recantation to save a heretic from burning. It may have been his recognition that by once again accepting transubstantiation and papal supremacy, he had rejected everything that had been the crowning achievement of his mature years. Or, he may possibly have remembered the saving clause in the homily on "Obedience": obedience to one's sovereign, yes, but only if it does not go against the will of God; if it does, then one must patiently suffer.

The ascension of a new pope, Paul IV, to the throne of St. Peter in 1555 marked the beginning of dissension between Mary and the papacy. One of Paul's first steps was to issue a bull condemning the expropriation of Church property, and only after difficult circumstances was Cardinal Pole able to gain an exception for England. Still, the papacy was anxious to recover the first fruits and tenths of all benefices which Henry had seized for the Crown. A statute in Mary's fourth Parliament (1555) freed the clergy from paying any first fruits either to the Crown or to the papacy. As for its provisions regarding the tenths of Church benefices, lay patrons continued to pay the Crown. All benefices where the queen was the patron, except for those exempted because they were very poor, had to pay their tenths to the papal legate. The tenths paid to the papal legate did not go to Rome but helped pay for monastic pensions. The papacy itself did not receive one farthing from England under Mary.

The chief problem Mary had with the papacy, however, arose from the Spanish marriage alliance. Pope Paul IV, originally made a cardinal at the intervention of Pole, intensely hated Spain because of Spanish military domination of Italy. When Philip became involved in a war with Paul in 1556, the pope denounced him as a heretic and threatened excommunication. The queen sided with her husband against the Holy Father, and England went to war with Rome's ally, France. In the following year Paul revoked Pole's legatine status (*legatus a latere*) and that of the see of Canterbury as well (*legatus natus*), the latter authority being one the papacy even recognized as still held by Cranmer when he was summoned to Rome for trial.[27] When the pope summoned Pole to Rome for trial on charges of heresy, claiming that the cardinal believed in the Lutheran view of justification, Mary refused to allow the papal messenger to land in England. When the pope replaced Pole with a feeble old man, William Peto, Mary told Paul that she knew better than he which men were best suited to the government of her kingdom.

Philip and the pope made peace in September, 1557, but it brought only a small amount of relief. The impasse between church and state prevailed until the deaths of Mary and Pole, both within just a few hours of each other, in mid-November, 1558. With their passing from the scene, England was not to have another Catholic sovereign for more than a century, but by then there was no chance—indeed no strong desire—to return to papal authority.

It has been asserted that Mary's reign marked the beginning of the Catholic or Counter-Reformation in England. There is some truth in this proposition. After all, one can cite Mary's reconciliation with Rome after the Henrician schism, the proclamation of an index against prohibited authors,[28] and the great number of burnings for heresy that recalled the Spanish Inquisition. Mary's first Parliament turned the church and state calendar back to 1536, and her third Parliament turned it even further back to 1529. There were two important exceptions to this movement, however, both affecting financial matters: the monasteries were not restored, and the papacy did not recover first fruits and tenths. Mary relinquished the title of supreme head of the Church, though only after using it for her own purposes, but she was not inclined to surrender control of the English Church to the pope, particularly one who ultimately excommunicated her husband. Instead, she retained those powers *vis à vis* the Church that the English Crown had acquired in the centuries before 1529. Among these powers was the same right to punish heretics that fifteenth century sovereigns had exercised against the Lollards. The horror of the burnings, preserved and possibly embellished for posterity by John Foxe in his famous "Book of Martyrs" (1563), helped to make Roman Catholicism an object of hatred for decades and centuries to come.

There is some evidence that Cardinal Pole, upon his return to England, tried to institute reforms by doing away with the nonresidence of the clergy and the alienation of Church land, as well as by issuing new books of religious instruction and an orthodox English translation of the New Testament. But Pole's program of Catholic reform never received the time nor the clerical commitment to meet the challenge of the Reformers which archbishop Laud's program in the next century offered to the challenge of the Puritans.[29] In fact, Laudianism in some ways more adequately fits the description of a true Counter-Reformation than does the achievement of Mary's reign. Mary's reign is better characterized as a Catholic reaction or a papal restoration, and a partial one at that.

The Marian Exiles

Nearly 800 men, women, and children who did not wish to subject themselves under Mary to the draconic punishment of the heresy laws emigrated to the continent. Of the 427 persons who have been identified by name, 116 were gentry (including two Elizabethan privy councillors: Sir Francis Knollys and Sir Francis Walsingham); sixty-seven were clergymen (including twelve Elizabethan bishops and three Elizabethan archbishops: Edmund Grindal, Edwin Sandys, and Thomas Young); 119 were theological students (including an Elizabethan Regius Professor of Divinity at Oxford, Lawrence Humphrey); and forty were merchants (including a leader of the Elizabethan Puritan classical movement, Thomas Wood.)[30] The Marian exiles emigrated to those Calvinist and Zwinglian centers in western Germany and Switzerland controlled by Reformed Church leaders. Bullinger was at Zurich; Calvin was at Geneva; Martyr was at Strassburg, Poullain was at Frankfort; and some of à Lasco's London congregation were in Emden.

Differences among the English exiles on liturgical matters appeared in the Frankfort church. William Whittingham and the minister, John Knox, whom Calvin had written that the Second Prayer Book was not as pure as it could be, supported a hybrid order of church service which combined the Second Prayer Book—minus the Litany and surplice, among other things—with parts of the Genevan order of service. With the arrival of John Jewel, who had escaped from England only after signing Catholic articles, and Richard Cox, who had twice served as a Prayer Book commissioner, the Frankfort congregation tried to restore "the face of an English church" by providing for the reading of the Litany.[31] Although Cox agreed to abandon such "indifferent" things as the surplice and kneeling, he would not give up on other things, especially the Litany. By exploiting Knox's comparison of Charles V to Nero, the Coxians succeeded in getting the Frankfort magistrates to expel Knox and to restore the Second Prayer Book with only minor changes. The secession of the Knoxians from the Frankfort congregation rapidly followed in the autumn of 1555, and within a few months, Cox, too, left Frankfort, confident that his side had won a permanent victory. Although there had been varying degrees of dissatisfaction with the Second Prayer Book, basically the Coxians had supported it and the Knoxians had opposed it.

Within two years, the Frankfort church divided once again, this time not over the Second Prayer Book, which continued to be used without some rites and ceremonies, but over a new Reformed discipline. After its adoption, the "New Discipline," which developed ideas promulgated in an "Old Discipline" used by the Knoxians, stated that Frankfort should have "a particular visible church" made up of the elect of God whose ministers and lay elders would be selected by and responsible to the congregation. Every prospective member had to make a confession of faith before the ministers and elders, indicating a willingness to accept the doctrine and discipline of the church. The doctrine for the catechizing of the youth was to be the Genevan Catechism, and the discipline was to correct both private and public offenses. The "New Discipline" directed the civil magistrate to ignore controversy within the church, but if neither the ministers and elders nor the congregation could make a peaceable settlement, then the church should refer such controversy to the civil magistrate for a final judgment. Conversely, neither the ministers and elders nor the whole congregation were to "meddle in any civil matters, as judges or determiners of the same, but only as arbiters for peacemaking."[32] The Frankfort congregational and polity was a prototype of seventeeth century Puritan Independency.

After Knox left Frankfort, Calvin welcomed Whittingham and other Knoxians at Geneva, where ultimately about 200 of the Marian exiles—one in four—spent some time. Anthony Gilby and Christopher Goodman served as pastors for the English congregation until Knox arrived, and they created a directory of worship and church government known as the *Form of Prayers* (1556). The *Form of Prayers* began with a confession of faith which set forth the Calvinist doctrine of the Eucharist as well as the full-fledged Calvinist doctrine of double predestination and election. It also prescribed a visible church organization similar to the one developed at Frankfort. But, unlike the complete independence of the church congregation at Frankfort, it provided for a weekly assembly, somewhat like the Genevan consistory, in which the ministers and elders in a given area would examine, admonish, and, finally, excommunicate not only those members of their congregations but also those of their own number who were found guilty of disciplinary "faults and suspicions." Another Calvinist influence appeared in the role of the civil magistrate who, as a member of the Church, was also subject to ecclesiastical censure. The magistrate was to defend the Church from such heretics as papists and Anabaptists as well as root out such concepts as the mass, purgatory, prayers to the saints, celibacy, and man's free will and good works. In return the congregation agreed that it "must render honor and obedience in all things, which are not contrary to the Word of God."[33]

This proviso regarding obedience to the magistrate was the subject of a number of marginal notes in the Geneva (or Breeches) Bible (1560), the most important contribution of Genevan exiles to succeeding generations of Puritans. The marginalia on the New Testament, revised from the Great Bible by Whittingham in 1557, provided the abstract principles. For example, to the passage from Luke 20:25 about giving unto Caesar the things which are Caesar's and unto God the things which are God's, the note adds; "The duty which we owe to Princes letteth nothing which is due unto God." Or again, where Acts 5:20 reads, "Then Peter and the Apostles answered and said, 'We ought to obey God than men,'" the note adds, "When they command, or forbid anything contrary to the word of God." The 160 editions of the Geneva Bible that were printed in less than a century indicate its popularity.[34]

Some of the Marian exiles extended the theme of obedience to the civil magistrate, except when contrary to the will of God, into a theory of rebellion against the sovereign. The most systematic of these writers was John Ponet, the Edwardian bishop who had supported Wyatt's rebellion and emigrated to Strassburg. Unlike Geneva, Strassburg and Zurich were centers of covenant theology, which stressed a conditional contract of mutual obligation entered into voluntarily by God and man for the latter's salvation.[35] Such contractual ideas may have influenced Ponet's *Short Treatise of Politic Power* (1556), which, though grounded in medieval and Catholic doctrines of natural law, foreshadowed Lockean concepts of a social contract and political trusteeship as guarantors of private property. Like John of Salisbury, Ponet believed that when a ruler becomes a tyrant, the people may, as a last resort, commit regicide, but, unlike John of Salisbury, Ponet did not believe that tyranny was God's punishment for sin because that would imply that God was the author of sin.

The political pamphleteers at Geneva—Gilby, Goodman, and Knox—placed more reliance upon the Word of God than upon natural law as the standard by which to judge erring monarchs—not so much tyrants as idolaters—but their conclusion was almost the same as Ponet's: a justification for rebellion. Gilby's *Admonition to England and Scotland* (1558) denounced the royal supremacy of Henry VIII. Goodman's *How Superior Powers Ought to Be Obeyed of Their Subjects* (1558) suggested that the true rebel is one who obeys an ungodly ruler. But the most famous of the Genevan pamphlets, Knox's *First Blast of the Trumpet Against the Monstrous Regiment of Women* (1558), argued that neither Queen Mary Tudor in England nor Queen Regent Mary of Guise in Scotland, both Catholics, was worthy of obedience. Calvin did not support the Genevan pamphleteers. In fact, he preached obedience to the civil ruler in several editions of his *Institutes*; however, in the last edition (1559) he stated that under certain conditions, the lesser magistrates might restrain tyrants.

It is an ironic twist that the English sovereign who achieved the reputation of being the greatest enemy to Protestantism should have inadvertently caused Englishmen to carry out religious experiments in continental laboratories that would inspire succeeding Puritan generations. In addition to the development of new forms of Church government and discipline by the Marian exiles, a new role for the magistrate was beginning to emerge. The Frankfort idea that the magistrate should not interfere with the Church, except when it had a crisis, defied a centuries' old stricture in church and state. Conversely, that the clergy should not interefere in the state, except as an arbitrator, suggested a kind of separation of church and state that the Puritan, Thomas Cartwright, elucidated with greater precision in the 1570s. Even more significant to the advocates of the royal supremacy was the Genevan idea that the magistrate as a Church member was subject to ecclesiastical censure like anyone, thereby reducing the power of the Crown to the protective role of a "nursing mother." But most startling of all was the transition from Tyndale's concept of "passive resistance," reaffirmed in Edward's reign to the "active resistance" of Knox and others. The revolutionary doctrine of "active resistance" reappeared in William Allen's *A Defense* in 1584 and received a Puritan re-articulation in the late 1640s. When Milton wrote *The Tenure of Kings and Magistrates* in defense of Charles I's regicide in 1649, the great English poet called Knox and Goodman "the true Protestant Divines of *England*, our fathers in the faith we hold." [36]

The Alteration of Religion

When Elizabeth, the daughter of Anne Boleyn, came to the throne at the age of twenty-five, the question was not whether the religious settlement would be Protestant, but just how Protestant it would be. Not a pious woman with zealous religious convictions like Mary, Elizabeth had expediently made the appropriate religious changes, under first her brother and then her sister, yet she had endeared herself to Protestants because of her imprisonment in the Tower for alleged complicity in Wyatt's rebellion. The foreign situation, however, prompted caution in the religious settlement. England was still at war with France, and a Franco-Spanish alliance was still something to be avoided. The royal title Elizabeth used when proclaimed queen on November 18, 1558, indicated her cautious response to diplomatic matters. Like Mary, Elizabeth used the ambiguous word "etc." after the title "Defender of the Faith," but, unlike Mary, she dropped the Henrician title of "Supreme Head" at the very outset.[37] Mass was celebrated in her chapel, but on Christmas Day and again at her coronation three weeks later, she walked out on the bishop of Carlisle when he refused her request not to elevate the Host, the customary act of sacrifice.

Two days after Christmas, the queen issued a proclamation prohibiting unlicensed preaching, a measure directed against those "wolves coming out of Geneva and other places of Germany" whom Bishop John White had foreseen in Queen Mary's funeral sermon.[38] The proclamation also prohibited any Church prayer, rite, or ceremony except "that which is already used and by law received," suggesting those religious ceremonies in force at the death of Mary. But the proclamation allowed the Litany of 1544, "used at this present in Her Majesty's own chapel," as well as the Lord's Prayer and the "Creed in English"—both contained in the *Primer* of 1545—until such time as the queen might consult with Parliament. It would almost seem as if Elizabeth wanted to reestablish religion, as she told Count de Feria, the Spanish ambassador, some months later, "as her father had left it." [39]

Yet, even if the foregoing statement to the Spanish ambassador was a true commentary on religious ceremonies rather than a reassertion of royal supremacy, and even if her own proclivities were for the First and not the Second Edwardian Prayer Book, neither of those religious goals was characteristic of the people to whom she entrusted her government and the Church. Elizabeth's key ministers in both church and state were convinced Protestants linked by close ties of friendship. First among her ministers was William Cecil, her principal secretary, who was married to the eldest daughter of the Marian exile, Anthony Cooke. Cecil gathered together a group of friends, most of whom had known each other either at Cambridge University (particularly St. John's College) in the 1530s—where they were called the "Athenian Tribe" because of an Erasmian interest in classical studies—or at the Inns of Court (particularly Gray's Inn) in the 1540s.

The government included Nicholas Bacon, Walter Mildmay, Francis Russell, William Parr, and Francis Knollys, among others. These men carried through the Acts of Supremacy and Uniformity in the House of Commons. The ministry included William Bill, Edwin Sandys, Richard Cox, Edmund Grindal, Matthew Parker, and William May, among others. Several of these clergy rose to important bishoprics: Grindal (London); Cox (Ely); Sandys (Worcester); May (nominated to York); and Parker (Canterbury). Some of the "Athenian Tribe" had gone into exile; some had not, but all were heirs of a Cambridge Protestant tradition that had coalesced around humanistic leadership, especially of John Cheke, a tutor for Edward VI, at St. John's College and, to a lesser extent, around Thomas Smith, the author of *De Republica Anglorum*, and Roger Ascham, a tutor for Elizabeth and author of *The Schoolmaster*. All of these friends of Cecil were committed to the royal supremacy and, as will become apparent, most of them to some form of the Second Prayer Book of 1552. [40]

From the very beginning of the reign, a number of plans for the "alteration of religion" circulated around the court. Most of these plans were concerned with how rapidly or slowly the queen should proceed. Nicholas Throckmorton urged her to move with caution and to avoid any religious innovation; Richard Goodrich suggested "dissimulation" with the papacy until her position was stable; and Armagil Waad suggested change "little by little" because of "the greatness of the Pope." Others, however, proffered contrary advice, particularly the anonymous author (possibly Cecil himself) of the "Device for Alteration of Religion," first found in a book of Thomas Smith and written a short time before the end of December, 1558. [41]

The "Device" called for the "alteration of religion" at the next Parliament and suggested the appointment of a committee, to be chaired by Thomas Smith, "to review the *Book of Common Prayer*." We do not know for sure which Edwardian Prayer Book the author of the "Device" had in mind, but, in an observation which might have been a subtle reference to the First Edwardian Prayer Book, he stated that "many people of our own will be very much discontented" if the "alteration of religion" is only "*a cloaked papistry or a mingle-mangle.*" As for the composition of the proposed committee, it consisted of Bill, Parker, May, Cox, Grindal, David Whitehead, and James Pilkington, the last four of whom were Marian exiles just returning from abroad, but not from Geneva. Although this particular committee may never have met, one made up of Sandys, Bill, and others did review "the old Common Prayer Book" at Thomas Smith's house for later presentation to Parliament.[42]

Elizabeth's first Parliament opened most auspiciously on January 25, 1559. When Abbot John Feckenham and the monks of Westminster Abbey greeted Elizabeth with candles, incense, and holy water, the queen ordered them to be put away. The clergyman chosen to deliver the sermon that day was none other than Richard Cox, the returned Frankfort exile who had supported the Second Prayer Book while abroad. Following the sermon, Nicholas Bacon, the lord keeper, speaking for the government in the presence of the queen, stated that Parliament should establish "an uniform order of Religion" that would avoid on the one side whatever might tend "to breed or nourish any kind of idolatry, or superstition," and on the other side any licentiousness, contempt, irreverence, or "any spice of irreligion."[43] Fine rhetoric for an Anglican *via media*, but the assent of both Houses of Parliament posed a practical problem.

Little opposition was expected in the House of Commons, where two-thirds of the members sat for the first time. Among their number were a dozen or so Marian exiles, including Knollys and Cooke, the father-in-law of Bacon as well as Cecil. The major difficulty was expected in the House of Lords, which contained Catholic bishops appointed by Mary. John Jewel wrote to Peter Martyr that the Marian bishops "reign as sole monarchs in the midst of ignorant and weak men, and easily overreach our little party." There was no indication that they would make the switch to the royal supremacy that had taken place under Henry in the 1530s; on the other hand, there was no indication that they would lead any policy of active resistance.[44]

The impending struggle between the two Houses of Parliament over a religious settlement began on February 9, when the government introduced a bill in the Commons "to restore the supremacy of the Church of England, etc., to the crown of the realm." No text of this bill survives, but when Knollys and Cooke reported it back to the House on February 21, it had been transformed from a bill of supremacy to a bill of supremacy *and* uniformity by including a revised prayer book, probably the Second Prayer Book. No text of this expanded bill survives either, but the Commons adopted it without any changes. The Lords purged the expanded bill of everything except the royal supremacy, and even on that issue it may have suggested that Elizabeth not take the title of supreme head. Although the purged bill passed the Lords after the third reading on March 18, all of the bishops present had voted against it. An incensed House of Commons responded by passing another bill "that no person shall be punished for using the religion used in King E's last year;" but, as was to be expected, this attempt to tolerate both

Catholics and Edwardian Protestants by abolishing the heresy laws came to naught in the Lords.[45]

Faced with a March 24 (Good Friday) dissolution of Parliament for Easter, a less defiant Commons passed the purged supremacy bill with an inserted proviso, and the Lords immediately followed suit, both Houses acting on March 22. The Commons' proviso may well have been the anachronistic provision in the purged supremacy bill for communion in both kinds. If so, this provision was not just an example of a deliberate "alteration of religion" by slow stages in successive Parliaments, since it appeared so suddenly and probably was not a part of the first supremacy bill. Nor was it an unnoticed leftover from the Lords' purging of the bill, since such an important provision would have been readily noticed. Nor was it just a timely response to the forthcoming Easter holiday need for direction, since a royal proclamation (also dated but as yet only printed on March 22) would recognize, if circulated, that the "Supremacy Act" (still unsigned by the queen) was too long to be printed and published by Easter.

The March 22 proclamation would also revive Edward VI's statute against revilers of the Blessed Sacrament and for communion in both kinds, even though the latter provision was not viable without the adoption of a new Prayer Book. *The Order of the Communion*, drawn up in 1548 in order to implement the Edwardian statute providing for communion in both kinds, had no legal status after Mary's repeal of both Edwardian Prayer Books into which it had been incorporated.[46] Even so, the last-minute insertion of the provision for communion in both kinds in the second supremacy bill (without *The Order of the Communion*) may have been a government attempt to insure at least a partially Protestant Church service, should the Lords defeat a future uniformity bill authorizing a new Prayer Book (with *The Order of the Communion*). The revival of the entire Edwardian statute by proclamation, instead of relying only on the communion in both kinds clause of the second supremacy bill, would permit the government, temporarily at least, to bring disciplinary action against those who reviled the Eucharist altogether, whether they were Catholics on the one hand or extreme Protestants on the other. The revival of the Edwardian statute, the March 22 proclamation noted, would "quiet the consciences of such great numbers," thereby enabling the government to allow the celebration of the Blessed Sacrament in a Protestant fashion.[47]

Even though the queen celebrated communion in both kinds in her chapel on Easter, she had withheld her assent to the second supremacy bill, had suppressed the March 22 proclamation, and on Good Friday had recessed (rather than dissolved) Parliament until 3 April. Why had Elizabeth changed her mind? One explanation is that she had received news on Palm Sunday that England and Spain were about to sign a peace treaty with the French at Cateau Cambresis, thereby encouraging the queen to drop her policy of dissimulation with Spain and announce to the Spanish ambassador, Count de Feria, that she could not marry Philip II because she was regarded as a "heretic." However, the supremacy bill was first introduced more than a month before news of an impending peace settlement reached England; there was no peace settlement until after Easter, and Henry II of France had been willing to make a separate peace with Elizabeth as early as January, 1559. There are more likely explanations for her change of mind. First of all, there was much unfinished business in the form of public and private bills, especially regarding economic problems of the Church, that required Parliament's further attention. Secondly, the supremacy bill that had already been passed needed to define the queen's supremacy position more precisely, particularly with reference to the replacement of bishops. And, finally, if Parliament was to complete the "alteration of religion," that is, to pass an Act of Uniformity, the government had to pursue a new strategy to counter the continued opposition of the Marian bishops.[48]

During the Easter recess, the government arranged a conference of Council and parliamentary members at Westminster, jointly chaired by Bacon and Heath. Nine Catholics and nine Protestants (all but one of the latter group had been in exile, and all but two of the latter group were to become bishops) discussed the following issues: the use of a language (Latin) unknown to the worshippers, the right of national churches to determine their own liturgy, and the authority for any propitiatory sacrifice in the mass. The Westminster Conference fell apart because of disputes over procedure—whether the arguments should be in Latin and in writing. Unfortunately, when the Marian bishops engaged in some verbal abuse, two of them ended up in the Tower charged with disobedience to authority, and six of their colleagues were called before the Privy Council and were forced to pay fines. "Promises, flattery, and bribes," according to Edward Rishton, may have also played a part in explaining the absence of several Marian bishops and Catholic laymen from the House of Lords, when the Lords voted on the uniformity bill after the recess. Also important, the unfortunate behavior of the Marian churchmen, as well as what Count de Feria called "roguery and injustice" on the part of the government, had cost the Catholic cause the votes of some members of the nobility. After the Commons passed the uniformity bill without a dissent, the Lords passed it by the very narrow margin of three votes, with nine bishops voting against it. Feria wrote to King Philip, saying that someone should tell the pope that during the Henrician Schism only the bishop of Rochester and Thomas More had protested, but under Queen Elizabeth not one bishop had agreed to the Uniformity Act and a great many laymen had opposed it on grounds of heresy. The government's strategy to discredit and intimidate the Marian bishops had worked.[49]

Elizabeth assented to a new supremacy bill (the third), which gave her the title of supreme governor (rather than supreme head), and to the new uniformity bill on 8 May, then promptly dissolved Parliament. But the government had extracted the Uniformity Act from the Lords at a very heavy price— namely, the altar and the traditional vestments of the Ornaments Rubric. And that Rubric was to provoke dissension for the next hundred years.

Once Elizabeth had appointed William Cecil as her principal secretary, it was only natural that he would surround himself with old friends from Cambridge and the Inns of Court. Cecil's associates, men of conviction, as we have seen, wanted to establish the royal supremacy and some version of Edward's Second Prayer Book as soon as possible. That does not mean, of course, that Cecil and the members of the Council did not recognize the need for dissimulation with the papacy and with Spain. The two policies were not necessarily incompatible. Even so, Elizabeth did not necessarily share all of the goals of her leading ministers regarding the "alteration of religion." Undoubtedly she and they wanted royal supremacy, but the evidence of their agreement on the forms of church worship is far less certain.

It is all the more difficult to distinguish between the queen's public actions and statements, many of which she seems to have made largely for the consumption of the Spanish ambassador, and her liturgical convictions, for which we have only her actions but no personal statements. Our dilemma is compounded even further by a tendency to see the inflexibility in religious matters of her later years as a conservatism characteristic of her earlier years. There is no convincing evidence that she had a clear preference in 1559 for the First Edwardian Prayer Book, or, for that matter, the Second Edwardian Prayer Book. But the queen's close advisors in church and state, who led a group of moderate reformers in the House of Commons, strongly favored the Second Edwardian Prayer Book. Whatever the queen's personal preferences, neither the religious radicals from Geneva nor a "Puritan choir" in the House of Commons forced her decision to go as far to the left as she did. Rather, opposition from an unreconstructed House of Lords (especially the Marian bishops) made any semblance of Catholicism, whether in liturgy or in doctrine, impossible to accept. Many members of the House of Commons may have been more fervently anti-Catholic than they were pro-reformation.

The Elizabethan Settlement

The preamble of the Supremacy Act of May, 1559, stated that many good laws had been made under Henry VIII for the extinction of foreign powers and for the restoration of the Crown to its ancient ecclesiastical superiority. Accordingly, the enacting clauses abolished all papal authority within the realm. Mary's Second Act of Repeal, which had repaired the breach with Rome, was itself repealed except for those clauses that had permitted Church lands and property to remain in lay hands. Also repealed was the Marian statute that had revived the medieval heresy acts. But the conservatives in the House of Lords hoped to protect their Catholic colleagues from having recognition of the pope or belief in transubstantiation turned into heresy by inserting words into the Supremacy Act which stated that nothing was to be adjudged heresy except by the authority of the "canonical Scriptures," the first four general councils, or by Parliament, with the assent of the clergy in convocation.[50]

In addition, the Supremacy Act's enacting clauses revived several Henrician statutes. These included Conditional Annates, Appeals, Absolute Annates, Submission of the Clergy, Suffragan Bishops, and Dispensations and Peter's Pence, but not the Supremacy Act of 1534. The restoration of the Act for the Submission of the Clergy did not revive the thirty-two member commission for canonical law reform because its authority had expired, and a fresh attempt to authorize a reform commission like the one which had produced the Edwardian *Reformatio Legum Ecclesiasticarum* was unsuccessful. By restoring the Absolute Annates Act, the Henrician method of a *congé d'élire* and a letter missive replaced the Edwardian method of selecting bishops by letters patent.

A clause of the new Supremacy Act provided that all spiritual and ecclesiastical jurisdiction, lawfully exercised heretofore by any spiritual authority in England, would be annexed to the "imperial crown" by the authority of Parliament. The latter phrase continued the trend, begun with Edward's Parliaments, of getting authorization from the king-in-Parliament rather than the king-in-Council. In order to carry out her ecclesiastical powers, the queen could appoint any person or persons by letters patent in order "to visit, reform, redress, order, correct, and amend all such errors, heresies, schisms, abuses, offences, contempts and enormities" within the Anglican Church. This was the legislative sanction for the early ecclesiastical commissions that later came to be called the Court of High Commission. No Elizabethan vicegerent, however, emerged.

One of the most striking features of the Supremacy Act—the imposition of an oath of loyalty upon all ecclesiastical persons and all secular officers in church and state—required a pledge of "faith and true allegiance" to the queen as the only "supreme governor" of the realm. According to the Spanish ambassador, Elizabeth had asked some members of Parliament for some other title than "Supreme Head"; and they had suggested, with an eye cocked to the fact that she was a woman, "Governess [Gobernadora] of the Church."[51] While the term "Supreme Governor," according to John Parkhurst, bishop-elect of Norwich, "amounts to the same thing" as Henry VIII's title,[52] Elizabeth may have preferred it in order to placate the consciences of Genevan Reformers and Marian Catholics, who believed Christ and his vicar the pope, respectively, to be the true head of the Church. It is also possible that Elizabeth's thinking may have approached that set forth many years later by John Selden in his *Table Talk* ("King of England"):

> There's a great deal of difference between head of the church and supreme governor, as our canons call the king. Conceive it thus: there is in the kingdom of England a college of physicians; the king is supreme governor of those but not the head of them, not the president of the college, nor the best physician.[53]

By applying Selden's distinction to Henry and Elizabeth, any possibility that Henry, as supreme head, may have had the right to exercise the *potestas ordinis*, in addition to the *potestas jurisdictionis*, was eliminated under Elizabeth as supreme governor.

The Oath of Supremacy had both far-reaching and short-run consequences. The first session of Elizabeth's second Parliament demanded the Oath of Supremacy in 1563 of all schoolmasters, all holders of university degrees, and all members of the House of Commons. An immediate consequence of the oath's administration meant deprivation of sixteen Marian bishops from their dioceses, ten bishoprics having already fallen vacant. The refusal of the sixteen bishops to take the oath was in sharp contrast to the compliance with a similar oath by the Henrician bishops twenty-five years before. Unlike the sixteen bishops, Bishop Anthony Kitchin and most of the lesser clergy were able to make the switch, but estimates of those who failed to do so have ranged all the way from 3 to 25 percent of the English clergy.[54] The comparatively light penalties for refusal to take the oath indicated that Elizabeth originally had no desire to make martyrs out of the recalcitrants as Mary had done even though the penalties were increased in 1563.

The Elizabethan Act of Uniformity not only revived the clause in Edward's Second Act of Uniformity that imposed compulsory attendance at church on Sunday and holy days, but, more significantly, it revived the Second Edwardian Prayer Book with a few basic changes. Most of these changes, as we shall see, were concessions to those of a more conservative religious persuasion, especially the Catholics in the House of Lords. One, however, was not. That was the dropping of the Black Rubric on kneeling, thereby ruling out the possibility of transubstantiation in the Eucharist. The Council had added the Black Rubric to the Second Prayer Book, but, unlike the rest of the Second Prayer Book, Parliament had never sanctioned it.

The new Prayer Book's concessions to those of a more conservative religious persuasion included the following provisions. First, an Ornaments Rubric for the churches and the ministers, "as was in the Church of England, by authority of Parliament, in the second year of the reign of Edward VI,"[55] brought back the altar and the vestments of the First Prayer Book until such time as the queen, upon advice of her ecclesiastical commissioners, wished to make changes. Second, the sentences of administration in the Communion service amalgamated phrases from both Edwardian Prayer Books: "The body of our Lord Jesus Christ which was given for thee, preserve thy body and soul into everlasting life" (from the First Book); and "take and eat this, in remembrance that Christ died for thee, and feed on him in thy heart by faith with thanksgiving" (from the Second Book). Third, it removed the prayer to be delivered from "the tyranny of the bishop of Rome, and all his detestable enormities." Despite these substantial adjustments, it was essentially the Second Prayer Book, not the First, that Parliament adopted against the known wishes of the convocation of the clergy and the Catholic bishops in the House of Lords. In the process of compromise, the government made the fewest concessions.

Elizabeth's first Parliament also had dealt with some economic problems of the Church.[56] Early in the session it repealed Mary's statute on First Fruits and Tenths and revived Henry's. Later, it dissolved the few chantries and monasteries, including Westminster, that Mary had been able to restore. But potentially most significant of all, it passed the Exchange Act, the first piece of legislation to attack the property of the secular Church. The Exchange Act empowered the Crown, whenever any bishopric fell vacant, to exchange royal impropriations, tithes, and tenths for the temporalities of an episcopal see. In effect, it permitted the exchange of royal ecclesiastical benefices, where the tithes were difficult to collect, for episcopal manors, where the value was underrated.

For those like Secretary William Cecil and Bishop Jewel, who envisioned the clergy primarily as pastoral shepherds, the Exchange Act was a step in the right direction, since it meant a loss of landed wealth, and hence political power, for the bishops. Actually, the bishops' surrender of manorial estates from 1559–1564 amounted only to about fifteen percent of their total holdings (most of this loss being sustained by five bishoprics), and the overall level of episcopal income, though prevented from rising, was not significantly reduced.[57] Partly because of the protests of the bishops, the momentum for further exchanges disappeared after the early years, and with it went some of the threat of further alienation of the Church's landed property. What did not stop, however, was the Elizabethan practice of plundering the Church by keeping episcopal sees vacant for long periods of time: Oxford was vacant for forty-one years; Ely, nineteen years; and Bristol, fourteen years. The Exchange Act had two consequences from a patronage standpoint. It gave the bishops control over additional ecclesiastical benefices that they could have used to provide decent incomes for the clergy. But more importantly, it enabled Elizabeth to reward her favorites through beneficial leases. There was a sound economic reason, therefore, why some of the queen's courtiers were frequently at odds with the Anglican hierarchy.

When Edward replaced several Henrician bishops (Bonner of London, Heath of Worcester, and Gardiner of Winchester) with Ridley, Hooper, and Ponet, respectively, these Protestant reformers gave the king several episcopal manors which he, in turn, granted to laymen. When Mary's commissioners reinstated the Henrician bishops, the alienated manors were to be restored as well. In order to sort out these legal tangles, a number of private-member bills in Elizabeth's first Parliament, particularly several dealing with manors of the bishop of Winchester, tried to give some relief to the deprived Edwardian laymen. Not all of these private-member bills passed, indicating that religious zeal was not always the prime motivation in Parliament. But of those that did pass, the claimant was able to show that the Marian bishop had acquired his manors through confiscation from a deprived predecessor. Consideration of these private-member bills took a great deal of time before the Easter recess, adding another reason for Elizabeth to continue the Parliament. The process also revealed that some leading members of Parliament, no matter what their feelings were about the liturgy, were strong advocates, as they had been in Henry's day, of the royal supremacy.[58]

The royal Injunctions of 1559, drawn up by Cecil and the Privy Council, made a few changes to the Elizabethan Acts of Supremacy and Uniformity, mostly in the direction of further reform. A case in point was the matter of clerical marriage. Even though the final draft of the Elizabethan Act of Supremacy had not revived the Edwardian statute for clerical marriage, as the second draft had done, one of the Elizabethan injunctions permitted such marriages after an extensive character examination of the prospective bride had taken place. Equally important was the case of the Ornaments Rubric for ministers and the churches, one of the concessions to the Lords in the New Prayer Book. The Ornaments Rubric had restored the altar and the sacerdotal vestments (the alb, chasuble, stole, and cope) deleted from the First Edwardian Prayer Book by the Second. One of the injunctions extended the Ornaments Rubric on outdoor vestments by prescribing the "seemly garments" (square caps and gowns) which had been used by ministers in the last year of Edward's reign. Another one of the injunctions amended the Ornaments Rubric for churches by prescribing the communion table of the Second Edwardian Prayer Book. An appendix to the injunctions further stated that communion tables should be placed where the altar had once stood except during Holy Communion, when they should be placed in the chancel in order to facilitate better communication between the minister and the communicants. Two of the injunctions, however, had a reactionary tone, providing for the licensing of all printed books and papers as well as the prevention of all "contentious disputations" in matters of religion.

The most significant part of the Elizabethan injunctions, however, contained another appendix (written by Cecil), explaining the Oath of Supremacy. In spite of the malicious reports that kings and queens "may challenge authority and power of ministry of divine offices in the church," Cecil declared, the oath required nothing but what Protestants acknowledged to be due to Henry VIII and Edward VI. But just in case there was some question as to whether or not Henry and Edward had assumed priestly functions, Cecil added:

> And further, her majesty forbiddeth all manner her subjects to give ear or a credit to such perverse and malicious persons, which most sinisterly and maliciously labor to notify to her loving subjects, how by the words of the said oath it may be collected, that the kings or queens of this realm, possessors of the crown, may challenge authority and power of ministry of divine offices in the church; wherein her said subjects be much abused by such evil disposed persons.[59]

Cecil claimed for Elizabeth the *potestas jurisdictionis* but not the *potestas ordinis*.

In order to put the Elizabethan injunctions into effect, the bishops carried out a visitation of the churches throughout the country. While Elizabeth was out of London in August and September, 1559, someone, presumably connected with the London visitation, removed a little silver crucifix and two candles from the royal chapel at Whitehall. Upon the queen's return to Whitehall, she recovered the crucifix and the candles, putting them back in place where they stood "altar-wise." Something of a controversy now developed over this episode, and Jewel wrote to Martyr.

The scenic apparatus of divine worship is now under agitation; and those very things which you and I have so often laughed at, are now seriously and solemnly entertained by certain persons, (for *we* are not consulted,) as if the Christian religion could not exist without something tawdry. Our minds indeed are not sufficiently disengaged to make these fooleries of much importance. Others are seeking after a *golden*, or as it rather seems to me, a *leaden* mediocrity; and are crying out, that the half is better than the whole.[60]

For the queen, it was not so much the ornaments themselves as it was the claim of the clergy to tell her what she should do, even if it did mean violating her own injunctions. In February, 1560, two of the common law judges listened to supporting and opposing arguments by four of the new bishops. The judges decided that the royal injunctions ruled out the crucifix and candles, and they also decided that those vestments of the clergy (namely the copes) that were restored by the Ornaments Rubric but ruled out by the royal injunctions should again be restored. Elizabeth accepted the judges' decision, but from this time forward her quarrels with and dislike of the clergy began.[61]

Besides writing the appendix for the injuctions, Cecil also assumed responsibility for commissioning an apologia in 1561 for the Church that would defend the Elizabethan settlement at home and abroad from the attacks of Roman Catholics and Anabaptists. The result was Bishop Jewel's short *Apology of the Church of England* (1562). A much lengthier *Defence of the Apology* appeared in 1567. Jewel's *Apology* is best remembered as a confession of faith for the Church at a time when it did not have an official statement. The doctrinal views set forth in the *Apology* included the following points, among others, which the later Thirty-Nine Articles incorporated: the two sacraments are baptism and the Lord's Supper; the body and blood of Christ are not corporeally present in the Lord's Supper; and salvation is by Christ alone but a lively faith calls men to good works. In addition, Jewel, drawing both from the early Church fathers and the Scriptures, attempted to show why the civil magistrates should serve as the governors of church establishments in their own countries. "A Christian prince hath the charge of both tables committed to him by God, to the end he may understand that not temporal matters only but also religious and ecclesiastical causes pertain to his office."[62] And what were these "religious and ecclesiastical causes"? Jewel did not give Elizabeth complete power within the Church, but he strongly intimated in the *Apology* that she was to have only the customary jurisdictional power which he later spelled out in detail in the *Defence*. Jewel thought of the queen as a "patron and nurse of the church," and that "we ought to obey princes as men sent of God."[63] Some of the ideas set forth in the *Apology* reappeared in the convocation of 1563.

By 1563 the Canterbury Convocation of the Clergy was ready to make some modifications to the religious settlement of 1559. Archbishop Parker and the bishops of the upper house, including Bishops Jewel and Cox, who had been Marian exiles—as well as a sizable block of precisianists in the lower house, including the prolocutor, Alexander Nowell, who had subscribed to the "New Discipline" at Frankfort—introduced various proposals regarding the doctrine, discipline, and liturgy of the Church. A precisianist book of discipline, similar in spirit to the *Reformatio Legum Ecclesiasticarum* of 1552, passed the lower house but never came to a vote in the upper house. A precisianist set of liturgical reforms—including the abrogation of holy days, the omission of the sign of the cross in baptism, the reservation of kneeling to the discretion of the ordinary, and the use of the surplice but not the cope—failed to pass the lower house by only one proxy vote. Both of these negative results meant that further attempts for disciplinary and liturgical reform in the Elizabethan period would probably have to come from Parliament rather than the Church.

But the convocation achieved some positive results in matters of doctrine. While nothing came of proposals to make some use of Jewel's *Apology*, the lower house of the Canterbury Convocation approved, although the upper house merely "allowed" and the queen never sanctioned, a Latin catechism written by Alexander Nowell, who was also the dean of St. Paul's. Nowell drew upon some parts of Ponet's catechism of 1552, but he relied most heavily upon the Genevan Catechism, which the "New Discipline" at Frankfort had endorsed.[64] The most important doctrinal statement of both convocations by far, however, indeed the most important in the entire history of the Anglican Church, appeared in its famous Thirty-Nine Articles.

Prepared and presented by Archbishop Parker and some of the other bishops, the Thirty-Nine Articles resulted from a revision of the Forty-Two Articles. This new declaration of faith authorized a second *Book of Homilies*, but it did not endorse the Elizabethan Prayer Book as the Forty-Two Articles had endorsed the Second Edwardian Prayer Book. It eliminated some of the earlier criticism of such Anabaptist positions as blasphemy, soul-sleeping, millenarianism, and universal salvation. It took a stronger anti-Catholic position by adding communion in both kinds, by designating only baptism and the Lord's Supper as "Gospel" sacraments, and by adopting a forthright statement that priests could lawfully marry. Yet, it made slight withdrawals from entrenched Lutheran and Calvinist doctrine by affirming that the free will of man is expected to cooperate with the grace of God instead of remaining inactive; by stating that good works, though ineffectual in putting away sins, are "pleasing and acceptable to God"; and by omitting a statement that the decrees of predestination are unknown to men. Some changes also took place in interpreting the Lord's Supper. In article twenty-eight, Cranmer's view of a true or spiritual presence was stated in positive terms: the body of Christ is eaten by faith "after a heavenly and spiritual manner only," but the Reformed statements that the body of Christ is in heaven, as well as the specific denial of the real presence, were dropped. A completely new article (article twenty-nine), which reflected the Reformed view of the precisianists, stated that the "wicked" are not "partakers of Christ," but it was dropped from the Thirty-Nine Articles when the queen gave her approval the following year to the remaining thirty-eight, the total number until 1571 when article twenty-nine was restored.

The twentieth article reaffirmed the *legislative* authority of the Church to decree rites and ceremonies, which is what Elizabeth as supreme governor participated in when she vetoed convocations' article twenty-nine. But when in her own hand she added to the twentieth article a *judicial* authority of the Church in matters of faith, she restricted herself from making the kind of declaratory judgment in matters of heresy that her father had made in Lambert's case.[65] On the role of the civil magistrate, article thirty-six claimed for Elizabeth the *potestas jurisdictionis* but not the *potestas ordinis*:

> we give not to our princes, the ministering either of God's Word, or of Sacraments, the which thing, the Injunctions also lately set forth by Eliza-beth our Queen, doth most plainly testify: But that only prerogative . . . that they should rule all estates and degrees committed to their charge by God, whether they be Ecclesiastical, or no, and restrain with the civil sword, the stubborn and evil doers.[66]

In general, the Thirty-Nine Articles gave the precisianists very little about which to rejoice.

The pendulum of religious policy, after having swung through wide arcs under Edward and Mary in accordance with the principle of *cuius regio eius religio* enunciated in the continental treaty of Augsburg (1555), reached a stability under Elizabeth that was to last for a number of years. An interesting question is at what point religious policy reached equilibrium. Clearly, that point was not within the confines of Marian Catholicism. By abolishing Mary's revived papal supremacy, Elizabeth had abolished the important religious changes of her stepsister: a revived papal supremacy, restored mon-asteries, modified first fruits and tenths, and reenacted medieval heresy laws. Since Henry VIII had first been responsible for all of these abolitions except the last, and since Elizabeth revived some of the Henrician statutes of the Reformation Parliament, she had seemingly returned to the religious policies of her father. In fact, however, these Henrician measures had been as much a part of Edward's reign as they were of Henry's. The only Elizabethan revivals of Henrician measures that had not continued through Edward's reign were the royal appointment of bishops by the *congé d'élire*, the licensing of printed books and papers, the partial implementation of Cromwell's plan to seize the secular land of the Church, and the delegation of ecclesiastical jurisdiction to any person or persons by letters patent—the last a power that Henry had exercised through Vicegerent Cromwell and that Elizabeth was to exercise through the Court of High Commission. But these exceptions are an insuffi-cient basis on which to conclude that Elizabeth had realized her expressed desire to return the Church to what it had been when her father died. Her father, after all, had left a Church in which he personally had tried heretics, had revised theological doctrine, and had come very close to claiming the *potestas ordinis*, none of which Elizabeth ever tried to do as her new title of "Supreme Governor" implied. The Elizabethan Church Settlement had moved much beyond that of Henry.

The question now becomes whether the pendulum came to rest at a point closer to the settlement of Somerset or to that of Northumberland. At first glance it would appear that the Elizabethan Settlement returned to the religious policies of Somerset. She and Parliament repeated his parliamentary repeal of the medieval heresy laws; she and Parliament maintained his parlimentary repeals of the King's Book and the Six Articles Act; she and Parliament reenacted his parliamentary reform on behalf of communion in both kinds; she reaffirmed his parliamentary reform in behalf of clerical marriage; and she and Parliament continued the practice, begun under Somerset, of asserting the authority of Parliament in religious legislation. But all of these policies, in addition to those mentioned earlier that Somerset retained from Henry, were continued through the protectorate of Northumberland as well. The one major reform under Somerset, not revived under Elizabeth, was, of course, the First Prayer Book. Whatever her personal attitude toward the Second Prayer Book under Northumberland, she accepted the latter, together with the compulsory church-attendance clause of Northumberland's Act of Uniformity. The few modifications to the Second Prayer Book in the direction of the First Prayer Book, contained in the Supremacy Act, were somewhat offset by the modifications in her injunctions. The other major reform under Northumberland, the Forty-Two Articles, was more extensively modified under Elizabeth than the Second Prayer Book. The net result, however, was only a slight retreat in the Thirty-Nine Articles from the moderate Reformed positions in doctrine and liturgy expressed in the Forty-Two Articles. Regarding canon-law reform, Elizabeth not only ignored the *Reformatio*, which Northumberland had rejected, but also would not renew the canon-law reform commission which both her father and her brother had supported. Elizabeth, then, was much closer to the religious settlement of Northumberland than to that of Somerset.

The Elizabethan Settlement—the famous *via media*—was not a compromise on the matter of royal supremacy between proto-Puritans and Catholics, since both sides opposed state control of the Church. Instead, it was a lopsided compromise on matters of Church worship and doctrine between conservative and moderate reformers in the Anglican Church. In the give-and-take, the former mostly gave, and the latter mostly took.

One of the questions to be asked about the Anglican Reformation is how, given the large arcs through which the religious pendulum was swinging in such a brief period, could it have achieved such stability so quickly? There are at least two possible answers to that question. First, the force and continuity of royal supremacy itself, even in spirit if not in name under Queen Mary, provided the guiding hand which shaped and molded the final religious outcome in 1563. It meant that three English sovereigns, including the Catholic Mary—who, like her father, was not about to let the pope dictate her personal life—called upon the traditional Erastian dominance of the Church by the state, with all of its built-in advantages and experience, to see them through a major period of religious reform. Second, the Anglican Reformation was tested under fire, literally and figuratively, before it hardened into

the settlement we essentially know today. Cranmer's whole program of reform, patiently introduced and enacted under Edward, was destroyed before
English men and women were hardly aware of it, but, like the phoenix rising
from the ashes, it was introduced and enacted once again, in slightly different
form, under a new Protestant sovereign, a determined group of leaders in
both church and state, and a willing House of Commons.

3

The Elizabethan Challenges

Two important challenges to the early Elizabethan settlement of religion threatened its existence during the course of the next three decades. "On the left hand with superstitious blindness," as Robert Cecil wrote later, there were the illegal activities of some English Catholics to restore the ancient faith under papal supremacy either by force of arms from without or by religious conversion from within. "On the right with unadvised zeal," he added, were the constitutional attempts of moderate and radical Puritans to purify the liturgy, but more especially, to reform the administrative structure of the Church either through Parliament or from within the Church itself.[1] Serious efforts to change the form of Church government had not been attempted in the previous three decades when doctrinal and liturgical matters had been to the forefront. Under Elizabeth the Anglican episcopate found itself more and more in the position of conducting a large holding operation—a policy that received at all times the wholehearted support of the queen but not always that of her more Puritan-inclined councillors. The bishops wanted to maintain a national church establishment in which the state, not the Church, was the dominant partner. What, one might ask, were the points of similarity and difference between Catholic seminarians and Puritan Presbyterians as they challenged the English Church and state? And which of the two, if either, had a reasonable chance of surviving against the prevailing Erastianism of the time?

The Puritan Threat

The English Puritan movement, as became increasingly apparent as Elizabeth's reign progressed, was made up of different groups of clerics and laymen. Yet they did share certain characteristics. They were antipapal polemicists who, having rejected many of the traditions of the Church Fathers, accepted primarily the authority of Holy Scripture as the revelation of God's will. They believed in an educated, preaching ministry. Many of them ac-

81

cepted an interpretation of Calvinist theology which led them to an assurance that they were predestined members of a "godly party." And some of them shared an evangelical intensity—sometimes manifesting itself as a religious conversion—indeed, a kind of spiritual metamorphosis that greatly heightened their religiosity. In a few instances, that intensity even had an apocalyptic vision whose millennial overtones became a strong characteristic of much Puritan thought in the 1640s and 1650s.[2] In matters of royal supremacy, the ecclesiastical organization of the Church, and the relationships of church and state, however, the Puritan clerics differed greatly.

Among these Puritan clerics were three basic groups: the moderate reformers, the Presbyterian radicals, and the Separatists. The moderate reformers, men such as Lawrence Humphrey, president of Magdalen College at Oxford, or Thomas Sampson, dean of Christ Church at Oxford, became deeply involved in the vestiarian controversy of the 1560s. The early moderates were interested in many relatively modest reforms of the Church, particularly in the Thirty-Nine Articles and the Prayer Book. They and their later successors, including William Whitaker, William Perkins, and John Reynolds, like the Anglican conformists such as John Whitgift, Thomas Bilson, and Thomas Cooper, generally accepted the royal supremacy and the established national Church. The moderate Puritans and the Anglican conformists also shared some form of Calvinist theology along with the rest of the Puritans. But the rest of the Puritans wanted substantial changes in the ecclesiastical organization of the Church, and frequently challenged the royal supremacy. Some Puritans were Presbyterian radicals, men like Walter Travers and John Field, who, for example, precipitated the admonition controversy of the 1570s. The Presbyterian radicals, especially Thomas Cartwright, hoped that from a system of Church courts a national assembly and ultimately an international Calvinist assembly would develop, which, somewhat like the Catholic Church, would transcend national boundaries but acknowledge only Christ as the head of the Church. Finally, a small number of the Puritans were radicals in a different sense than the Presbyterians. As Separatists, these radical Puritans, men like Robert Browne, Robert Harrison, Henry Barrow, and John Greenwood, forsook any episcopal or Presbyterian ecclesiastical structure, working toward separate authorities in church and state. With the Presbyterian radicals, however, they shared a "vision of a truly reformed church of Christ," and an attitude toward the civil magistrate in which "obedience was due only so far as the Word of God allowed."[3]

Although these three models suggest focal points where Puritan theory and practice tended to cluster, they are by no means exclusive since, as has been suggested, they shared several points of view that distinguished them from the Anglican conformists in the Church and Roman Catholics outside of the Protestant spectrum altogether. And, there were some fascinating and at times influential individuals who do not fall easily into any category. Such a man was Edward Dering, a fellow of Christ's College at Cambridge during the 1560s, who moved from a moderate position to "the very edge" of the Presbyterian position. Still another was Lawrence Chaderton, also a fellow of

Christ's and the first master of Emmanuel College at Cambridge, who, as Dering's successor in a sense, wrote as a Presbyterian at the peak of the subscription crisis in 1583–1584, yet played the moderate at the Hampton Court Conference in 1604. Defining Tudor religious categories too rigidly or precisely obscures their overlapping nature, but eschewing differentiation, viewing these people altogether merely as Protestants, obscures the rich religious diversity of the Elizabethan age.[4]

Among the Puritan laymen in the House of Commons were moderate reformers (Thomas Norton and Walter Strickland) and radical Presbyterians (the Wentworth brothers, Anthony Cope, and a future Speaker, Christopher Yelverton). In addition, some aristocrats, such as the Earl of Huntingdon, and some members of the gentry like George Carleton, largely adhered to the moderate reformers, as did those Puritan-inclined privy councillors, including Sir Francis Knollys, Sir Walter Mildmay, the Earl of Leicester, the Earl of Warwick, and Sir Francis Walsingham. Sooner or later Puritans would attack all of Cranmer's program (the Prayer Books, the Ordinal, the Homilies, and the Thirty-Nine Articles) except the one thing, the *Reformatio*, which was never adopted. Although the aforementioned Puritan members of the Commons were oftentimes very outspoken in their views, as we shall repeatedly see, they did not constitute a "Puritan choir"—a mythical term mistakenly attributed to a supposedly sizable Puritan pressure group devoted to reformist legislation.[5] Nevertheless, they constituted a threat to the religious order of things that had been established in Parliament at the beginning of the reign.

The Vestiarian Controversy

The Puritan threat—indeed the term "Puritan" itself—emerged outside of Parliament during the vestiarian controversy of the mid-1560s. In 1564, two eminent Marian exiles, Sampson and Humphrey, led the criticism about clerical vestments. These precisianist or vestiarian Puritans maintained that even though clerical vestments were *adiaphora*—things indifferent to salvation—as most of the bishops admitted, they were associated nevertheless with Catholicism (and were hence idolatrous) as well as unauthorized by Scripture (and hence not subject to Church regulation). In January, 1565, Queen Elizabeth pointed out to Archbishop Parker the "open and manifest disorder" in the Church brought about by "diversity of opinions," especially regarding the "external, decent, and lawful rites and cermonies." The queen also charged the archbishop and the ecclesiastical commission to bring about a "uniformity of order" in every church in accordance with the law. By March, Parker responded with a "book of articles"—a prototype of the *Advertisements*.[6]

The "book of articles," as far as vestments were concerned, was a compromise between the Ornaments Rubric of the Elizabethan Prayer Book and the contemporary practice of many of the Puritan clergy. Parker did not relax the requirement of the injunctions for outdoor apparel (caps and gowns); but the requirement of the Ornaments Rubric for eucharistic vestments (the alb, chasuble, stole, and cope), though still necessary in cathedral and collegiate churches, was reduced to only a surplice in parish churches. This concession more nearly met the proposals of the precisianists than those of the bishops, which had produced the very close voting in the Convocation of 1563. The queen, although approving, would not formally assent to the new articles, and the Privy Council did not extend the "helping hand" to Parker, which he mistakenly thought it "once did in Hooper's days." Actually, in Bishop Hooper's case, the Edwardian Privy Council had superceded, not corroborated, episcopal authority on the vestments issue. Since neither Sampson nor Humphrey would accept the new articles, Parker ordered them to leave their livings, although only Sampson was finally deprived.[7]

Not much further action was taken for a year, but Elizabeth did not let the matter rest. In March, 1566, Parker, together with the bishops of the ecclesiastical commission, issued the *Advertisements*, the first of the Church's four subscription tests imposed upon all of the clergy during Elizabeth's reign. Shortly afterwards, Parker and the reluctant Bishop of London, Edmund Grindal, a protégé of Bucer and an exile at Strassburg, sought written promises of conformity from more than 100 London preachers. Thirty-seven refused to sign and were suspended from their livings, thereby bringing nearly all of the preaching exercises in the city to an end. The *Advertisements* required all holders of ecclesiastical livings to subscribe to the doctrine and ceremonies of the church according to the law of the realm and to subscribe to the clerical vestments in accordance with the concessions made in the "book of articles."

Elizabeth refused to give her assent to the *Advertisements* just as she had refused to assent to the earlier "book of articles." Although she approved of both documents as an expedient course of action, the queen did not wish to give her authorization to anything less than the settlement of 1559; that is, she would accept nothing less than the vestiarian requirements of the Ornaments Rubric and the injunctions. If she had given her consent, she might have found it increasingly difficult to resist further encroachments by the Puritans upon her religious settlement. Refusing to change her standards permanently, Elizabeth convinced the archbishop to carry out her wishes, but in doing so he asserted her ecclesiastical authority free from the interference of the Privy Council or of Parliament.[8]

Some of the Puritans who had suffered at the hands of Parker in the vestments controversy decided to consult continental reformers or write pamphlets stating their position. Neither Humphrey nor Sampson was under any illusion that the queen was not the force behind the *Advertisements* when they wrote to Henry Bullinger, one of Zwingli's successors at Zurich. Humphrey asked Bullinger whether he could become involved in the bondage of the Church "by the authority of a royal edict" after having enjoyed a freedom in liturgical matters; Sampson asked Bullinger if any religious ceremony could "be prescribed to the church by the sovereign" without the "free concurrence of churchmen." Much to their disappointment, Bullinger told Humphrey that if he refused to comply with a "civil ordinance," he would "expose the churches to wolves, or at least to teachers who are far from competent," and he told Sampson that "if the consent of the clergy is always to be waited for by the sovereign," it is probable that "godly princes" would never have been able to bring the churches into "proper order." When Bishop Grindal made public a copy of Bullinger's responses to Humphrey and Sampson, it served to deter some bishops and ministers, most of them Marian exiles, who otherwise might have left their livings. Humphrey and Sampson, however, told Bullinger that they were "not merely disputing about a cap or a surplice" since there were other popish blemishes on the Church of England. When Sampson and Humphrey, joined by the old Henrician reformer, Miles Coverdale, appealed to Theodore Beza, one of Calvin's successors at Geneva, the reaction was more sympathetic; but Beza felt helpless to intervene, partly because of the queen's hostility toward Geneva ever since the publication of the Genevan tracts on regicide written by Knox, Goodman, and Gilby.[9]

Bullinger and Beza urged the Puritans to seek some relief in the second session of Elizabeth's second Parliament (1566–1567). None of the religious bills brought before this Parliament, nearly all without the knowledge of the queen, dealt with vestments. But one of them, giving statutory authority to all of the Articles of Religion of 1563 (Bill A), the queen withdrew, much to the consternation of fifteen bishops, including the two archbishops. She did so, to Cecil's regret, not because she disliked the Articles themselves but because she opposed "the manner of putting forth the book," that is by the authority of Parliament. One governmental religious bill, drafted by the attorney general, though vigorously opposed by eleven Catholic peers that both houses of Parliament passed, provided for the consecration of bishops. Queen Elizabeth signed the bill because Queen Mary's rejection of the Edwardian Ordinal had left no legal procedure for creating new bishops.[10]

A few precisianists like Gilby, Thomas Crowley, and John Bartlett tried to keep the vestiarian issue alive with pamphlets that called into question the royal supremacy itself. Bartlett's *Fortress of Fathers* (1566), which pointedly included some early statements of Bullinger against vestments, further argued:

> Christ is only the head of his mystical body which is the church, as the Prince or chief Magistrate is the head of the Politique body of his Realm and country. The supreme magistrate is bound to obey the word of God, preached by Christ's messengers, and he is also subject to the discipline of the Church.[11]

Here is one of the earliest manifestations of that radical view of royal supremacy which was to become an integral part of Presbyterian Puritanism.

The Articles of 1571

Elizabeth's third Parliament (1571), like the session of 1566–1567, provided the opportunity for both Puritans and bishops to make changes in Elizabeth's settlement of religion. Proposed parliamentary measures included the adoption of Cranmer's *Reformatio Legum Ecclesiasticarum*, the reform of the Prayer Book, the repeal of part of the Henrician Dispensations Act, the modification of the requirement for church attendance, and the denial of benefit of clergy in some felonious cases. A bill by Thomas Norton, Cranmer's son-in-law, would have adopted John Foxe's new translation of the *Reformatio*, but it died in committee, probably because reform of the canon law generally came under the jurisdiction of convocation or an ecclesiastical commission. Walter Strickland's attempt in the Prayer Book bill to eliminate copes, surplices, wedding rings, kneeling at communion, and private baptism failed when Sir Francis Knollys noted that ceremonial matters were part of the queen's prerogative. The Puritan George Carleton introduced a measure to modify part of the Dispensations Act (1534). The act had given the archbishop of Canterbury full power to issue licenses and dispensations except those that were contrary to the law of God. Carleton's bill, which never emerged from the Lords, would have added to the exception edicts of Convocation or acts of Parliament. Bishop Grindal's bill for church attendance, which would have increased the fines but lessened the frequency of church attendance as pre-scribed by the Act of Uniformity, passed both houses. The queen refused to give her assent, perhaps because she did not like to consent to bills that had not been cleared with her. Of these parliamentary measures, only the one denying benefit of clergy to "cut-purses or pick-purses" became law.[12]

The Parliament of 1571 also dealt with two bills on the Articles of Religion. The first, which had been called Bill A in the Parliament of 1566–1567 but later called a "bill for conservation of order and uniformity in the Church," confirmed the Articles which Convocation passed in 1563. Whether this new Bill A, whose exact provisions are unknown, would have given approval to *all* of the Articles, as the old Bill A had done, or to a lesser number, is uncertain. The latter possibility, however, seems unlikely in a bill whose title called for "uniformity." The second bill, which had been called Bill B in the Parliament of 1566–1567 but later was called a "bill to reform certain disorders touching ministers of the Church," provided two options for the clergy. They could either subscribe to all of the Articles or to "so much of the said Articles" as would be ratified in the current sessions of Parliament or convocation. Most Protestants wanted a subscription bill so that crypto-papists surviving from Mary's reign could not hold clerical positions.

The evidence that the Puritans were interested in a new Bill B requiring subscription to less than all of the Articles comes from an account which Peter Wentworth wrote four years later. The day before the new Bill A was read in the Commons, a group of six Puritan members met with Archbishop Parker. When the archbishop asked them why they exempted from the new Bill A those articles which dealt with the "Homilies, consecrating of bishops, and such like," Wentworth replied that the Puritan members had had no time to examine them to see how they agreed with the Word of God. When Parker told them that that examination was the function of the bishops, Wentworth hurled back, "No, by the faith I bear to God . . . we will pass nothing before we understand what it is, for that were but to make you Popes."[13]

Meanwhile, bishops, but not the lower house, of the Canterbury Convocation of the Clergy were themselves acting on the Articles of Religion. Quite early in the parliamentary session, convocation passed a set of twelve canons, thereby adding the Church's second subscription test of the reign to the first, the *Advertisements*. Number six of the twelve canons called for ministers to subscribe to the Ordinal, the Book of Common Prayer, and *all* the Articles of Religion as set forth in the 1563 version of the Articles. The queen never signed these Canons of 1571, perhaps because they prescribed the vestments of the *Advertisements* and the mild Calvinist theology of Nowell's Catechism for schoolmasters. Later in the session convocation turned to two revisions of the 1563 Articles themselves. The first revision reinstated article twenty-nine—the one which said that the "wicked" are not "partakers of Christ" and which the queen had deleted in 1563—thereby bringing the number of articles back to thirty-nine. Convocation also incorporated Elizabeth's penciled amendment to article twenty, which gave the Church authority in matters of faith and, hence, a small part of the *potestas jurisdictionis*. Before long the York Convocation also ratified the twelve canons and the slightly revised Articles. Although the queen did not sign the canons, she did approve the revised Articles.[14]

Back in Parliament, the Commons passed the new Bill A. Elizabeth, however, stated that although she liked the revised Articles she was not going to have Parliament handle them. The queen's withdrawal of the new Bill A provoked the Commons to eliminate the two options of the new Bill B. In their place new phraseology required every "Priest or Minister of God's holy Word and Sacraments" who had not been ordained by the Ordinal of Edward VI, and all new clergy, including those with Catholic patrons, to subscribe "to all the articles of Religion which only concern the confession of the true Christian faith and the doctrine of the sacraments." The ambiguity of just what articles the new phraseology covered produced a religious textual controversy that reverberated well into the Stuart period, indeed, among historians into our own time. The passage by both houses of Parliament of this revised new Bill B, and the queen's signing of it especially after she had withdrawn the new Bill A, could be interpreted as one of the most stunning reversals of religious policy in Elizabeth's reign or of any other English sovereign's reign in the early modern period.[15]

A hasty reading of the amended phraseology in the revised subscription bill could leave a strong impression that subscription is required only to those Articles of Religion that deal with "the confession of the true Christian faith and the doctrine of the Sacraments." Indeed so the eminent seventeenth century legal writer, John Selden, wrote in his famous work, *Table Talk*. In the absence of any appended list of supposedly excludable articles, however, one is left to speculate upon which of the Articles may not have dealt with faith and doctrine.

One possible line of speculation is to examine Peter Wentworth's list that appeared in his *contretemps* with Archbishop Parker—the same list that

Wentworth had said the Puritans did not have time to examine carefully. That list included (1) the "Homilies" (mentioned in article thirty-five), which the Puritans intensely disliked but which the article says contains a "godly and wholesome" doctrine; (2) the "consecrating of bishops" (mentioned in article thirty-six), which Parliament had just extended in a government bill; and (3) the nebulous phrase—"and such like." Wentworth's phrase "and such like" may have implicated article thirty-seven, which, as we have seen before, excluded any priestly authority for Elizabeth but reaffirmed her ecclesiastical authority in religious matters. It is inconceivable that the queen would have signed any authorization bill that in her judgment would have exempted the foregoing articles, thereby seriously jeopardizing royal supremacy.[16]

The idea that Puritans during the subscription process might have wished to extend their alleged exemption from certain articles to anything that in their judgment was not "agreeable to the Word of God" was anathema to the eminent seventeenth-century judge, Sir Edward Coke. In his famous *Institutes*, he stated that such a subscription "was *not according to statute* of 13. Elizabeth" because that statute required an "*absolute*," not a "*conditional*," subscription. In this discussion, much depends on the interpretation of the word "only" in the statute's phrase "all the Articles of Religion which only concern the Confession of the true Christian faith."

Some argue that the word "only" was not used in a restrictive sense, that is, to limit the number of articles, but rather in a demonstrative sense, that is, to declare the nature of the subjects handled in the entire book of Articles. The phrase "Priests and Ministers of God's holy Word and Sacraments" in the very opening of the statute has been seen to imply what all priests and ministers were expected to do. It closely matches the statute's later use of the phrase "the Confession of the true Christian faith and the Doctrine of the Sacraments" as a broad statement of what all the articles cover. Perhaps more persuasive is the suggestion that the word "only" was meant to distinguish subscription to all the Articles of Religion from other documents, such as the Ordinal or the Book of Common Prayer, to which subscription might have been required in all of their parts. (In fact, the Canterbury Convocation of the Clergy had just required subscription to all three.)[17]

Finally, the subscription bill of 1571 surfaced, as we shall see, just after the Catholic Rebellion of the Northern Earls and the papal bull excommunicating Elizabeth. The most plausible explanation of the queen's decision to sign the revised Bill B seems to be that she was embroiled in a Catholic crisis of far greater magnitude than any challenge which the parliamentary Puritans presented. Had she withheld her assent to the revised Bill B, she would have announced to the world, and particularly to the Roman Catholic part of it, that she had substantially rejected the doctrine and sacraments of the Anglican Church. By accepting the revised Bill B, Elizabeth indicated her preference for an effective subscription process for Catholics and Protestants alike. It is very difficult to imagine that she would have ever accepted a subscription bill that would have retreated one iota from all of the Thirty-Nine Articles that the Convocations of 1571 had just approved. Having conceded to Parliament, for pragmatic reasons of state, the right to participate once again in the process of determining religious policy as in 1559, Elizabeth was not about to approve any bill that would have weakened that earlier settlement of religion.

The Admonition Controversy

In the first session of Elizabeth's fourth Parliament (1572), the Puritans introduced a bill on rites and ceremonies that led directly to the Admonition Controversy of the early 1570s. The preamble of the original draft of the bill noted that a number of ministers, with the consent of some bishops, had introduced prophesyings or preaching exercises for the edification of their congregations, thereby departing from the Prayer Book. The enacting clauses of the original draft of the bill provided that the Act of Uniformity of 1559 would apply only to Catholics, whereas others, with the permission of their bishops, might omit parts of the Prayer Book or adopt the Genevan *Form of Prayers* used in the Stranger congregations (both French and Dutch) of London. Modifications of the bill in the Commons did not alter the queen's dislike for the bill. Once again, she prohibited any further measures concerning religion not first approved by the bishops or by Convocation.

Immediately after the withdrawal of the bill, two radical Puritans, John Field and Thomas Wilcox, issued *An Admonition to Parliament* (1572). Parts of the *Admonition* outlined the marks of a true church: the "pure" preaching of the Word, the "sincere" administration of the sacraments, and the "severe" enforcement of ecclesiastical discipline. But other parts of the *Admonition* were inflammatory attacks upon the remaining "popish abuses" in the Anglican Church. For example, Field and Wilcox contended that the Prayer Book, to which some "godly" ministers had refused to subscribe in accordance with the Canons of 1571, had been "culled and picked out of that popish dunghill, the Mass book." Yet not only the Prayer Book came under attack. The *Admonition* also called for the removal of the *Homilies*, the Thirty-Nine Articles, and the injunctions as well as advowsons, patronages, and impropriations. One of the ways proposed to establish the true church was to abolish the titles and authority of all archbishops, bishops, deans, and archdeacons—in short, the whole Anglican hierarchy. How would such an action affect the royal supremacy? Without spelling out the details, Wilcox wrote:

> Not that we mean to take away the authority of the civil Magistrate and chief governor, to whom we wish all blessedness, and for the increase of whose godliness we daily pray: but that Christ being restored into his kingdom, to rule in the same by the scepter of his word, and severe discipline: the Prince may be better obeyed, the realm more flourish in godliness, and the Lord himself . . . more sincerely . . . served then . . . yet at this present is.

Field went one step further by stating that "civil offices, joined to the Ecclesiastical, is against the word of God." What these radical Puritans, a small but vocal minority, hoped to substitute for the Anglican hierarchy was nothing less than the Presbyterian form of church government that was more fully elaborated in the *Second Admonition* (1572), attributed to Job Throkmorton, and in Walter Travers' *A Full and Plain Declaration of Ecclesiastical Discipline* (*Ecclesiasticae Disciplinae*) (1574).[18]

Both Cartwright and Travers had just returned from the Genevan Academy where they had drawn out the Presbyterian implications of Beza's neo-Calvinism: the New Testament revealed the presbytery as the true apostolic form of the Christian church. The presbytery's claim to govern the Church was based upon a divine right, and divine right was the basis of Rome's, but as yet not Canterbury's, claim for bishops to govern the Church. In England the term "presbytery" primarily referred to the disciplinary court or local consistory of a particular congregation. It consisted of a triple ministry of deacons (instead of overseers of the poor), ruling lay elders (instead of churchwardens), and preaching pastors or ministers (instead of vicars or rectors).

The congregations initially elected their ministers, among whom there was a parity and not a hierarchy as in Anglicanism, and their ruling elders by common consent. This elective procedure differed greatly from the Anglican parish, where the lay or ecclesiastical patron, through the possession of the advowson, had the right of presentation of a clergyman to a benefice. Presbyterians disputed whether or not the officers of a congregation, once elected, were responsible to the members of the congregation. Both Travers and Cartwright, however, thought that the distribution of power within the congregation should be aristocratic, or theocratic, rather than democratic. Free elections within Presbyterian churches, even with a Puritan patron, became increasingly uncommon, since the choice of a minister came to be made in a classis or conference.[19]

The classis, together with the provincial synod and the national assembly, constituted a series of additional church courts ranging above the presbytery, each representing a larger geographical area. These additional church courts were to hold the supreme power under Christ in ecclesiastical affairs. The temporal ruler of the land would be merely a member of a particular congregation, not a supreme governor, of a reformed national church. Moreover, as John Field wrote in a published collection of family prayers, the queen should be taught "to be humble under thy hand, to kiss the rod, and to profit under thy corrections, which thou hast or shall hereafter in mercy lay upon her." It is no wonder that in 1573 the dean of York, Matthew Hutton, wrote to Cecil (now Lord Burghley): "At the beginning it was but a cap, a surplice, and a tippet; now, it is grown to bishops, archbishops, and cathedral churches, to the overthrow of the established order, and to the Queen's authority in causes ecclesiastical."[20]

Most of the vestiarian Puritans, such as Humphrey and Sampson, did not approve of the *Admonition*, but most of those Puritans who became more radical, such as Edward Dering, gave their support to Field and Wilcox. Dering, who had the audacity in 1570 to tell the queen in a sermon in her chapel that "you sit still and are careless" about the Church, visited Field and

Wilcox in prison. Although the earl of Leicester blamed both sides in the Admonition Controversy, he and the earl of Warwick secured the prisoners' release. In May, 1573, Dering, together with Field and Wilcox, appeared before the Council in Star Chamber. After much debate the Star Chamber suspended Dering from lecturing, but not before he told Burghley that "the lordship or civil government of a bishop . . . is utterly unlawful in the Church of God" and that in the spiritual sphere "the worldly power of the prince hath no place."[21] In June, a royal proclamation ordered all copies of the *Admonition* to be turned over to the bishops or to the Council.

In October, 1573, a Puritan fanatic, Peter Birchet, mistook the celebrated sea dog, John Hawkins, for Christopher Hatton, the queen's new favorite and staunch opponent of the Puritans. Birchet stabbed Hawkins in the Strand. Birchet, though mentally deranged, paid with his life, and the queen issued another proclamation. She called for the imprisonment of anyone who criticized the Prayer Book, and the Council consequently set up special commissions to detect nonconformity. A few days later, Burghley noted that "a number of persons young in years, but over-young in soundness of learning and discretion" had enticed Her Majesty's subjects "to think it a burden of conscience to observe the orders and rites of the Church established by law."[22] Although the Puritan movement temporarily lost its momentum, the government's response did not turn into a wholesale persecution. The English Puritans were in no danger of extreme action like that carried out against the Huguenots in France on St. Bartholomew's Day the preceding year.

Thomas Cartwright and John Whitgift engaged in a famous polemical duel over the relationship between church and state during the later stages of the Admonition Controversy (1574–1577). Cartwright, whom vice-chancellor Whitgift had dismissed from his post as Lady Margaret Professor of Divinity at Cambridge, put forward the radical Puritan theory of the two kingdoms. Church and state, like the twins of Hippocrates (separate but related), should prosper and languish together. Just as in the temporal realm it is unlawful for a minister of the Church to make civil laws or to hold political office, wrote Cartwright, so in Christ's spiritual realm it is unlawful for the civil magistrate to proclaim ceremonies and doctrine pertaining to the Church. Ceremonies and doctrine, of course, were the two areas of religious jurisdiction which the queen had already turned over to the bishops in the twentieth article of the revised Thirty-Nine Articles.

Whitgift, who became the first bishop under Elizabeth to hold a seat on the Privy Council, replied, "I am fully persuaded . . . that there is no such distinction betwixt the church of Christ and a christian commonwealth, as you and the papists dream of." (Whitgift's comparison with Catholicism was somewhat inaccurate since Cartwright did not claim exemption of ministers from the civil jurisdiction of the magistrate, as the Catholic Church had done in England). Contrary to Cartwright's position, Whitgift asserted the authority of the civil magistrate to determine the ceremonies of the Church as well as to execute laws and to maintain discipline. He did not include the doctrine of the Church, however, as part of the magistrate's authority, and there was still enough of the reformer in him to add a qualifying phrase: "(so that he do nothing against the word of God)."[23] Whitgift specifically disavowed any authority of the Crown to preach the Word of God, or, for that matter, to administer the sacraments or excommunicate from the Church. The queen's power stopped with the *potestas jurisdictionis*; it did not extend to the *potestas ordinis*.

Whitgift's fear of Cartwright's two-kingdom theory went beyond the possible loss of royal supremacy in ecclesiastical affairs; it envisioned the possible loss of royal supremacy in civil affairs as well. Much in Cartwright's flamboyant rhetoric would confirm these fears. Despite his enjoinder to obey the civil magistrate who "governeth the church of God," Cartwright urged his readers to remember that civil magistrates were "nurses" as well as "servants" to the Church. "They must remember to subject themselves unto the church, to submit their sceptres, to throw down their crowns, before the church, yea, as the prophet speaketh, to lick the dust of the feet of the church.' This is the "kind of speech the pope himself useth," wrote Whitgift, "and under the same pretense hath trodden kings under his feet." Cartwright immediately explained that he did not mean to be taken literally, but Whitgift assumed that what he meant was that the prince should "be content to be ruled and governed, to be punished and corrected, to be excommunicated and absolved," by the seniors or elders of a Presbyterian church.[24] The right of the church to excommunicate the sovereign was the very doctrine that Beza had asserted against Thomas Lieber or Erastus, although the term Erastianism came to stand for the broad control of most aspects of religious affairs by the secular power.

With a metaphor that succeeding generations of Puritans were to pass along to their descendants, Cartwright continued, "as the hangings are made fit for the house, so the commonwealth must be made to agree with the church, and the government thereof with her government." For Whitgift, these words meant that Cartwright "would have all monarchies over thrown, and reduced either to a popular or an aristocratic state." Cartwright, however, expressed no desire to transfer either the elective principle of pastors or the governing principle of elders to the Tudor monarchy, "granted that the government of one be the best in the commonwealth, yet it cannot be in the church." What he had in mind with the analogy of the "hangings" was the responsibility of the prince to submit to the Church in the application of civil disabilities to the excommunicate, in the suppression of false religions, and in the punishment by death for offenses against the Mosaic code. And what this means, wrote Whitgift, is that "all the laws of this land, that be contrary to these judicial laws of Moses, must be abrogated: the prince must be abridged of that prerogative which she hath in pardoning such as by the law be condemned to die."[25] It seemed as if Cartwright wanted a civil government founded upon the judicial law of the Old Testament. Here, then, was the basis for a church state instead of a state church. Not surprisingly, Elizabeth and her churchmen became greatly concerned about the Presbyterian threat to her Erastian settlement.

The Prophesyings

One of the outward marks of a true Christian church, according to the first *Admonition*, was the preaching of the Word of God. Any attempt to improve the preaching ability of the clergy appealed to both radical and moderate Puritans. In most of the southern dioceses in the mid-1570s, Puritans conducted exercises or prophesyings for the improvement of preaching. These prophesyings produced still another controversy in Elizabeth's reign.

Prophesyings had originated in Zurich and other continental reformed centers, but in England the Stranger congregations of London had first conducted them during the reign of Edward VI. Parker's *Advertisements* had curtailed these exercises in London in the mid-1560s, and a parliamentary bill of 1572 mentioned them as a departure from the Prayer Book. Although practice varied from diocese to diocese, the exercises usually consisted of weekly or fortnightly meetings led by a moderator who allowed ministers to expand their interpretations of the Holy Scriptures through sermons and commentaries for the edification of the laity. The laity, who attended in considerable numbers and gave generous financial support, frequently left after the sermons and commentaries, whereupon the clergy would engage in a strict examination not only of the views propounded but also of their own lives and morals. Sometimes, as in Norwich, where a modified episcopacy was developed with the consent of the bishops, the prophesyings bestowed on a permanent moderator the powers of a rural dean or a suffragan bishop, the latter being an office created by parliamentary statute during the height of the Henrician schism. The rural dean examined candidates for the ministry, dealt with minor disorders at monthly meetings of the ministers and church wardens, and sat with the bishop when rebukes or suspensions were to be given to the clergy and the laity. Sometimes, as in Northampton, where an attempt was made to replicate Calvin's Geneva with the consent of the bishop, the prophesyings were turned into weekly meetings in which the minister, the mayor, and others attempted to regulate the morals of the townspeople.[26]

A prophesying, particularly as a disciplinary device to regulate morality, can be viewed as the Presbyterian classis or conference in embryo; a prophesying, particularly as a form of church organization that stressed the notion of hierarchy rather than parity, can also be seen as a modification of Anglican diocesan episcopacy. Either way, however, prophesyings emanated primarily from the moderate and radical Puritan clergy, not from the Anglican bishops, and resulted invariably in a greater discussion of religious issues by both the Puritan clergy and laity than the queen was prepared to tolerate. In 1574, Elizabeth ordered Archbishop Parker to put an end to the prophesyings, but rather than comply completely, he limited his prohibition only to the diocese of Norwich. In the last months of his life, the archbishop's private letter to Cecil indicated that Parker felt that he no longer possessed what he called the "supreme government ecclesiastical" since the queen, especially in connection with some ecclesiastical appointments about which she did not consult with him, had exceeded her powers as supreme governor.[27]

When some eight months after the death of Parker in April, 1575, Cecil finally succeeded in getting Elizabeth to issue a *congé d'élire* for Grindal, the archbishop of York, to become archbishop of Canterbury, he undoubtedly had no idea that his friend Grindal would soon become involved in one of the sharpest disagreements between an archbishop and the Crown since the days of Becket and Henry II. The "unlearnedness of the ministry" and other Puritan grievances arose in a petition to the queen during the second session of Elizabeth's fourth Parliament (1576). This was the same Parliament, incidentally, in which the Puritan Peter Wentworth delivered his famous oration on free speech—"Sweet indeed is the name of liberty"—as a safeguard against messages from the queen prohibiting the discussion, among other things, of religious matters.[28]

Elizabeth referred the petition to Grindal and the bishops meeting in Canterbury Convocation, which quickly drew up a new set of fifteen canons. One of the new canons stated that bishops should not admit "unlearned ministers" to any ecclesiastical benefice, and a second called for ministers diligently to "teach their auditors sound doctrine." Yet another canon, which provided the Church with its third subscription test, required ministers to subscribe only to the Articles of Religion. Elizabeth, who had not approved the Canons of 1571, agreed to the Canons of 1576 only after deleting a canon authorizing marriage during Advent, Lent, and other special times, and after she had stricken another limiting the administration of private baptism only to ministers and deacons (not lay people).[29]

The Canons of 1576 disappointed the Puritans, but they liked Grindal's attempts to reform the medieval archiepiscopal courts, especially the Court of Faculties, and his grant of permission to print the Geneva Bible in England for the first time. But Elizabeth cut this reforming activity short when, at the prompting of Sir Christopher Hatton, she ordered Archbishop Grindal to reduce the number of preachers in each shire to three or four and to end all prophesyings in the Canterbury province. As she told her bishops later, the prophesyings "schismatically divided" the "vulgar sort" into a variety of "dangerous opinions" and encouraged "the violation of our laws" and "the breach of common order."[30]

Before drafting his famous reply to Elizabeth, Grindal tried to save the prophesyings. First, he learned from his questionnaire to the bishops under his jurisdiction that the prophesyings were indeed being held except in London, Salisbury, and a few other places; that while not closely supervised, they often had the sanction of a bishop; that they enjoyed strong lay support, both in attendance and financially; that the clergy and laity had had some strong disagreements about them; and that most of the bishops felt that the prophesyings should continue. Second, he drew up eight "Orders for the reformation of abuses about the learned exercises and conferences among ministers of the Church," which strictly limited prophesyings by requiring the authorization of a bishop, official approval of moderators and speakers, no speaking by laymen, no discussion of public or private affairs, and no "invections" against the laws, rites, and discipline of the Church.[31] But the queen would not have prophesyings, not only because she genuinely feared them as a disruptive force in both church and state, but possibly also as a way to discredit Grindal's attempts at reform.

Like Dering in his sermon before Elizabeth a few years earlier, Grindal, too, found the courage to disagree openly with the queen. Responding to the queen's command to decrease the number of ministers, Grindal argued in a 6,000 word manifesto of May, 1576 that the reading of homilies, while useful, was "nothing" compared to preaching. "By preaching also due obedience to Christian princes and magistrates is planted in the hearts of subjects . . . where preaching wanteth, obedience faileth." Regarding the queen's command to eliminate prophesyings, Grindal flatly stated, "I cannot with safe conscience . . . give my assent to the suppressing of the said exercises" because they increase knowledge among the clergy and edify the laity. It was no cause for alarm to Grindal that different men found different "senses" of one sentence of Scripture just as long as "all senses be good and agreeable to the analogy and proportion of faith"—a standard that the archbishop did not stop to explain.[32]

If this overt act of disobedience by her archbishop had not outraged Elizabeth, the two requests he made next certainly must have done so. He requested that she should refer all matters relating to the doctrine and discipline of the Church to the bishops. And he also requested that she should not "pronounce so resolutely and peremptorily" in religious matters as she might do in civil matters. Then, in phraseology which suggested the "hangings" analogy, though not the Presbyterianism, of Thomas Cartwright—"princes ought to bow their sceptres to the Son of God"—Grindal concluded. "Remember, Madam that you are a mortal creature. . . . And although you are a mighty prince, yet remember that He which dwelleth in heaven is mightier." Grindal was exercising in the ecclesiastical sphere what Peter Wentworth was claiming for the members of Parliament.[33]

The impasse between the queen and the archbishop reached a climax in the Privy Council. The queen apparently informed Sir Walter Mildmay that when Grindal appeared before the Council meeting in Star Chamber, he should either confess his fault or be deprived. When the Council sent Mildmay and another councillor to sound out Grindal, he stated that before he would confess any guilt "he would be torn in pieces with horses." Lord Keeper Bacon prepared a stern rebuke for the archbishop, but the confrontation was avoided because of Grindal's illness on the days scheduled for his appearance. As far as we know, he was never brought before any court which might have attempted to deprive him.[34]

After the failure of Cecil and the Council to get Grindal to compromise his semi-Puritan position, the queen placed the archbishop under house arrest and sequestered him from office. She did not remove him from his post, partly because many of the members of the Privy Council, both gentry and aristocracy alike, sympathized with Grindal's conception of the Church, partly because deprivation by legal process had not been undertaken before, and partly because any further punitive action could only bring additional comfort to the Catholic Church and disappointment to Elizabeth's friends abroad (Protestants in the Low Countries and France). A matter of conscience, even in the case of the archbishop of Canterbury, seemed insufficient reason under the circumstances to bring in the full force of royal supremacy.[35]

In May, 1577, Elizabeth bypassed Archbishop Grindal and ordered the bishops of the Canterbury province to carry out the commands she had given him, permitting no form of public and divine service except that which agreed with orders established by law. Not one bishop raised his voice in protest as indeed none had when Grindal was sequestered. By her action Elizabeth brought the royal supremacy into the immediate foreground in a way that she had not done since the first year of her reign. She was prepared to remain in the background only as long as she could get the bishops to do her will.

The main characteristic of the Elizabethan supremacy in the years after 1563 was the queen's unwillingness to significantly change her earlier religious settlement. She did not wish to claim any spiritual powers for the Crown, as her continued disavowal of the *potestas ordinis* attested, and she still wished to leave matters of liturgy and doctrine to the Church. It was as if she had assumed that the compromise that she had worked out would last as long as she lived. At first she tried to remain in the background on most religious matters, hoping that the Church would carry out her will without question. She supported the bishops' *Advertisements* and Convocation's Canons of 1571 (which included the *Advertisements*) because of their resolution of the vestiarian controversy and because they required subscription to the royal supremacy, the Prayer Book, and all of the Articles of Religion. She did not, however, give either document her formal approval, probably because of the bishops' slight concession to the Puritans in the Ornaments Rubric of the Prayer Book and, in the case of the canons, the inclusion of Nowell's Catechism.

If the bishops had not met the queen's standard on ceremonies, Elizabeth fell only slightly below her own standard when she signed a parliamentary bill in 1571 (revised Bill B), requiring subscription to all of the Thirty-Nine Articles. Yet Elizabeth's acceptance of revised Bill B, in the face of other religious bills that with one exception she either withdrew or withheld assent, was designed, as we have already seen, to meet the threat from Roman Catholicism in 1569 and 1570. Elizabeth's approval of the Grindal Canons of 1576 confirmed her belief in the idea of subscription to all of the Articles of Religion. And although her approval of Grindal's Canons (which also included the *Advertisements*) at last marked her formal concession to the vestiarian Puritans in the Ornaments Rubric, she nevertheless crossed out at the same time several liturgical reforms proposed by Convocation.

Both Elizabeth and her bishops adamantly opposed any of the radical Puritan petitions to change the Anglican form of church government during the Admonition controversy. Yet, if there was any doubt that Elizabeth was less lenient than her bishops, that doubt was completely dispelled by her suspension of Grindal during the dispute over prophesyings. Grindal regarded the prophesyings as a matter of discipline which the queen should refer to her bishops, while Elizabeth regarded them as improper ceremonial variations on her earlier settlement. Until Elizabeth could get rid of Grindal and appoint an archbishop more sympathetic to her point of view, such as Whitgift, she felt she had to assume personal direction of the Church. As a result, the Elizabethan supremacy during this brief time looked something like the supremacy of Henry VIII.

The Separatists

The suppression of the prophesyings was a serious blow to the cause of moderate Puritanism, just as the issuance of the *Advertisements* had been earlier. The suppression also gave fresh impetus to the Puritan Presbyterian movement within the church and to a Puritan Separatist movement away from the Church. Although there had been earlier Separatist congregations, not until the early 1580s did Separatism find two outstanding spokesmen in Robert Browne and Robert Harrison, both graduates of Corpus Christi College at Cambridge. Against considerable opposition, Browne and Harrison formed a Separatist congregation at Norwich in 1580 in which the godly members of the congregation covenanted together and with God to obey the divine law. The bishop of Norwich complained to Burghley, a distant relative of Browne, about the Separatists' activity in encouraging "the vulgar sort of people" to gather together in private houses and conventicles.

After spending some time in prison, Browne, with Harrison and their followers, left for Middelburg in the Netherlands. At Middelburg, Browne published *A Treatise of Reformation Without Tarrying* (1582), a title which indicated his disapproval of the Presbyterian policy of waiting for the magistrate and for Parliament to undertake a godly Reformation. In his *Treatise*, Browne argued that the queen's authority in civil matters was the highest under God within her dominions; therefore, "she may put to death all that deserve it by Law, either of the Church or Commonwealth, and none may resist her or the Magistrates under her by force or wicked speeches." But the religious matters of the church were something different. In the church she and her magistrates had no authority "to be Prophets or Priests, or spiritual Kings"—no authority to exercise the *potestas ordinis*. Browne did admit that the queen and the magistrates might "reform the Church and command things expedient for the same," but he added the important proviso that they could do nothing concerning the churches except "civilly, and as civil Magistrates." They could act on its "outward provision and outward justice," such as protecting the churches from their enemies, "but to compel religion, to plant churches by power, and to force a submission to Ecclesiastical government by laws and penalties belongeth not to them."[36]

Although his use of language was not always explicit, Browne had gone a long way in denying the Crown's authority of the *potestas jurisdictionis*, and hence of the Elizabethan religious supremacy itself. No wonder that Elizabeth issued a proclamation in June, 1583, against the "seditious, schismatical, and

erroneous printed books" of Browne and Harrison. Shortly afterwards, two
men were hanged for distributing Separatist writings. Browne had quarreled
with Harrison by the end of 1583, and after a brief sojourn in Scotland, where
he also quarreled with the Scottish Presbyterians, he returned to England to
sink into nearly half a century of obscurity after recognizing the Anglican
Church as the true Church in 1585. Harrison, who negotiated unsuccessfully
with Cartwright about a union of English Puritans, died in Middelburg the
same year. It was not long, however, before a new group of Separatists began
to plague the Anglican Church.

The writings of Browne and Harrison illustrate three aspects of the term
"Separatism." [37] First, it has designated the voluntary gathering of the Elect
or visible Saints through a church covenant between themselves and/or with
God so as to separate themselves from the non-elect or ungodly persons. On
this basis the Brownists qualify. They hoped to hive themselves off into
unattached conventicles, bound only by a voluntary church covenant where
the Saints in congregation would be able to select and censure, and in turn be
censured by, the pastor. Second, in the most common contemporary usage,
the term "Separatism" referred to the separation of independent church
congregations from the centralized discipline of an Anglican bishop or a
Presbyterian synod. On this basis, also, the Brownists qualify, although
Browne separated from the Church of England because he regarded it as a
corrupt, albeit a true, Church. Brownists were not only impatient with the
Presbyterian tactic of waiting for the magistrate to proceed with a more godly
reformation, but they also did not believe in identifying the church with the
nation, both Saints and sinners alike. Third, the term "Separatism" has
depicted the separation of church and state—the freedom of the church from
control by the temporal magistrate, and vice versa. On this basis, none of the
Brownists qualify; yet Browne came very close to it in his argument against
royal supremacy in religious affairs. But his position was flawed by his
admission in the *Treatise* that the magistrate might put to death those who,
once having received the covenant, fell away and no longer sought the Lord.

The toleration that emerged from Browne, then, was to be a toleration
only for the true religion as he and his followers conceived it. Browne's
toleration was not a theoretical statement on behalf of all those who wanted
to worship as their particular consciences might direct. It did not aspire to
that liberty of conscience achieved by a later Separatist, Roger Williams.

With such diversity of thought and behavior among lay and clerical Puritans
during the Elizabethan period, it is pertinent to ask, as with the Catholics
later, just what was it that they all had in common? They certainly did not all
support the complete separation of church and state. Despite the Presbyterian advocacy of the theory of the two kingdoms (separate but related), only
the Separatists came close to a complete separation. All Puritans certainly
not support the creation of a Calvinist or Presbyterian form of church
government; neither the moderate nor the Separatist clerics, to say nothing of
some of the Puritan parliamentarians, wanted that. Certainly all Puritans did

not wish the overthrow of royal supremacy; neither the moderate ministry nor some of the Puritan parliamentarians would go that far. But the members of the Elizabethan Puritan community could all agree with the liturgical or precisianist demands of the moderates. All of the members of the Puritan community wanted to make purifying changes of some kind that would increase the distance between themselves and Roman Catholics.

But they wanted more than that. Both the moderates and radicals supported the prophesyings because they strongly wanted a preaching ministry, a characteristic in which the Separatists joined them. And all of the Puritans wished to modify royal supremacy so that some different forms of liturgical services and ecclesiastical organizations could be employed. In short, they had no use for the queen's inflexibility in these matters, seeking instead a toleration of the true religion, as each of the Puritan groups perceived it, but not a general toleration for all. Since the Separatists shared these goals with the moderates and radicals, it seems pointless to arbitrarily exclude them from the Puritan spectrum. And this is especially true after the Elizabethan period when the covenanting idea, so characteristic of the Separatists, came to be shared by the dominant Puritan groups—Presbyterians and Independents—of the 1640s. Also, by that time, the dismantling of the Anglican episcopal organization was well underway, and the question of whether Puritanism was a reform movement within the Anglican Church was purely academic. By then all Puritans, one way or another, had separated from the Anglican Church.

The Catholic Threat

The English Catholic community, too, consisted of groups of laymen and clerics. Among the laymen were those with bastard-feudal connections in the border country who, standing for the "Old Religion," had participated in the aristocratic debacle of the Rebellion of the Northern Earls in 1569. Also among the laymen were those gentry and lesser peerage with "parish" households, usually located in the more populated areas of the country, who, on the whole, disapproved of the Babington plot and professed their loyalty to the queen at the time of the Spanish Armada. Lord Henry Howard even led a small group of Catholics at Court. Still another lay group, mainly from the lower orders of society and the rural areas of Lancashire and Yorkshire, also stood for the "Old Religion" with the aid of overworked secular priests. Among the clerics were those like William Allen, who, though critical of the unreformed Marian regime and once attracted to Protestantism, regarded the Elizabethan settlement as intolerable and stressed, in addition to the traditional forms of Catholic worship, the salvation of souls. For this Catholic missionary effort, Allen established seminaries abroad so that English seminarians could return home to gentry households, primarily in London and the Thames valley where Catholicism was not the strongest, in order to provide pastoral care and, in some cases, engage in soul-saving. Without access to

Parliament to make the changes they desired, these seminarians ultimately relied upon foreign intervention as the means to achieve their ends. Joining the seminarians was a smaller number of Jesuits, men such as Edmund Campion and Robert Parsons, who, dedicated to militancy and conversion not unlike that of later Puritanism, supported themselves as an arm of the Counter-Reformation.[38]

The Rebellion of the Northern Earls

During the first ten years of Elizabeth's reign, English Catholics generally followed a policy of secular loyalty and political nonresistance. With the Rebellion of the Northern Earls in 1569, however, there was an abrupt change, thereby producing the first major Catholic threat to the Elizabethan settlement. For the next five years the comparatively peaceful relations of the first decade were marred by Catholic polemics and political resistance to the established government. The change began in 1568 when the Catholic Queen of Scots, Mary Stuart, whose claim to the English throne made her the focal point of numerous plots against Elizabeth for nearly the next twenty years, fled to England. Supported by promises of assistance from Spain, a group of northern earls, disaffected with the policies of Cecil in the Council, hoped to bring about the marriage of the Protestant Duke of Norfolk with the captive Queen of Scots; they also wished to obtain recognition of Mary Stuart as Elizabeth's heir. With the meek surrender of Norfolk, the bolder Catholic earls of Northumberland and Westmoreland rose in a rebellion that had some outward resemblances to the Pilgrimage of Grace some thirty-five years before. Wearing the old banners that displayed the five wounds of Christ crucified, the rebels broke the communion table in Durham cathedral and ripped the Prayer Book into shreds; they restored the altar and sang mass. But the earls were not military tacticians, and they had no plan. Elizabeth's troops soon put an end to the uprising, and the vanquished earls suffered dreadful retribution.

After the rebellion, the government issued *Queen Elizabeth's Defense of Her Proceedings in Church and State* (1569), outlining the queen's authority in the Church:

> But that authority which is yielded to us and our Crown consisteth in this; that considering we are by God's grace the Sovereign Prince and Queen next under God, and all the people in our realm are immediately born subjects to us and our Crown and to none else, and that our Realm hath of long time past received the Christian faith. We are by this authority bound to direct all estates, being subject to us, to live in the faith and the obedience of Christian religion, and to see the laws of God and man which are ordained to that end to be duly observed, and the offenders against the same duly punished, and consequently to provide, that the Church may be governed and taught by archbishops, bishops and ministers according to the ecclesiastical ancient policy of the realm, whom we do assist with our sovereign power. . . .[39]

When compared with the statements of Henry VIII, this is a modest claim for royal authority. But *Queen Elizabeth's Defense* also stated what Elizabeth did not claim in connection with the Church. She specifically disavowed, as she had done in an appendix to the Injunctions of 1559 and in article thirty-six of the Articles of 1563, "the use of any function belonging to any ecclesiastical person"—the *potestas ordinis*. And she took one further step, for she disavowed any supposed claim "to define, decide or determine any article or point of the Christian faith and religion, or to change any ancient ceremony of the church from the form being received and observed by the Catholic and Apostolic church." Those were matters, as Elizabeth's penciled modification of article twenty of the Articles of 1563 had stated, reserved for the Church.

In response to a request for assistance from the northern earls, Pope Pius V issued a bull, *Regnans in Excelsis* (1570). The papal bull both excommunicated Elizabeth from the Roman Catholic Church as a heretic, without the usual prior warning, and immediately deposed her from the throne, without the usual lapse of a year following excommunication. John Felton, a Roman Catholic layman, posted a copy of the bull on the gate of the palace of the Bishop of London. Received in England after the rebellion was quashed, the papal bull released all English men and women from any obligation or allegiance to the queen and commanded them never to obey her laws. Although it did not specifically state that Catholics should take up arms against a heretical queen, it condoned uprisings by Catholics, who previously might have found unconscionable a rebellion against a *de facto* sovereign. The papacy was too late in coming to the assistance of the northern earls, but it strongly supported, as did Philip II of Spain, the unsuccessful Ridolfi Plot (1571). As a result of the Ridolfi Plot, Mary Stuart narrowly escaped with her life, but the Duke of Norfolk was tried and executed the following year.

The dilemma of English Catholics, whom the papal bull forced to choose between their patriotic allegiance to England and their devotional loyalty to the Roman Catholic Church, was exacerbated by new legislation passed by Elizabeth's third Parliament (1571). The Treasons statute of 1571 prohibited any spoken words or writing that called the sovereign a "heretic, schismatic, tyrant, infidel or an usurper"—a phrase which had been a part of Henry VIII's Treason statute (1534), passed shortly after his own excommunication. But the 1571 statute also prohibited any spoken words or writing that denied Elizabeth was the lawful queen or that affirmed somebody else—phrases designed to silence the advocates of Mary Stuart. A second statute made it a treasonable offense for anyone such as Felton to attempt to execute a papal bull or for anyone by such papal authority to absolve and reconcile to Rome those persons who would forsake their obedience to the queen. Cuthbert Mayne, a seminary priest found guilty under this statute, was executed in 1572. The third statute, directed against the property of Catholic exiles, especially fugitives who fled abroad after the Rebellion of the Northern Earls, specifically exempted exiles who returned under prescribed circumstances.

The Canterbury Convocation provided the theological justification for this new legislation when it added a homily "Against Disobedience and

Willful Rebellion" to the second *Book of Homilies* (1563). The new homily, which drew upon the biblical chapters of Romans 13 and 1 Peter 2, stated that "Kings, Queens, and other Princes . . . are ordained of GOD, are to be obeyed and honored of their subjects: that such subjects, as are disobedient or rebellious against Princes, disobey GOD, and procure their own damnation."[40]

By the late 1560s, after a decade of peace with the Catholic Church, it became readily apparent that the queen was not going to abandon the Anglican communion or, indeed, modify the *via media* in any significant way. As something of a sequel to the Pilgrimage of Grace, the Rebellion of the Northern Earls was the last military action, apart from the Spanish Armada, that attempted to restore England to the old faith. Its failure, like that of its predecessor, stands in marked contrast to the military success of that other international religious movement, Puritanism, against the Crown in the mid-seventeenth century.

The Catholic Mission and Catholic Martyrs

The failure to restore England to Roman Catholicism by force of arms signaled the return after 1574 to a policy of political nonresistance for a period of about ten years. It also marked an alternative strategy for Catholic missionaries to try to win English souls back to Rome by religious conversion. While the missionary effort achieved some modest gains, the government extracted a fearful price—the execution of both Catholic priests and laymen who became, like their Protestant predecessors under Mary, martyrs to their cause.

The Catholic mission began in the mid-1570s with the return to England of seminarians educated by William Allen at the English College of Douai (1568) in the Spanish Netherlands (afterwards moved to Rheims), and, later, at the English College in Rome (1579). As patrons of the colleges, the pope and the king of Spain gave a strong presumption to the government's view that the Catholic mission intended to carry out the provisions of the papal bull of excommunication. The dispatch of Jesuit missionaries in 1580 under the leadership of Robert Parsons and Edmund Campion gave further sustenance to that view.

Before leaving Rome, the seminarians attempted to free the mission from the dilemma of allegiance in which the papal bull had placed it. Campion and Parsons encouraged the new pope, Gregory XIII, to issue an *Explanatio* that became a part of their "faculties" or spiritual powers granted by Rome. The *Explanatio* stated that Pius V's bull against Elizabeth did not bind Catholics until they could feasibly carry out her deposition. Meanwhile, English Catholics could recognize Elizabeth as a *de facto* sovereign, thereby rendering ineffective the Treasons Act of 1571. The *Instructions* to Campion and Parsons from the head of the order stated:

> They must not mix themselves up with affairs of state, nor write to Rome
> about political matters, nor speak, nor allow others to speak in their

presence, against the queen—except perhaps with those whose fidelity has been long and steadfast, and even then not without strong reasons.[41]

Only a year later, the head of the order deleted the exception. The *Instructions*, however, insisted that no dispensations would be forthcoming for those Catholics who obeyed that provision of the Act of Uniformity requiring attendance at Anglican services.

In January 1581, just before a meeting of Parliament, much delayed because of the queen's marriage project with the Duke of Alençon, a French Catholic, Elizabeth issued a royal proclamation taking notice that the pope had created seminaries for the training of English priests. These seminaries, the proclamation continued, not only corrupted Her Majesty's subjects in matters of religion but also withdrew them from obedience to the Crown. Should anyone give them succor, or fail to report them to the local justices, he would be prosecuted by the laws of the land. But the government soon realized that the laws of the land were inadequate to meet the new Catholic threat, so the third session of Elizabeth's fourth Parliament addressed itself to this problem. In order to counteract the Catholic mission, the Parliament of 1581 brought forward two anti-Catholic measures which, after modifications, became law.

The first of these measures was a bill that Sir Francis Knollys introduced to "Retain Her Majesty's Subjects in Due Obedience." Because the Catholic laity's nonattendance at Anglican church services was a persistent form of resistance, Knollys' bill raised recusancy fines from a modest one shilling per Sunday to a prohibitive £20 per month. Although non-Catholic recusants had to pay only £10 per month, any person who usually attended Anglican services in his or her own house only needed to attend the parish church four times a year, a form of occasional conformity. This possibility raised an important moral decision for a conscientious Catholic. Indeed, cases of conscience were studied in the casuistic curricula of the English seminaries on the continent, and manuals of casuistry viewed occasional conformity as a kind of lawful equivocation, a practice which became an important issue for Protestants under Queen Anne.[42]

Another provision of the Knollys' bill made it treason for any person, including seminarians, Jesuits, and their converts, to withdraw any of the queen's subjects, or himself be withdrawn, from natural obedience to the queen, or to convert any subject, or himself be converted, "for that intent" to Roman Catholicism. Those three words, "for that intent," had not appeared in the earlier drafts of the bill, but, probably at the insistence of the queen, they had been inserted into the final draft which became law. By this insertion, the statute, like the 1571 Act Against Reconciliation to Rome by Papal Bulls and Writings upon which it was based, refrained from defining conversion to Catholicism per se as treason. It had to be conversion accompanied by withdrawal of national allegiance.[43]

Whatever leniency Catholics had gained from this provision stressing the political rather than the religious aspects of conversion was offset by still another provision which must have been a carryover from an earlier and harsher draft of the act. It provided fines and imprisonment to anyone who would say or hear the Catholic mass. By this provision Catholics could not comply with the law without ceasing to be Catholics. The government may have thought, as did King James II later, that once a large number of English men and women practiced the Catholic faith, an increasing demand for a political sovereign of the Roman faith would naturally follow. So the government enacted a law which prosecuted Catholics for both political and religious reasons, but the political prosecutions carried the harsher penalties.

The second anti-Catholic measure of 1581 legislated "Against Seditious Words and Rumors Uttered Against the Queen." Based upon a similar statute passed in 1554, during Mary Tudor's reign, its penalties were much more severe than those of the Marian statute. The penalty for slanderous statements in the 1554 Act, for example, amounted to imprisonment and loss of both ears, with an option of a fine in lieu of the ears, but the 1581 bill dropped the option and increased the imprisonment period from three months to the queen's pleasure. For a second offense, the 1581 bill raised the penalty from life imprisonment and forfeiture of all goods to death. A new provision of the 1581 bill also made it a felony to write or to print words dealing with how long the queen would live or who would reign after her death, both topics of great interest to Puritans and Catholics alike.[44]

The increased severity of these penalties prompted the Puritans in the Commons to wonder if the government wanted to catch them in the net as well as Catholics. Accordingly, Thomas Norton tried to amend the bill by making it a seditious rumor to state that the doctrine of the Church as established by law, with which the Puritans had relatively little quarrel compared with the Catholics, was either heretical or schismatical. If accepted by the Lords, Norton's amendment would have transferred the jurisdiction of disputes over doctrine from the ecclesiastical courts to the civil courts, a situation which had prevailed while Henry VIII's Six Articles Act was in force (1539–1547). Before the bill was enacted into law, however, the Lords rejected Norton's amendment and kept the felony penalty for second offenses and for slanderous writing and printing. But the Commons succeeded in including provisions to repeal the earlier Marian statute, to restore the option of a fine or loss of ears, to reduce the penalty for imprisonment from the queen's pleasure to three months, and to insert the phrase "with a malicious intent" in connection with all slanderous offenses as well as the phrase "at the election of the offender" in the ears option—all with the hope of sparing their Puritan friends from unwarranted prosecution and excessive punishment. As it turned out, Puritan zeal against the Catholics boomeranged ten years later, when the foregoing Puritan modifications were insufficient to keep the Puritan printers in the Martin Marprelate case from being tried and severely punished under this same statute.

Despite the 1581 legislation, the government decided to bring Campion and several others to trial in November, 1581 under the basic treason statute of Edward III (1352) because it did not wish to get drawn into the sticky relationship between political allegiance and religious conversion. Although Parsons had eluded the government, a priest-hunter had pried Campion out of a secret hiding place in a Catholic household at Lyford Grange, Berkshire. When Campion appeared before the Privy Council for interrogation, Elizabeth asked if he acknowledged her to be his queen. Campion replied that he did and added that she was his "lawful governess" as well. But when she asked him if the pope might lawfully excommunicate her, he casuistically confessed himself to be "an insufficient umpire between her majesty and the Pope, for so high a controversy, whereof the certainty is as yet unknown." The ecclesiastical commissioners asked Campion these same questions, more refined on the point of religious supremacy, plus some "supposals"—the bloody questions, as Campion called them. These may have included a query on whose side he would choose, the pope's or the queen's, in the event of a Catholic invasion of England. But Campion's answers remained essentially the same even after he was tortured on the rack three times. He told the commission he would willingly give to Her Majesty what was hers, which included the supremacy of the state, but he must pay to God what was his, which included the supremacy of the Church.

Campion and a small number of Catholics, including Allen and Parsons (in absentia), were brought to trial on November 12 for conspiring to kill the queen, to overthrow the established religion, to subvert the state, and to encourage foreigners to invade the realm. No good evidence showed that Campion and the others were guilty of any of these charges, all of which Campion denied. When the jury found the defendants guilty, the lord chief justice asked Campion if he had a statement to make. "If our Religion do make us Traitors," spoke Campion, "we are worthy to be condemned; but otherwise are and have been as true subjects as ever the Queen had."[45] On December 1 at Tyburn, Campion, along with two others, was hanged, drawn, and quartered. Parsons fled the country never to return. In a royal proclamation on April 1, 1582, Elizabeth stated that the deaths were an example of what had happened to those who contemptuously violated her proclamation of January 10, 1581. Henceforth, all Jesuits and seminarians who merely entered England automatically became traitors to the Crown.

The government's claim that it prosecuted Catholics for political reasons highlighted Lord Burghley's tract, *The Execution of Justice in England* (1583). Burghley argued that the seminarians and Jesuits of the Catholic mission, like the papally-instigated northern earls in 1569, regarded themselves as "well warranted to take arms to rebel against Her Majesty when they shall be thereunto called, and to be ready secretly to join with any foreign force that can be procured to invade the realm." All of these Catholics, he said, have rightly suffered death under the Treasons Act of Edward III because they maintained, as the papal bull stated, that Elizabeth was not the lawful queen of England. Unlike the seminarians and Jesuits, Burghley continued, some Catholics, such as the Marian bishops or wealthy laymen, though differing in religious views from the Church of England, had professed loyalty and obedience to Queen Elizabeth; such persons had not been prosecuted.

As proof for his position, Burghley asserted that the papal "faculties" granted to Campion and Parsons, which contained the *Explanatio* suspending the implementation of the papal bull for English Catholics until it could be executed, contained evidence that the two Jesuit priests had been actually charged with imparting the contents, and hence paving the way for, the ultimate implementation of the papal bull. As additional proof, he claimed that Campion and other priests, when asked the now famous (or infamous) bloody questions, would not give direct answers. Finally, in a desperate move to counter criticism of the government, Burghley claimed that Mary's burning of many Protestants for heresy, unlike Elizabeth's execution of a few Catholics, had been "beyond all heathen cruelty," and an addendum, possibly not written by Burghley, stated that Campion "was never so racked but that he was presently able to walk and to write."[46]

Parsons offered a critique of Burghley's pamphlet in his vituperative *Leicester's Commonwealth* (1584), but the main attempt to refute Burghley came in Allen's *A True, Sincere, and Modest Defense of English Catholics* (1584). In the latter work, Allen highlighted the Catholic Mission's claim that the government's prosecution of Catholics was for religious reasons. Indeed, Allen argued that a number of Catholics, including Cuthbert Mayne, had not been executed for reasons of state under the statute of Edward III, but rather "for mere matter of religion" under the laws of 1571 and 1581. Furthermore, the execution of some other Catholics for simply denying royal supremacy in religious affairs had nothing to do with "disloyalty or old treasons." And, in an aside on the oath of supremacy, Allen said that the disclaimer by Elizabeth in her injunctions to possessing the powers of a priest (*potestas ordinis*) made her spiritual jurisdiction (*potestas jurisdictionis*) no less an usurpation of the pope's headship of the church.

As for Burghley's evidence that the papal "faculties" given to Campion and Parsons enjoined an implementation, albeit later, of the papal bull, Allen stated that Campion had felt that the bull was actually "troublesome to them," indicating that it was good that it had been mitigated by the *Explanatio*. In regard to Burghley's evidence regarding the refusal or failure to answer the "bloody questions," Allen wrote that all princes and Christians should bear witness that Catholics suffered death only for "cogitations and inward opinions," and we "never took arms in all England upon the bull of Pius the Fifth." As for Burghley's comparison with persecution under Mary, Allen wrote that Mary found Cranmer guilty of both treason and heresy, but no Elizabethan Catholic could be burned for strictly religious reasons because Elizabeth had repealed all of the heresy laws.

In the last part of *A Defense*, however, there is an interesting shift in Allen's argument. Although he had maintained that Campion and other Catholic priests had not been involved in political activity, he categorically stated that "anointed and lawfully created kings may be deposed." Even Protestant doctrine, including the writings of Luther, Zwingli, Calvin, Beza, Goodman, and Knox, he wrote, justified resisting and deposing princes in matters of religion. Allen's lines are reminiscent of those of Thomas Cartwright:

And although . . . the Church and civil state, the magistrate ecclesiastical and temporal, concur in their kinds together (though ever of distinct regiments, natures, and ends), there is such a concurrence and subalternation betwixt both that the inferior of the two (which is the civil state) must needs (in matters pertaining any way either directly or indirectly to the honor of God and benefit of the soul) be subject to the spiritual and take direction from the same.[47]

Using sixteenth century English precedents, Elizabethan Catholics could draw more and better examples of religious and political resistance from the Protestant martyrs and exiles of Mary's reign than they could from the Catholic martyrs of Henry's reign.

Indeed, *A Defense* may have revealed two William Allens: the ardent defense attorney for the Catholic priests and the earnest theorist for the papacy. But within a year Allen privately told the papacy about invasion plans as follows: "We have now (although many have been recently deported) almost three hundred priests in the households of noblemen and men of substance and we are daily sending others, who will direct the consciences and actions of the Catholics in this affair when the time comes."[48] The theorist of royal deposition attempted to transform his theory into practice just as Burghley suspected he would.

By the time Elizabeth's fifth Parliament met (1584), it seemed as if the queen's fears about the threat from international Catholicism had been realized. In the fall of the preceding year, Walsingham had unraveled the Throckmorton Plot against Elizabeth in which the pope, Mary Stuart, and King Philip of Spain were implicated. And the preceding July, William, the Protestant Duke of Orange, who had been put to the ban by Philip, fell victim to an assassin. In addition to forming the Bond of Association—a group of gentry who pledged themselves to track down anyone who threatened harm to the queen—the government decided that it needed additional legislation to control the Catholic Mission.[49]

The government based its bill upon the assumption of guilt by association, or more specifically guilt by allegiance to an external power, the papacy, which, the government felt, threatened to destroy the state. The main provision of the new bill, like the royal proclamation of January, 1581, made the very presence of a Jesuit or a seminary priest in the land, irrespective of whether or not he was converting souls or withdrawing their allegiance from the queen, a treasonable offense. One member of Parliament observed, "It might seem a very hard case to make it treason for a man to come into the realm without doing of any other thing."[50] The only way for a Catholic priest to escape prosecution for treason was to stay out of England, thereby cutting back drastically on the mission, or to take the oath of supremacy—an impossible task, since it would have meant forfeiting the principal of papal supremacy. Another provision mandated the death penalty for anyone who received or aided priests.

The bill against Jesuits and seminarians became law in early 1585, despite a declaration of allegiance to Elizabeth by Catholic gentry, including Sir

Thomas Tresham and Sir John Arundel. Unlike previous anti-Catholic measures, which had not been drastically enforced, this one was. Out of 189 Catholic clerical and lay martyrs found guilty of treason during Elizabeth's reign, the statute of 1352 condemned only 24, but as many as 123 were condemned by the statute of 1585, largely from 1585 to 1588.[51] Whereas Elizabeth executed nearly two hundred Catholics for treason, mostly over a ten-year period, Mary executed nearly three hundred Protestants for heresy, mostly within a three-year period.

Allen linked his politics with his religion, but Burghley insisted that Elizabeth's government tried to keep the two separate. Elizabeth's advisors liked to claim that Catholic persecution resulted only from treasonable actions affecting the state—not from purely religious beliefs. A hackneyed statement frequently cited comes from Francis Bacon:

> Her Majesty, not liking to make windows into men's hearts and secret thoughts, except the abundance of them did overflow into overt and express acts or affirmations, tempered her law so as it restraineth only manifest disobedience, in impugning and impeaching advisedly and maliciously her Majesty's supreme power, and maintaining and extolling a foreign jurisdiction.[52]

Bacon implies that Elizabeth carried out a modicum of religious toleration. The evidence seems to belie this interpretation.

There is a sense in which Elizabeth's government tolerated Catholics more than Mary tolerated Protestants. In practice, Elizabeth did not inquire into theological views—for instance, the issue of the Holy Eucharist—as Mary had done. But Elizabeth remained uninterested in theology per se; she concerned herself with the outward manifestations of a total religious position, whether it took the form of Puritan prophesyings or Catholic conversions. Understandable as her Draconian policy may have been in terms of reasons of state, the penal provisions of the 1581 statute to Retain Her Majesty's Subjects in Due Obedience made it impossible for Catholic priests to say, or Catholic laity to hear, mass without fear of prosecution. And the statute of 1585, as well as the 1581 proclamation which preceded it, made the mere presence of seminary priests or Jesuits in the land a treasonable offense. Catholics simply did not have the right to worship as they pleased. Therefore, in her way, Elizabeth indeed peered into "men's hearts and secret thoughts."

The Catholic Crusade

As the ranks of the Catholic Mission suffered setbacks throughout England, particularly in London and York, plans were formed in Madrid and Rome for a Spanish Armada to invade England. Elizabeth's sixth Parliament, meeting in 1586 under the influence of the Armada scare, decided to act. Because the number of recusancy cases and receipts from fines had been so low—in the period from 1581 through 1585, only fifty-five recusants from eighteen counties and two cities had contributed only £6,356—Parliament permitted the government to tighten its recusancy procedures and to take two-thirds of the estates of Catholic recusants upon default of the £20 that the 1581 recusancy act authorized.[53] But the issue which definitely propelled Philip to carry out a crusade against England was the execution of Mary Stuart in February, 1587. Mary had been beheaded because she would have become queen of England had the Babington Plot (summer, 1586), like the Throckmorton and other plots in which she was also implicated, been successful.

No evidence links the Catholic Mission to any part of the Babington Plot, or, indeed, to any political organization of English Catholics that might have been formed to assist the invading forces. This was true despite the government's statement that a considerable number of Catholics had answered, in reply to the last of the bloody questions, that they would side with an invading force. Allen assured Philip in March that English Catholics wanted the invasion, but the leading Catholic laymen, brought into custody just before the Armada sailed, pledged their loyalty to the queen and expressed their desire to be placed in the front lines of the queen's troops if the Spanish should land. Pope Sixtus V and Philip reached an agreement in July on papal support for the crusade. The pope gave Philip one million gold ducats on condition that the future ruler of England, when nominated by Philip, should have the pope's consent; that Philip would receive England, as King John had done over three centuries before, as a papal fief; and that all Church property, whether episcopal lands, monasteries, or chantries, should be restored.

Philip also asked the pope to lend his official support to the Crusade by saying that the Armada would carry out the papal bull of excommunication and deposition. The pope's response, drawn up by Allen—now a cardinal—was a manifesto printed in English that renewed Elizabeth's previous excommunication and announced her imminent deposition. Cardinal Allen, perhaps assisted by Parsons, elaborated upon the manifesto in a vitriolic pamphlet written for distribution in England after the forthcoming invasion. Entitled *An Admonition to the Nobility and People of England and Ireland* (1588); it stated:

> All the virtuous priests of your country, who, by the long tyranny of this time, have suffered manifold miseries and martyrdoms, both at home and abroad, to save their own souls, and win their dearest countrymen to salvation, they also stretch forth their consecrated hands night and day for your victory, and be present divers of them to serve every man's spiritual necessity, by confession, counsel, and all consolation in Christ Jesus, giving you testimony by their readiness to live and die with you, how just the cause of this holy fight is, and how happy and glorious is the blood that shall be shed therein.[54]

By advocating a "just" war, Allen at long last publicly revealed his missionary efforts and potential treason. But Allen's hope, as well as those of the pope and the king of Spain, for a military invasion of England came to naught. The defeat of the Armada temporarily averted the attempt to execute the papal bull and to bring England back to the Catholic Church.

The continuing war with Spain in the 1590s prevented relaxation of persecution against the Catholics, especially since Philip threatened a new invasion. Accordingly, in the fall of 1591 Elizabeth issued a proclamation reiterating the government's policy of bringing Jesuits and seminarians, including those from the new seminary at Valladolid, to trial for traitorous activity but "not for any points of religion."[55] Because Parsons and Allen had allegedly given the pope and the king of Spain the names of Jesuits and seminarians willing to help Philip's invading force, the proclamation called for new local commissions to examine these "venomous vipers" after all Englishmen had made a "particular inquisition" of anyone who had joined a household during the preceding year.

The Catholic response to the proclamation divided itself between a moderate majority and a radical minority, whose differences were accentuated by the death of the mellowing Cardinal Allen two years later (1594). Robert Southwell, the Jesuit poet whom the government subsequently executed for treason, struck a conciliatory note in his *Humble Supplication to Her Majesty* (unpublished until 1600). Just before his arrest, he wrote, "we do assure your Majesty, that what Army soever should come against you, we will rather yield our breasts to be broached by our Country swords, then use our swords to the effusion of our Country's blood." But from his sanctuary on the Spanish peninsula, the more radical Parsons took a much harder line on the deposing power than he and Campion had displayed ten years before.

> 'Tis certain, we must believe it, and it is the opinion of all Divines and lawyers, that if any Christian prince fall from the Catholic faith, and could have others to follow him, he himself thereby, doth forthwith, both by Divine and Human Law, though the Pope do no way censure him, fall from all his Authority and Dignity, and his subjects are freed from all their oaths of Allegiance which they swear to him as a lawful prince; and so they may, nay and ought (if they have force enough to overcome) pull him down from the Throne, as an Apostate, Heretic, a forsaker of Christ, and an enemy to the Commonwealth."[56]

Parson's reply, as well as the success of the 1586 statute against recusants, must have encouraged the government to introduce additional legislation against Catholics. During the years from 1587 to 1592, the government collected over £36,000 from 167 lay recusants residing in thirty-two counties. Nearly three-quarters of the fine money, however, was paid by only sixteen gentlemen who, as "token recusants," became scapegoats for the entire Catholic lay community—perhaps the government's tacit admission that it could not, or would not, enforce the penal laws against all Catholic laymen. Still, the Act Against Popish Recusants (1593) provided that all Catholics refusing to attend Anglican church services were not to leave a five-mile radius of their homes. Should they do so, they would forfeit *all* property—not just the two-thirds the recusancy act of 1586 prescribed—or, in the absence of property, be banished from the realm. If the enforcement of the laws against Catholic laymen may have been somewhat equivocal, the enforcement of the penal laws against Jesuits and seminarians was not.[57]

Although this recusant statute was the last piece of Elizabethan legislation against Catholics, and in some respects the most severe of the queen's reign, what finally emerged from the Parliament, which seemed more concerned about Separatist recusants, was less drastic than what the government had proposed. The government, for example, had wanted to exclude all Catholics from political office and the professions. This proposal, like the five-mile provision for nonconformists, did become the law of the land during the Caroline restoration.

With such diversity of thought and behavior among lay and clerical Catholics during the Elizabethan period, it is pertinent to ask, as with the Puritans earlier, what it was they had in common. They certainly did not all want the restoration of the Marian regime. While restoration might have appealed strongly to the bastard-feudalism of the northern border and, perhaps, to some Jesuits, the "parish" household had no interest in offending Elizabeth in that way, and the seminarians wanted a reformed Catholic Church, which Mary had not given them. Certainly all Catholics did not want papal suprem-acy. While papal supremacy received the support of a large number of Jesuits and seminarians, most of the lay Catholics were not interested in placing their religion under the control of clerics, including the pope. Certainly all Catho-lics did not wish the overthrow of Elizabethan government. Apart from the northern earls, the Jesuits, and most seminarians, Catholics, especially lay-men, were profoundly loyal to their queen. As a result, the English Catholic community divided sharply on the course of action to take. The clerical community, like the northern earls before them, finally sought military intervention to take England back to the Roman Catholic communion and the supremacy of the pope. The lay Catholics, unlike the northern earls, would go no further than seeking a royal supremacy tolerant of their Catholic forms of worship. Catholic laymen in the *Petition Apologetical* (1604) pub-licly requested religious toleration in exchange for an oath of allegiance by priests. After the Gunpowder Plot (1605), when Catholic violence again emerged, Parliament enacted an oath of allegiance, but the Catholics did not gain religious toleration."[58]

The Puritan Threat Again

Conflict between the queen and the archbishops of the Anglican Church did not characterize the later Puritan threat to the Elizabethan settlement as it had the earlier one. Two important controversies (the vestiarian and the admonition) had dominated the earlier Puritan threat, and two important controversies (the subscription and the Martin Marprelate) would dominate the later one. The earlier controversies, like the prophesyings that gained support from Grindal, resulted from innovative attempts to reform the Anglican Church by moderate, radical, and Separatist Puritans. The later controversies, in which Whitgift took the lead, resulted from a recriminatory campaign by the queen, the Church, and the prerogative courts, which provoked the radical and Separatist Puritans to respond with a satiric, indeed slanderous, assault on the establishment. The burgeoning creativity of the earlier Puritan period had yielded, except for instances like the Dedham classis and Cope's bill, to a retreat to defensive positions that debilitated the whole Puritan community, ultimately forcing it to go underground for the remainder of Elizabeth's reign.

The Subscription Controversy

Upon the death of Grindal in 1583, the appointment of John Whitgift to the see of Canterbury—the first bishop under Elizabeth to hold a seat on the Privy Council—gave the queen at long last an archbishop who would run the Church to her liking. Whitgift, in a Paul's Cross sermon preached in November, set the tone of his archiepiscopate. The queen's supremacy, he declared, did not pertain to such functions "as to preach, minister the sacraments, or consecrate bishops." Indeed, she had conceded all of that, and much more, to the bishops in her *Queen Elizabeth's Defense* at the time of the Northern Rebellion. Whitgift's strong belief that the queen's ecclesiastical "office is to see God served, and honoured, and obeyed by [her] subjects" must have pleased Elizabeth.[59]

In order to carry out that office for the queen, Whitgift, with the advice of some bishops and the approval of the queen, had issued his Eleven Articles. The main thrust of the Eleven Articles, which called for execution of recent laws against Catholic recusants, was directed against the radical Puritans. They authorized the Bishops' Bible (1568) rather than the Geneva Bible, and prescribed the clerical apparel stipulated in the Injunctions of 1559 (as modified by Parker's *Advertisements*). The Eleven Articles also set forth a new subscription test, the Church's fourth and last of the reign. Some of the remaining articles dealing with abuses of ordination and penance, plus two new ones dealing with abuses of excommunication and pluralities, became the basis for Convocation's Canons of 1585, which received the assent of the queen. The new subscription test abandoned the less demanding requirement of the Grindal Canons of 1576 that churchmen subscribe only to the Articles of 1563 and reverted to the more rigorous requirements of the Parker Canons of 1571 that they subscribe to the Prayer Book and the Ordinal as well. According to Whitgift's threefold subscription test, no minister could perform any ecclesiastical function unless he subscribed to the ecclesiastical supremacy of the Crown and the exclusion of all foreign powers, the Book of Common Prayer, and the Ordinal as containing nothing contrary to the Word of God, and *all* of the Articles of Religion as set forth by the Convocations of 1563. Most Puritans, except for some Separatists, could subscribe to the first; the same was true of the third, if the hierarchy and the ecclesiastical commissions continued to observe the limited subscription of the statute of 1571; but the second offended all Puritans, effectively uniting the moderate majority and the radical minority.[60]

Whitgift attempted to carry out his subscription policy through the ecclesiastical commission of December, 1583. It was one of numerous ecclesiastical commissions at both the diocesan and provincial level that came to be called, in the case of the southern province, the Court of High Commission. Before a trial actually began at the High Commission, some preliminary steps had to be taken. All ministers were required to take the subscription test of the Eleven Articles in their local dioceses. Most ministers conformed, but throughout 1584 about 300 or 400 Puritan ministers gave only a conditional subscription, one accompanied by a protestation, to the Prayer Book. Largely as a result of pressure from the Puritan-inclined privy councillors, Whitgift did agree at the end of the year to accept a conditional subscription from the moderate Puritans, hoping to split them and the radicals.[61] The archbishop summoned a few radicals before an ecclesiastical commission where he used the oath *ex officio mero* in the pre-trial procedure.

By the oath ex officio—by virtue of their office as ecclesiastical commissioners—the bishops on the High Commission tried to get the radical Puritans to swear to answer truly all questions that might subsequently be put to them with no knowledge of the accuser or the accusation, and without legal counsel. A Puritan who took the oath ex officio and told the truth to the bishops acting as prosecutors during such an interrogation, might well be brought to trial, where he would be found guilty by the same bishops acting as judges, for the trial considered exclusively the pretrial answers of the defendant. If he took the oath and perjured himself, he not only violated his conscience but laid himself open for further prosecution. If he refused to take the oath, as Cartwright did, thereby stopping any further judicial proceedings, he could be cited for contempt of court and imprisoned. The Puritans thought the oath tyrannical. The bishops of the High Commission contended that the only reason for refusing the oath, or for refusing to answer a particular question, was the Puritan's own knowledge that he had violated ecclesiastical law. But the Puritan maintained that the oath bound him to give answers incriminating himself and his neighbors before any trial began. When Lord Burghley found out about the twenty-four interrogatories used in the pretrial examination, most of which dealt with the Prayer Book, he wrote to Whitgift: "this judicial and canonical sifting of poor ministers," who are fearful of "captious interpretation," is a proceeding "too much savouring of the Romish inquisition." Whitgift replied that he had not "done anything in this matter, which I do not think myself in duty and conscience bound to do; which her majesty hath not with earnest charge committed unto me."[62]

The use of the oath ex officio also raised questions about the legality of the Court of High Commission. Puritans had generally supported ecclesiastical commissions before 1581, when the activities of such commissions were largely confined to ferreting out Catholic priests. Ten years later, a test case arose over the lawfulness of the prerogative Court of High Commission in the trial of Robert Cawdrey, a Puritan who refused to take the oath ex officio. In Cawdrey's case (1591) the judges of the Court of Queen's Bench upheld the legality of the Court of High Commission. They stated that the Uniformity Act of 1559, upon which the High Commission was based, merely declared what had been the ancient law of the land in ecclesiastical causes. Those ancient laws, said the judges in words that paraphrased the 1533 Act of Appeals, divided the "body politic . . . into two general parts, that is to say the clergy and the laity," each with its separate jurisdiction—the ecclesiastical law and the common law—but both vested "next and immediately after God" in the supremacy of the crown.[63]

The Classical System

The underlying difference between the Puritans and the bishops over the ex officio oath is best revealed in the interpretations each side placed on what the liturgy and government of the Church should be. Many of the clashes from 1583 to 1589 in the Court of High Commission arose over the radical Puritan attempt to set up a classical system within the structure of the existing Church. An outgrowth of one form of the exercises or prophesyings, the classis (or presbytery as the Scots called it) developed as a conference of ministers who frequently worked to set up a Presbyterian system of ecclesiastical government within the Anglican Church (*ecclesiola in Ecclesia*). The lay component was absent in England as compared with the Reformed churches elsewhere. A short outline of the Presbyterian ecclesiology, perhaps edited by Travers or Cartwright, called the Book of Discipline (*De Disciplina Ecclesiae*) circulated among the various classes, such as Dedham in Essex, where the local Minute Book has survived.[64]

The Dedham classis advocated emendations in the Prayer Book ceremonial, refused to accept all of the Thirty-Nine Articles, assumed advisory powers for (and sometimes the right to place) the twenty or so ministers, usually university men, of its member congregations. It did not wish to be ruled by higher provincial synods or national assemblies. The latter tendency, characteristic of later Independency, made Dedham something less than a distinctly Presbyterian classis. The Dedham classis also engaged in political activities. Just before the election to Elizabeth's Parliament of 1586–1587, one of its leaders wrote to the coordinator of the radical Puritan opposition, John Field:

> I hope you have not let slip this notable opportunity of furthering the cause of religion, by noting out all the places of government in the land; for which Burgesses for the Parliament are to be chosen: and using all the best means you can possibly for the procuring the best gentlemen of those places, by whose wisdom and zeal, gods causes may be preferred: confer amongst your selves, how it may best be compassed. You are placed in the highest place of the Church and land, to that end: even to watch for all occasions of procuring good and preventing evil. Quit your selves worthily.[65]

A national assembly met in London in November, 1586 in order to launch the forthcoming parliamentary campaign. No Parliament of Saints, however, emerged.

In February, 1587 the Presbyterian Anthony Cope, whose election to the new Parliament radical Puritans may have aided, introduced a bill that would have brought about nothing less than a revolution in the Church. After a lengthy preamble reviewing the history of the Henrician schism and the Anglican reformation, the brief text proposed to make "utterly void and of none effect all former laws, customs, statutes, ordinances and constitutions" providing for the government or religious practices of the Church. One stroke would have erased the religious slate. This unprecedented bill would have abolished the Court of High Commission, the ex officio oath, the Prayer Book, the legislation against popish recusants, the royal supremacy in religious affairs, and much more.[66]

Cope's bill, like that of Dr. Peter Turner in the preceding Parliament of 1584–1585, also would have adopted a revised version of the Genevan *Form of Prayers*—that directory of worship and church government first drawn up by the Genevan exiles in 1556. This second version of the *Form of Prayers* suggests a Henrician view of the royal supremacy. But alterations in the book actually presented to Parliament, especially in the section on the authority of the magistrate in matters of religion, appeared before its publication.[67] Within a few hours after the introduction of Cope's bill, Elizabeth had confiscated it and Turner's bill as well. As a direct result of her action, Peter Wentworth once again raised the issue of whether or not freedom of speech existed in the House of Commons. Both he and Cope were sent to the Tower.

When the 1586–1587 Parliament returned to the moderate Puritan proposals to bring about a learned ministry and to curb the oath ex officio, which had been raised without any success in the Parliament of 1584–1585, one of the privy councillors delivered a message from the queen.

> Her Majesty is fully resolved, by her own reading and princely judgment, upon the truth of the reformation which we have already . . . Her Majesty hath fully considered, not only of the exceptions which are made against the present reformation—and doth find them frivolous . . . Her Majesty thinketh that though it were granted that some things were amiss in the Church . . . [yet] to make every day new laws . . . were a means to breed great lightness in her subjects, to nourish an unstaid humor in them of seeking still for exchanges.[68]

There had been no change in her view that the Anglican reformation was completed and further change unnecessary.

Cope's bill also met opposition because it would have transferred the advowson or patronage of church livings to the presbyteries. As Christopher Hatton said in a speech written by his chaplain, Richard Bancroft, "It toucheth us all in our inheritances." The queen would have lost her revenue from First Fruits and Tenths as well as from royal ecclesiastical benefices, although the latter slowly declined in number as a result of the Exchange Act of 1559. The gentry, who, together with the queen, controlled nearly five-sixths of the ecclesiastical livings, would have lost their income from impropriated tithes which they regarded as lay property that could be bought or inherited. Their opposition to this radical measure was just as implacable as it had been to Queen Mary's proposal to restore the monastic lands. Caught in an economic squeeze since the days of Henry VIII as a result of the inflationary movement of prices, the gentry pocketed much of the income from livings rather than passing it along to the clergy. Consequently, more than half of the approximately 9,000 ecclesiastical livings in England were worth no more to the clergy than £8 to £10 annually, an amount so low that kitchen scullions and stable grooms earned more; about a thousand of these livings yielded only a stingy £2 per annum; only about 5 percent of the total numbers was worth more than £30 yearly. Such income in most instances would not attract a learned divine or prevent some clergymen, especially bishops, from holding more than one benefice. Many Puritans like the Welshman John Penry complained of "dumb dogs" in the pulpits, if indeed there was anyone there at all.[69] In Elizabeth's seventh Parliament of 1588–1589, a few Puritans had begun to attack Whitgift and the bishops for these and earlier complaints in several tracts written by Martin Marprelate.

The Martin Marprelate Controversy

As the author's pseudonym suggests, the Martin Marprelate tracts brought the whole episcopal hierarchy under a scurrilous, yet sometimes clever, attack. Men like the Presbyterians John Penry and John Udall anticipated Marprelate in their writings, but it now seems unmistakably clear that another Presbyterian, Job Throkmorton, wrote the tracts. Since the Injunctions of 1559, all printed books and papers were to be licensed. And in 1586, Whitgift had obtained a decree from the Court of Star Chamber that prevented any printer from setting type for any manuscript unless the archbishop or the bishop of London licensed it. The first two Marprelate tracts—*The Epistle* and *The Epitome*, as they are known in their abbreviated titles—appeared without license immediately after the dispersal of the Spanish Armada. In February, 1589, the queen ordered the destruction of these "seditious books, defamatory libels, and other fantastical writings . . . against the godly reformation of religion and government ecclesiastical established by law."[70]

The Church responded to *The Epistle* and *The Epitome* with *An Admonition to the People of England* by "T.C." The first two words of the last title and the initials facetiously suggest the author to have been Thomas Cartwright, especially since he, together with Travers and other Presbyterians, was anxious to disassociate himself from Marprelate. Actually, the author was Thomas Cooper, bishop of Winchester. Drawing upon Bishop Jewel's views as expressed in the *Apology*, Bishop Cooper wrote that a subject owed obedience to the prince in all of those things—such as lands, goods, and possessions—that are not against the Word of God and His commandments. But even if the prince should do something against God's law, the subject, although he might assume a passive disobedience, could not engage in any active resistance by violence. Marprelate's reply, parodying a London street cry, was entitled *Hay* [*Ha'ye*] *Any Work for* [*the*] *Cooper*. In it Marprelate did not advocate active resistance to the supreme governor, but he did maintain that the government of the Church—"petty popes and petty Antichrists"—was contrary to the law of God and, therefore, should be abolished by Her Majesty.[71] The Earl of Derby's agents discovered and seized the press near Manchester, and the printers, found guilty under the statute of 1581 against seditious words, received fines and imprisonment.

At the height of the attack upon the bishops, Richard Bancroft preached a sermon at Paul's Cross which marked a turning point in the theory of Anglican Church government. Most of the sermon attacked the Presbyterian form of church government, but numerous comments referred to Martin Marprelate. For instance, Bancroft accused Marprelate of syllogistic argument in behalf of rebellion. "No petty Pope is to be tolerated in a Christian common-wealth: But her Majesty is a petty Pope: Therefore her Majesty is not to be tolerated in a Christian common-wealth." Despite Bancroft's unmistakable assertion of the royal supremacy—almost in the very words of the Henrician Act of Supremacy—his critics accused him of setting forth the idea of episcopacy by divine right. One of his critics, the lord chancellor, Sir Christopher Hatton, complained to Lord Burghley that the bishops should not claim their dignity "from a higher authority than directly from her majesty's grant." Sir Francis Knollys, who strongly supported the royal supremacy, repeatedly complained to Burghley that Archbishop Whitgift supported the *jus divinum* of bishops when he asserted, in a book against Cartwright, "this superiority of bishops is God's own institution." Actually, the divine right of episcopacy was not what Bancroft had preached. What he had preached was something Archbishop Whitgift also believed: the modest notion that the Church had been governed by a hierarchy of bishops, not by a party of presbyters, ever since apostolic times. What he had omitted, however, was something else that Whitgift believed, namely, that the precise form of church government was not provided by Scripture.[72]

By the 1590s, however, some writers like Anthony Marten and Thomas Bilson had gone beyond the position taken by Bancroft in his Paul's Cross sermon. Indeed, in 1593 Bancroft stated that episcopacy had existed under Jesus Christ, and in 1594 Whitgift wrote to Beza that episcopacy was both apostolic and divine. Elizabeth did not appear to be bothered by these early statements about episcopacy as a divine institution, since other statements, asserting the royal supremacy in ecclesiastical affairs, accompanied them. Indeed, they may have been partly devised to counteract the Presbyterian claim to divine right. Ironically, it is the Erastian, Knollys, whom historians have come to call a "Puritan" privy councillor because of his support of

Cartwright, whereas it is the establishment figure, Whitgift, who supported in some sense the divine right of episcopacy, an innovative idea that would take root in the next century.[73]

While Bancroft and others were making incipient statements about divine right episcopacy, Richard Hooker tried to mute his own reluctant support of that position when he penned an important defense of the royal supremacy in ecclesiastical affairs in his *Laws of Ecclesiastical Polity*. Whitgift appointed Hooker, who had enjoyed Jewel's patronage while a student at Oxford, to the vacant office of the master of the Temple Church in London in 1585 over the incumbent deputy master or afternoon lecturer, Walter Travers. According to Thomas Fuller, "what Mr. Hooker delivered in the morning, Mr. Travers confuted in the afternoon."[74] Hooker had problems with the rigid Calvinist theology that Whitgift later accepted in the Lambeth Articles (1595).

In the eighth book of the *Laws*, written by 1593, Hooker set forth his views on the relations between church and state. He attacked the Presbyterian concept, eloquently enunciated by Cartwright, of separate but coordinate authority between church and state (the two-kingdom theory). Nor did Hooker have any use for the notion, especially strong among the Separatists, that the Church should consist only of the elect of God. Instead, he believed that "there is not any man of the Church of England but the same man is also a member of the commonwealth; nor any man a member of the commonwealth, which is not also of the Church of England." This argument in behalf of a single society (the one-kingdom theory), which logically required a single governor (the queen), had been used earlier by Stephen Gardiner in his *De Vera Obedientia* and by John Whitgift against the Puritans. Hooker also drew upon the views of Jewel and Whitgift by excluding the *potestas ordinis*, as well as matters of faith necessary to salvation, from the control of the sovereign.

Hooker, like Whitgift, contended that external or outward religious matters—"things indifferent" to salvation—should be limited by positive or man-made law. "We are to hold it a thing most consonant with equity and reason, that no ecclesiastical law be made in a Christian commonwealth, without consent as well of the laity as the clergy, but least of all without consent of the highest power."[75] The consent of Parliament, as has been repeatedly observed, was one of the last things that Elizabeth desired for the Anglican Church. It was probaby fortunate for Hooker that Elizabeth never saw Book VIII of the *Laws*, but, upon its first publication in 1648, Parliament, without the sovereign, had already gone a long way toward carrying out a revolution in the Church.

Bancroft's search for the press of Martin Marprelate in the Midlands turned up additional evidence about the Presbyterian movement. On the basis of this evidence, which included information about the network of classes as well as the text of the Presbyterian Book of Discipline, Cartwright and eight other ministers, mostly Presbyterian, appeared before the Court of High Commission for examination in 1590. This move was made much easier because Cartwright no longer enjoyed the patronage of Leicester, who had died in 1588. (The death of Sir Walter Mildmay in 1589 and the earl of Warwick and Sir Francis Walsingham in 1590 left only Sir Francis Knollys as a Puritan supporter, albeit an Erastian, at court). All of the nine ministers, when asked to take the ex officio oath, refused.

After months of harassment, the preachers suffered removal from their ecclesiastical offices, and in May, 1591, the Queen's Council, sitting as the Court of Star Chamber, brought the ministers before it. The charge against the ministers was a seditious attempt to supersede the queen's supremacy in ecclesiastical matters with the discussion and use of the Book of Discipline in classes, synods, and assemblies. Under the advice of their lawyers, the ministers denied any intention of separating from the Anglican Church or of holding meetings for any seditious purpose. Furthermore, they said that the Book of Discipline, which they thought had been drawn partly from Cranmer's *Reformatio Legum Ecclesiasticarum*, had not been implemented, and their subscription to it indicated only a desire to see it legally established by queen and Parliament. After all, they argued, if the writing of the Book of Discipline was seditious, so also was Cranmer's writing of the *Reformatio*.

In the middle of the trial, two supporters of the defendants, Edmund Copinger and Henry Arthington, proclaimed in Cheapside that the queen had forfeited her Crown and that one William Hacket was the "new Messiah and King of Europe." Despite this association with the excesses of messianic Anabaptism, the Court of Star Chamber seemed unable to find the necessary evidence to convict the ministers of a seditious act. After a long imprisonment, the defendants, still proclaiming their innocence, signed a submission in 1593 indicating their regret that the classical meetings had been offensive to the queen and promised not to provoke her displeasure in the future. Eventually they secured their release, but the trial and imprisonment had taken a heavy personal toll. Although the trial was an immediate victory for the ministers, its effect greatly curtailed Presbyterian activity.[76]

In addition to the Presbyterian Puritans, the government also brought to trial a new group of Separatist Puritans. Two Cambridge men led the Barrowists, as they came to be called: Henry Barrow, a relative of the Bacon family, and John Greenwood. Arrested in the fall of 1587, both men spent most of the next six years in various prisons. Like the Brownists, the Barrowists believed in the separation of the elect from the nonelect within each church congregation. Like the Brownists, the Barrowists also believed in the separation of the church congregation from the Anglican hierarchy, chiefly because they found the Church of England a false church.

On the separation of church and state—more specifically on the role of the civil magistrate in ecclesiastical affairs—Barrow did not go as far as Browne, but Greenwood went further. During Barrow's fifth examination before the civil authorities in 1589, he acknowledged Elizabeth as the "supreme governor over the whole land, and over the church also, both of bodies and goods," but he added the important qualification that the prince should not make any laws for the church except those that Christ had left in His Word. Barrow also believed in the power of the church to excommunicate the prince for any transgression of God's law.[77] Consequently, Barrow's conception of the magistrate turned out, after all, to be quite similar to that of the Presbyterians.

In his examination before the civil authorities in 1589, Greenwood, too, advocated the right of the church to excommunicate the civil magistrate. But, when they asked him if the queen was "supreme head" of ecclesiastical causes, he said no, adding that Christ was the "only head of his church." When they asked him if he would take the Oath of Supremacy to "the laws in the church as it is now established," he said he would "not answer to approve thereof."[78]

During the debate on a Bill Against Seditious Sectaries in Elizabeth's eighth Parliament (1593), Barrow and Greenwood were put to death under the 1581 statute Against Seditious Words and Rumors. At about the same time, Penry, who had become a Separatist in 1592, was tried and hanged under the same statute. When the bill Against Seditious Sectaries became the law of the land, anyone, Puritan or Catholic, who obstinately refused to go to church, or who in word or print impugned the royal supremacy, or who was present at "any unlawful assemblies, conventicles, or meeting" contrary to law, was to be imprisoned. If a Puritan dissenter—Catholic recusants were taken care of in another statute—did not submit after three months, he was banished; if he returned, he was to be tried as a felon without benefit of clergy. It is little wonder that many of the Separatists now made their way to Holland, some of whom eventually sailed to the New World as the Pilgrims.

By the mid-1590s, the Anglican bishops, strongly supported by the queen, appeared to be lined up on the side of suppression, persecution, and coercion, whereas the radical Puritans seemed to be lined up on the side of free speech and freedom from self-incrimination; the Separatists seemed to be leaning heavily toward the separation of church and state. For instance, when the queen had suppressed debate in Parliament over Cope's bill, the parliamentary Puritans, including Peter Wentworth, protested that their freedom of speech had been violated. Or, when the bishops used the ex officio oath in the Court of High Commission in order to persecute the supporters of the Book of Discipline and the classical system, the Presbyterian Puritans such as Thomas Cartwright claimed a freedom not to testify against themselves. Or again, when Elizabeth's government forced the Brownists and Barrowists to submit to the ecclesiastical government of the Anglican Church, some of the Separatists like John Greenwood came close to advocating the complete separation of the church from the state. Such Puritan rhetoric and strategy can be viewed as prototypes for the first and fifth amendments to the American Constitution.

But there is evidence that would lead to a countervailing conclusion as well.[79] For instance, it is one thing to state that the parity or equality of ministers in Presbyterianism sharply contrasted with the Anglican ecclesiastical hierarchy of church offices, as indeed it did. But it is quite another thing to realize that Presbyterianism wished to establish its own ecclesiastical hierarchy of church courts, indeed its own version of a national church related to other Calvinist national churches. It is one thing to state that the Presbyterian election of ministers sharply contrasted with the Anglican system of impropriations, as indeed it did. But it is quite another thing to realize that the classes or conferences usually chose the Presbyterian ministers and that the ministers and elders retained effective control of a Presbyterian congregation—indeed, of the classical system. Again, it is one thing to state that the discussions for the edification of the ministers and laity at Puritan exercises or prophesyings sharply contrasted with the *pro forma* reading of Anglican homilies by "unlearned ministers," as they did. But it is quite another thing to realize that the Puritans imposed a Calvinist system of discipline and corporateness upon their individual interpretations of Holy Scripture. And again, it is one thing to state that Presbyterians believed in a two-kingdom theory of church and state, as they did. But it is quite another thing to realize that the same godly people who would have power in the church would also hold it in the state.[80] Indeed, the goals of the radical and Separatist Puritans, which had received numerous setbacks at the hands of Parliament and the courts by the 1590s, echo earlier theocratic societies. Yet the means, and sometimes the rhetoric, to achieve some of these goals, which often had been provoked by the repressive measures of the queen, the bishops, and her councillors, presaged later democratic societies.

Although there are hazards in making generalizations about large religious communities, especially when there is a wide range of groups within each, there are some striking similarities between Catholics and Puritans. The differences are more obvious. Puritanism was essentially a reform movement within Anglicanism bent upon moving the church further from Roman Catholicism and closer to Reformed Protestantism. Catholicism, however, at least in its clerical form, was an underground resistance separate from the Church as established by Elizabeth, bent upon restoring the ancient faith. Consequently, the Puritans attempted to carry out their religious reforms mostly, though not exclusively, by legal means, either within the Church through prophesyings and the classical system or by introducing legislation such as Turner's and Cope's bills in Parliament. The Catholics, however—and here we must exclude most household laymen—attempted to conduct their resistance mostly by illegal means, either by religious conversion or by such military force as the Rebellion of the Northern Earls and the external invasion attempts that Spain could muster. When one adds to these dissimilarities the profound differences over transubstantiation, justification by faith, and papal supremacy, it would appear that Catholics and Puritans had very little in common.

Yet they shared some positions, particularly in connection with the royal supremacy. Unlike the Anglican hierarchy, who believed in a state church, the militant Catholics and radical Puritans believed in the ultimate dominance of the church over the state despite all of their talk about two swords and two kingdoms. William Allen was no less emphatic than Thomas Cartwright on this point. Their ecclesiastical conceptions of a church state transcended national boundaries (more so with Catholicism than with Puritanism) so that they drew sustenance, both in theory and practice, from abroad—from Rome and Geneva, respectively. Unlike Anglican clergy such as Jewel, Whitgift, and Hooker, who generously gave the *potestas jurisdictionis* into the hands of the queen while withholding the *potestas ordinis* for themselves, the militant Catholics and radical Puritans appeared to claim the *potestas jurisdictionis* as well. Furthermore, they both claimed a divine right for their clergy, whereas the Anglicans, except for a few who followed after Bancroft, upheld the royal supremacy. Not only did each group try to obtain complete control over its own church (the new edition of the *Form of Prayers* marked a slight retreat from the Puritan position), but each hoped to be influential in the conduct of civil affairs (Catholics more so than Puritans). Although Catholic churchmen such as Cardinals Wolsey and Pole had long taken an active role in temporal matters, the Puritan clergy, who did not hold political office, tried to work in conjunction with the Puritan laity, who exerted a clerical influence in temporal affairs through Parliament.

Unlike the Anglican hierarchy, both the militant Catholics and radical Puritans believed in the excommunication of the civil magistrate, should the church's will be violated; and though the radical Puritans never attempted to depose the queen, as the militant Catholics tried to do, the Catholic Allen employed the proto-Puritan theory of deposition (Knox, Goodman, and Ponet) which Independent Puritans were to act upon a half century later. The response of Elizabeth's Erastian government to these anti-Erastian moves brought militant Catholics and radical Puritans under heavy questioning through the "bloody questions" and the ex officio oath. These interrogations frequently resulted in prosecution for both groups under the same statutes (1581 and 1593) for sedition. Finally, both groups failed in what they set out to do, just as the Puritans were to fail in 1660, and the Catholics in 1689.

4

The Jacobean Consolidation

In the last few years of Elizabeth's reign, Catholics, Puritans, and Anglicans alike had a long time to speculate about the religious changes which James VI of Scotland might make when he ascended the throne of England. And changes, it seemed, would certainly take place, because all Henry VIII's offspring had made some changes immediately upon their respective assumptions of power in church and state. Somewhat hopeful were the Catholics who, even though James had not adopted the Catholic faith of his mother, Mary Stuart, thought that his ecumenical views would be a vast improvement over the persecution of Elizabeth's reign. That possibility was severely tested with the Gunpowder Plot of 1605, but the retributive legislation, including a new Oath of Allegiance, seemed to be directed primarily at those radical Catholics who sought the king's deposition.

Slightly more hopeful were the Puritans. James' early training by his Calvinist tutor, George Buchanan, as well as the strength of Presbyterianism within the Scottish Kirk, were encouraging factors. But the Reformed Church leaders' rough handling of James, and their dislike of his exalted political views, more than offset whatever they might have had in common with him. Still, James did agree, after receiving the Millenary Petition, to meet with the moderate Puritans at the Hampton Court Conference, but they quickly found out that he would make very few concessions.

Most hopeful of all were the Anglicans. Anglican clergy realized that their Erastian tradition accorded with James' own opposition to the claims of some Catholics and Puritans that the spiritual realm was superior to the temporal realm. The Canons of 1606, as well as James' support of the Anglican bishops against the writs of prohibition of the common law courts, redeemed that hope. But the king's notion of divine right monarchy seemed to be on a collision course with that small group of Anglicans who had come to believe in a divine right of episcopacy, and his Calvinism jarred those few Anglicans who were just beginning to advocate Arminianism. Potentially, James' reign could represent minor alterations of positions the Crown took under Elizabeth or new views which might be the portent of things to come.

The Last Years of Elizabeth

Although the last years of Elizabeth have been characterized as ones of relative peace between church and state—indeed a period, as she liked to state, in which she ruled with the love of her subjects, it was a period of critical importance for Puritans and not so quiet desperation for Catholics. The Puritans, who had suffered serious defeats across their spectrum, were attempting a serious modification to the Thirty-Nine Articles at Cambridge in the form of the Lambeth Articles. These Lambeth Articles would become the subject of debate for years to come. The Catholics, also in retreat, were badly split. Their failure to act in a unified way may have indicated the seeming hopelessness of their cause.

The Lambeth Articles

In the mid-1590s, a doctrinal dispute among the scholars of Cambridge University resulted in an attempt to impose a rigid Calvinist theology—a new Protestant scholasticism—upon the loose Calvinist theology of the Anglican Church, particularly that reflected in the Thirty-Nine Articles. This Protestant scholasticism—derived from Peter Martyr and Calvin's disciple, Theodore Beza—featured a theological system that included a double predestination, which militantly stressed reprobation, limited atonement, and the indefectibility of the elect. William Perkins, Fellow of Christ's College; William Whitaker, the Regius Professor of Divinity; Lawrence Chaderton, Whitaker's brother-in-law; and the heads of some of the colleges had endorsed this rigid Calvinism.[1] John Overall, Fellow of Trinity College, and Peter Baro, Lady Margaret Professor of Divinity, opposed their Cambridge associates.

The dispute reached a crisis in 1595 when William Barrett, a young disciple of Baro, preached a sermon attacking some of the rigid Calvinist doctrines. He asserted, among other things, that grace was given to all men, that the elect could lose their faith totally but not finally, and that no man could be so certain of faith that he could be assured of salvation. Whitaker took great offense at Barrett's sermons, and Baro observed in the ensuing debate that Perkins tried to confute Overall's contention that Christ had died for all men. In May, the heads forced Barrett to recant his views and to state that he believed in the statements on election and reprobation as set forth in the Articles of Religion. Archbishop Whitgift, who was still operating within the loose Calvinist consensus of Elizabeth's first two decades, could not find that Barrett had violated any of the Thirty-Nine Articles. In fact, article sixteen says that "we may depart from grace given," and article seventeen refers only to predestination to life (not reprobation to death). Before long, however, Baro lost his professorship, and Barrett retracted his recantation and went abroad to become a Catholic. Barrett eventually returned to England and was still alive in the late 1620s when Puritans like William Prynne and Francis Rous claimed that Catholicism was the logical outcome of those same theological views (since labeled as Arminian) that Barrett had proclaimed in the 1590s.[2]

As a result of the theological controversy in Cambridge, Archbishop Whitgift called a conference at Lambeth Palace in November, 1595, to discuss a set of rigid Calvinist propositions that Whitaker had drafted. The archbishop, in all likelihood influenced by Matthew Hutton, archbishop of York, accepted six of Whitaker's propositions virtually without change. These included propositions (one and three) that God had "predestined" a "certain number" of men to eternal life and "reprobated" some to eternal death. Again, Whitgift accepted the propositions (eight and nine) that no man can "come to Christ . . . unless the Father draws him . . . and all men are not drawn" nor is it in "the will or the power of each and every man to be saved." Whitgift also accepted the proposition (four) that those not predestined to salvation are inevitably condemned "on account of their sins," perhaps because Lancelot Andrewes, his chaplain and master of Pembroke College, said that the phrase "on account of their sins" meant "because they sin." Again, Whitgift accepted the proposition (seven) that "saving grace" is "not granted . . . not made common, is not ceded to all men, by which they might be saved."

Yet, the archbishop, who wished to assert his own authority, altered three of Whitaker's propositions, thereby toning down somewhat the rigid Calvinism. For example, although Whitgift agreed that the elect could be saved only by the will of God and not by man's will, nor the "foreseeing of faith, or of perseverance," nor good works, nor "anything innate" in the predestined, the archbishop changed the word "Predestination" to the phrase "predestination to life," thereby implying that reprobation was caused by man's own sins. Or again, while agreeing that faith never fails finally nor totally in the elect, the archbishop's substitution of the "elect" for "those who once have been partakers of (faith)" left the implication that the reprobate might enjoy faith for a while before losing it. Or still again, while agreeing that "the truly faithful man" is "sure" of the remission of sins and eternal salvation through Christ, the archbishop stated that this is known by an "assurance of faith," as Barrett implied, and not, as Whitaker had stated, by a "certainty of faith." Apart from this substitution of "assurance" for "certainty," which may be the most significant of Whitgift's alterations in all of Whitaker's propositions, the Lambeth Articles did not represent Whitgift's attempt to move away from Calvinism toward Barrett's Pelagianism, but rather Whitgift's support for Whitaker's attempt to impose a rigid Calvinist doctrine upon the Thirty-Nine Articles.[3]

When Whitgift told Lord Burghley, the aged chancellor of Cambridge University, that the Lambeth Articles corresponded to the professed doctrine of the Church of England, Burghley, though disapproving, confessed that such "matters are too high mysteries for [my] understanding." Elizabeth stated that predestination was a "matter tender and dangerous to weak ignorant minds" and promptly suspended the Lambeth Articles. According to tradition, the queen told Whitgift, probably in jest, that he had violated the statute of Praemunire for having called a Church council without her consent. Still, the rigid Calvinism of the Lambeth Articles had a "close connection" with the thought of such Puritans as Thomas Cartwright, Lawrence Chaderton, Walter Travers, and, of course, William Whitaker.

As the previous chapter reflects, there was very little discussion about Calvinist theology among Puritans and Anglicans during the middle decades of Elizabeth's reign. In the mid-1590s, however, the display of proto-Arminian ideas at Cambridge produced the conference which resulted in the Lambeth Articles of 1595. The Lambeth Articles represented a rigid Calvinst theological framework for such Puritan theologians as Whitaker, Chaderton, and Perkins, as well as such Anglican archbishops as Whitgift and Hutton. That bishops and their critics could reach such agreement in part depends upon the different conclusions they drew from the same Calvinist theology. The bishops were essentially credal Calvinists who, emphasizing the invisible church, did not wish to implement their theological views in the popular pulpit or in particular religious communities. Alarmed by the antinomian possibilities of a rigid Calvinism, they stressed the Erastian domination of the Church by the civil magistrate. The Church's critics tended to be experimental Calvinists who emphasized various ecclesiastical forms of the visible church, and who used their rigid Calvinism to define more precisely the godly community in the pulpit and in the congregation. Restricting active church membership only to the visible godly, they saw little need for an Erastian magistrate who, in the final analysis, was just one of them. A crucial issue is how long the credal Calvinists could maintain a cohesive Anglican Church in the face of the fissiparous tendencies of experimental Calvinism.[4]

Elizabeth's ninth Parliament (1597–1598) did not debate any of the foregoing issues, but the Church received some unforeseen criticism over the subject of marriage licenses. Because these licenses replaced the publication of banns before marriage, some unscrupulous persons, including priests, had recently misused them in order to foster the abduction of heiresses. Also, debate over other ecclesiastical abuses, such as the probate of wills, seemed imminent. Rather than forbid debate as she had so often done in the past, the queen requested evidence from the Commons about unlawful marriages so that she could act in her role as supreme governor of the Church. The Commons complied, but it also proceeded to draft its own bill on marriage licenses as well as a bill against excessive fees in ecclesiastical courts. Shortly after the appearance of these anticlerical measures, the Puritan Henry Finch introduced a bill to make changes favorable to Puritans in the Act of Uniformity of 1559 and the Subscription Act of 1571.

      None of these bills reached the statute books, but the Canterbury Convocation of the Clergy attempted to remedy the Commons' anticlerical grievances in the Canons of 1597. These canons, like the Canons of 1576 and the Canons of 1585, which they supplemented, received the queen's signature. In the second half of her reign, Elizabeth had finally learned to make some adjustments in her Church settlement, preferably through the convocations of the clergy rather than the Houses of Parliament.[5]

Three issues dealing with the Church arose in Elizabeth's tenth and last Parliament (1601): the sabbath, pluralism, and recusancy. Regarding the stricter keeping of the sabbath, the Parliament of 1584–1585 had passed a bill forbidding Sunday markets or fairs and banning unlawful games—bearbaiting, wakes, hawking, hunting, and rowing with barges—during church service. Parliament had acted partly in response to the accidental death of eight persons on a Sunday afternoon when a scaffold collapsed around a bear ring in Paris Garden. The queen vetoed the bill. The Puritan Nicholas Bownde, in his *Doctrine of the Sabbath* (1595), had insisted that Sunday should be given over completely to meditation and spiritual exercises, but Thomas Rogers had labeled such sabbatarian views as "antichristian," preferring to call Sundays the queen's days.[6] The Commons passed a new sabbatarian bill in 1601, which included only the clause forbidding markets and fairs from the 1584–1585 bill, but the proposal died in the Lords.

On the question of pluralism, the pluralities statute of 1529 had allowed dispensations to the Crown, the Church, the nobility, and academics. Even though the Canons of 1585 and 1597 had called for the general restraint of pluralism in ecclesiastical benefices, a Commons pluralities bill in 1601 provided for the elimination of the Henrician dispensations. The new bill, with many of the same clauses as the one the queen had opposed in the Parliament of 1588–1589, allowed only one benefice to a minister unless it was worth less than £8 and the second benefice was within three miles of the first. Whitgift, however, told the queen that under the present system there were more learned men in the Church than ever before; and some Anglicans outside Parliament argued that the intellectual quality of the Church, especially among clergymen at colleges and cathedral churches, would decline without pluralism. Still another pluralities bill raised the limit from £8 to £20 and retained all of the dispensations of the Henrician pluralities act. In all likelihood the latest pluralities bill met the same fate as the pluralities bill of 1588–1589. Tempting as it may have been to sign a bill that would have actually increased pluralism, the queen was not about to surrender her ecclesiastical prerogative to Parliament on this issue.[7]

On the question of recusancy, the Act of Uniformity had levied fines of one shilling for failure to attend church on Sunday. The shilling fine, collected usually from the poor, had fallen into disuse since the passage of the recusancy act of 1581 with its fines of £20 levied against the wealthy. When the government introduced a new bill in the Commons for the better collecting of the shilling fine in 1601, it included a clause requiring husbands to pay for the absence from church of wives, and masters for servants. The bill, however, failed to pass by three votes. Even when the husband and master clauses were dropped, and a new occasional conformity clause required attendance only eight times a year—four more than the recusancy statute of 1581—the bill still failed by one vote. Puritans in this session not only suffered one of their worst defeats, failing even to get an anti-Catholic recusancy measure, but they seemed to have lost the religious fervor and leadership, even on outright ethical issues, that had carried them through so many Elizabethan parliamentary debates.[8]

The Appellant Controversy

The decline in anti-Catholic feeling reflected in the Parliament of 1601, after the death of Cardinal Allen in 1594, accompanied the development of a sharp division between the dozen or so Jesuits and the approximately 300 secular clergy, which affected English Catholicism for the remainder of Elizabeth's reign. Three things aggravated the differences between the two groups: the establishment of a strict Jesuit rule among all the Catholic prisoners at Wisbech Castle, which produced the "Wisbech Stirs"; the pro-Spanish conduct of affairs by the Jesuits at the English College in Rome; and the Jesuit proposal for a Spanish succession to the English throne.

But the crucial problem facing English Catholics was the need for some kind of effective ecclesiastical organization—the Jesuits wishing a closer tie, and the seculars a looser tie, with Rome. When the papacy ignored Robert Parsons' request for two bishops, it adopted the Jesuit's alternative proposal for an archpriest with twelve assistants. Cardinal Cajetan, the protector of England, appointed George Blackwell, an unknown but pro-Jesuit secular priest, as archpriest with limited powers over the secular clergy. In all important matters Blackwell should consult with the Jesuit superior in England, Henry Garnet. Blackwell sought confirmation of his appointment by Pope Clement VIII, but two secular priests—William Bishop, who believed in "the subordination of the spiritual to the secular power," and Robert Charnock— ironically appealed to the pope, in violation of the 1533 Act of Appeals, for the appointment of a bishop chosen by the secular clergy. Bishop and Charnock, somewhat naively, also sought to strip the Jesuits of control of the College in Rome and to forbid the publication of books written against Queen Elizabeth. It is a curious expression of national loyalty to violate the very statute that is the incarnation of national self-sufficiency, but equally interesting is the attempt to raise an ecclesiastical issue, where undoubtedly the pope had the final authority, into a political issue—a clerical issue into one affecting laymen.[9]

When the two appellants arrived in Rome, Robert Parsons, the Jesuit rector, placed them under house arrest at the English College. Cardinal Cajetan and Cardinal Borghese, the vice protector of England, tried them in a papal court. When they were found guilty, one English secular priest observed, "Our statute of *praemunire* may well be repealed now."[10] Although neither of the appellants had seen the pope, a papal letter stated that the pope had ordered Blackwell's original appointment as archpriest. The papal decision temporarily stifled all of the opposition to Blackwell, but the deep differences no longer allowed any hope for Catholic unity.

Had Blackwell not attempted to discipline the secular priests who had appealed to the pope against him, he might have avoided one of the most astonishing developments in all of the Tudors' relations with the Catholic Church. Instead, the archpriest sought an admission of guilt for schism from the dissident secular priests. Little wonder, then, that thirty-three secular priests sent a second appeal to Rome, charging Blackwell with misgovernment as well as favoring the Jesuits. In order to raise funds for their appeal, the dissident secular clergy began unprecedented negotiations on an informal basis with the Elizabethan government. The path had been opened by such secular priests as William Watson.

> We wish with all our hearts (and groan every day at the contrary) that her Majesty had continued in her obedience to the See Apostolic, as Queen Mary, her sister of famous memory, had left her a worthy example; but seeing that God for our sins would have it otherwise, we ought to have carried ourselves in another manner of course towards her, our true and lawful queen, and towards our country, than hath been taken and pursued by many catholics, but especially by the Jesuits.[11]

Richard Bancroft, now bishop of London, sensing the opportunity to exploit the Catholic disunity, assisted the appellants in raising the necessary funds for this appeal. Thomas Bluet, a dissident secular from the Wisbech "Stirs," hoping for some kind of toleration from Elizabeth's government, worked for the recall of the Jesuits from England. Backed by the French court, which opposed a Spanish candidate for the English succession, the appellants were able to get some redress from the pope in October, 1602. Although Blackwell remained as a reprimanded archpriest, he could not consult with the Jesuits and reported directly to the pope.[12]

Clement VIII did nothing about withdrawing the Jesuits from England, and Elizabeth did not issue Catholics the equivalent of an Edict of Nantes. In fact, in a royal proclamation of November 5, 1602, Elizabeth explicitly denied that she had ever intended to give toleration to Catholics, but she observed that the government in recent years had exercised some forbearance in the administration of the penal laws. However, because of the recent treason of the Jesuits and their adherents, and the disloyalty of the secular clergy, she ordered the former group to leave the realm at once and the latter group at the latest by February 1, 1603.[13] The secular priests might submit themselves to the mercy of the Crown. Only thirteen did so. Their "Protestation of Allegiance" of January 31, whereby they hoped to escape the fate they wished for the Jesuits, not only acknowledged their political loyalty to the queen and their spiritual loyalty to the pope, not only answered all of the old "bloody questions" to the Crown's satisfaction, but also explicitly denied the papal deposing power. Nevertheless, Bishop Bancroft found the Protestation inadequate, probably because it was not an oath of allegiance, and even if it had been, the seculars would continue exercising their priestly powers; it was soon forgotten in those last days of the dying queen.

In the closing years of Elizabeth's reign, much of the thrust was spent that had so animated the Puritans and, to a lesser extent, the Catholics during the reign's three middle decades. The government's unprecedented negotiations with secular priests had successfully exploited the division within the Catholic ranks. More and more Catholics had come to accept the government's distinction between royal political authority and papal ecclesiastical supremacy. As for the Puritans, the Court of High Commission had chastened many of their old leaders, some of whom had died, and the rest had lost nearly all their old friends at court either through retirement or death. It seemed as if a new generation of Puritan leaders, hesitant and inexperienced, was waiting for the queen and the archbishop to die before it would undertake another siege against the citadel of Anglicanism. The Puritans made some attempts in Parliament to revive the old ecclesiastical fervor. But a temporary exhaustion, even a sense of deja vu, with these issues, and the continued intransigence of the queen, stymied any notable success, even against their traditional whipping boy, the Catholic recusant. The one sector, however, in which a truly fresh development had taken place was theology. The Lambeth Articles dampened the proto-Arminianism of Cambridge University, but it was to flare up again during the last years of James' reign and to burst into flame under Charles I.

King James and the Puritans

Both in his native Scotland and in his adopted England, James Stuart ran a gauntlet made up of those who opposed the established churches of each nation. As James VI of Scotland, he formulated his ideas of divine right monarchy to withstand the Presbyterian (radical Puritan) ideas of theocratic monarchy that dominated the Kirk toward the end of the sixteenth century. As James I of England, he received the complaints of the moderate Puritans against the Anglican Church in the Millenary Petition and gave them a forum at the Hampton Court Conference. As supreme governor of the Anglican Church, he attempted to impose an ecclesiastical uniformity with the Canons of 1604, which the Presbyterians and moderate Puritans regarded as uncompromising in some instances and accommodating in others. Also, as supreme governor of the Anglican Church, James had to confront those Separatist Puritans who would not conform to the Canons of 1604. How James fared in his running of the Puritan gauntlet goes a long way in telling us what kind of churches he was to bequeath to his successor.

James VI and the Scottish Presbyterians

During the second half of the sixteenth century, the Scottish Kirk had alternated between episcopal and Presbyterian forms of church government. When James was still a boy, the General Assembly of the Kirk (the governing body of the Scottish Church) adopted the Concordat of Leith (1572). The

Concordat reflected Regent Morton's plan to approximate the Kirk to the Church of England as much as possible. For example, bishops swore allegiance to James as "supreme governor." When the king was a teenager, Andrew Melville, later principal of St. Mary's College at St. Andrews University (after years of teaching with Travers and Cartwright in Beza's Geneva), reversed Morton's policy by getting the General Assembly (but not the Crown) to adopt the second version of a Scottish *Book of Discipline* (1578). It set forth the principles and organization of what has since come to be known as Scottish Presbyterianism. Although the Scottish second *Book of Discipline* lacks the overall clarity of the English Book of Discipline, the first section states the theory of the two kingdoms, the "Power of the Sword" and the "Power of the Keys." Moreover, "as ministers are subject to the judgment and punishment of the magistrate in external things, if they offend; so ought the magistrates to submit themselves to the discipline of the kirk if they transgress in matters of conscience and religion." [14] Although the second *Book of Discipline* did not claim the superiority of the spiritual over the temporal sphere, as Cartwright had done, it did state that the ministers, though not having the power to exercise civil jurisdiction, should "teach the magistrates how to exercise it according to the Word of God."

Within two years, the General Assembly declared the office of bishop unlawful, and Cartwright and Travers had taken up positions at St. Andrews. James' answer to the second *Book of Discipline* was the group of "Black Acts" passed by the Scottish Parliament in 1584. These "Black Acts" eliminated all ecclesiastical jurisdiction (including the second *Book of Discipline* not approved by Parliament, gave that ecclesiastical jurisdiction back to the bishops, and returned the power over both the temporal and spiritual realms to the Crown. But as the General Assembly had reversed itself earlier, Parliament reversed itself in 1592 by passing an act authorizing Presbyterian church government once more under the General Assembly through synods, presbyteries (like the English classes), and particular church sessions. The office of bishop, though curtailed in function, was not abolished; and the Crown could determine the meeting time and place of the General Assembly. Still, it was a victory for Melville, and four years later he could take the king by the sleeve in Falkland Palace and call him "God's silly vassal." But Melville did not stop with name-calling, for this "Hildebrand of Presbyter" lectured James somewhat in the fashion that John Knox had lectured James' mother, Mary Stuart, nearly forty years before. "And, therefore, Sir. . . . I must tell you, there is two Kings and two Kingdoms in Scotland," spoke Melville. "There is Christ Jesus the King, and his kingdom the Kirk, whose subject James the Sixth is, and of whose kingdom not a king, nor a lord, nor a head, but a member." [15]

Confronted by this Presbyterian "Hildebrandism," James VI made a theoretical defense of his tenuous position by dusting off the medieval doctrine of divine right monarchy. Wycliff had already employed a modified form of this doctrine against the temporal claims of Boniface VIII, and Tyndale had used a modified form of it against the spiritual claims of Clement

VII. James published a book in 1598 that denounced the clerical claims of both Catholics and Protestants. In *The True Law of Free Monarchies*, he stated that "Kings are called Gods by the prophetical King *David*, because they sit upon God his Throne in the earth, and have the count of their administration to give unto him." [16] In addition to administering justice, establishing good laws, and procuring peace, he continued, it is within the office of the king to serve as a "good Pastor." Here was an opportunity for a statement that might have claimed for the Crown not only the *potestas jurisdictionis* but also the *potestas ordinis* as well. But the king did not avail himself of the opportunity then or later. Instead, he said that kings at their coronations take an oath to maintain the religion "presently professed" according to the law whereby it is established and to punish all those who would alter or disturb the practice of religion. Scottish religious practice was a long way from the theory of James VI.

Within a year (1599) James secretly published *Basilikon Doron* which was to serve as a set of instructions for his young son Henry regarding various matters of church and state. In what seems to be a reference to John Knox and the events of 1559 and 1560, the king noted with some distaste that the Scottish Reformation had been undertaken by "a popular tumult and rebellion" rather than "proceeding from the Prince's order, as it did in our neighbor country of England." And in what seems to be a reference to Melville and the Presbyterians, he explained that "some fiery spirited men in the ministry" began "to phantasy to themselves a Democratic form of government" by pressing for a "parity in the Church." "For if by the example thereof, once established in the Ecclesiastical government, the Politic and civil estate should be drawn to the like, the great confusion that thereupon would arise may easily be discerned." Therefore, James advised his son to take heed of proud Puritans, "very pests in the Church and Common-weal" and to preserve himself from their poisons by advancing "godly, learned and modest men of the ministry. . . . to Bishoprics and Benefices." As might be expected, Melville was irate at what he called the "Anglo-pisco-papistical conclusions" of the *Basilikon Doron*.[17]

When the first public edition appeared in 1603—just a few days after Elizabeth's death—James, with an eye cocked toward the English Puritans, had added a new preface. In it he explained that by his use of the term "Puritan" he had not meant those preachers who are persuaded "*that their Bishops smell of a Papal supremacy, that the Surplice, the cornered cap, and such like, are the outward badges of Popish errors.*" He noted that he had always regarded such things as "indifferent." What he had meant by the term "Puritan" was that group of preachers, such as Browne, Penry, and others who had "*come into Scotland, to sew their popple amongst us.*" And whether or not they were actually members of that Anabaptist sect, the Family of Love, argued James, they still held the common Anabaptist concept—contempt for the civil magistrate—which was the last thing that the theory of divine right would allow.

The experience of James VI with Presbyterians in Scotland gave him a good taste of what it would be like as James I to break bread at a conference table with Puritans in England. His advocacy of divine right government in response to the Scottish Presbyterians had been as far removed from his actual conduct of religious affairs north of the border as it would become with the English Puritans south of the border. Actually, James looked forward to a "new found land" where there was an established Church that seemed to accord more closely with his own Erastian notions of church and state.

The Hampton Court Conference

When James traveled southward from Edinburgh in April, 1603 to take up his duties at Westminster, he received a petition, allegedly supported by a thousand ministers, to call a conference for the reformation of certain ceremonies of the church. The Millenary Petition, which bore no signatures, disclaimed that it represented "factious men affecting a popular parity in the church" (Presbyterians) or "schismatics aiming at the dissolution of the State ecclesiastical" (Separatists).[18] Instead, it represented for the most part those moderate Puritans who, ever since the Vestiarian controversy, had accumulated a number of grievances throughout Elizabeth's reign, most of which were regarded as "things indifferent" to man's salvation.

It is significant that the Millenary Petition did not ask for the drastic remodeling of church government along Presbyterian lines. But it did contain two phrases from radical Puritans that were suggestive of the Scottish second *Book of Discipline*: "discipline . . . may be administered according to Christ's own institution" and "that none be excommunicated without consent of his pastor." Other Puritan petitions followed, including a London radical petition in July, which asked for church reform "according to the rule of God's Holy Word, and agreeable to the example of other reformed Churches." This radical Puritan petition contained almost the exact wording that was to appear in the Solemn League and Covenant in 1643, after the Independents forced the Presbyterians to add the phrase about the Word of God. At the July, 1603 conference of ministers, however, the moderates forced the radicals to delete the phrase about the example of the Reformed Churches before the petition went forward to the king. Those changes are indicative of the compromises with their rivals which Presbyterians had to make when they were weak in 1603 and strong forty years later.[19]

Divided into four sections, the Millenary Petition first treated the church service and ministers. In the church service the moderate Puritans wished to do away with confirmation, the ring in the marriage ceremony, the sign of the cross in baptism, baptism by women, the compulsory use of the cap and surplice, bowing at the name of Jesus, the reading of the Apocrypha, the use of terms like "priest" and "absolution," the strictness of rest on holidays, the profanation of the sabbath, and the "longsomeness" of the service itself, which prevented long sermons from being preached. They wished to add an examination before communion, more edifying church songs and music, and a uniformity of doctrine. Concerning ministers, they advocated the encouragement of all able preachers and the removal of those who could not preach, the prohibition of all nonresidency, the revival of Edward VI's statute allowing ministers to marry, and ministerial subscription to royal supremacy and only those doctrinal articles of the Thirty-Nine which they thought the 1571 subscription statute required.

The Millenary Petition then turned to the two remaining topics. In connection with church livings and maintenance, the moderate Puritans asked for bishops not to hold livings in *commendam*, that is, in addition to their original preferment, not to receive the income of a vacant living. They also requested the avoidance of clerical pluralities, the conveyance of impropriated tithes (annexed only to bishoprics and colleges) to the resident ministers for the old rent, and the taxation of impropriated tithes of laymen at a sixth or a seventh of their value in order to maintain a preaching minister. As to church discipline, the moderate Puritans asked that excommunication not be administered under the name of lay officials or without the consent of one's pastor or for "trifles, and twelve-penny matters." Also, licenses for marriage (without banns asked) should be more cautiously granted, and the "popish canons" for restraints of marriage should be reversed at certain times. Moreover, they asked that the delays from two to seven years of suits in the ecclesiastical courts should be restrained, and the oath ex officio used "more sparingly." The latter request, like the bulk of the document, indicated that radical Puritans had not drafted the Millenary Petition, even though they had been able to insert the vague phrase that discipline was to be "administered according to Christ's own institution," perhaps an indirect reference to the *Form of Prayers* or to the Book of Discipline. As a summary of the grievances of the moderate Puritans, the foregoing is about as complete a list as one could wish. As an agenda for a conference, here were enough issues to keep the king and clergy occupied for months.

Probably with the hope of driving a wedge between the radical and moderate Puritans, James decided to reinforce his image as supreme governor by presiding over a conference of the bishops and a few of the moderate Puritans at Hampton Court in October, 1604. The concluding passage from a royal proclamation, probably drafted by Whitgift and Bancroft, delaying the conference until mid-January, 1605 offered no hope to the radical Puritans, and only a little to the moderate Puritans: "our purpose and resolution ever was, and now is to preserve the estate as well Ecclesiastical as Politic, in such form as we have found it established by the Laws here, reforming only the abuses which we shall apparently find proved."[20] The moderates might have taken a little more hope about the possible outcome had they known that James had altered the original draft of the proclamation at several key points. For example, the king changed earlier references to "abuses" in the Church in one instance to "corruptions" and in another to "scandals," and the bishops' reference to the "constitution and doctrine" of the Anglican Church as "nearest" to the condition of "the Primitive Church" was changed to "near." But, more significant for opening the dimensions of the debate a little wider, the king added in his own hand to the model of the "Primitive Church" the phrase that the moderates had added to the July petition of the radical Puritans: that which is "agreeable to God's word." Agreement with Holy Scriptures as an example or standard for the Church would have been inconceivable as a concept in any Tudor sovereign's proclamation.[21]

The fairly large representation of the Anglican hierarchy, which attended the king on the first day, included the aging Archbishop Whitgift and the son of the great Lord Burghley, Robert Cecil. A small group of four (mostly moderate) Puritans, led by John Reynolds and nominated by the government, received no invitations for the discussions until the plenary session on the second day. With the Puritans not present, James delivered an opening speech in which he thanked God "for bringing him into the promised land, where religion was purely professed, where he sat among grave, learned and reverent men, not, as before, elsewhere, a king without state, without honor, without order, where beardless boys would brave him to his face."[22]

When the king asked what needed to be reformed, the bishops fell upon their knees and beseeched the king not to make any changes in the government or divine service of the Church. They further asserted that any changes would give both Catholics and Puritans grounds for complaining that they had been unjustly persecuted for the past forty years. James responded that there was no state, either ecclesiastical or civil, into which some corruptions might not creep over a period of forty years. After all, said James, if a man has been sick of the pox for forty years, there is no reason to believe that he might not be eventually cured.[23] On some special points raised by the king, the bishops agreed to consider adding the phrase "remission of sins" to the general rubric of absolution, to refuse lay officials any jurisdiction over excommunication, and to restrict the administration of baptism to ministers, thereby excluding women (midwives). After about four hours of discussion, the bishops once again asked the king not to listen to the Puritan ministers, but James said that if he refused to hear them, they could justly call him an unjust king. The Puritans were to have their day in court after forty years of tarrying for the magistrate.

John Reynolds, master of Corpus Christi College at Oxford, began the second day's proceedings with the Puritan presentation of four areas of reform somewhat similar to the four demands of the Millenary Petition: doctrine, the ministry, the Prayer Book, and the government of the Church. On the question of doctrine, Reynolds asked to have the Lambeth Articles incorporated into the Thirty-Nine Articles, thereby indicating that the Puritans wanted to move closer to rigid Calvinism. More specifically, to the wording of article sixteen of the Thirty-Nine Articles ("we may depart from grace given"), Reynolds wished to add the words "yet neither totally nor finally," which Whitgift had earlier accepted from the rigid Calvinists. Bishop Bancroft felt that ministers like Reynolds—who "presumed too much of persisting of grace" by arguing from predestination that "If I shall be saved, I shall be saved"—neglected the element of holiness in a person's life.[24] According to Thomas Sparke, a representative of the Puritan group at the Hampton Court Conference, James "granted, that the words in the sixteenth Article . . . should be explained, by addition of some such words, as whereby plainly it might appear, that it taught not, that the regenerate and justified either totally or finally fall at any time.[25] Despite Bancroft's objection that the incorporation of the Lambeth Articles into the Thirty-Nine would make the composite book too large, James nevertheless agreed to consider the enlargement. The king also agreed to other Puritan demands: a more perfect catechism in place of that in the Prayer Book and that of the late Dean Nowell, a prohibition (supported by Robert Cecil) against the importation of popish books, and a new translation of the Bible providing it contained none of the marginal notes of the Geneva Bible that allowed disobedience to kings. It began to look as if things might go well for the Puritans, at least on matters of doctrine.

The conference next turned to the second and third general areas on Reynold's agenda. In the second area—the ministry—Reynolds asked for able and learned men who could preach the Word of God in all parishes and for the elimination of non-residence and pluralism in all benefices. Bishop Bancroft stressed a praying rather than a preaching ministry with emphasis on the service rather than the sermon, urging the use of homilies until learned men could be placed in every parish. James agreed with the Puritans that a preaching ministry was best. They concluded that learned ministers and maintenance for them should be provided wherever a need appeared, with as few double benefices as possible and with the nonresidents being called home.[26] When Reynolds protested against lay chancellors conducting disciplinary matters such as excommunication, the king argued that the ministers should deal directly with the bishops assisted by the deans.

In the third area—the Prayer Book—Reynolds complained that the Church lately had required many ministers to subscribe to more than just the doctrinal articles, which he believed were the only ones prescribed in the 1571 statute. James did nothing about relaxation of such subscription, nor did he change the wearing of the surplice and the use of the ring in marriage. He agreed to give further thought to the making of the sign of the cross in baptism. Although the king would not ban the reading of the Apocrypha in the church service, he called for the correction of its errors. And although James agreed to have local pastors catechize children, the act of confirmation remained in the hands of the bishops. Otherwise, it would make "every one in his cure to be Bishop." This attack on the authority of the bishops prompted James to state for the first time his famous aphorism: "No bishop, no king."[27]

The last general area on Reynolds' agenda was the crucial question of the government of the Church. The Puritan leader asked for the revival of a form of those prophesyings that Archbishop Grindal had allowed for a short time. Pastors of churches were to be divided into classes that would meet every fortnight to hear and censure the offenses committed within their circuits. Whatever problems the classes could not solve would be referred to an ascending hierarchy of church courts, including episcopal synods made up of the bishop and a presbytery. For a fleeting moment the image of Andrew Melville might well have replaced that of John Reynolds in the king's eye. Visibly angered, the king called this suggested structure nothing else but the "presbytery of Scotland." But John Knewstubs, one of the Puritans present who had been active in the Elizabethan Presbyterian movement, added that Reynolds had meant only a presbytery of ministers and not of laymen. James replied, "When I mean to live under a presbytery, I will go into Scotland again. But while I am in England, I will have Bishops."

> Therefore, content yourselves in this matter, for I will think of this matter seven years before I resolve to admit of a presbytery, and by that time happily I may wax fat, and if then I think it behooveful for me to have any to stir me up and awaken me, I will then have a presbytery by me. Till then I will have the Bishops to govern the church.[28]

But the king had misjudged the Puritan spokesman. The moderate Reynolds was not the radical Melville. What the Puritans wanted was a reduced episcopacy rather than the abolition of episcopacy. What the king feared was a loss of his ecclesiastical supremacy. What he had said earlier, he now repeated: "No bishop, no king."[29]

Although we cannot be sure, a discussion of the oath ex officio and the Court of High Commission was probably the anticlimatic end of the activities for the second day rather than the beginning of activities for the third day. One of the lay lords present, citing Lord Burghley's letter to Archbishop Whitgift in 1584, noted that because of the oath, the defendants in the High Commission ended up accusing themselves and that the Court's proceedings "were like unto the Spanish inquisition."[30] Beset by a very short memory in his last years, Whitgift responded that the High Commission's defendants might refuse to answer questions and that his reply to Burghley, which had been followed by the archbishop's moderation of the Court's persecution, had satisfied Burleigh and would satisfy His Majesty. The argument ended, but the king had already agreed to a review of the High Commission.

On the third and last day, James summarized the conclusions of the Conference, exhorting everyone to a unity within the Church and declaring that "he would have the Bishops to govern and the ministers to obey." In his concluding remarks, the king indicated his disposition of some of the matters upon which he had delayed his decisions the previous day. He agreed that absolution was a "remission of sins," that catechizing was the "examination of the children's faith," that the cross was only a "significative," not an effective, sign in baptism, that the oath ex officio was only for "great and public slanders," and that the High Commission should be made up of "men of honor and good quality."[31] One of the moderate Puritan spokesmen, Lawrence Chaderton, the "pope of Cambridge Puritanism" as master of Emmanuel College, asked James for a special dispensation from the ceremonies of the Church in Lancashire because of their disuse there for some time. Over the opposition of the bishops, James granted the request. When Knewstubs asked for the same dispensation for Suffolk, the king, somewhat annoyed, said that the Lancashire dispensation was "not generally for all." Finally, the king told the bishops to deal gently with their Puritan brethren and "not when they were gone to use fire and sword and make a vacuum lest the Devil enter in."[32] Bishop Bancroft ended the proceedings with a prayer of thanksgiving for James, and the bishops retired to choose committees for the items that James had referred to them.

From the number of concessions James made, the moderate Puritans at the Hampton Court Conference apparently had a considerable success. Examination of the substance of these concessions, however, plus following what happened to them later, reveals quite a different conclusion. First, while the three-day conference touched upon a surprisingly large group of items from the Millenary Petition, another group of items received no attention. The latter included topics relating to the church service, sabbatarianism, marriage (of both priests and laity), maintenance of ministers in *commendam* or by tithes, and delays in the ecclesiastical courts. Second, while several items from the Millenary Petition had been raised, James neither accepted them nor recommended that they be given further consideration. These included the banning of the ring in marriage, the removal of the surplice, the elimination of the Apocrypha, the abolition of confirmation, and subscription only to some of the Articles of Religion. Third, while the Puritans raised two items at Hampton Court that, at least, had not been included in the Millenary Petition, the king finally accepted neither one, the second probably because Bancroft totally opposed it. These were the reintroduction of prophesyings and the grafting of the Lambeth Articles onto the Thirty-Nine Articles. Fourth, while James agreed to several general principles at Hampton Court about the ministry and the ecclesiastical courts, the bishops could not agree about any specific plan to implement them. These included pluralism, nonresidency, and adequate maintenance, as well as the oath ex officio, the Court of High Commission, and the jurisdiction of lay officials over excommunication. Fifth, while James agreed to make a number of changes at the Hampton Court Conference, which the bishops incorporated into a revised edition of the Prayer Book, the proclamation authorizing that Prayer Book stated, despite the "weak and slender proofs" brought forward by the Puritans at Hampton court, that "some small things might rather be explained than changed."[33] These "small things" included absolution defined as a remission of sins, confirmation defined as catechizing of children, baptism administered by ministers only, readings retained from the Apocrypha that Reynolds had specifically asked to be removed, and a new catechism that suggested there might be more valid sacraments than baptism and Holy Communion. Finally, while the Puritans had not asked for a new translation of the Bible in the Millenary Petition, the appearance of the "Authorized Version" in 1611, based upon the revised edition of the Bishops' Bible (1572) and the work of fifty-four translators including Overall, Reynolds, and Chaderton, was the only truly significant result of the Hampton Court Conference. The introductory "Epistle" of the King James or "Authorized Version" blocked out the Erastian position that the Church of England continued to hold between the claims of both Rome and Geneva. All in all, the moderate Puritans finally had very little to show for their confrontation with the bishops. Not surprisingly, the Puritans looked once more, as in Elizabeth's day, for assistance from Parliament.

The Canons of 1604

James called the first session of his first Parliament on March 19, 1604. On that same date Archbishop Bancroft, who had just succeeded to the province of Canterbury upon the death of Whitgift, summoned meetings of the convocations of the clergy. In his opening speech from the throne, James referred to that "Sect" of Presbyterian "Puritans and Novelists" who do not differ from Anglicans except in their "confused form of parity and polity," being "discontented with the present government, & impatient to suffer any superiority."[34] But the king was soon to learn that a number of moderate Puritans in the House of Commons were becoming distressed with the Canterbury Convocation's new canons on the surplice and the sign of the cross in baptism. On April 16, Sir Francis Hastings moved for a select committee to consider the confirmation of the established religion as well as the maintenance of a learned ministry. Much to the consternation of Bancroft, James immediately expressed his hope that the Commons would confer with the Canterbury Convocation before meddling any further in such matters. The Commons found no precedent for such a conference, but they indicated their willingness to meet with the bishops as members of the House of Lords. On April 17, the king sent another message to the Commons, indicating that he wanted an "absolute reformation," presumably meaning that any reform should come through the absolute power of the supreme governor.[35]

About three weeks later, a Commons' committee presented several articles for the bishops' consideration: subscription to the doctrinal Articles of Religion, which they believed were the only ones prescribed in the 1571 statute; admission to the ministry only for persons holding the Bachelor of Arts degree; no more dispensations for pluralism and nonresidence; increases for all ecclesiastical livings under £20 a year; no punishment of faithful ministers for not wearing the surplice or making the sign of the cross in baptism; and official authorization of the Lambeth Articles (which the committee did not press). The conference between the bishops and the Commons achieved nothing, nor did anything come from two bills passed by the Commons against pluralism and for a learned ministry. Parliament passed a statute deleting manslaughter cases from benefit of clergy, however, just as robbers and rapists had lost their protective clerical mantle in Elizabeth's reign. In addition, Parliament revived two statutes from Edward's reign. The first provided that the king (not the bishops) would issue writs for heresy cases in the ecclesiastical courts; and the marriage of the clergy, which Elizabeth had tolerated and the Millenary Petition requested, achieved legal sanction. The second piece of legislation stopped the alienation of episcopal lands, which had been going on with Parliament's approval since 1559.

At the end of the session, some members of the Commons summed up their complaints against the king in the famous "Form of Apology and Satisfaction." The religious section of the Apology chastized the king for having claimed an "absolute power" to alter religion, but it quickly acknowledged James as the supreme governor in church and state. The Apology disclaimed any intention, in a Presbyterian "Puritan or Brownist spirit," to introduce a "parity" or to subvert "the state ecclesiastical as now it standeth." Instead, it indicated a desire only to "reform certain abuses."[36] The tone of the Apology, like that of the moderate Puritans throughout the session and at Hampton Court, was nonbelligerent and conciliatory. Still, Parliament had much less to show for its weeks of deliberation on the question of religion than the Canterbury Convocation.

The Canons of 1604 were the result of the most comprehensive attempt ever made by the Anglican hierarchy to codify the Church's constitutional position. Reformers had raised many of the issues as far back as Thomas Cromwell's day. Of the 141 canons, ninety-seven were old and forty-four were new, but nearly one half of the new canons dealt only with the Church courts, while more than two-thirds of the old canons dealt with both church ritual and church discipline. The ninety-seven old canons came from a variety of sources: injunctions, advertisements, articles, and earlier canons. Three of the canons originated in Cromwell's Injunctions of 1536, five in his Injunctions of 1538, and twelve in Edward VI's Injunctions of 1547. They surfaced because they had been retained in Elizabeth's Injunctions of 1559. In addition to twenty-five canons taken from the Injunctions of 1559, twelve canons came from the *Advertisements* of 1566, and twenty-five canons came from the Canons of 1571. Also, nine of Whitgift's Articles of 1583 and twelve of the Canons of 1585, which were repeated *verbatim* in the Canons of 1597, entered the final codification. While these figures are somewhat deceptive, since some of the Canons of 1604 embodied two or more topics from more than one earlier source, the bulk of the final document was a consolidation of the piecemeal documents written at various intervals throughout Elizabeth's reign.[37]

What was the nature of the forty-four new canons? The twelve opening canons dealt with the membership of the Church, mostly in a negative way. The opposition to the Anglican Church by the Puritans and Catholics had necessitated new efforts to establish an ecclesiastical uniformity. Other canons, especially those dealing with the Church courts, for the first time provided penalties for offenders who disobeyed Church law. As a matter of fact, many of the new canons enumerated specific penalties ranging from penance to excommunication. In some of the new canons, fashioned with the Puritans in mind, the Anglican hierarchy took uncompromising stands on subscription, vestments, and the Holy Table, while yet other new canons attempted accommodation with the Puritans on sabbatarianism, pluralism and nonresidence, and the sign of the cross in baptism. It remained to be seen whether or not these accommodations would keep the Puritans in the Church.

Divided into several sections, the Canons of 1604, both old and new, dealt with the Church of England, divine service and the sacraments, ministers, church accoutrements, and church courts. The section on the Church reaffirmed the Crown's "Ancient jurisdiction over the state ecclesiastical," and provided for the excommunication of those who impugned the supremacy of any of the Thirty-Nine Articles, the lawful rules, ceremonies, and government of the Church, as well as those who separated from the Church or maintained conventicles.

The section on divine service specified the keeping of Sundays and holy days with "godly and sober conversation" (but without the performance of any work as Elizabeth's Injunctions had allowed); authorized the wearing of copes in all cathedral and collegiate churches for Holy Communion in accordance with the *Advertisements* (but surplices were sufficient when there was no Holy Communion); required kneeling for the reception of Holy Communion (but omitted the qualifying statement of Knox's Black Rubric in 1559); and, in the longest canon of them all, called for the use of the sign of the cross in baptism (yet "purged from all popish superstition and error," as Jewel's *Apology* had stated in principle, and without being any part of the "substance of that sacrament," as James' concluding speech at Hampton Court had implied in particular).

In the section on ministers, canon 36, drawn heavily from Whitgift's Articles, required every clergyman to subscribe "willingly and *ex animo*" to the royal supremacy, the Book of Common Prayer, and "all and every" one of the Thirty-Nine Articles. Other canons in this section stated that no ministers should hold pluralities, except those with Master of Arts degrees, able to reside in each of his benefices a "reasonable time" each year; that ministers should wear a decent surplice with either academic hoods or black, silkless tippets; and that every child should render an account of its faith "according to the Catechism" in the Prayer Book before the bishop will "lay his hands upon" it during confirmation—a modification toward the bishops' position at Hampton Court.

In the section on church accoutrements, each church was to provide a Bible, the Prayer Book, the two books of homilies (not Erasmus' *Paraphrases* as in the Elizabethan injunctions), a font of stone for baptism, and a decent communion table for the celebration of Holy Communion ("within the church or chancel" for the convenience of communicants—a slight modification of the Elizabethan Injunctions). In the section on church courts, only those having special authority could issue marriage licenses without publication of the banns.

In summary, then, most of the Canons of 1604 took positions that the Anglican hierarchy had consistently held. Where a few accommodations were made, they were so meager that they almost seemed an affront to Puritans. On September 6, 1604, the king, in accordance with the authority given by the Henrician statute for the Submission of the Clergy, approved the canons, and they became Church law. The York Convocation did not ratify the canons until the following year.[38]

On July 16, James issued a proclamation to force compliance with the Canons of 1604. Reviewing the background of the canons, the proclamation stated that "no well grounded matter" had appeared at Hampton Court as to why the state of the Church of England should be altered in any material point, nor had the protagonists there greatly insisted on change after the king and bishops had spoken. It also noted that the Commons had recently renewed a discussion of the earlier issues, particularly in a conference with the bishops, but the results once again had shown no reason to change the Prayer Book or the Church discipline, and so the Commons, too, had desisted from requesting further change. Everyone was admonished, therefore, to conform without listening to "certain Ministers, who under pretended Zeal of Reformation, are the chief Authors of Divisions and Sects among our people." If people did not conform, the proclamation continued, then "what untractable men do not perform upon admonition, they must be compelled unto by Authority" of "the Supreme power resting in our hands, by God's ordinance." Accordingly, the ministers had until November 30 either to conform or to be deprived. Finally, in a gesture that would have been uncharacteristic of Queen Elizabeth, the proclamation enjoined "all Archbishops, Bishops, and other Ecclesiastical persons, to do their uttermost endeavors by conferences, agreements, persuasions, and by all other ways of love and gentleness to reclaim all that be in the Ministry, to the obedience of our Church Laws."[39]

Puritan petitions and manifestoes throughout October and November showed considerable opposition to the canons. On December 10, therefore, the Privy Council ordered Bancroft to take action against those who would not conform. About two weeks later, the archbishop addressed a circular letter to the bishops, directing that all curates and lecturers should subscribe to canon 36, whereas beneficed clergy were only asked to conform. Of the four Puritans at the Hampton Court Conference, John Reynolds refused to subscribe but did conform, John Knewstubs and Lawrence Chaderton went unmolested, and Thomas Sparke admitted his errors at the king's personal entreaty. The Council ordered the parliamentary Puritan, Sir Francis Hastings, who had drawn up a petition in favor of the deprived ministers from Northamptonshire, to retire to his country estate. A bill to restrain the execution of the canons passed in the Commons but failed in the Lords during the second session of James' first Parliament (May, 1606). The number of ministers deprived has been estimated as high as 300 and as low as forty-nine. The actual number was probably about eighty, perhaps ninety.[40] It was not high enough to run the risk of uniting the Puritans through heavy persecution nor low enough to indicate that the government was not serious about conformity.

The adoption of the Canons of 1604 nearly completed the Jacobean Church consolidation, insofar as the Puritans were concerned. The Millenary Petition had conveniently listed many of the grievances that the moderate Puritans had been collecting for over half a century. By agreeing to act on the petition, James had given the Puritan grievances a dignity that Elizabeth would never have deigned to give. The Hampton Court Conference had provided a forum for moderate Puritans and the Anglican hierarchy to air their differences in the presence of the king. By debating the religious issues with both parties, James had permitted that personal confrontation with the Crown which Elizabeth had scrupulously avoided. He also promoted a meeting between the parties that had been only mildly approached by a Lambeth disputation staged by Leicester in 1584. The first session of James' first Parliament had tried to do something about the Puritan failures at Hampton Court. By suggesting that a Commons' committee meet with the bishops, James had presided over an unprecedented (albeit unfruitful) attempt to reach some agreement between Parliament and the convocations. The Canons of 1604 had resolved most of the issues which James or the various ecclesiastical committees, including the one to revise the Prayer Book, had not decided at Hampton Court. By relying upon the convocations of the clergy to make a thorough codification of the canon law, James had been able to forego the unilateral device of employing royal injunctions that had characterized the reigns of Henry VIII, Edward VI, Mary, and Elizabeth. Instead, he had been able to implement at long last that thorough revision of the canon law, which, despite the drafting of the Henrician Canons of 1535 and Cranmer's *Reformatio Legum Ecclesiasticarum*, had never been fully carried out in accordance with its first authorization in the Henrician statute for the Submission of the Clergy. In all the foregoing procedural matters, the king had departed from Elizabethan, indeed Tudor, practice. But the substantive results of all these actions meant that conditions were essentially the same as those which had prevailed at the end of the preceding reign.

The Jacobean Exiles

Although the Hampton Court Conference had considered a number of points of theology, one concept, the idea of the covenant, had received no mention, either as a covenant of grace or a covenant of works. The latter covenant was designed for everyone, whether they were of the elect or not. Formulated in Heidelberg in the 1560s, the covenant of works was closely identified with the law, especially the Ten Commandments. Every son of Adam and daughter of Eve—including the unregenerate or immoral majority—was thereby brought into a legal relationship with God. A Puritan preacher found the covenant of works a wonderful way in which to enforce a moral discipline upon all members of English society and, perhaps, through their obedient striving, to evince credentials of righteousness.[41]

The covenant of grace, on the other hand, existed only for those who were God's elect. As a concept, it had developed earlier from two separate streams, both of which antedated the 1560s. The first stream flowed from Zwingli and Tyndale, stressing a *conditional* covenant of grace as a mutual agreement between God and man, which placed a part of the responsibility for its fulfillment upon man, the sacraments being vows of obedience to God. The second stream flowed from Calvin, stressing an *absolute* covenant of grace as God's promise to man that the covenant had already been fulfilled by the sovereignty of God, and that the sacraments served as signs or seals of that continuing fulfillment. In both types of the covenant of grace, God's grace is overwhelming; but in the conditional covenant, grace *enables* the Saints to repent and believe, whereas in the absolute covenant grace *moves* the Saints to faith and repentance. The Calvinist absolute covenant of grace had become more influential after its incorporation into the Geneva Bible in 1560, but the Separatist Robert Browne and the Presbyterian Thomas Cartwright kept the Zwingli-Tyndale conditional covenant of grace very much alive.[42]

In the writings of William Perkins (*A Golden Chain*, 1591) and the writings of John Downame, among others, one can find a disquisition on both the covenant of works and the covenant of grace. Perkins, who had argued at Cambridge against Overall's contention for universal salvation, seemed to embrace both streams of the covenant of grace. For instance, he wrote that "the covenant of grace is that whereby God freely promising Christ and his benefits, exacts again of man that he would receive Christ and repent of his sins." But on the same page he also wrote that the covenant of grace is "a testament or will" as well, in which "we do not so much offer, or promise any great matter to God, as in a manner only receive."[43]

In the early seventeenth century, however, the two streams (conditional and absolute), which had come together in the writings of Perkins and Downame, appeared mostly as one or the other stream in the writings of some of Perkins' successors, including William Ames and John Preston. Ames, later followed by such Independents as John Owen and Thomas Goodwin, leaned toward the absolute covenant of grace. Preston, later followed by such Presbyterians as Richard Baxter and Samuel Rutherford, leaned toward the conditional covenant of grace. Although none of the Jacobean divines tried to extend the conditional covenant of grace between God and men to a social contract between the ruler and subjects based on mutual political limitations, Downame, for one, used the covenant of works in relation to Englishmen, as it had been for ancient Israel, as a theological basis to fuse "public order with moral reform." The time would come, however, in the late 1630s and early 1640s when the conditional covenant would be useful to those theologians who opposed the Crown and supported the Scottish National Covenant or the Solemn League and Covenant of the Scots and the English.[44]

Puritan believers in covenant theology, a number of whom left England for Holland because of the religious climate after the promulgation of the Canons of 1604, included Ames, William Bradshaw, and Henry Jacob. These semi-Separatists, as their contemporaries sometimes called them, accepted an ecclesiastical counterpart of covenant theology, the church covenant. In 1605, Jacob claimed that a true visible church is only a "free mutual consent of Believers joining and covenanting to live as Members of a holy Society."[45] The semi-Separatist Puritans tended to follow a path that ultimately led to the non-Separating Congregationalism of New England or the Independency of old England.

Presbyterians and Anglicans opposed the idea of a church covenant, prevalent among the Brownists in the 1580s, largely because both Presbyterians and Anglicans were committed to churches for everyone. Like the Presbyterians and the Separatists, the semi-Separatists believed in the election of church officers by the congregation rather than a patron's nomination or a bishop's investiture. Like the Separatists, they had no use for any superior ecclesiastical jurisdiction, whether it was the Anglican hierarchy of archbishops and bishops or the Presbyterian hierarchy of church courts, although semi-Separatists did believe in "voluntary" synods of churches later associated with non-Separating Congregationalism and Independency. Unlike the Separatists, however, many of whom held that the Church of England was a false church, semi-Separatists did not believe in separating from the Anglican communion. In his book, *English Puritanism* (1605), Bradshaw admitted that the civil magistrate ought to have supreme power over all the churches within his dominions, but, as a member of a particular congregation (and this had been the Presbyterian position as well) the king could be censured, suspended, and denounced by the congregation. Conversely, ecclesiastical officers could be punished if they intruded upon the rights of the civil authority.[46] Following a lengthy sojourn in Amsterdam, Jacob returned to England to set up in Southwark what was probably the first semi-Separatist congregation in England.

After the death or defection of the first generation of Brownists and Barrowists under Elizabeth, a second generation of Separatists under James decided to leave England for Holland. Among these Separatists who believed in a covenant of grace and a covenanted church were Francis Johnson, John Smyth, and John Robinson. Although Johnson had led a Separatist church at Amsterdam during the later years of Elizabeth's reign, at the same time two congregations of Separatists flourished in a triangle along the borders of Yorkshire, Nottinghamshire, and Lincolnshire. The leader of the Gainsborough congregation of Separatists was John Smyth, and two of his church members were Thomas Helwys and John Murton, future leaders of the Baptists. The teacher of the nearby Scrooby congregation of Separatists was John Robinson, who had studied with Perkins and Whitaker at Cambridge; two of his followers were William Brewster, the future leader of the Pilgrims, and William Bradford, the future governor of Plymouth colony.

In 1606, the Gainsborough congregation left for Amsterdam, and the Scrooby congregation settled in Leyden shortly afterwards. According to their historian, Bradford, the Separatists had been forced to flee from England because some of them "were taken and clapped up in prison" while "others had their houses beset and watched night and day."[47] The Scrooby-Leyden congregation was Separatist in the sense that its members constituted a covenanted church of believers separate from nonbelievers. It was also Separatist in the sense that it felt no binding tie with the Anglican Church. But the Scrooby-Leyden congregation was not Separatist in the sense that it advocated a complete separation of church and state. Robinson, who was an exponent of the absolute, rather than the conditional covenant of grace, contended that a magistrate may "use his lawful power lawfully for the furtherance of Christ's Kingdom and Laws." But such power, he added, was extremely limited since magistrates had "no power against the laws, doctrine, and religion of Christ."[48] The followers of John Robinson signed the Mayflower Compact while en route to the Plymouth colony.

From the ranks of the English Separatists abroad, and specifically from the Gainsborough-Amsterdam congregation, there soon emerged still another group of Puritans, the Baptists. The Baptists included Smyth, Helwys, Murton, and Leonard Busher. These men came to believe that the best way to enter into a covenant with God or with a congregation was through the baptism of all professed believers. Since repentance and faith must precede baptism, according to Smyth's long *Confession of Faith* (c. 1612), there was no point in baptizing infants, especially since infant baptism was not even mentioned in the New Testament. But, Smyth believed, God had given those adults old enough to understand baptism freedom of will either to receive or to reject his grace. For God predestined no man to eternal damnation nor was he the author of sin. Such beliefs in general redemption and the resistability of grace led these Baptists (called General Baptists because of their rejection of Calvin's principle of election for only a few) to a defense of liberty of conscience for all—including Jews, Turks, and pagans. In article eighty-four of his *Confession of Faith*, Smyth wrote that the civil magistrate was not "to meddle with religion, or matters of conscience, to force and compel men to this or that form of religion or doctrine; but to leave the Christian religion free to every man's conscience, and to handle only civil transgressions, injuries, and wrongs of men against man."[49] Smyth believed that if the civil magistrate persecuted any man for erroneous religious beliefs, that man might be unable to participate in God's plan for his salvation. Helwys, who upon Smyth's death in 1612 brought the General Baptist congregation in Amsterdam to Spitalfields outside London, believed that the tares should be allowed to grow alongside the wheat, not because it was impossible to distinguish them from the wheat, as Roger Williams (a Particular or Calvinist Baptist) argued later, but because they might actually *become* wheat.[50] The General Baptists went further than any of the other Separatists, including Browne, by standing for a complete separation of church and state.

The Jacobean exiles went to the continent of Europe under pressure from the Crown just as the Marian exiles had gone a half century earlier. Instead of turning to the cities of Switzerland and western Germany, however, the Jacobean exiles chose the cities of Holland in order to find a measure of religious toleration. Unlike the Marian exiles, who opted for either the Erastian conception of church–state relationships as at Frankfort or for the theocratic conception as at Geneva, a few of the Jacobean exiles were inclined toward or actually arrived at a complete separation of church and state. Some of the Jacobean exiles later returned to England, ultimately to influence events there, just as the Marian exiles had done though more quickly and more dramatically. But some of them moved on to the New World to settle permanently, just as the Laudian exiles of the 1630s were to do.

By several standards of judgment James dealt most successfully with the English Puritans. He silenced discussion of the goals of radical Presbyterian Puritans and made practically no concessions to the moderate Puritans at Hampton Court. With the enforcement of the Canons of 1604, a number of semi-Separatist or Separatist Puritans left the country, some of them permanently. Despite this consolidation and obvious strengthening of the Anglican Church's historic position, especially through the constitutional changes of the canons, there were some ominous signs for the future. While the Puritan movement in England, especially Presbyterianism, would reach the nadir of its power and influence vis-à-vis the Crown in the next decade or two, the dispersion of the semi-Separatist and Separatist movements abroad and at home finally led to the Independent and sectarian movements that transformed church and state in the 1640s and 1650s.

James I and the Catholics

In the very early years of his reign, James showed that same willingness to reach an accommodation with at least some of the Catholics as he had tried to do at the outset with the moderate Puritans. Although he continued in May, 1603 to collect recusancy fines, thereby resulting in the Bye Plot—an unsuccessful attempt to seize James and force him to grant toleration to all Catholics—James agreed to remit the penal laws against Catholics because most of them disassociated themselves from the Bye Plot. In the autumn of 1603, and for some months thereafter, James proposed to Pope Clement VIII the calling of an ecumenical council, a kind of international Hampton Court Conference, for the purpose of uniting Catholics and Protestants into one universal Church. By renouncing the Puritan extremists on the one side and the Jesuits on the other, James hoped that some kind of religious and political compromise might be achieved in which the king would recognize the pope as the spiritual head of Christendom if the pope would renounce all temporal claims to power.

In his opening speech before the first session of Parliament on March 19, 1604, James declared that his mind was free from the persecution of Catholics. He even said, "I acknowledge the Roman Church to be our Mother Church, although defiled with some infirmities and corruptions." However, he stated two points of which the Catholic clergy, as distinguished from the Catholic laity, were chiefly guilty. The first was the claim that the pope has "an Imperial civil power over all Kings and Emperors, dethroning and decrowning Princes with his foot as pleaseth him," and the second was the assassination and murder of kings.[51] This speech encouraged Parliament to put into execution in June all of the penal laws passed during Elizabeth's reign against the Jesuits and secular priests. But, once again, the government did not stringently enforce the penal laws, and James told the Catholic Sir Thomas Tresham that the recusancy fines would not be collected. Besides, England's lengthy war with the king of Spain ended in the late summer of 1604.

Before long, however, a number of irritations with the Catholics, in part stemming from excesses encouraged by his lenient policy and the false news of his own imminent conversion to Catholicism, provoked James to declare in Council in February, 1605 his utter detestation of this "superstitious religion." A royal proclamation issued on February 22, not unlike Elizabeth's proclamation of November 5, 1602, ordered all Jesuit and seminary priests to leave the realm by March 19. Such reversal of policy led to the "Powder-Treason" or the Gunpowder Plot.

Robert Catesby, a Catholic gentleman, formulated the Gunpowder Plot as early as 1603, and brought several other Catholics, mostly gentry, into his conspiracy: Thomas Percy, a cousin of Robert Cecil's great rival, the earl of Northumberland; his cousin, Thomas Winter; his friend, Thomas Wright; and Guy Fawkes, a soldier returned from the Spanish Netherlands. The plotters placed barrels of gunpowder under the Parliament House in order to blow up the king, the queen, Prince Henry, the councillors, the Lords, and Commons at the opening of the second session of James' first Parliament on November 5, 1605. The Catholic gentry of the Midlands were to gather after the explosion in a hunting party at Dunchurch in Warwickshire to formulate plans to take over the government. Work began in London during May, 1604 on a subterranean passage under the chamber of the House of Lords, but later the plotters rented a house whose cellar connected with that of Parliament House. To this cellar Fawkes brought some thirty-six barrels of gunpowder.

As the work progressed, the number of conspirators expanded to thirteen, including Francis Tresham, son of Sir Thomas Tresham. Tresham probably betrayed the plot by writing a warning letter, delivered on October 26, to his brother-in-law, Lord Monteagle, one of the Catholic peers who would have been present at the opening of Parliament on November 5. Monteagle promptly informed Robert Cecil (now Lord Salisbury), who decided to postpone a search until later. Only two days before the scheduled opening of Parliament, the king saw the letter. A thorough search of the cellar of the Parliament House on November 4 resulted in the arrest of Fawkes, who stood guard over the gunpowder. Four days later at Holbeach House in Staffordshire, troops of the sheriff killed Catesby and Wright, mortally wounded Percy, and took Winter prisoner after having wounded him. Those who survived, including Fawkes, were tortured, tried, and then executed for high treason. Father Garnet, the head of the English Jesuits, revealed at his trial that he had learned of the plot only under the seal of confession, *sub sigillo*, which should have saved him from execution, but it did not.

A couple of unanswered questions about the Gunpowder Plot have caused some difficulties with the traditional interpretation. For example, where did the gunpowder, under a government monopoly after 1601, come from? Or again, why did Salisbury wait so long before taking any action after he first discovered the existence of the plot? Such questions and the lack of crucial information at critical junctures have allowed some historians to speculate that either Cecil instigated the plot with the aid of *agents provocateurs*, such as Fawkes, because he wanted to convince James that Catholics could not be trusted, or, like Walsingham under Elizabeth, having become aware of it fairly early, he encouraged it until he could expose it. Although there is a certain plausibility in the latter conjecture, there is no conclusive evidence that Salisbury employed either of these methods. Surely, however, the plot inspired terror in the king and provoked horror among many people.[52]

When James finally addressed the second session of his first Parliament, he thanked God "for the great and miraculous Delivery he hath at this time granted to me, and to you all." In addition, he stressed that only one religion in the world thought that "it was lawfull, or rather meritorious (as the *Romish* Catholics call it) to murder Princes or people for quarrel of Religion." Parliament reacted by passing two severe measures against popish recusants. One of the two recusancy statutes added new disabilities in order to prevent any future dangers. For instance, it included that clause prohibiting Catholic recusants from educating their own children, which had been deleted from the 1593 Act Against Popish Recusants. In addition, convicted recusants could not practice law and medicine, serve in the army or navy, or hold minor political offices. Although they could keep weapons necessary for self-defense, they had to surrender any gunpowder they possessed.

The preamble of the second recusancy statute stated that

> many [of] his Majesty's subjects that adhere in their hearts to the Popish religion . . . by the wicked and devilish counsel of Jesuits, seminarians, and other like persons dangerous to the Church and State . . . are ready to entertain and execute any treasonable conspiracies and practices, as evidently appears by that more than barbarous and horrible attempt to have blown up with gunpowder the . . . House of Parliament assembled.[53]

Enacting clauses of the second recusancy act stiffened earlier Elizabethan penalties. Specifically, they added another condition to the Elizabethan Act of Uniformity's requirement to attend church services: the obligation to receive the Lord's Supper at least yearly. The enacting clauses also allowed the king to refuse to take from recusants £20 a month, the statute of 1581 penalty, so that he might seize two-thirds of their lands, as a 1587 statute authorized, if the fine were not paid. But most important of all, the second recusancy statute directed Catholic recusants to take not only the Oath of Supremacy of 1559 but also a new Oath of Allegiance. Salisbury mentioned the two new recusancy statutes, as well as the plot that provoked them, in a royal proclamation of June 10, 1606, which, like a proclamation of February 22, 1604, called for all Jesuits and seminary priests to leave the country. In 1610, Parliament passed still another act, which instructed all subjects over eighteen to take the Oath of Allegiance.

The Oath of Allegiance was Bancroft's version of several forms of submission that Catholic priests had proposed at various times over the last ten years or so. Their central theme was a promise of loyalty to the king without detracting from the spiritual authority of the papacy. In that sense, the new oath was less comprehensive than the old Oath of Supremacy, which called for the denial of all authority of anyone outside the realm in spiritual affairs. Specifically, the Oath of Allegiance required all Catholic recusants to declare that King James I was the "lawful and rightful King of this Realm" to whom they would "bear faith and true allegiance." The oath further required all Catholic recusants to declare "without any equivocation or mental reservation whatsoever" that the pope did not have any power to depose the king, to dispose of his dominions, to invade his realm, to discharge his subjects of their allegiance and obedience, or to give license to anyone to bear arms, to raise tumults, or to bring harm against His Majesty's "Royal Person." Interestingly enough, James excluded from the provisions of the oath, against the wishes of the Commons, any denunciation of the pope's spiritual power to excommunicate a prince—a concession which neither Henry VIII nor Elizabeth would ever have allowed.

In addition to requiring Catholics to deny the papal claim of deposing or murdering an excommunicated king, the Commons inserted a clause in the oath which required Catholic recusants to swear that they did "abhor, detest, and abjure" such doctrines as "impious and heretical."[54] Since Paul V held these doctrines, the implication of the last three words was in effect to ask Catholic recusants to swear that the pope was a heretic. After initially opposing the Oath of Supremacy, Archpriest Blackwell finally defended it on the grounds that papal deposition could not be carried out anyway. But on September 22, the pope, at the urging of Robert Parsons, denounced the Oath of Allegiance as containing many things contrary to salvation. A second papal brief reiterated the first, and the pope, after asking Cardinal Robert Bellarmine to convince the archpriest of the error of his ways for having taken the oath, removed Blackwell from his position.

The king and his churchmen now became involved in a pamphlet warfare with a group of theologians from various parts of western Europe. In his *Apology for the Oath of Allegiance* (1608), James' reply to the two papal briefs as well as Cardinal Bellarmine's letter to Blackwell, the king asserted that the oath was merely civil, "ordained for making difference between the civilly obedient Papists, and the perverse disciples of the Powder-Treason." Then James asked of Bellarmine: "can there be one word found in all that Oath, tending or sounding to matter of Religion?"[55] Obviously not! In his reply to the king, Bellarmine denied that the oath was merely civil, stating his view that anything affecting the papacy was a matter of faith.

But Bellarmine also set forth an attenuated version of the medieval doctrine of the plenitude of papal power. Whereas Boniface VIII had contended in his bull, *Unam Sanctam*, that all spiritual and temporal power belonged to the pope, Bellarmine distinguished between the direct power of the papacy over the church and the indirect power of the papacy in temporal affairs. The pope should use his temporal power, Bellarmine conceded, only in very exceptional cases when the salvation of souls was at stake. This line of argument subsumes the indirect temporal power of the papacy under the direct spiritual power of the papacy where—as with the old belief in the deposition of kings by Rome—it was regarded as a doctrine essential to salvation. In a revised edition of his *Apology* called *A Premonition* (1609), addressed to the sovereigns of western Europe, James denied Bellarmine's doctrine of the *potestas indirecta* because, like John Wycliffe, James regarded the hierocratic claims of the papacy as incompatible with divine right monarchy. At the same time Lancelot Andrewes, now bishop of Chichester, wrote at James' request a lengthy reply to Bellarmine, *Tortura Torti* (1609). Bellarmine had remarked to Blackwell that the authority of the head of the Church of England had been transferred from the successor of St. Peter to the successor of Henry VIII. Andrewes now replied that Henry VIII's recovery of the supremacy of the Church from the pope had given English sovereigns the ecclesiastical supremacy only—the *potestas jurisdictionis*—whereas the spiritual supremacy—the *potestas ordinis*—as well as points of doctrine and modes of worship, had reverted to the archbishops and bishops.[56] Other papal supporters included the Jesuits, Robert Parsons and Martin Becanus; other royal supporters included Isaac Casaubon and John Donne. Donne's *Pseudo-Martyr* (1610), for example, argued that *"nothing required in this Oath, violates the Pope's spiritual jurisdiction; And that the clauses of swearing that Doctrine to be Heretical, is no usurping upon his spiritual right."*[57] The assassination of King Henry IV of France in 1610 by a Catholic fanatic gave the issues of this controversy an ironic poignancy.

While the second session of James' first Parliament addressed the Oath of Supremacy, the Canterbury Convocation debated some canons on *civil* government at the king's request. To the anti-Catholic George Abbot, who was appointed archbishop of Canterbury in 1611, James explained his request: "I was of the mind to call my clergy together, to satisfy not so much me, as the world about us, of the justness of my owning the Hollanders at this time."[58] In other words, he wondered how far a Christian and Protestant king might go in helping his Dutch neighbors shake off their obedience to the king of Spain, a tyrannical and oppressive sovereign. Both convocations answered the king's question in a series of canons known as *Bishop Overall's Convocation-Book*—a work that was not published until 1690. Canon twenty-eight affirmed the wickedness of eschewing obedience to a sovereign as well as the unlawfulness of a king invading his neighbor's territory. However, canon twenty-eight concluded that when any "new Forms of Government, begun by Rebellion, are after thoroughly settled, the Authority in them" is of God.[59]

What must have seemed to the bishops to have been a happy solution to the king's dilemma about the Dutch rebellion against Spain seemed to James to reduce his own claim to his subjects' obedience from *de jure* to *de facto*. He had claimed to be king by divine right, not by conquest, and the *Convocation-Book* made no clear statement of the divine right theory of monarchy. The line of reasoning adopted in canon twenty-eight, James wrote to Abbot, meant that "if the king of Spain should return to claim his old pontifical right to my kingdom, you leave me to seek for others to fight for it; for you tell us upon the matter beforehand, his authority is God's authority, if he prevail."[60] Such an argument, justifying tyranny as by God's authority, James wrote, approximated the view that makes God the author of evil. Like Elizabeth, James wished to preserve the right to fuel fires in other people's houses without allowing them to do the same in his own. The king did not approve the Canons of 1606 as he had the Canons of 1604, even though *Bishop Overall's Convocation-Book* repeatedly asserted the authority of the king over the pope in ecclesiastical and temporal affairs, and even though canon twenty-six specifically disapproved of the right of "high priests" to depose kings.

Some striking similarities between the reigns of Elizabeth and James regarding the treatment of Catholics suggest a considerable degree of continuity. The differences, with one important exception, are less striking, but do suggest the modest changes that had taken place. On the whole, Jacobean policies toward the Catholics, like Jacobean policies toward the Puritans, offered a consolidation of Elizabethan practice rather than innovation and new departures.

   Both sovereigns held the high position that the persecution of Catholicism was carried out for political rather than spiritual reasons. Some of Elizabeth's statutes and proclamations, as we have seen, seriously infringed upon the spiritual rights of the papacy and English Catholics. Since James' first Parliament confirmed all of Elizabeth's anti-Catholic statutes, besides adding a few of its own, and since the king issued his own proclamations which, like Elizabeth's, simply expelled Jesuits and secular priests from the land, James, too, can be charged with infringing spiritual rights. Indeed, the Oath of Allegiance was largely a formal articulation of what Lord Burleigh had been arguing in his *Execution of Justice*. But the Jacobean government led people to believe that the Oath of Allegiance would be sufficient for any priest or lay person, even though theoretically the requirement to take the Elizabethan Oath of Supremacy still remained. The Oath of Allegiance, despite the inclusion of the phrase "impious and heretical," was more tolerant than the Oath of Supremacy.

   Also, James' strategy was essentially the same as Elizabeth's. That strategy called for the government to divide and weaken the Catholic opposition over the question of political allegiance so that they would be more vulnerable to prosecution. Whereas Elizabeth succeeded in drawing a very large number of Catholic laity away from their priests, whether Jesuits or seculars, James succeeded in drawing away many of the seculars from the Jesuits. The prosecution of Catholics continued in James' reign with some forty of them, mostly seminarians and Jesuits, losing their lives and many imprisoned. This is a considerably smaller number than those Catholics who lost their lives under Elizabeth, but the threat of invasion from Spain came to an end after 1604. Still, James, like Elizabeth, wanted to help the Dutch, but, also like her, he did not want to derogate from his own sense of the royal prerogative in religious affairs, as the Canons of 1606 clearly indicate.

Even the Catholic response under James had its points of similarity with the response during Elizabeth's reign, whether at the official or semiofficial level. In both reigns, the Catholic hierarchy modified its official position in order to withstand the persecution of the government. Whereas the *Responsio* modified the execution of the Elizabethan papal bull of excommunication until such time as deposition could be put into effect, so did Cardinal Bellarmine's doctrine of the *potestas indirecta* modify the papal right of deposition for circumstances most unusual in nature. In both reigns, a number of Catholic plots, usually with some kind of semiofficial sanction, plagued the government. Elizabeth, of course, had her share, including the Ridolfi, the Babington, and the Throckmorton Plots, whereas James had the Bye and Gunpowder Plots. It is quite possible, however, that the Gunpowder Plot, which embellished a long-standing Catholic tradition of plotting against the government, may have ultimately done more than any other preceding event to undermine the Catholic cause in England. In succeeding decades, two ritualistic events came to symbolize the historic association of Catholicism with treason: the traditional search of Parliament by the yeomen of the guard on the occasion of its annual opening, and the special thanksgiving service for the fifth of November, abolished only in 1859.

The Church and the Common Law

The common law judges, like the Puritans and the Catholics, challenged the bishops and the king on religious matters. In his *Certain Articles of Abuses* (1605), dubbed the *Articuli Cleri* by Edward Coke, Archbishop Bancroft appealed to the king against the practice in the common law courts of issuing writs of prohibition against proceedings in ecclesiastical courts, which the common law judges regarded as properly falling under their own jurisdiction. As the *Articuli Cleri* pointed out, in forty-five years of Elizabeth's reign, there had been 482 writs of prohibition issued against the Court of Arches, but in only two years of James' reign there had already been eighty-two (a 400 percent increase). With considerable exaggeration, Bancroft concluded that "the authority of his majesty in causes ecclesiastical" had been "so impeached by prohibitions" that it was "in effect thereby almost extinguished."[61] The common law judges, according to Bancroft, were perfectly willing to leave testamentary and matrimonial cases in the hands of the church courts, but cases involving the collection of tithes, which dealt with property, were the object of many writs of prohibition.

Bancroft's interest in prohibitions stemmed from his attempt to improve the economic status of the clergy—a reform which the Puritans also advocated in the Millenary Petition—by bringing suits in the church courts for the recovery of impropriated tithes, the restitution of payment of tithes in kind, and the restoration of tithes commuted into fixed money payments. When Bancroft complained in the *Articuli Cleri* that writs of prohibition had been improperly used in violation of provisions of the Edward VI tithe statute

(1549) for double and treble penalties, among other things, Coke and the common law judges responded that they "never heard it excepted unto heretofore that any statute should be expounded by any other than the judges of the land." And when Bancroft argued that the same Edwardian statute provided that only ecclesiastical judges should hear tithe cases, the common law judges replied that the "temporal courts have always granted prohibitions . . . in discharge of tithes, or the manner of tithing." In fact, as Coke pointed out, the same Edwardian statute that Bancroft cited stated that prohibitions had been used for some time and actually had provided for their use under certain circumstances.[62] The archbishop reported to the lower house of Convocation on November 21, 1606, that the king had agreed to put a restraint upon prohibitions. Two years later, when Bancroft brought out his *Articuli Cleri* once again, the king would not support him because of the great strength of the common law judges. Meanwhile, James had raised Coke to the post of chief justice of the Court of Common Pleas. The appointment was a blow to the Church's quest for independence.

Although the common law judges had recognized the legality of the Court of High Commission in Cawdrey's case, they had also attacked this highest of ecclesiastical courts through writs of prohibition. In one such case Nicholas Fuller, a Puritan lawyer, obtained a writ of prohibition from the Court of King's Bench in July, 1604, after having been arraigned for "heresy, schism, and erroneous opinion" before the Court of High Commission. On hearing about Fuller, James wrote to the Earl of Salisbury, "whensoever the ecclesiastical dignity shall be turned in contempt and begin to vanish in this kingdom, the kings thereof shall not long prosper in their government and the monarchy shall fall in ruin, which I pray God I may not live to see."[63] King's Bench issued a consultation in October which in effect returned the case to the High Commission, but Coke and the common lawyers took up Fuller's argument that the High Commission had no right to fine and to imprison—punishments Coke himself was to endure at its hands. Coke and the common lawyers argued that the Elizabethan Act of Uniformity did not give the High Commission such powers, and they also denied the legality of the oath ex officio except in testamentary or matrimonial cases. On the other side, John Cowell, Regius Professor of Civil Law at Cambridge and the author of the absolutist law dictionary, *The Interpreter* (1607), along with the civilian lawyers who practiced in the ecclesiastical courts, urged the king to stop the abuse of prohibitions.

In 1608 and 1609, James held a series of conferences between the common law judges and bishops, hoping again, as at Hampton Court, to reconcile differences. At a conference in November, 1608, Bancroft, who believed the survival of the Church was at stake, advised James that whenever there was a question over the jurisdiction of the Church courts—"the statute concerning tithes, or any other thing ecclesiastical, or upon the statute 1 Eliz. concerning the High Commission"—the king should "decide it in his royal person."[64] But Coke emphatically denied James' claim to decide between rival jurisdictions, stating that only the judges could interpret the law. James' wrath exploded; Coke fell to his knees. At a conference in June, 1609, Attorney General Henry

Hobart proposed that parliamentary statutes that modified or amended some part of the ecclesiastical law should be interpreted solely by the ecclesiastical courts, except when common law penalties had been prescribed. But Coke argued that acts of Parliament were laws of England and were not to be interpreted by any ecclesiastical judge. The conferences ended inconclusively, but the parliamentary Puritans hoped to raise the question of the Commission's practices in the next Parliament.

When the fourth session of James' first Parliament met in 1610, it became the forum for causes dear to both the lawyers and the parliamentary Puritans. Many of the ecclesiastical grievances that had arisen in one or more of the first three sessions appeared once again in a Commons' petition: failing to enforce the penal laws against Jesuits, seminarians, and popish recusants; requiring subscription to the comprehensive canon 36 of the Canons of 1604; tolerating pluralism and nonresidency; and allowing the excommunication of a large number of people for very small causes. In fact, the Commons passed bills, as they had in earlier sessions, against nonresidence and pluralism (introduced by Nicholas Fuller) as well as for the restraint of canons not ratified by Parliament. The Lords, however, ratified neither of these bills. Nor did the king mention any of these grievances in his opening address to Parliament, but he did speak about the problem of prohibitions. Referring to his recent conferences on that subject, James said that he had informed the concerned parties to distinguish between the "true use" and the "abounding abuse" of prohibitions.

On July 7, the Commons sent another petition to the king, which not only complained about writs of prohibition but also listed a number of grievances against the Court of High Commission. The petitioners thought it most unreasonable that the ecclesiastical commissioner, by forcing a man upon the oath ex officio to accuse himself, should hand down, without appeal, fines and imprisonment for actions that were to be tried in the common law courts, according to Parliament's own penal laws. Moreover, they objected to the High Commission's practice of breaking into men's houses in its search for supposedly scandalous books. Concerning writs of prohibition, the king promised: "*I will yet take more pains that every jurisdiction shall know her own.*" Concerning the High Commission, he promised "*to set down new instructions,*" which appeared in letters patent issued at the appointment of George Abbot as archbishop of Canterbury a year later. Although the letters patent provided for a new appeal procedure through a commission of review, they also spelled out the current practices of meting out punishment through fines or imprisonment as well as employing the oath ex officio. In addition, the letters further empowered the High Commission to enforce the penal laws against Catholics. When invited to join the Court of High Commission, Coke responded to the letters patent: "if the High Commissioners might have fined and imprisoned men for offences against the ecclesiastical laws, to what end were the statutes of 23 Eliz., 28 Eliz. &c., made against men?"[65] Coke declined to serve on the Court, and the common law judges went on issuing prohibitions though with considerably less aggressiveness and provocation.

Coke's quarrel with the king over prohibitions and the High Commission reached a climax in two ecclesiastical cases that, combined, resulted in Coke's dismissal as chief justice of the Court of King's Bench, a position to which he had been transferred in 1613. In the first case, Edward Peacham, a rector from Somerset, refused to contribute to the benevolence or voluntary gift that the bishops had asked the clergy to give to the king's depleted treasury. Convocation had granted a benevolence after the failure of James' second or Addled Parliament (1614) to supply additional funds to the Crown. The Court of High Commission imprisoned Peacham for libelous statements against his bishop. While in prison Peacham's study was ransacked—a practice condemned in one of the Commons' petitions of 1610—revealing notes for a sermon that, according to Attorney General Francis Bacon, encompassed the king's death. In order to decide whether or not Peacham had committed an act of treason, the king's Privy Council wished to consult with the judges, but James, suspecting what their opinion might be, insisted that the consultation should be only on a separate and individual basis. Coke strongly opposed what he regarded as a fresh procedural interference with the independence of the judicial bench. When he finally gave his separate and individual opinion in 1615, it was against the Crown, but Peacham died in prison shortly before he was to be executed for treason.

In a second case, Richard Neile, bishop of Lichfield, received from James a rich ecclesiastical benefice in addition to his poor see, that is, in *commendam*, a pluralistic practice condemned in the Millenary Petition. After two men contended that the right of presentation to the benefice was theirs and not the king's, the case came before the common law judges gathered together in the Exchequer Chamber. At the command of the king, Bacon requested the judges to withhold their opinion about this doubtful exercise of the advowson until the king had consulted with them about his prerogative in the case. When Coke refused to delay the case for such a consultation, the king summoned all the judges into his presence and told them that he had a right to be heard in all cases of which he was a party. Nearly all the judges fell to their knees and asked the king's forgiveness, but Coke alone stated that in the future he would do what would befit a judge to do. There were to be no future cases for Coke, however, and following his dismissal from the bench, and after numerous attempts to regain royal favor, he joined the parliamentary opposition. Although Bishop Neile lost the Commendam's case, the kings' right of presentation in *commendam* was not jeopardized.[66]

Coke was not the only exponent of the common law to meet humiliation at the hands of the king and the Court of High Commission. In 1618, John Selden, one of the most learned men in England, published his *History of Tithes*, which attempted to justify the payment of tithes on the basis of manmade law. Selden cited the statutes passed during the reigns of Henry VIII and Edward VI, calling for the levy of tithes according to the custom of the parish. In addition, Selden argued that it was only "the *Secular* or *Common Laws*" that "permit or restrain the Canons in legal exaction" of tithes. As a result, the Anglican hierarchy easily construed his argument as an attack upon its largely unsuccessful attempt since Bancroft's day to increase the Church's revenue by tithes using the canon law and the ecclesiastical courts. Yet Selden insisted that he had not written his book "*to prove that Tithes are not due by the Law of God.*"[67] After all, he wrote, that question was only within the purview of divines or civilian lawyers, for he must have been well aware that Bishop Andrewes' thesis for the doctor of divinity degree had defended the collection of tithes on the basis of a *jus divinum*.

Selden's explicit case for positive law was so overwhelming, and his inferential case against divine right so disturbing, that Richard Montagu, rector of Stanford Rivers, Essex, urged James to take action. After three lively interviews with the king, Selden appeared before the Court of High Commission. In the Court he acknowledged his error for having published the book, especially if he had offered any opportunity for argument against tithes by divine right. With his recantation the book was suppressed, and the High Commission enjoined the author not to answer Montagu. In the years to come, Selden, too, became a powerful member of the parliamentary opposition.

The Elizabethan connections between the Crown and the Anglican hierarchy on the one hand, and Parliament and some Puritans on the other hand, developed even further under James. The Crown-Anglican connection received active support from some civil law lawyers and the Parliament–some-Puritan connection received active support from at least one common law judge. The institution over which the two sets of lawyers had their greatest differences was the Jacobean Court of High Commission. And within the Court, the issue that gave rise to so many of the writs of prohibition was, of course, that of tithes. Increased tithes were to be used for the better mainte-nance of the clergy, and the better maintenance of the clergy was a goal upon which both Anglican and Puritans could agree. They differed over the finan-cial means to achieve this end. The Anglican hierarchy believed that impro-priated tithes should be restored in kind and that customary tithes should revert to the original tenth. With these goals the civilian lawyers hoped to increase the Church's total income by administering the canon law through the Court of High Commission. The Puritans believed that the wealthier benefices (including the cathedral and collegiate churches) that were not controlled by the gentry should be deprived of some of their income, and that multiple benefices (including those held in *commendam* should be eliminated in order to take care of the poverty-stricken parishes.

By withstanding the Church's challenge to the property rights of the gentry class who dominated Parliament, the common lawyers and judges upheld the superiority of statutory law against a key prerogative court of the Crown. Coke and the common law judges played an important role in helping the Puritans check the power of the king. But the Court of High Commission and the canon lawyers played an important role in helping the Anglican hierarchy try, albeit unsuccessfully, to check the power of Parliament.

As in its disagreement with the Puritans and the Catholics, the Jacobean Crown did not move much beyond the Elizabethan Crown in its relationships with the common lawyers on religious matters. It is true that there had been an increase from Elizabeth to James in the number of times the common law judges took cases, especially regarding tithes, out of the Courts of High Commission through writs of prohibition. And it is also true that the chief protagonists between the Church and the common law courts—Archbishop Bancroft and Chief Justice Coke—were much abler spokesmen for their respective causes than were any of their counterparts under Elizabeth. But James never could quite distinguish between the "true use" and the "abounding abuse" of writs of prohibition. Like Elizabeth, who encountered the issue of writs in an incipient form, James did not wish to allow too much independence to his bishops—that would derogate from the royal supremacy—nor too much independence to his common law judges—that would derogate from the royal prerogative. In the final analysis, James forthrightly opposed the common law judges—both Coke and Selden experienced humiliation— but he did not show correspondingly strong support for the bishops. And the questions about writs of prohibition were left unresolved. While Jacobean policies demonstrated continuity with those of Elizabeth, her reign did not consolidate her position on the common law and the Church as much as it did her positions on the Puritans and the Catholics.

The Synod of Dort

The alliance James had enjoyed with the Court of High Commission in England provoked him to create two similar courts in Scotland in 1610, which were symptomatic of a larger plan to pattern the Kirk of Scotland after the Church of England. In the same year, Anglican bishops consecrated three titular Scottish bishops, who had been appointed by James a decade before, but whose power as bishops had been made moot by the Scottish Parliament's approval of a Presbyterian form of church government in 1592. This consecration was a sanction for episcopacy which neither the king nor the Scottish Parliament could bestow. At the same time, an attempt to require episcopal ordination for Scottish Presbyterian ministers was unsuccessful. By 1616, along with the imposition of episcopacy in the Scottish Kirk, James became interested in promulgating a new confession of faith, a new liturgy, a new catechism, and a new set of canons. That same year, the General Assembly of the Scottish Kirk adopted a new confession (less strident but still Calvinistic in tone), and during his 1617 visit to Scotland James tried to bring the Scottish Book of Common Order (1562) more closely in line with the English Book of Common Prayer.[68]

While in Scotland, James convoked a session of the Scottish Parliament, which debated several bills dealing with the Kirk. One controversial proposal called for Parliament to declare that the king, "after consultation with the bishops and a 'competent number' of ministers, could make binding decisions on 'all matters decent for the external policy of the kirk.'" Some ex-Melvilleans and some moderate Presbyterian ministers strongly protested this unprecedented aggrandizement of ecclesiastical power by the Crown because they realized that James planned important changes in the liturgy, which would eventually become the Five Articles of Perth. Confronted by this opposition, the king withdrew the bill, but he stated "that he could act as he chose in questions of church government anyway, by virtue of his prerogative."[69] This claim, however, was never put to a test in Scotland.

In August, 1618, after James' return to England, the archbishop of St. Andrews, John Spottiswood, persuaded a majority of the General Assembly of the Scottish Kirk, packed with lay appointees, to enact the Five Articles of Perth out of obedience to the king. Three of the articles—private baptism, commemoration of holy days, and episcopal confirmation—were either noncontroversial or not strongly opposed. But two of the articles, both dealing with Holy Communion, aroused strong opposition.[70] One authorized private communion, and the other, requiring every communicant to kneel to receive the sacrament, raised an old controversy which Knox and Hooper had tried to avoid with the Black Rubric in 1552. The Black Rubric had stated that kneeling to receive the sacrament did not mean an adoration of the elements in and of themselves, nor the doctrine of the real presence. When the Scottish Court of High Commission summoned some ministers, including John Scrimegour of Kinghorn, Archbishop Spottiswood remarked, "I tell you, Mr. John, the king is Pope now, and so shall be."[71] Although the Scottish Parliament ratified the Five Articles of Perth in 1621, James abandoned any further attempts to revise the Book of Common Order. The wisdom of this decision was one of the many lessons Charles I did not learn from his father; otherwise, he would not have attempted to impose a new Prayer Book on the Scottish Kirk in 1637.

En route from Scotland, James addressed the problem of Puritan sabbatarianism, which had also arisen at the end of Elizabeth's reign. Shortly before his arrival in Lancashire, the Puritan magistrates suppressed many of the sports and recreations which customarily followed Sunday service. Not content with changing the religious service of the Church, the Puritans wished to transform the social fabric to their literal conception of the Jewish Sabbath as set forth in the Mosaic Code. "Remember the sabbath day, to keep it holy." No distinction should exist between the world of grace and the world of nature, at least on Sundays. After listening to the advice of the bishop for Lancashire, Thomas Morton, James issued a declaration later applied to all of England.

The Declaration of Sports, or Book of Sports, permitted all those who had attended divine services to engage in dancing, archery, leaping, vaulting, "May-games, Whitsum-ales, and Morris-dances," but not bear and bull baiting or, for "the meaner sort of people," bowling on the green. The king defended his action because he felt that the prohibition of recreation would encourage some men to convert to Roman Catholicism and because he felt that the "common and meaner sort" of people would turn instead to "filthy tippling and drunkenness," which breed "idle and discontented speeches in their ale-houses."[72] In order to give force to the *Declaration*, James ordered each bishop to publish it throughout all the parish churches of the land, but many Puritan clergymen and others, presumably even Archbishop Abbot, refused to read it. Confronted with this opposition, James prudently withdrew the order to read the *Declaration*. The wisdom of this decision was one of the many lessons that James II did not learn from his grandfather, especially in connection with his attempt to impose a second Declaration of Indulgence on the Anglican hierarchy in 1688.

Shortly after James' return from Scotland, the Dutch convened an international synod at Dort (1618–1619). The Dort debate over the ability of man to resist God's ordinances outlined the difference between the Arminians and the Calvinists. Arminius, who believed that the elect could fall finally and totally from grace and that the non-elect were damned because of their own sins, had raised much the same kind of opposition to the theology of Calvin as Archbishop Bancroft had raised against the rigid Calvinism of the Lambeth Articles at the Hampton Court Conference. Bancroft had not recommended acceptance of the Lambeth Articles for incorporation into the Thirty-Nine Articles. But James Ussher (later archbishop of Armagh) had gotten the Lambeth Articles approved by the Irish Convocation of the Clergy and the lord deputy in the name of King James I. The appointment in 1611 of George Abbot (the candidate of the earl of Dunbar), rather than either of the proto-Arminians, Lancelot Andrewes or John Overall, as the successor to Archbishop Bancroft also had revealed James' inclination toward a more rigid Calvinist theology.[73] Two years later Archbishop Abott wrote that Andrewes, the bishop of Ely, had "*inclined*" to the view that a "*truly justified and sanctified*" man could fall totally but not finally from grace. James, Abbot asserted, believed that such a view of a fall from grace "was as well *finaliter* as *totaliter*,"[74] meaning that Andrewes' belief—halfway between the Arminian position that man could resist God's grace and the rigid Calvinist tenet that such grace was irresistible—was an unwelcome concession to Arminian views.

Upon the death of Arminius in 1609, James and his Calvinist Archbishop Abbot strongly opposed the nomination of the Arminian Conrad Vorstius to the divinity chair at the University of Leyden. Vorstius had been tinged with Arianism, the same heresy charged against two Englishmen, Bartholomew Legate and Edward Wightman. James had personally cross-examined Legate, as Henry VIII had John Lambert; but James, unlike Henry, had returned Legate to the consistory court where he was convicted with Wightman, the last two Englishmen to be burned for heresy. Had it not been for Vorstius' theology, an offshoot of the "corrupt seed which that enemy of God, Arminius, did sow amongst you some few years ago," and had not Martin Becanus, a Jesuit, linked Vorstius with James as atheists at the time of the Oath of Allegiance controversy, the king might have been able to look much more kindly toward Vorstius because of his Erastian views. Vorstius had praised a treatise of another Arminian, John Uitenbogaert, for advocating the full authority of the state over the church.[75] The facts are that the Erastian

James, who had a reputation abroad as a Calvinist in theology, was much more of an Arminian than a Calvinist when it came to church–state relationships.

In the fall of 1618, James sent a small group of British clergy to the Synod of Dort, the Dutch international conference divided between Remonstrant Arminians and Contra-Remonstrant Calvinists. The British delegation, which mostly agreed with the Contra-Remonstrant Calvinists, included Bishop George Carleton of Llandaff, cousin to the pro-Calvinist English ambassador, Sir Dudley Carleton, at the Hague; Joseph Hall, dean of Worcester and fellow of Emmanuel College at Cambridge; Samuel Ward, master of Sidney Sussex College at Cambridge, and a great admirer of the Calvinists, Whitaker and Perkins; Thomas Goad, who had opposed Baro and Overall at Cambridge in the 1590s, was chaplain to Archbishop Abbot, and replaced the ill Hall; John Davenant, Lady Margaret Professor of Theology and master of Queen's College at Cambridge, whose lectures attempted to confute the doctrines of Arminius; and Walter Balcanqual, a Scottish episcopalian and fellow of Pembroke College at Cambridge. The king's choice of theological Calvinists as the English representatives is a further indication that he was basically unsympathetic to the theological views of the Arminian Remonstrants at Dort.[76] At the same time the king did not wish to offend those Arminians who held Erastian views, nor to encourage the Puritans at home by approving the church discipline of the Calvinist Contra-Remonstrants.

The Arminian Remonstrance, which became the basis of theological discussion at Dort, contained these five principles of Arminianism: (1) God through His foreknowledge *conditionally* elected those who would believe through His grace in Jesus Christ and persevere in faith and obedience, rejecting the unconverted and unbelievers to eternal damnation; (2) Christ died for each and every man, but none but the faithful should enjoy this pardon of sin; (3) man could not obtain saving faith by himself or by the strength of his own free will, but needed God's cooperating grace; (4) the grace of God is not irresistible; (5) and true believers might fall away from God totally and finally. It is possible to see how these Arminian principles might give renewed though somewhat misplaced impetus to optimistic beliefs in universal redemption and freedom of the human will through an exaltation of natural reason.

The members of the synod rejected the Arminian principles of the Remonstrants, but the British divines, at James' request, urged the synod to avoid harshness and rigidity in judging the Remonstrance, especially the second article, which distinguished between the sufficiency and efficiency of Christ's death. While the British divines agreed with the synod in rejecting nearly all the principles of Arminianism, Ward and Davenant, after checking with King James, urged the acceptance of that loose Calvinist interpretation of article two, which stated, as *both* Calvin and Arminius had believed, that Christ died for each and every man even though only the elect would achieve eternal life. However, Bishop Carleton and the other two British delegates, after checking with Archbishop Abbot, adhered to the rigid Calvinist contention formulated by Beza, that Christ had died for the elect only. Despite this difference within the British delegation, none of the five delegates could be characterized as Arminian. The Calvinist Contra-Remonstrants defeated the Arminian Remonstrants at the synod on all of the issues. No agency of church or state in England ever ratified the decisions of the Synod of Dort, but the debates at Dort sharpened the issues between the dominant Calvinist faction and the rising Arminian faction within the Anglican Church.[77]

John Selden summarized the difference between Puritans and Arminians most succinctly in his *Table Talk*.

> The Puritans who will allow no free-will at all, but God does all, yet will allow the subject his liberty to do or not to do, notwithstanding the king, the god upon earth. The Arminians, who hold we have free-will, yet say, when we come to the king there must be all obedience, and no liberty must be stood for.[78]

James' Calvinist theology of determinism and his Arminian emphasis on obedience might have been consistent with each other, but they were in conflict with the two prevailing sets of ideologies, and the conflict spread within the Anglican Church as well. A Calvinist community of Saints was not necessarily incompatible with the church concept of a national church. After all, they had coexisted in the small city-state of Geneva although, admittedly, the two sets of ideas did not fit together easily elsewhere. Calvinist churches everywhere in Europe wished to have an influential voice in both religious and civil affairs, a tradition that defied the divine right temper of James and the Erastian heritage of England. Cartwright and Perkins had developed this tradition. Yet, an Arminian theology with its suggestion of free will and good works, which could be interpreted to mean universal salvation, was much more compatible with a national church concept. Here the invisible church of believers corresponded to the visible church that all of His Majesty's subjects were legally required to attend. Bancroft and Andrewes had developed this tradition. In addition, many Calvinist Puritans in the Separatist tradition had begun to feel that their emphasis on a well-disciplined community of God's pre-ordained elect was incompatible with a national church ideal that allowed the predestined sinners to mix with the predestined Saints. For that reason they hived off into church communities that had little or nothing to do with the Anglican hierarchy. Browne and Robinson had developed this tradition. Even Scottish Presbyterianism and, later, New England Congregationalism, theocratic as they were, found it necessary to adopt a covenant theology, a compromise between an all-embracing Arminianism and a restrictive Calvinism. When William Laud came to ecclesiastical power in the 1620s and 1630s, he had a splendid opportunity to combine Arminian theology with the national church concept. However, in attempting to do so, he did not heed the advice of James to his Parliament in 1610: "I never found, that blood and too much severity did good in matters of Religion."[79]

The early years of James I's reign in church and state were, for the most part, the culmination of developments that had been going on since the middle decades of Elizabeth's reign. For example, the Canons of 1604, which added very little that was actually new, were largely consolidations of the Elizabethan Injunctions, Parker's *Advertisements*, Whitgift's Eleven Articles, and the Canons of 1571, 1576, 1585, and 1597. Also, the Jacobean Oath of Allegiance, which modified the Elizabethan Oath of Supremacy, was essentially a recognition that government was interested in political subversion and not religious heresy. Again, the Court of High Commission (with its oath ex officio), which shifted its primary concern from heresy to tithes, continued to make life unpleasant for the Puritans despite the writs of prohibition from the common law courts. Even James' concept of divine right monarchy, which made no claim to the *potestas ordinis*, was in the Erastian tradition of Elizabeth's opposition to presbytery *jure divino* and episcopacy *jure divino*, to say nothing of the divine claims of papal supremacy.

Almost the only marked development in James' reign was the new emphasis on theological matters. The attempts very late in Elizabeth's reign and in the first two-thirds of James' reign to polarize the official theology of the Anglican Church received serious setbacks when first the queen and then the king rejected the Calvinist articles from Lambeth Palace and the king rejected the Arminian articles from the Synod of Dort. In short, for the first time since Henry VIII, a new sovereign had succeeded to the English throne without a major change in religious policy. Furthermore, for the last time until Queen Anne, a new sovereign succeeded to the English throne without a major change in religious policy. The Jacobean Consolidation, therefore, does not mark an epoch in the English Church comparable with the Henrician Schism, the Edwardian Reformation, the Marian Persecution, or the Elizabethan Settlement. Nor will it stand in importance with the events of the Laudian Counter-Reformation. It was not even a major reconstruction of the English Church—only a minor alteration. But it did mark a short period of stability in church and state relationships that was not to be seen again until the eighteenth century.

5

The Laudian
Counter-Reformation

The Synod of Dort had rejected the Arminian Remonstrants in 1619. But a number of English clergymen like John Hales, who "bade John Calvin 'good-night,'" welcomed the Arminianism which had been slowly growing ever since Whitgift's attempt to check loose Calvinism at the Lambeth Conference. In the 1630s, adherents to Arminianism held—besides "all the best bishoprics and deaneries in England"—views about free will and good works that led Puritans to fear a doctrinal return to the Thomistic synthesis of the Catholic Church. In the words of the anonymous author of *The Arminian Nunnery* (1641), "*Arminianism* is a bridge to *Popery*." While the Roman Catholic mass was gone, except at court where every English queen from 1603 to 1688 was a Roman Catholic, the liturgical position of the Catholic Church resembled the liturgical position of the Anglican Church enough to cause consternation among the Puritans, especially within the five Parliaments which met between 1621 and 1629. This was most true of the reforms associated with William Laud under the phrase, "the beauty of holiness." Indeed, the period of Laud's hegemony, first as a bishop and later as an archbishop, could be seen as the English Protestant equivalent of the earlier Catholic Counter-Reformation.[1]

The Last Years of James I

Foreign and domestic concerns that arose from the marriage of James' daughter Elizabeth to Frederick, the Calvinist elector of the Palatinate, and the proposed marriage of James' son Charles to Donna Maria, the infanta of Spain, occupied to a great extent the closing years of the king's reign. The Spanish ambassador in England, Count Gondomar, hoped the proposed marriage would woo James away from the Union of Protestant Princes and obtain relief for English Catholics from the penal laws. James advocated the marriage to maintain peace in Europe through an alliance between the major Catholic and Protestant powers; he also wanted to obtain a substantial dowry to ease his acute financial needs. In August, 1619, Frederick accepted the

164

crown of Bohemia without consulting his father-in-law, but a year later he lost it to the Austrian Hapsburgs at the battle of White Mountain. James did not intervene in his behalf. When Spanish Hapsburg armies invaded the Palatinate, James hoped that negotiations with Gondomar would bring about the withdrawal of the armies and the restoration of Frederick to the Palatinate in exchange for the Spanish marriage. To meet the demands of his foreign policy, especially to pay for an English army in the Palatinate, James summoned his third Parliament in January, 1621 for the granting of supplies.

The House of Commons was in an anti-Catholic and anti-Spanish mood. For example, it sentenced a Roman Catholic barrister, Edward Floyd, to a fine and the pillory for allegedly stating that Frederick had no more right to the Bohemian crown than he did. Most of the members favored a maritime war with Spain, the leading nation of the Catholic League, and a Protestant wife for the Prince of Wales as the best ways to strike a few blows for Frederick. Although concerned primarily with foregin affairs, Parliament also saw Catholicism as an internal danger. Both Houses adopted a petition, which had first appeared in the parliamentary session of 1610, asking James to put various penal laws into effect against Jesuits, priests, and popish recusants. James rejected the petition, not because of any "slack of my self" regarding the promotion of the "true Religion" but because "any new or stricter course against the Papists . . . is like to induce [them] to the like against our Religion" in the Palatinate. And when James warned that both Houses should also look "on the left hand to the Puritans," as well as "on the right hand to the Papists," he was probably referring to the Commons' recent expulsion of a member, Thomas Shepherd, who had defended James' Book of Sports against the provisions of a new but unsuccessful sabbatarian bill.[2]

After the summer recess John Pym, in his first Parliament, addressed the Catholic danger. So concerned was Pym about protecting James from the Catholics that he actually proposed reviving the Elizabethan Bond of Association to ensure that all public officers were loyal to the established Church and the king's person. In a passage whose substance Pym often delivered to Parliament, he said:

> the King cannot think there is any safety in this connivancy. . . . For having gotten favor they will expect a toleration, after toleration they will look for equality, after equality for superiority, and having superiority they will seek the subversion of that religion which is contrary to theirs.

The Commons addressed these sentiments with a statement that Prince Charles should marry someone "of our own Religion" in a revised petition. James told Parliament not "to meddle with anything concerning our government or deep matters of State, and namely not to deal with our dearest son's match with the daughter of Spain." The Commons next petitioned for freedom of speech, telling James that the "patrimony of your children . . . the welfare of religion, and [the] state of your kingdom" were indeed matters for the deepest consideration in Parliament. James likened these plenipotentiary claims of the Commons to those he had encountered from the Scottish

Presbyterians, who "hooked in to themselves the cognizance of all causes," and to those claims of Cardinal Bellarmine, who had given the Pope "all temporal jurisdiction" over kings. The members of the House reasserted their right to freedom of speech on December 18 in their Great Protestation, which James answered by tearing the Great Protestation from the Commons' *Journal*.[3]

Through his responses to parliamentary petitions, James had imposed restrictions upon free speech for members of Parliament. Later, the royal Directions Concerning Preachers (1622) imposed similar restrictions upon free speech for ministers and Church lecturers. Drawn up by John Williams, lord keeper and bishop of Lincoln, the Directions attacked schismatical tendencies in church and state, especially those stemming from university students who were reading "late writers and ungrounded divines" from abroad like David Pareus. For example, an Oxford divinity student named John Knight had preached that a lesser magistrate might take up arms against the king in behalf of the true religion. Arrested, Knight received a light sentence because of his youth, but any justification of rebellion horrified James. The Directions prohibited "indecent railing speeches" from the pulpit against Catholics or Puritans, but they also declared that no preacher was to delineate "the power, prerogative, jurisdiction, authority, or duty of sovereign princes, or otherwise meddle with these matters of state" except as he was instructed by the Thirty-Nine Articles or the homilies, particularly the one "Against Disobedience and Willful Rebellion."[4]

University students were also reading books on theological issues raised at the Synod of Dort. The Directions accordingly forebade any minister under the rank of a bishop or dean to preach about "the deep points of predestination, election, reprobation, or of the universality, efficacy, resistibility or irresistibility of God's grace." In addition, Sunday afternoon sermons, important to Puritan lecturers, were generally to be replaced by expounding points of the catechism to children. And the Directions requested greater care in licensing preachers, especially the lecturers. In order to defend the Directions, James enlisted some Anglican divines, among them the Dean of St. Paul's, John Donne. Donne stated that James did not want preachers "*To soar in points too deep, To muster up their own Reading, To display their own Wit, or Ignorance in meddling with Civil Matters.*" Like Elizabeth, James probably felt that any discussion of theological issues would ultimately raise questions about royal supremacy.[5]

Shortly after these attempts to curtail the religious freedom of the lesser clergy, and particularly the Puritan lecturers, James was determined to extend some measure of religious freedom to English Catholics. He was insistent, despite the opposition of his previous Parliament, on having Charles marry the Spanish infanta. In a gesture to Spain, he issued writs for the release of numerous Roman Catholics from prison. The Spanish court insisted that the infanta have a public church served by a Catholic bishop and priests as well as control over the religious education of her children. To speed up the negotiations, Charles and George Villiers, the duke of Buckingham, journeyed to Spain in the spring of 1623. In the subsequent marriage treaty, Spain made no definite commitments regarding the dowry nor its withdrawal from the Palatinate, but James conceded all of the Spanish demands in public articles of the treaty. In private articles he took an oath, partly at the insistence of Pope Gregory XV—who issued a dispensation for the impending marriage—never to enforce the English penal laws (including the Oath of Allegiance), to encourage Parliament to repeal them, and never to agree to any new penal laws. Finally, the infanta would stay in Spain during a year's probationary delay to test English good faith.

These exacting terms, as well as difficulties that Charles and Buckingham encountered in Spain, turned them and many of the privy councillors against the marriage treaty. Even James hesitated "to marry his son with a portion of his daughter's tears."[6] Indeed, Charles and Buckingham, whose influence over the aging James was now paramount, had become so hostile toward Spain that they were determined to go to war, a sentiment which Puritan members of the House of Commons shared.

Even though James' fourth Parliament (1624) spent much energy on working out the subsidies necessary for the war against Spain and on some important domestic issues, it sometimes focused, like the Parliament of 1621, on specifically religious matters. The Commons brought forward the perennial sabbatarian bill, which the king vetoed, and a bill for the termination of the right of sanctuary for any cause whatsoever, which James signed. Parliament revived the antirecusant petition, but this time the petition requested that "upon no occasion of marriage, or treaty, or other request in that behalf, from any foreign prince or state whatsoever," will you "take away or slacken the execution of your laws against the popish recusants."[7] Puritan members of the Commons were concerned about negotiations undertaken with France, as part of a grand alliance against Spain, for a marriage treaty between Prince Charles and the Catholic French princess, Henrietta Maria. Charles apparently told his father that the best way to get the Commons to loosen its purse strings was by granting its petition.

Instead of rejecting the petition, as he had done three years before, James granted the substance of what was asked, adding something of his own. He agreed to issue a proclamation, as he had done in 1606, fixing a day by which all Jesuits and seminary priests should be gone from England; to command the judges, as he had done in 1610, to execute all of the penal laws against Catholic recusants; and to prohibit English Catholics from resorting to the chapels of foreign ambassadors for mass. In addition, he offered to prevent the education of recusant children in foreign seminaries. On the matter of future concessions to Catholics in treaties, James said: "I will be careful that no such condition be hereafter foistered in upon any other treaty whatsoever."[8] James subsequently issued the proclamation ordering all Jesuits and seminary priests to leave England by June 14, but the final draft of the marriage treaty with France gave the French princess almost the same religious privileges which had been granted to the Spanish infanta. In fact, a secret clause, upon Cardinal Richelieu's insistence, guaranteed to English

Catholics the same religious freedom as the marriage treaty with Spain had provided.

Before it adjourned, the Parliament of 1624 opened up the question of Arminianism, a subject which increasingly claimed the attention of the next three Parliaments. The leader of the Arminian movement in England after the Synod of Dort was the bishop of Durham (1617–1628), Richard Neile, who had been involved in the Commendams case. Neile sided with the Cambridge Calvinists in the 1590s against John Overall and Peter Baro. But by 1618, the Dutch Arminian, Oldenbarnevelt, requested the Dutch Ambassador in London to appoint the anti-Calvinists Neile and John Buckeridge, bishop of Rochester, together with Overall, as English representatives to the Synod of Dort. The previous year Neile had moved the Durham cathedral communion table to an altar-wise position and about 1620 replaced it with a stone altar. In addition, he appointed anti-Calvinists to clerical positions in his diocese, including the prebendary John Cosin, who developed strong ties with Arminianism through Bishop Overall and Grotius. At his London residence in the Strand, Bishop Neile assembled a circle of Arminian churchmen including Bishops Buckeridge, John Howson (Oxford), and William Laud (St. David's) as well as his protégé Richard Montagu, archdeacon of Hereford, who, like Cosin, later encountered extensive difficulties with the Parliaments of Charles I. The Durham House-in-the-Strand group intended to exercise extensive court influence and patronage. In 1623, Neile, together with the aging Bishop Andrewes and the up-and-coming Bishop Laud, invited Matthew Wren, chaplain to Prince Charles, to brief them on the religious views of the future monarch. From Wren they learned that Charles, who had been under considerable pressure to turn Catholic in Spain during the marriage fiasco, was more committed to their Arminian religious views than to his father's Calvinist views.[9]

A Puritan attack on Richard Montagu, who had been associated with the Cambridge theology of Bishop Overall and who had urged James to take action against Selden, occasioned a discussion of Arminianism in the 1624 Parliament. In response to a Catholic tract entitled *The Gag of the Reformed Gospel* (1623), which stated that the doctrine of the Anglican Church was Calvinist, Montagu wrote a reply subtitled *A New Gag for an Old Goose* (1624). *A New Gag* stated that the Catholic Church, while unsound on transubstantiation, was a true church, that free will and good works played a role in man's salvation, and that the elect can lose God's grace totally, but not finally. John Pym and other Puritans in the Commons, supported by Archbishop Abbot, denounced Montagu, whose book had been printed by a royal warrant without the king's "privity," as a papist and an Arminian, although Montagu apparently had not yet read Arminius at this time. The Commons, as yet reluctant "to become judges in so deep points of religion," asked Abbot to handle the matter. As a good double predestinarian Calvinist, the archbishop admonished Montagu, advising him to alter his views, but the archbishop's influence had suffered from his anti-Catholic diplomatic intrigues as well as his accidental killing of a gamekeeper with a bow and arrow a few years before. The attenuation of Abbot's influence permitted Neile to achieve James' support for Montagu. In fact, James told Montagu, "If thou be a Papist, I am a Papist." Before the king died the following year, he assured Montagu that he would approve the archdeacon's reply to his critics, *Appello Caesarem* (1625).[10]

In the last few years of his reign, James appeared to have retreated from some religious positions of his earlier years. These included his long-standing support of the penal laws against the Catholic recusants. His treaties with Spain and France to suspend the penal laws appeared to betray the reputation he had earned throughout Europe as the champion of Protestantism. The dynastic and fiscal exigencies of his foreign policy had caused this slackening of the reins, but James, never one to use the spur without first using the bridle, had always believed, as he told the Parliament of 1621, that it was best to use persuasion before resorting to compulsion.[11] Also, the king seemed to distance himself from Calvinist theology when he banned theological topics so dear to Calvinist preachers in 1622. James' Directions of 1622 perhaps stemmed from a fear that preachers might draw from those theological topics some seditious implications which would jeopardize his Erastian notion of church and state relationships.

James's failure to suppress Montagu's *A New Gag* is puzzling because Montagu had done exactly what James had prohibited in his Directions of 1622. Perhaps James was simply repaying a past favor—Montagu's reply to Selden's *History of Tithes*. Of course, it is possible that if James had actually read *A New Gag* or if he had discussed theology with Montagu, the king became more sympathetic to some of Montague's theological ideas, especially if they offered a better chance for eternal salvation in those few months before his death. But much more likely, the king may have realized that his Calvinistic views put into jeopardy his desire for an Anglo-Spanish alliance. Whatever truth there may be in such speculation, Buckingham—still the royal favorite—under the influence of his chaplain, Bishop William Laud, had thrown his support behind Montagu. James' patronage of Montagu foreshadowed the transformation in the Crown's theological stance that would take place with Charles' succession to the throne.[12]

Charles' Early Parliaments

Because of the urgency to obtain money to continue the war against Spain and the Hapsburgs, Charles I called his first Parliament (1625) into session only a few months after he had succeeded to the throne. The new king, who had just married Henrietta Maria after France received the same kind of religious concessions that had been given to Spain, told Parliament that the wishes of his dying father had quickened his zeal for the defense of religion. An equally zealous Commons drew up a petition on religion which included most of the old anti-Catholic provisions from the petitions of 1621 and 1624, plus a new one stating that recusant fines from the Elizabethan Act of Uniformity should be given to the poor. But the petition also called for several measures to strengthen "our own religion" including the restoration of the freedom of ministers to preach the Word of God (presumably those topics banned in the Directions of 1622), the restraint of nonresidency, pluralism, and *commendams*, and the raising of maintenance for parish ecclesiastical livings. The Commons passed the petition and voted two subsidies, then turned to the matter of Richard Montagu.[13]

A Commons' committee believed that Montagu's *A New Gag* had slighted such "great lights in the Church" as Calvin, Beza, Perkins, and Whitaker. More specifically, the committee felt that the book had dishonored the late king by upholding Arminian views that, it claimed, James had tried to stymy with his censure of Arminius and Peter Bertius, with his divines' assent to the conclusions at the Synod of Dort, and with his issuance of the Irish Articles. Number thirty-eight of those Irish Articles—the one about "justifying faith cannot be lost"—which the committee particularly noted, contained the words "totally and finally." That wording, the committee incorrectly added, "was likewise contained in the sense and intention of the Articles of England, but not so fully explained." The committee also argued that Montagu had created disturbances in church and state by arguing that "a Puritan is worse than a Papist" and had given offense to the jurisdiction of the Commons by printing his second book, *Appello Caesarem*, while there was a complaint pending against him in Parliament. For the last offense, Parliament committed Montagu to the custody of the sergeant-at-arms, but Charles soon appointed him as one of the royal chaplains.[14]

During a brief adjournment because of the plague in London, three of Charles' Arminian bishops—Laud, Howson, and Buckeridge—wrote to Buckingham that some of Montagu's opinions were indeed the "resolved" doctrine of the Church of England. Furthermore, the bishops added, according to Henry VIII's Submission of the Clergy, a convocation of the clergy or a national synod, and not Parliament or an international synod (such as the Synod of Dort), should settle any doctrinal differences. Besides, "all or most of the contrary opinions were treated of at Lambeth," and Queen Elizabeth had suppressed the 1595 Articles because "of how little they agreed with the practice of piety and obedience to all government." As to Montagu's person, the bishops added, "only thus much we know, he is a very good scholar, and a right honest man; a man every way able to do God, his Majesty, and the Church of England great service." But four months later, John Davenant, now bishop of Salisbury, wrote to Samuel Ward, his colleague at Dort, that Montagu's opinion "concerning predestination and total falling from grace is undoubtedly contrary to the common tenet of the English Church ever since we were born."[15]

When the Parliament of 1625 resumed its proceedings at Oxford, the Montagu case was allowed to simmer, but Buckingham made one last attempt to get the Commons to act on additional subsidies. He announced that the king had fully and freely granted all of the provisions of the petition on religion. Yet this was to no avail. No more financial aid, not even the traditional tonnage and poundage duties for life, was forthcoming, although Parliament confirmed the two subsidies that the convocation of the clergy granted. The king, nonetheless, did sign the perennial sabbatarian bill into law. It was, however, carefully drawn up so as not to conflict with James' Book of Sports, and therefore was not the Puritan victory it might have been.[16]

A few days after the calling of a new Parliament in early February, 1626, the duke of Buckingham held a two-day conference of some Arminians and Calvinists at his London residence (York House) to conciliate Montagu's critics in the House of Lords. Speaking for the Calvinists were Bishop Thomas Morton (Coventry), a former student of William Whitaker at Cambridge; John Preston, the Puritan clergyman who had suggested to Buckingham in 1624 that dissolving the cathedral churches was the way to solve the financial problems of the Crown; and the two Puritan lords who had requested the conference, Viscount Saye and Sele plus the earl of Warwick. Representing the Arminians were Bishop Buckeridge, a member of the Durham House-in-the-Strand group; Dean Francis White (Carlisle), a protégé of Bishop Neile, who had licensed *Appello Caesarem*; Cosin, who had assisted Montagu with both of his books; and Buckingham. The earls of Pembroke and Carlisle, both privy councillors, led a middle group of peers.[17]

In the course of the two days, the disputants ranged over a number of topics, especially the doctrine of perseverance in grace and conditional election. During the first day, Dean White argued for the Arminian view that any man could fall from grace and suffer eternal punishment if, for example, he committed adultery as the biblical David had done. Preston contended that if an elect or regenerate man sinned he would not lose God's grace because, like the biblical prodigal son, he would still remain God's son even though his father might be angry with him. Bishop Morton replied that David's adultery did not affect his election, which was unchangeable. Bishop Buckeridge observed that this was "a most licentious, a sensual and a dangerous doctrine." Pembroke and Carlisle allegedly deplored setting up such a "school of sin." Montagu attended the proceedings on the second day when the subject returned to the doctrine of election. Preston challenged White to defend Montagu's denial in the *Appello Caesarem* of an "absolute, necessary, determined, irresistable . . . decree of God . . . without any consideration had of faith, obedience, [and] repentance." Some years before, White had committed himself against election "on account of works foreseen," and now stated that he had nothing to say in defense of conditional election. Stripped of White's protection, Montagu contended that no declaration of the Church of England spoke against conditional election, whereupon Preston stated that article seventeen of the Thirty-Nine Articles supported unconditional election. This apparent Calvinist success prompted the Puritan lords to renew their hope that the Calvinist conclusions at Dort might be received and established as the doctrine of the Church of England, just as Reynolds had asked to have the Lambeth Articles added to the Thirty-Nine Articles at Hampton Court. But the York House Conference broke up when the duke indicated that he was not interested in a theology, especially one which denied universal salvation, prescribed by a "village in the Netherlands."[18]

Although an attempt to impeach Buckingham for the disastrous expedition to Cadiz the previous autumn dominated Charles' second Parliament (1626), the Commons gave some attention to the case of Montagu, from whom Buckingham was now anxious to disassociate himself. Bishop Laud sounded a note of warning in the opening sermon: "take heed of breaking the peace of the Church. The peace of the State depends much upon it." John Pym, a friend of John Preston and stepbrother of the Puritan, Francis Rous, brought in a report from a Commons' subcommittee on April 17 charging Montagu with publishing doctrines contrary to the Thirty-Nine Articles and the homilies of the Church of England, tending to create seditious disturbances in church and state, and inclining the "well affected in religion"— indeed attempting to reconcile them—to the Church of Rome. Although the subcommittee stated that it did not wish to meddle with the theological doctrines of Montagu's work except "as they disturb the peace of the Church and Commonwealth," it did accuse Montagu of affirming that "men after grace received may fall and rise again" when "the Article of the Church of England denieth the falling from grace."

It was probably a good thing that the subcommittee felt some reluctance to enter into this point, since it had mistakenly attributed to Montagu what the Thirty-Nine Articles (article sixteen) actually said about perseverance of the saints. On April 20, the king announced to the Commons that he disliked the writings of Montagu—probably because he wished to slow down the impeachment proceedings—adding that he would refer Montagu's books to the convocation of the clergy. On April 29, the Commons found Montagu guilty of the charges brought in Pym's subcommittee.[19]

While preparations were being made to put the Montagu case before the Lords, the Commons discussed a bill to deal with the problem of Arminianism in general. The bill for "the Better Continuing of Peace and Unity in the Commonwealth" would have added the Irish Articles of 1615 to the Thirty-Nine Articles as the official doctrine of the Church of England. The Irish Articles, it may be recalled, had incorporated the Lambeth Articles of 1595, and the Lambeth Articles had incorporated a more rigid Calvinist theology than that in the Thirty-Nine Articles. The Lambeth Articles called for predestination to death (as well as life) and stated that the elect could fall neither totally nor finally from grace. Nothing came of the Irish Articles bill, however, since Charles dissolved the Parliament of 1626, even though no subsidies had been granted, in order to save Buckingham from impeachment.

The day after the dissolution Charles issued a proclamation to stifle the opposition against Montagu. It was prompted by an earlier suggestion of Bishops Laud, Andrewes, Neile, Buckeridge, and George Montaigne (London) to prohibit recent books critical of Montagu. Such books included those by two of the English representatives at Dort—Bishop Carleton and Thomas Goad. The Proclamation of 1626 commanded that "neither by Writing,

Preaching, Printing, Conferences or otherwise" were Charles' subjects to "raise any doubts, or publish, or maintain any new inventions, or opinions concerning Religion than such as are clearly grounded, and warranted by the Doctrine and Discipline of the Church of England, heretofore published, and happily established by authority." While such a proclamation might have been applied indiscriminately to all in James' day, under Charles the Arminian bishops used it to control "*Rigid Calvinians.*"[20]

Not long after Charles had issued his Proclamation of 1626, he called upon Laud to "tune the Pulpits" by issuing certain instructions in behalf of the king of Denmark who was then militarily "much distressed by Count *Tilly*" of France. Laud's Instructions of 1626 began with a single kingdom theory about the proper relationship between church and state.

> *We have observed that the Church and the State are so nearly united and knit together, that though they may seem two bodies, yet indeed in some relation they may be accounted but as one, inasmuch as they both are made up of the same men, which are differenced only in relation to Spiritual or Civil ends. This nearness makes the Church call in the help of the State, to succor and support her, whensoever she is pressed beyond her strength: And the same nearness makes the State call in for the service of the Church, both to teach that duty which her Members know not, and to exhort them to, and encourage them in that duty which they know.*

Laud cited the Proclamation of 1626 as an example of how the state could serve the Church, and his Instructions of 1626 as an example of how the Church could support the state by advocating "*peace and unity at home*" when a "*Foreign Force*" was "*uniting and multiplying against it.*" Charles was so pleased with Laud's instructions that he informed him that he planned to appoint him as his next archbishop of Canterbury.[21]

As the nation drifted into war with France in 1627 over naval provocations, Charles desperately needed money. Bishop Laud, appointed to the Privy Council with Bishop Neile in April, called upon the clergy to support the levy of an extraparliamentary forced loan. Robert Sibthorpe had already told his Northampton congregation, "he that resisteth the *Prince*, resisteth the power and ordinance of God, and consequently shall receive damnation." When Archbishop Abbot refused to license Sibthorpe's sermons for publication, a commission of Arminian bishops including Laud took over Abbot's ecclesiastical jurisdiction. At Laud's request, Roger Manwaring, rector of St. Giles-in-the-Fields in London, restated the theme of the Elizabethan homily "Against Disobedience and Willful Rebellion" in two sermons preached before the king: "no Subject may without hazard of his own Damnation . . . *question*, or *disobey* the will and pleasure of his *Sovereign*." Furthermore, added Manwaring, "the *Laws* . . . take their binding force from the *Supreme* will of their *Liege-Lord*." Although Laud felt that Manwaring's two sermons would be "very distasteful to the people," he instructed Bishop Montaigne to license both of them, plus Sibthorpe's, for printing. There was no necessary connection between Manwaring and Sibthorpe on the one hand

and Arminianism on the other, but to their enemies it certainly seemed, despite Sibthorpe's disclaimer, that he and Manwaring were making "*Divinity* . . . the Handmaid of *Policy*; or *Religion* the Stalking-horse of the State."[22]

Once the first session of Charles' third Parliament (1628) had secured a satisfactory answer from the king to its famous Petition of Right, which forebade forced loans, gifts, benevolences, or taxes without its consent, it turned to Manwaring and religious grievances. The Commons impeached Manwaring, and the Lords found him guilty of subverting the "Frame and Fabric" of the commonwealth for having given to the king a lawless, tyranni-cal power and for having robbed the subject of the propriety of his goods. The clergyman was condemned to prison, fined one thousand pounds, suspended from ministerial duties for three years, prohibited from any "Ecclesiastical Dignity, or Secular Office," and prevented from preaching at Court. Man-waring had to acknowledge his offenses, his book was to be burned, and the remaining copies confiscated.[23]

Meanwhile, the Commons drew up a remonstrance condemning both the disastrous military policy of Buckingham in behalf of the French Huguenots and the Arminian attempt to introduce "Innovation and Change of our Holy Religion." Roman Catholics, such as Buckingham's mother, enjoyed a "Tol-eration, odious to God," it said, and Arminians were "Protestants in show but Jesuits in opinion." Arminianism, the remonstrance continued, was "(as your majesty well knows) but a cunning way to bring in popery" as well as to achieve preferment and promotion in the Church. The remonstrance further stated that the 1626 proclamation's restraint of "Orthodox Books" had fa-vored the Arminians, whose spokesmen "near about the King," Bishops Laud and Neile, are "justly suspected to be unsound in their opinions that way." Before any decisive action could be taken on the remonstrance, Charles prorogued Parliament.[24]

Prior to the king's prorogation of Parliament, some Puritans attempted, as they had done in the Parliaments of 1625 and 1626, to pass a bill calling for the observance of the subscription statute of 1571. That Elizabethan act had required clerical subscription to those Thirty-Nine Articles "which only con-cerned the confession of the true Christian faith and the doctrine of the sacraments." As we have seen, the intended phraseology of that statute in all likelihood applied to every one of the Thrity-Nine Articles, but various Puritans, starting with Peter Wentworth, believed that the requirement ap-plied only to the so-called doctrinal articles. Number thirty-six of the Canons of 1604 had called for clerical subscription to all the Articles of Religion that Convocation had approved in 1563, a condition which considerably annoyed the Puritan members of Charles' earlier Parliaments. Of twenty-seven known anti-Arminians in the Parliament of 1628, at least twelve favored the bill. Among them were Pym, Rous, and Sir Nathaniel Rich. Rich expressed the sentiment of several members of the Commons when he stated, "I will never give my consent that a canon should be of more power than an act of Parliament." Interestingly, the former jurist Sir Edward Coke, who in his

Institutes had interpreted the 1571 statute as applicable to all the Articles of Religion, said that he liked the proposed bill. And John Selden, who had argued in his *Table Talk* (published posthumously) for the more restricted interpretation, said that he was "against passing it." Like the remonstrance, the Commons' bill for the observance of the 1571 statute did not come to a vote.[25]

After Parliament's prorogation the king suppressed Manwaring's sermons, but, at the solicitation of Bishop Neile, Charles pardoned Manwaring (as well as Sibthorpe) and presented him to the rich rectory of Stanford Rivers vacated by Montagu. The king also pardoned Montagu and appointed him to Chichester, the see vacated by the death of his Calvinist antagonist, Bishop Carleton. But in January, 1629, another royal proclamation suppressed *Appello Caesarem* and, like that of 1626, called for no further disputes about "these unnecessary questions." Although Charles restored Archbishop Abbot to his ecclesiastical functions, the archbishop had not recovered the substance of power as the promotion of the following Arminian bishops to larger sees indicated: Neile to Winchester, White to Norwich, Howson to Durham, Buckeridge to Ely, and Montaigne to York (quickly followed by Samuel Harsnett) in order to make way for Laud at London. In sum, the king tried to avoid theological controversy with the Puritans by suppressing controversial writings, but his Arminian advisors clearly retained control over the Church through the exercise of the king's patronage, even after their own patron, the duke of Buckingham, fell victim to an assassin's knife (1628).[26]

In the hope of avoiding "unnecessary disputations, altercations, or questions to be raised, which may nourish faction both in the Church and Commonwealth," Charles, on the advice of a conference of bishops, reissued the "Articles of the Church of England (which have been allowed and authorized heretofore, and which our clergy have generally subscribed unto)." Prefixed to the Thirty-Nine Articles was a declaration, stating that Charles was the supreme governor of the Church, and if any differences should arise over the doctrine and discipline of the Church, the clergy in convocation should settle them. The Declaration of 1628 also observed, quite erroneously, that clergymen within the realm always had subscribed most willingly to the Articles. But it further observed with considerable truth that "in those curious points, in which the present differences lie, men of all sorts take the Articles of the Church of England to be for them." In the future no one should "put his own sense or comment to be the meaning of the Article, but shall take it in the literal and grammatical sense."[27] When the second session of Charles' third Parliament (1629) convened, the Commons became suspicious of the 1628 Declaration's assumed impartiality because a booksellers' petition indicated that Bishop Laud was using the declaration to restrain books against popery and Arminianism.

The 1628 Declaration's statement that only the clergy in convocation and not Parliament should determine the doctrine and discipline of the Church also disturbed the Commons. In fact, a Commons' petition raised a question about two lines of the twentieth article of the Articles of Religion. The two lines, which Elizabeth had inserted in the twentieth article immediately after the Convocation of 1563, declared, "The Church hath power to decree Rites or Ceremonies, and Authority in controversies of Faith." The Commons petition stated that the statute of 1571 "did confirm the Articles that were set out in a printed book in which those two lines are not." As even Laud later admitted, an English and a Latin printing of the Articles in 1571 did not contain the disputed lines. The 1571 Convocation, however, authorized the disputed lines, as we have earlier observed, and they did appear in many editions of the Articles—not only in Latin in 1563, as the Commons' petition admitted, and twice in English in 1571, but also throughout the remainder of the Elizabethan as well as the Jacobean reigns. Although the Commons may have been technically correct on the point they were trying to make, the clergy's claim to determine doctrine was historically much more sound.[28]

Charles called the second session of his third Parliament in January, 1629 in order to request tonnage and poundage duties, but the issue of Arminianism was a major concern of its members. In one of the most eloquent speeches uttered in the Commons, Francis Rous spoke:

> I desire that we may consider the increase of Arminianism, an error that maketh the grace of God lackey it after the will of man, that maketh the sheep to keep the shepherd, that maketh mortal seed of an immortal God. Yea, I desire that we may look into the belly and bowels of this Trojan horse, to see if there be not men in it ready to open the gates to Romish tyranny and Spanish monarchy.

Pym pushed Parliament to lay down "the established and fundamental truths" of religion by confirming specific writings and actions of the Church of England sympathetic to rigid Calvinism. Sir John Eliot warned Parliament not to make a new religion nor "to alter the body of the truth which we now profess;" furthermore, disquisitions on individual divines could lead into "a labyrinth that we shall hardly get out." Something of a compromise was reached in January when the Commons passed their Vow in response to the king's Declaration of the preceding November.

> We the Commons in parliament assembled do claim, profess, and avow for truth that sense of the 39 Articles of Religion which were established in parliament *An° 1571* being in the *13 Eliz.* which by the public acts of the Church of England and the general and current expositions of the writers of our Church hath been delivered unto us; And that we do reject the sense of the Jesuits, Arminians, and all others wherein they differ from it.

Laud's answer to the Commons' Vow included two questions. "Will you reject all sense of Jesuit or Arminian? May not some be true?"[29]

The imprecision of the Commons' Vow was rectified when Pym's committee on religion drew up a list of "orthodox" doctrinal statements and when the House launched an attack upon John Cosin. The list of doctrinal statements was designed to show "wherein the Arminians differ from us and the other

Reformed Church." It included the 1571 restricted interpretation of the Articles of Religion, the Book of Common Prayer, the Homilies, the Nowell catechism, Bishop Jewel's works, the Lambeth Articles, the Irish Articles, and the conclusions of the Synod of Dort. The attack upon Cosin was based upon his *Collection of Private Devotions* (1627), written for the queen and based upon the *Primer* of 1545. Cosin was charged with substituting the word "priest" for "minister" and omitting the word "elect" in a special printing of the Prayer Book, introducing popish doctrine and ceremonies as prebendary of the cathedral church at Durham, and, most serious of all, stating that the king was not the "supreme head," having "no more to do with Religion than he that rubs his horse's heels." Apparently, Cosin had claimed that the king was the supreme governor of church and state in matters of external jurisdiction (*potestas jurisdictionis*) but added that "the power of spiritual jurisdiction [*potestas ordinis*] itself was from Christ" and his successors by ordination.[30]

Before Parliament could act upon Pym's list or the Cosin charges, Charles decided to adjourn the Houses. Eliot hurriedly prepared three short resolutions against innovations in religion as well as against the collection of tonnage and poundage duties. On March 2, with the Usher of the Black Rod pounding at the door with a message from the king, and with the Speaker forcibly held in the chair, the Commons resolved that anyone who sought to introduce or extend Arminianism and popery would be a capital enemy to the kingdom. A week later the king dissolved Parliament, thereby ending nearly a decade of futile parliamentary criticism of the Arminian Counter-Reformation. What does seem increasingly clear by 1629 is that the religious polarization between Puritanism and Arminianism was beginning to unite with a constitutional polarization between king and Parliament over extraordinary taxation.[31]

Implicit in the whole discussion of Arminianism during the first few years of the reign of Charles I was the question of which body—Parliament or convocation—should have the final say in matters of Church doctrine. Charles, unlike Henry VIII or James I, had no taste for theological disputation even though it was considered to be part of the *potestas jurisdictionis*. And like Elizabeth, who interpolated the two lines in article twenty of the Articles of Religion, he was quite willing to leave matters of doctrine and ceremony in the hands of the clergy. The doctrinal issues in Montagu's case, however, did not come to a vote in convocation, perhaps because the Arminians did not yet dominate that body.[32] The members of Charles' early Parliaments hesitated to get involved in the specifics of theological questions, and for the most part they refrained from doing so. When they did investigate Montagu's interpretation of the perseverance of the saints, they misunderstood it. They were much more inclined to lay down general principles (the Commons' Vow) or to ratify doctrinal statements (the Irish Articles) already devised by the clergy. There was a good precedent for them to do this, albeit a distant one, since they had ratified the Thirty-Nine Articles—or, as they thought, some of them—in 1571, a belief they frequently asserted.

Both the Calvinist parliamentarians and the Arminian hierarchy claimed to be orthodox in their views, and each sought to label the other an "innovator." Laud had listed the leading clergy of the realm for Charles in 1625, adding to each name an "O" for orthodox or a "P" for Puritan. And Sir John Eliot told the Parliament of 1629 that not all of the bishops were "so free, sound, and orthodox in Religion as they should be."[33] Neither Puritans nor Arminians could truly claim to be theologically more orthodox than the other, since both groups had been innovating upon the loose Calvinism of the Thirty-Nine Articles of Elizabeth's reign. The Arminian innovations, as set forth by Montagu and the Remonstrants at the Synod of Dort, represented a slightly greater departure from the Thirty-Nine Articles than the more rigid Puritan innovations, as set forth by the Lambeth Articles, the Irish Articles, and the Contra-Remonstrants at Dort. In this way Eliot was somewhat more correct than Laud.

However, consideration of the theological issue of innovation versus orthodoxy for a much longer period, extending as far back as the reign of Henry VIII, suggests a quite different conclusion. Viewed from this longer perspective, Montagu and the Arminian bishops returned the Church theologically to a pre-Elizabethan period, back almost to the time of the Christian humanists.[34] Inspired by unrepresentative proto-Arminians like Bishops Overall and Andrewes, the Arminian bishops referred to such early documents as the Henrician Litany, *Primer*, and some of the Injunctions of 1538. Their views were akin to such Erasmian doctrines as good works, free will, and universal salvation. In that sense, Laud was far more accurate than Eliot.

Economic Reforms of the Church

In early December, 1629, Laud wrote to secretary Dorchester that Charles was thinking of reviving the Elizabethan Injunctions of 1559. Instead, Laud and the king, drawing heavily upon Archbishop Harsnett's "Considerations for the Better Settling of Church Government," drafted the Instructions of 1629. These instructions ordered the bishops, as the "Considerations" had done, to "strictly" observe the Declaration of 1628 prefixed to the reissue of the Thirty-Nine Articles. The Instructions of 1629, however, omitted the provocative statement in the "Considerations" that Cambridge's "*Emmanuel* and *Sidney* Colleges . . . are the nurseries of Puritanism."[35]

The main part of the Instructions of 1629 consisted of regulations for those Puritan lecturers, both single and in combination, who had come to occupy such an important place in the Church's ministry. Single lecturers usually were unbeneficed ministers who received stipends for traveling from one pulpit to another to read lectures. The Canons of 1604 required single lecturers to be licensed by a bishop or archbishop and to make the usual subscription required of all ministers (canon 36) as well as to read divine service biennially and to administer the sacraments according to the Prayer Book (canon 56). In his Directions of 1622, James had substituted catechizings for afternoon sermons, which the lecturers often delivered, and had tightened up the procedure in the archbishop of Canterbury's Court of Faculties for the licensing of single lecturers, who constituted "a new body severed from the ancient clergy of England." The Instructions of 1629 resurrected the Jacobean catechizings ordered in the Directions of 1622.[36]

Combination lecturers were usually members of a rotating panel or a combination of beneficed clergymen, drawn from the vicinity of a market town, who preached a weekly or monthly sermon followed by a clerical exercise or voluntary conference of ministers. Although Elizabeth had banned prophesyings or exercises altogether in 1577, in the Canons of 1604 (canon 72) Bancroft had banned them only if unlicensed men preached. The Elizabethan prophesyings had developed into combination lectures, and Bancroft, like Laud later, hoped to confine them to the clergy over whom he had some ecclesiastical control. During the Jacobean period, both the single lecture and the combination lecture manifested a Puritan (rather than an Arminian) outlook theologically, and the combination lecture possessed some of the attributes of the Presbyterian classis organizationally.[37]

Small wonder, then, that in 1629 Laud wanted to reform the lecture system. The Instructions of 1629 prevented all single lecturers from preaching until they had agreed to take up an ecclesiastical living with a cure of souls. Also, the instructions authorized combination lectures in market towns by "grave and orthodox divines"—dressed in academic gowns and cloaks—drawn from the same diocese, and required single and combination lecturers—dressed in surplices and hoods—to read divine service before each of their lectures "according to the liturgy printed by authority." Laud was attempting to impose upon the lecturers a canonical liturgical and vestiarian uniformity. Although the number of Puritan lecturers in the city of London declined from fifty-eight in 1629 to forty-six in 1633, they still preached about sixty sermons a week within a square mile.[38] Laud's annual provincial reports recorded much information from bishops about attempts to regulate lecturers in accordance with the modified royal instructions, but few of the bishops, except Matthew Wren, bishop of Norwich, showed any genuine effort, fewer still success.

Bishop Laud had considerably greater success in eliminating the Puritan feoffees for impropriations than he had in regulating the Puritan lecturers. The feoffees for impropriations, a group of twelve trustees, banded together in 1625 to help maintain the Puritan ministry. Among the feoffees, or closely associated with them, were such Puritan ministers as John Preston, William Gouge, Richard Sibbes, John Davenport, and Hugh Peters. Instead of taxing the tithes from impropriations at one-sixth or one-seventh of their value, as the Puritans had advocated in the Millenary Petition, the feoffees wished to buy up impropriations from the laity. They could then pay stipends to Puritan single lecturers and augment the income of Puritan beneficed clergy, whether lecturers or not. Between 1625 and 1633, the feoffees collected the modest sum of about £6,000, a fourth of which financed six lectureships in the London parish of St. Antholin's. St. Antholin's served as a kind of small

Puritan seminary for the training of a godly ministry. By 1633, the feoffees held thirty-one church properties and patronage in eighteen counties.[39]

The field of activity for the feoffees was potentially quite large because lay gentry owned nearly 40 percent of the benefices in England, many acquired as a result of Henry VIII's dissolution of the monasteries. The gentry, however, often opposed Puritan attempts to create a strong church independent of the Crown, preferring an Erastian church under parliamentary control. Laud's opposition to the feoffees did not rest upon the principle of purchasing impropriations, for he keenly supported the return of impropriations from lay to clerical control in order to augment the finances of Anglican curates and rectors. To Laud, the activities of the Puritan feoffees seemed "a cunning way, under a glorious pretence, to overthrow the Church Government, by getting into their power more dependency of the clergy, than the King, and all the Peers, and all the Bishops in all the kingdom had." Besides, Laud argued, "most of the men they put in, were persons disaffected to the discipline, if not the doctrine, too, of the Church of England." Laud directed the matter to the Court of Exchequer, which dissolved the feoffees in 1632. Of the Puritan clergymen who had been active in the project, Preston was dead and Sibbes would die within three years, but Davenport and Peters, together with Thomas Hooker, eventually emigrated to New England after participating with William Ames in a Congregational classis in Amsterdam.[40]

Laud was especially interested in augmenting the income of impoverished vicars and bishops. The Commons in 1625 had stated that a 1540 statute had negated a bishop's right to increase the stipends of vicars by charging impropriators. In James I's reign, the common law judges, through the use of prohibitions, successfully withstood attempts by Archbishop Bancroft and others to increase tithes. Laud, however, convinced Charles in 1629 to issue a proclamation limiting the use of prohibitions. And in the case of *Thornborough and Hitchcock* v. *Hitchcock*, a church court decided that Bishop John Thornborough could raise the stipend of Vicar John Hitchcock, who held an ecclesiastical benefice, when the lessee of the impropriation (his namesake) failed to get a prohibition from both the Courts of King's Bench and Common Pleas. The work of Coke against Bancroft seemed about to be undone.

Laud began with the augmentation of ecclesiastical benefices leased to laymen, as in the case of *Thornborough and Hitchcock* v. *Hitchcock*, but later tried to augment lay benefices. Shortly after Chief Justice John Finch issued his first prohibition against the Court of High Commission, Laud persuaded Charles to order the common law judges not to meddle with the ecclesiastical courts without an archbishop's approval. Finally, he prompted the king to order the augmentation of financial support for all needy vicars and curates. Even so, Laud had scant success in increasing vicars' stipends.[41]

Laud wished to do two things about the incomes of poorer bishops. First, he wanted to shorten the length of leases of diocesan lands that tenants held. Shorter intervals would allow more frequent raising of rents as well as more frequent renewal fees that the bishop could collect. Accordingly, Laud persuaded Charles in 1633 to forbid leases for as long as the customary period of three lives with their heavy entry fees, rather than the usually shorter period of twenty-one years, with its lighter renewable fees every seven or ten years. Second, Laud wanted to annex some *commendams, sine cura,* for the smaller bishoprics. Accordingly, Charles wrote to the bishops of Bristol and St. David's, providing for the perpetual annexation of rectories in *commendam.* At his trial, Laud would state that he had thought it "good Church-work to settle some temporal lease, or some benefice *sine cura,* upon the lesser bishoprics . . . that so no other man's patronage might receive prejudice by the bishop's *commendam.*" Laud justified the old practices of pluralism and absenteeism to bring about the economic reform of the Church.[42]

Another economic matter, the insufficient payment of tithes, affected the London clergy. The Henrician statutes of 1536 and 1546 levied a rent charge of 2s. 9d. per pound on the City of London in lieu of personal tithes due to the Church. Over the years, many, especially the wealthier people, avoided the full rate. The London clergy were far from receiving their 10 percent for a variety of reasons, including the withdrawal of support by some Puritans, the issuance of prohibitions by the common law courts, and the decisions of the lord mayor in tithe disputes. The 1618 decision of the Court of Exchequer that the 2s. 9d. rate should be paid on the true yearly value of all property had not been enforced. Laud was determined, as he wrote in his diary, to see "the tithes of London settled, between the clergy and the city." Laud's efforts to enforce the 1618 decision led him to support the appointment of William Juxon, his successor as bishop of London, to the post of lord treasurer. A survey of London showed that the average paid tithe was about £80 a parish, the average true tithe was about £1,800 a parish, and the average requested tithe was about £125 a parish. The dispute between London parishioners and the clergy spread to other parts of the realm, especially Norwich. Here both parties agreed to royal arbitration, and Charles set a rate of 2s. per pound for all house rents. While strong opposition kept the king from extending that ruling to London, the troubles with Scotland developed. The ensuing financial crisis made it difficult to continue opposing the wealthy parishioners of London.[43]

Laud directed his most creative efforts toward improving the economic fortunes of the clergy. Some of these efforts were in the spirit of the early reformers, but Laud did not hesitate to use pluralism and absenteeism, for example, when it was to his financial advantage to do so. To be sure, he spared no efforts in curtailing the Puritan feoffees with the assistance of the courts. And, like Bancroft, he tried hard to control the prophesyings (combination lectures) with the assistance of the Crown. Also like Bancroft, he strove to limit prohibitions and to recover tithes for the Anglican clergy—and with more success. Indeed, he surpassed Bancroft in his efforts to recover impropriations and to augment stipends for poor vicars and rectors as well as for low-income bishops. In his effort to recover personal tithes, Laud accepted the late Henrician legislation allowing the substitution of a rent charge for the tithe, but he was determined to collect the rent charge at the risk of alienating laymen from London and other cities. In Laud's quest to augment the stipends of vicars and rectors, his lawyers, much to the consternation of laymen, challenged the Commons' claim that late Henrician legislation removed the bishops' authority over lay impropriations. Once again, Laud had gone back 100 years to the early Reformation (post-Henrician Schism) for guidance in carrying out his reforms. In the process of being "at least a century out of date,"[44] Laud succeeded in alienating the common lawyers, Parliament, and the City of London. Charles, however, followed his bidding in all of this, but, significantly enough, the king did not give up the royal impropriations to the Church except in Scotland.

The Early Persecution

During the furor over the proroguing of Parliament in 1628, Alexander Leighton, a Scottish minister, had issued a pamphlet entitled *An Appeal to the Parliament, or, Sion's Plea Against the Prelacy*. In a flamboyant rhetoric similar to that of Francis Rous in the 1629 Parliament, Leighton argued that the calling of the Anglican bishops, which he said they claimed by *jure divino*, was both unlawful and anti-Christian. "If the Hierarchy be not removed, and the *scepter* of Christ's government, namely *Discipline* advanced to its place, there can be no healing of our sore, no taking up of our controversy with God."[45] Leighton's call for the extirpation of bishoprics and their replacement by the offices of Presbyterianism brought him in 1630 before the Court of Star Chamber, where Bishops Neile and Laud sat in judgment as privy councillors. While admitting only to have written his book for Parliament's consideration, Leighton nonetheless was heavily sentenced. The Court ordered that he be degraded, fined £10,000, and set in the pillory and whipped, have his ears cut off and his nose split, and be branded on the face with an "SS" (sower of sedition), and imprisoned for life. After the Court of High Commission stripped him of his clerical garb, he escaped from the Fleet Prison, thereby ending any possibility of clemency. A royal proclamation called for his arrest, and upon his capture, most of the rest of his punishment was carried out.

A Calvinist bishop also got into trouble with the Church and the state authorities a few weeks later. The Privy Council summoned John Davenant, bishop of Salisbury, who had preached before the king on the subject of predestination. The Council claimed that Davenant had violated the Declaration of 1628, prefixed to the Thirty-Nine Articles, enjoining the clergy to give the literal meaning rather than their own interpretation to the Articles.[46] Article seventeen proved to be Davenant's nemesis. Although Davenant and Samuel Ward had sided at the Synod of Dort with the Arminians against the Calvinists on the scope of Christ's atonement, they had voted on the other theological points, including predestination, with their British colleagues against the Arminians. For these services, James had raised Davenant to the bishopric of Salisbury and Ward to the Lady Margaret Professorship of Divinity at Cambridge.

If Davenant expressed before Charles the same views on predestination that he had approved at Dort in 1619 and that he would expound in his *Animadversions* in 1641, he would have asserted the rigid Calvinist view of predestination to both election and reprobation. After his examination before the Privy Council, however, Davenant wrote to Ward that his exposition of the doctrine of "election" had not offended Archbishop Harsnett and Bishop Neile. The Arminian bishops, nevertheless, disliked his preaching on a topic prohibited by the Declaration of 1628. It is quite possible, however, that his anti-Arminian views provoked Harsnett and Neile "*to make him fall totally and finally from the king's favour.*" In one of his rare pronouncements on theology, Laud told Lord Saye and Sele in 1641, the year of Davenants' *Animadversions*, "my very soul abominates" the view "that God from all eternity reprobates by far the greater part of mankind to eternal fire, without any eye at all to their sin." Davenant's silence and obedience for the next ten years testified to the anti-Calvinism of the Laudian bishops.[47]

Bishop Davenant did not have long to wait before he had an opportunity to display his submission to the Arminian hierarchy. Henry Sherfield, who had criticized the pardons given to Montagu, Manwaring, Sibthorpe, and Cosin, was disturbed upon his return to Salisbury by a stained-glass window in St. Edmund's church, which depicted "*God the Father*" as a "little old Man in a blue and red Coat." The vestry voted to remove the window as idolatrous, but Bishop Davenant ordered the church wardens to ignore the order of the vestry. Sherfield, a leader of the local Puritan oligarchy, promptly smashed the window with his pikestaff. When the iconoclast was called before the Court of Star Chamber for this relatively trivial issue in 1633, two defense witnesses stated that Sherfield had broken the window because there was an "image" in it, presumably in violation of both the Elizabethan Injunctions and the homily "Against Idolatry." Although Laud later said that the picture was "not one of God the Father," he was adamant about Sherfield's violation of ecclesiastical authority, as well as of the royal authority, "for the Church derive their authority from the King." Star Chamber decided unanimously against the defendant, but the two chief justices, Sir Thomas Richardson and Sir Robert Heath, were less vindictive about the appropriate punishment than were Laud and Neile, the latter now archbishop of York. Sherfield escaped with a £500 fine, the costs to repair the window, and an acknowledgment of his fault.[48]

Sherfield's case was not the only occasion when Laud differed with Chief Justice Richardson and a local Puritan oligarchy. Upon the petition of some Somerset justices of the peace, Sir John Denham, the judge of the western circuit, banned church-ales or wakes in 1632. Customarily held on Sundays, wakes sometimes resulted in drunkenness and other infractions of the law. Laud, now elevated to archbishop of Canterbury, complained to the king about this intrusion upon his authority. He also asked the bishop of Bath and Wells, William Pierce, for further information. After surveying seventy-two members of the clergy in his diocese, Pierce reported that church-ales had practically vanished, but orderly dedication feasts or revels were still popular. Pierce echoed both Queen Elizabeth and James I when he claimed that "if the people should not have their honest and lawful Recreations upon Sundays after evening Prayer, they would go either into tippling houses . . . talk of matters of the Church or State, or else into Conventicles."[49]

Before Laud received Bishop Pierce's reply, Charles had already acted. He reissued his father's *Declaration of Sports*, permitting lawful recreations and sports for those who attended Sunday church services. Under James, the order to have the *Declaration* published in all churches had been rescinded because of the difficulty of enforcement, but under Charles the Court of High Commission either suspended or deprived ministers who failed to comply. Meanwhile, Laud ordered Richardson to revoke the order against the church-ales. At first the Chief Justice—though no Puritan—refused to comply. Later, Richardson complied with the qualifying phrase "as much as in him lay." Summoned before the Privy Council for having revoked the order "in such a slight manner," Richardson emerged from the session, protesting, "*I am like to be choked with the Archbishop's Lawnsleeves.*"[50] Laud's success with Richardson contrasts markedly with Bancroft's failure with Sir Edward Coke.

A few days after the reissue of the Book of Sports, controversy over the communion table erupted in the church of St. Gregory's, nestled in the shadows of St. Paul's cathedral. During extensive repairs to the church, the ordinary of St. Gregory's, who was also the Laudian dean of St. Paul's, decided to move the communion table from the middle to the east of the chancel against the wall, turn it altarwise (the ends facing north and south), raise it two or three steps, and surround it with rails in order to prevent defamation. Five parishioners appealed to the Court of Arches, whose dean had been appointed by Archbishop Abbot. When the dean of the Court appeared ready to decide in favor of the parishioners, Charles stopped the proceedings and called the case before the Privy Council, where Archbishops Neile and Laud sat.

Responding to complaints about the mass, the Elizabethan Injunctions of 1559 had been very clear about the location of the communion table. The appendix to those injunctions stated that the table should stand where the altar had once stood—against the east wall—except during Holy Communion, when it should stand in the chancel to allow better communication between minister and congregation. The Canons of 1604 were based upon, but less specific than, the Elizabethan injunctions on this matter. Canon 82 stated that during the celebration of Holy Communion the table "shall be . . . placed in so good sort within the church or chancel, as thereby the minister may be more conveniently heard of the communicants in his prayer." Although the St. Gregory parishioners appealed to canon 82, the king decided in favor of the ordinary. Charles' action erased whatever remained of the Elizabethan compromise over the communion table. Despite the violation of canonical authorization, Laud supported the ordinary's action in turning the communion table into an altar. The new practice at St. Gregory's (or rather the return to the practice prior to the Edwardian Reformation) provided the impetus for Charles, aided by Bishops Matthew Wren (Hereford, Norwich, and Ely) and William Pierce (Bath and Wells), to encourage altars throughout the land.[51]

As both bishop of London and archbishop of Canterbury, Laud systematically persecuted individuals and groups who opposed his views on Church government, iconography, doctrine, sabbath-keeping, and ornaments. Chiefly through the Court of Star Chamber, he stifled Leighton's withering criticism of episcopacy and Sherfield's iconoclasm at Salisbury. Chiefly through the Privy Council, he muzzled the Calvinist predestinarianism of Bishop Davenant, opposed sabbatarianism by humiliating Chief Justice Richardson, and went along with the turning of a communion table into an altar at St. Gregory's in London.

Despite his sympathies with many aspects of the Anglican Reformation, Laud did not attempt one or two changes that he might have been expected to try. He did not, for example, try to restore those medieval vestments of the Church, such as the chasuble, that were used throughout most of Edward's reign. Nor did he try to reinstitute the doctrine of the real presence as set forth in the first Edwardian Prayer Book.[52] On the whole, his ceremonial and liturgical reforms were very small in number as compared with the great variety demanded by the Puritans at Hampton Court. But Laud's general policy of conformity to the Anglican ecclesiastical formularies in the Court of High Commission caused considerable distress to Puritans—so much so that many of them began to leave England for America. Only the case of Alexander Leighton as yet showed the brutal lengths to which the Court of Star Chamber was prepared to go. But he alone of the Puritans called for the extirpation of the office of bishop.

The Puritan Proto-Martyrs

The Puritan attempt to transform society into its own moral image of a biblical ideal extended beyond sabbatarianism. William Prynne, a Presbyterian lawyer who had attacked Montagu's Arminianism in 1627 and Cosin's "cozening" *Devotions* in 1628, published a series of ethical tracts which culminated in *Histrio-mastix* (1633), a scurrilous attack upon stage plays and all people associated with the theater. Disclaiming any "puritanical singularity" of purpose, Prynne called stage plays and masques the "chief delights of the Devil" and the "most mischievous plagues that can be harboured in any Church or State." With the confidence that can come from one convinced that he will never fall finally nor totally from grace, he regarded as equally sinful and wicked the plays' concomitants:

effeminate mixed Dancing, Dicing . . . lascivious Pictures, wanton Fash-
ions, Face-painting, Health-drinking, Long hair, Love-locks, Periwigs,
women's curling, powdering and cutting of their hair. Bonfires, New-year's
gifts, May-games, amorous Pastorals, lascivious effeminate Music, excessive laughter, luxurious disorderly Christmas-keeping, Mummeries.

The pretext for Prynne's prosecution for seditious libel in 1634 before the
Court of Star Chamber arose from a careless entry in the book's index,
"Women-Actors, notorious whores." This entry caused considerable consternation at court, since Queen Henrietta Maria was herself going to act in a
play.[53]

What most disturbed the Court of Star Chamber was Prynne's implication that Charles (more like Nero than Constantine) and the bishops had
failed to impose a godly discipline upon the realm. Or, as Lord Cottington
noted at the trial: "the truth is, Mr. Prynne would have a new church, a new
government, a new king, for he would make the people altogether offended
with all things at the present." Actually, Prynne did not attack the royal
supremacy, as the Separatists had done, only the bishops' encroachments
upon it. Nor did he even attack the bishops' office, as Alexander Leighton
had done; only their misuse of it. Therefore, Prynne seemingly had no
intention of justifying rebellion against tyrannical princes as Laud had
charged him. Prynne's judges, however, including Chief Justice Richardson
of the Somerset wakes, sentenced him almost as brutally as Leighton. After
Prynne's ears were cropped, he wore long hair, ironically one of the attributes
of the stage players he had assailed.[54]

From his cell in the Tower, the compulsive Prynne began to spew forth
more books on his grievances against the Crown and the bishops. Prynne
concentrated on the Laudian bishops, and in this anti-prelatical enterprise a
clergyman, Henry Burton, and a physician, John Bastwick, soon joined him.
In *News from Ipswich*, a 1636 tract written possibly by Prynne or by Burton
or by both, the author(s) asked Charles "to behold these desperate innovations, purgations, and Romish practices of thy Prelates, in open affront of
these thy *Declarations*." If you do not take vengeance on these prelates, the
author(s) continued, they will have "pulled thy Crown off thy Royal head, to
set it on their own traitorous, ambitious pates, by exercising all ecclesiastical
power, yea Papal jurisdiction over thy Subjects in their own names."[55]

In two 1636 sermons entitled *For God and the King*, Burton, whom
Charles on his accession had dismissed as clerk of the closet, specifically
condemned the bishops for innovations. There were innovations in doctrine
(Arminianism), in discipline (the Book of Sports), in worship (erecting altars
and bowing toward them, as well as at the name of Jesus), in the Thirty-Nine
Articles (inserting article twenty), in the Prayer Book (eliminating Calvinist
words from the Collect on the Prince), and in civil government, "which they
labor to reduce and transfer to Ecclesiastical" government under the claim of
a *jure divino* authority. Burton also came very close to a theory of popular

resistance to the Crown when he wrote that God's children should "hinder and stop the beginning and creeping in of Idolatry and Superstition."[56]

In a style reminiscent of Martin Marprelate, the physician Bastwick argued in his *Letany* (1637) that the aphorism from the Hampton Court Conference, "no bishop, no king," was just as great an impiety as the aphorism, "no devil, no king." Why? Because the claim of the bishops to a *jure divino* authority defied the king as supreme governor of the Church. Of this *jure divino* authority, Bastwick remarked:

> *Such insolency was never known before*: that obscure fellows, not born to three halfpence a year of inheritance and merely advanced, by the free donation of gracious Princes, to places of eminency and splendor, in their dominions and Kingdoms, *should now dignify themselves above their masters*, or at least be checked with them, *for they said, they were Princes, and had their thrones, and that by divine authority, and were before Christian Kings.*[57]

With this statement Bastwick had drawn the full Puritan implication of *jure divino* authority: archbishops and bishops, as the papacy had long maintained, had authority over kings in ecclesiastical matters.

The Court of Star Chamber found Prynne, Burton, and Bastwick guilty of libel in June, 1637. The Court sentenced all three to lose their ears—in Prynne's case the remaining stumps—to pay £5,000, and to be imprisoned for life in separate castles far from London. The public apathy at Prynne's punishment three years earlier was transformed into a crowd-gathering drama which must have rivaled the best performances in the London theater. As the three proto-martyrs sat in the three pillories, Burton pointed out the similarity to the three crosses on Calvary, but no one attempted a more detailed application of the analogy. Branded on both cheeks with an "S.L." (Seditious Libeler), Prynne referred to his disfigurement as *Stigmata Laudis*, the Scars of Laud.[58]

After the Court sentenced Prynne, Bastwick, and Burton, Archbishop Laud addressed the defendants' charges of innovation. He admitted that his insistence upon order and conformity resulted from his desire to settle the Church according "to the rules of its first reformation." Therefore, the Puritans were the innovators, not Laud and the bishops. He demonstrated that he had not introduced article twenty into the Prayer Book in 1628. His response to several other accusations, however, was much less convincing. On the charge of deleting Calvinist words in the Collect for the Prince, as well as the slight change in wording about bowing ("in" for "at" the name of Jesus), Laud defended the right of bishops to make small changes at will. On the charge of locating the communion table "altarwise" in the east of the church, Laud cited the appendix of the Elizabethan Injunctions, canon eighty-two of the Canons of 1604, and the latest intructions of the chastized Bishop Davenant. He did not mention, however, the clear statement in the appendix or the less specific one in canon eighty-two about bringing the table into the chancel during the Holy Eucharist so that parishioners could more conveniently see it. That was the position of Laud's old rival, the Calvinist Bishop John Williams, whose book, *The Holy Table, Name and Thing* (1637), the archbishop attacked before the assemblage.[59]

Laud readily admitted the charge of advocating episcopacy *jure divino*. As a theory, it extended back to such Elizabethan bishops as Bancroft, Andrews, and Bilson, whose book, *The Perpetual Government of Christ's Church* (1593), Laud later cited. In 1640, Bishop Joseph Hall wrote on the subject under the archbishop's tutelage in *Episcopacy by Divine Right*. In his Star Chamber speech during the trial of Prynne, Bastwick, and Burton, Laud stated:

> our being bishops *jure divino*, by divine right, takes nothing from the King's right of power over us. For though our office be from God and Christ immediately, yet may we not exercise that power, either of order or jurisdiction, but as God hath appointed us, that is, not in his Majesty's or any Christian king's kingdoms, but by and under the power of the King given us so to do.

While Laud admitted on this occasion, and again at his trial seven years later, that the *exercise* of his power, either the *potestas ordinis* or the *potestas jurisdictionis*, derived from the Crown, he steadfastly maintained at both times that the *power itself* came by "Divine apostolical right." Laud's position can be interpreted as a reconciliation of episcopacy *jure divino* with royal supremacy, as some Anglicans may have thought, but it can also be seen as a forthright assertion of episcopal "godly rule," as radical Puritans certainly thought.[60]

After making his statement about the theory of episcopacy *jure divino* in 1637, the archbishop must have shocked his audience, as well as Prynne, Bastwick, and Burton, when he stated that

> we live under a gracious and a religious King, that will ever give us leave to serve God first, and him next. But were the days otherwise, I thank Christ for it, I yet know not how to serve any man against the truth of God, and I hope I shall never learn it.

Although the homily on "Obedience" provided for obedience to one's sovereign except when he or she obstructed the will of God, archbishops and bishops under Elizabeth and James were not inclined to make such anti-Erastian statements, especially in public courts of judicature. What Laud probably meant was that he had found a sovereign who would let the Arminian episcopal bench independently carry out innovations—though he would have called them changes—in the ecclesiastical jurisdiction of the Church. In view of these attitudes, it is not too surprising that the authors of *The News from Ipswich* had charged the prelates with wanting to exercise all ecclesiastical power. And, in view of the activities of Laud and Neile on the Privy Council, it is also not too surprising that Burton had charged them with wanting to transfer civil government to ecclesiastical government. The final straw had been Laud's success in getting the bishop of London, William Juxon, to replace the earl of Portland as lord treasurer. Laud was so pleased at Juxon's appointment—the prospect of increased clerical influence in government—that he wrote in his diary on March 6, 1636, "No Churchman had it since Henry 7. time . . . And now if the Church will not hold up themselves with God, I can do no more." [61]

Ironically, Laud felt that Burton, Bastwick, and Prynne had done some of the very same things that they had accused him of doing. In his Star Chamber speech to them, for instance, Laud complained that "no men . . . have been more guilty of innovation than they, while themselves cry out against it." As has been already observed, *both* the Puritans and Arminians had attempted theological innovations upon the Elizabethan settlement. The Puritan changes from loose to rigid Calvinist theology, however, occurred *before* Anglican changes from loose Calvinist theology to Arminian theology. In addition, the Puritan attempt to bring about the classical system of church government, that is, to move from credal to experimental Calvinism, had preceded the Laudian attempt to change the liturgy toward Roman Catholicism. If innovation after 1559 rests with those who make the first substantial moves, rather than those who make the most extensive ones, then the Puritans, not the Laudians, were the innovators. [62]

Later, at his own trial, Laud told Burton, "if bishops and presbyters be all one order (as these men contend for), then bishops must be *jure divino*, for so they maintain that presbyters are." The anti-episcopal Puritans, whether radical presbyterians or separatists, must have deeply resented the later Laudian claims to episcopacy *jure divino* (confined to bishops only) because it invalidated their own earlier claims to forms of church government as having been prescribed by God. The moderate Puritans, who were far less ambivalent about the royal supremacy than either the Laudian bishops or, indeed, than Presbyterian Puritans, were much more concerned about clerical influence in civil government than either of the other groups. [63]

Laud wrote to Thomas Wentworth, lord deputy of Ireland, at about the time of the trial of Burton, Bastwick, and Prynne, that "these men do but begin with the Church, that they might after have the freer Access to the State." But while both radical Puritans and Laudians did try to shape the state in accordance with their religious beliefs, many other Puritans specifically excluded the clergy from participation in affairs of state. The Laudians, though nearly as hierocratic in their aims as Cardinal Wolsey had been at the beginning of the Tudor period, did not possess as bright a vision of a godly society as that which infused the Puritan recollection of the Genevan theocracy. [64]

Once again, as under Mary in the 1550s and under Elizabeth in the 1590s, courts or commissions had prosecuted English Protestants. In several respects, the prosecutions of the 1630s resembled those of the 1590s more than they did those of the 1550s. In the Elizabethan and Laudian periods, the Courts of High Commission and Star Chamber arraigned Puritans but not all Protestants; the most serious charges involved sedition and seditious libel; the number of Puritans found guilty was fairly small; and the punishments usually involved fines, imprisonment, and, in extreme cases, mutilation (Prynne) or execution (Penry).[65] There are striking differences, however, between the prosecutions of the 1550s and the 1630s. The Puritans under Laud were not prosecuted by a Catholic sovereign and a Catholic commission for heresy, which in the 1550s had resulted in about 1,000 burnings at the stake for members of the Church hierarchy as well as laymen from most social groups. But these differences do not mask the important similarities between the prosecutions under Mary and those under Laud. During both of these periods, the Crown, whether leading the way as in the 1550s or mostly following the archbishop as in the 1630s, wanted to take the Anglican Church back to a theology, a liturgy, and a form of church government that it had enjoyed previously in its history. Both Mary's many martyrs and Laud's few proto-martyrs, either by the example of their cruel deaths in the 1550s or their imprisonment and suffering in the 1630s, kept their respective causes alive for a few years until Parliament could vindicate the principles for which they had suffered. Meanwhile, the prospect of life-threatening persecution encouraged those embarkations from England that we know as the Marian exile and the Great Migration to New England.

The New England Theocracy

In the late 1620s, a small number of Englishmen under the leadership of the Puritan squire, John Winthrop, emigrated to the New World when they became desolate about the fate of the Church and despondent over economic distress. Gaining control of the newly chartered Massachusetts Bay Company through the influence of Puritan noblemen like the earl of Warwick and Viscount Say and Sele. Winthrop and leading members of the company made a civil covenant with one another. This Cambridge Agreement formed the temporal counterpart of the church covenant of the elect. In order to free themselves from an overzealous government in England, the Cambridge signers stipulated that the government of the company, together with the charter, should be transferred to New England. Before sailing for America in 1630, however, they declared their intention of not separating from the Church of England. By this act they placed themselves squarely in the tradition of those covenanting Puritans like Ames and Bradshaw—covenanters in both theology and the church—who had embraced semi-Separatism or nonseparating Congregationalism. They wished to conduct a holy experiment in the wilderness of America in accordance with certain ideals that Puritans in old England had found impossible to implement.[66]

Soon after their arrival at Massachusetts Bay, the colonists transformed the government of the trading company into a Puritan commonwealth. "It is of the nature and essence of every society," Winthrop wrote, "to be knit together by some Covenant, either expressed or implied." God's implied covenant with Massachusetts took an express form that allowed the freemen to elect the small group of magistrates, and later a large group of deputies, who, in turn, elected the governor and deputy governor. Like ministers elected by their church congregations, Winthrop and other elected civil officials did not feel bound to represent the views of their constituents. They believed, rather, that they possessed broad discretionary powers to carry out the law of God. But, like the ministers, they realized that they could be voted out of office if they did not pay attention to those who felt that the civil officers possessed specific delegated powers.[67]

In order to make sure that all officeholders were honest and God-fearing men, the General Court (the magistrates and the deputies) decided in 1631 that only members of a Congregational church could become freemen and, hence, have the right to vote. They assumed that the ministers would be able to advise church members about the selection of officeholders. The Puritan colony of New Haven followed Massachusetts in making church membership a requirement for freemen, but their sister colony of Connecticut required church membership only of the governor. Although everyone had to attend church (as in England) as well as pay taxes for its support, the General Court in 1636 passed another law stating that a person could not become a member of a Congregational church unless he or she satisfied the elders and the congregation of his or her regeneration through a conversion experience. The New Haven colony under John Davenport enforced a similar requirement of visible sainthood for church membership, but Thomas Hooker's Connecticut was more lenient about church admissions. The new statute gave the churches tighter control over those who could vote and hold civil office. Although church membership in Massachusetts provided a broader base for the franchise than the forty-shilling freehold qualification in English counties, only about half or slightly more of the free adult males in Massachusetts were able to participate in the early political life of the colony. As the colony grew, the percentage of church members actually declined.[68]

The religious restrictions imposed upon the elective process were designed to give Massachusetts a form of government that can best be called a theocracy. Both Winthrop and John Cotton, the colony's leading minister after 1633, decried democratic forms of government. "If the people be governors," wrote Cotton, "who shall be governed?" Winthrop and Cotton believed in a theocratic form of government whereby the will of God would be made manifest through the rule of His Saints. In fact, Cotton wrote to Lord Saye and Sele that theocracy was "the best form of government in the commonwealth as in the church."[69]

As in the two-kingdom theory of Thomas Cartwright, but unlike the single-kingdom theory of Laud in the Instructions of 1626, Cotton thought that church and state were separate but related aspects of a holy commonwealth. He described the proper relationship between church and state in a letter to Lord Saye and Sele in 1636:

> Mr. Hooker doth often quote a saying out of Mr. Cartwright (though I have
> not read it in him) that no man fashioneth his house to his hangings, but his

hangings to his house. It is better that the commonwealth be fashioned to the setting forth of God's house, which is His church than to accommodate the church frame to the civil state.[70]

That point of view did not mean that Cotton would allow the clergy to participate directly in the management of civil affairs. Such hierocratic government aroused the old fears of Roman Catholicism and the newer ones of Archbishop Laud.

While the Massachusetts clergy held no political office, there was considerable interaction between the church and state. The clergy influenced civil government not only through election sermons but also through continuous solicited counsel and recommendations so that the elected leaders might be informed of the mind of God in particular issues. In fact, ministers ordinarily attended sessions of the General Court. Of Cotton and Hooker one contemporary wrote, "such was the authority they (especially Mr. Cotton) had in the hearts of the people, that whatever he delivered in the pulpit was soon put into an Order of Court, if of a civil, or set up as a practice in the church, if of an ecclesiastical concernment.[71] Conversely, the state acted as a "nursing-father" to the churches. Since there were no church courts as in old England, the state exclusively handled testamentary and matrimonial cases. But the state also tried cases growing out of both the first and second tables of the Ten Commandments. Usually, however, churches first disciplined their own members for infractions of the Mosaic code, including heresy, before the state took its action. Whether the church or the state had the responsibility for a particular activity, society was organized so that decisions were made only by the Saints and the godly party rather than the unbelievers and disenfranchised.

Roger Williams, the Separatist minister, disliked the contacts that Massachusetts Puritans maintained between their Congregational churches and the Church of England, between the regenerate and the unregenerate while attending services within their churches, and between their churches and the state in its role as "nursing-father." Shortly after Williams' arrival in Massachusetts, the Boston church invited him to serve as teacher, but he refused to minister to people unseparated from the Church of England. When Salem, which had some Separatist tendencies, offered him the same post, Governor Winthrop told the Salem authorities that Williams believed the civil magistrate might not punish any breach of the first table of the Ten Commandments. After Salem withdrew its offer under pressure from Winthrop and Cotton, Williams moved on to the self-proclaimed Separatist colony of Plymouth, but he soon protested the contamination of the Plymouth Saints when they attended Anglican Church services on visits to England.

Upon Williams' return to a more independent Salem in July, 1635, the General Court (advised by the colony's ministers) summoned him to answer for the extreme positions that grew out of his uncompromising Separatism. The ministers unanimously declared that Williams ought to lose his pastorate at Salem. But they ignored the principle of the independence of each congregation by recommending that the other churches ought to request the magistrates to remove Williams. When the General Court prepared to act upon this advice from the clergy, Williams told his Salem congregation not to communicate with the colony's other churches unless they wished him to leave. Faced with his ultimatum to isolate their church and anxious to obtain the land of Marblehead Neck from the General Court, a majority of the Salem church members failed to support Williams. In October, the General Court with all of the ministers in attendance banished Williams from the colony. Williams fled to Plymouth in January, 1636, but the following spring he journeyed to Narragansett Bay where he founded Providence, the nucleus of the future colony of Rhode Island. In Providence, Williams, a Calvinist but no covenant theologian, carried on the tradition of the separation of church and state as set forth by Browne, Barrow, and the later Separatists.[72]

A second and more serious challenge to the Bay Colony theocracy came from Anne Hutchinson and her Antinomian followers. Antinomianism was a theological reaction against covenant theology. Instead of stressing man's preparation of the heart for salvation, Antinomians stressed the immediate and personal revelation of the Holy Spirit to those who were already saved. Unlike most New England ministers, John Cotton (Hutchinson's teacher in both Bostons—Lincolnshire and Massachusetts) and John Wheelwright (her brother-in-law) spoke of the theological covenant as if God's grace or Holy Spirit were absolutely free and conditionless. In weekly discussions of Cotton's sermons, Hutchinson told her adherents, including many members of the Boston church, that behaving in a sanctified way—through a legalistic obedience to the moral law of Holy Scripture—was not necessarily evidence of salvation. To assume that such evidence of sanctification was valid was to confuse the proper man with the pious man, to subscribe to a covenant of works instead of a covenant of grace. For magistrates like Winthrop, Mrs. Hutchinson's views were an invitation to licentious conduct, something not to be tolerated in either church or state. By February, 1637, Winthrop noted, "it began to be as common here to distinguish between men, by being under a covenant of grace or a covenant of works, as in other countries between Protestants and papists." In Cotton's context, those who believed in a conditional covenant of grace were preaching a covenant of works.[73]

The counterattack against the Antinomians began with the General Court's conviction of Wheelwright for sedition because of inflammatory language preached against those under a covenant of works. The ministers in attendance had agreed to have the Court proceed "without tarrying for the church." In May, Winthrop was again elected governor, succeeding Henry Vane the Younger, the twenty-two-year-old friend of Cotton and Hutchinson. Fearing the arrival in the colony of some Grindletonians (English followers of the Antinomian preacher, Roger Brearly), the General Court passed an alien act which gave the civil officials power to screen newly arrived candidates for church membership before their examination by the elders.[74]

In an effort to recover the initiative from the magistrates in defining matters of heresy, Cotton and other ministers agreed to participate in a synod of Massachusetts divines called by the General Court in Newtown. While responding to a series of searching questions, Cotton removed even the condition of faith from God's promise of salvation: man's salvation took place "before our faith doth put forth it self to lay hold on him." This Antinomian conception of faith by justification, which reversed the traditional conception of justification by faith, shocked the assembled clergymen. Shortly afterwards, however, they must have been pleased when Cotton admitted that "the Spirit doth Evidence our Justification both ways, sometime in an absolute Promise, sometime in a conditional."[75]

With the retreat of Cotton at the synod, the General Court brought Hutchinson to trial—with the clergy in attendance, as in the case of Williams. The Court accused Hutchinson chiefly of maligning the ministers of the Colony, including Hugh Peters (Williams' successor at Salem), for having labored under a covenant of works, a charge that Cotton denied under oath as he sat at her side. However, when she said she determined a true ministry "by an immediate revelation"—"by the voice of his own spirit to my soul"— she sealed her fate.[76] She had cast aside the authority of Holy Scripture. Winthrop banished her from the colony in the name of the General Court, and Cotton censured her shortly afterwards in the name of the Boston church. Congregational Massachusetts would not tolerate that kind of heresy.

The extensive power which the General Court exercised in religious affairs during the 1630s led the ministers to support the Court's codification of the law known as the "Body of Liberties" (1641). Written by the minister-lawyer, Nathaniel Ward, the *Body of Liberties* contained a section on the "Liberties the Lord Jesus Christ hath given to the Churches." The "church liberties" attempted to guarantee the traditional Puritan quest for the independence of the churches from state control. Some of the church liberties verified Samuel Stone's statement that the church was a "speaking *Aristocracy* in face of a silent *Democracy*." These church liberties included the gathering together in a "Church Estate" in the first instance, the election and ordination of "able, pious, and orthodox" church officers, the admission of members as well as the expulsion of them and the church officers through the free exercise of "the Discipline and Censures of Christ," and the quarterly meetings of the elders of the churches "for conferences and consultations about Christian and Church questions." Other church liberties appear to have grown out of the Antinomian controversy. These church liberties included the disallowance of private meetings for religious edification; the prohibition of any state injunction upon churches, church officers, or chuch members regarding points of doctrine, worship, or discipline; and, in order to prevent the growth of heresy in any one of the churches, the calling of consultations or conferences of ministers and elders from adjoining churches, not altogether unlike the synod called in the Antinomian controversy, to resolve "cases of conscience" concerning doctrine, worship, or church government.[77]

Both of these sets of church liberties were somewhat offset, however, by articles from the section on "Liberties more peculiarly concerning the free men." One of these articles enlarged the traditional Puritan role of the state beyond a mere "nursing-father" to the churches. It gave the civil authority power to maintain "the peace, ordinances, and Rule of Christ observed in every church according to his word," just as long as it was done in "a Civil and not in a Ecclesiastical way." Despite the imprecision of this article, other articles in this section defined the boundaries between church and state much more precisely in two instances. First, the civil authority had the power to mete out "Civil Justice" to any church member, and that included violations of the Mosaic code; but churches could deal with their own members already in the hands of "Civil Justice," presumably by passing a church censure *before* the state acted. Second, while every church could pass censure upon any of its members who were magistrates, deputies, or other officers of the state for an "offense given in their places," no church censure could result in their removal from political office. The *Body of Liberties* reflected much of the practical experience that the Massachusetts Puritans acquired in the 1630s. Still, it is significant how closely they adhered to the two-kingdom theory (separate but related) of Cartwright and the early Puritans.

Once again, as in the 1550s and to a lesser extent as in the first decade of the seventeenth century, a group of Englishmen escaped abroad from the persecution of the state in religious matters. Unlike the two earlier instances, the New England Puritans did not seek refuge in established Reformed cities of western Europe. They fled, instead, to the wilderness of America, where they could set up their own civil governments as well as their own churches. No longer did they have to seek toleration from foreign city and state governments where they would be small minorities, however friendly their reception.

In New England, Puritans formed the dominant religious and political group from the outset, unencumbered by a royal court, an entrenched social aristocracy, or a religious hierarchy. Crown control amounted largely to a royal proclamation forbidding the emigration to America of anyone "under the Degree of Subsidy-men" unless they had taken the oaths of Allegiance and Supremacy and had testified to their conformity to the Anglican Church. Aristocratic influence consisted of advice from Lord Saye and Sele, who finally decided against joining the thousands who made up the Great Migration of the 1630s. Archbishop Laud referred to the way of religion in New England as "the presbyterial government as it seems established there." According to Laud's chaplain, only the development of hostilities in England kept him from sending a bishop to keep the Massachusetts Puritans in line.[78]

Just as the Separatist ideals of Roger Williams had grown out of the refinements that the Jacobean exiles in Amsterdam and Leyden made upon the ideas of Browne and Barrow, so the theocratic ideals of the Massachusetts Congregationalists had grown out of those refinements that Cartwright and his colleagues made upon the ideas of the Marian exiles in Frankfort and Geneva. Frankfort had provided the concepts of freedom of the church from the state, except in a crisis, and freedom of the state from the church, except as an arbitrator. Geneva had provided the idea of ecclesiastical censure of the civil magistrate, but the New England Congregationalists did not make any use of the Genevan doctrine of "active resistance" to the civil magistrate. As long as they dominated the civil government, the Congregationalists did not need to develop a theory of revolution or, for that matter, a theory of toleration. These theories achieved a high priority only when a minority of Puritan Independents in old England took up the New England way and found leadership in the 1640s from such former residents of Massachusetts as Henry Vane and Hugh Peters.

The Resurgence of Catholicism

While the Puritans in New England were building a new Jerusalem, many Puritans in old England perceived a resurgence of Catholicism because of the proto-Catholic changes in the churches and the Church service, the spread of anti-Calvinist theology, the claims of the bishops to episcopacy by divine right, and the increase in episcopal influence at the highest levels of government. Their conclusion was right, but their reasons were wrong; the resurgence of Catholicism came in another way. After the partial suspension of the penal laws when Charles married, Henrietta Maria pressed the king to suspend them. Although the Queen exercised a strong influence over Charles, he never suspended all of them because he wanted his commissioners to be able to negotiate with Catholics for payment of recusancy fines so necessary for the Crown's weakened financial situation. Henrietta Maria's chaplains said mass daily in her household, and the queen became the rallying point for Catholics at court. New creations of Catholic aristocrats, particularly under James I, brought their numbers to about one-fifth of the peerage. Some notable conversions to Catholicism included Laud's godson, William Chillingworth, and Lady Newport, the wife of a prominent Puritan peer. But more important, three of Charles' chief ministers were perceived as having close ties with Roman Catholics: Chancellor of the Exchequer Francis, Lord Cottington; Secretary of State Sir Francis Windebank; and Lord Treasurer Sir Richard Weston (earl of Portland).[79]

Quarrels between the Jesuits and the regular priests had continued to plague the Jacobean successors of Archpriest Blackwell as well as each man who, as Catholic bishop of Chalcedon, held the new post of vicar apostolic for England. Of these underground bishops, William Bishop (1623–1625) had been one of the Elizabethan appellants, and Richard Smith (1625–1631) had been the subject of a royal proclamation in 1629, calling for his arrest for high treason. In 1634, Dom Leander Jones, who had shared university rooms with Laud, tried unsuccessfully to get Pope Urban VIII to rescind the papal bull of 1626, which forebade Catholics to take the Oath of Allegiance in any form. By 1635, the unofficial papal emissary, Gregorio Panzani, observed that Bishop Godfrey Goodman of Gloucester, who had once been summoned before Convocation for preaching transubstantiation or something akin to it, said divine offices out of the Roman breviary every day. And Bishop Montagu told Panzani that he would subscribe to all of the Pope's articles except for transubstantiation and communion in one kind. Panzani's most important act resulted in the first exchange of diplomatic relations between England and Rome since the days of Henry VIII. Auspiciously, Charles promised to permit the Catholic Church to have a legal bishop in England if the pope would allow the Catholics to subscribe to a more lenient Oath of Allegiance. The Roman Catholic Church had reason for guarded optimism.[80]

For a short time between 1636 and 1638, George Conn, the new agent from Rome, had seemingly replaced Laud as the most important religious adviser at court. While he plied Charles with gifts of paintings by renowned Italian Renaissance artists, Conn tried to bring about the king's conversion and the reconciliation of the Anglican Church with Rome. With Charles he discussed a book published in Passau which called the kings of England Antichrists because they had claimed the headship of the Church. The king objected to Henry VIII's title—supreme head of the Church of England—because of his dislike of schism. Charles believed himself to be a Catholic (but not a Roman Catholic), one who belonged to the whole body of orthodox Christendom. And he further stated that there was no essential difference between the Roman Catholic creed and the Thirty-Nine Articles.[81]

In his negotiations with Conn, Charles expected Rome to yield on such points as communion in one kind, the mass in Latin, the celibacy of the clergy, and, especially, the power to depose heretical princes. In return he agreed to drop the phrase from the Oath of Allegiance that required Catholics to declare that papal deposition was "impious and heretical" and to require only an "unconditioned fidelity to the king . . . against all invasion, *deposition*, rebellion etc. by any prince, *priest*, or people." But Rome balked at the words "deposition" and "priest" as well as at all other attempts to compromise. Laud astutely warned Charles that if he "wished to go to Rome, the Pope would not stir a step to meet him." Reunion with Rome, on equal terms rather than in a submissive sense, was a naive hope that Charles shared with his father, but conversion to Rome was something that he never seriously contemplated.[82]

Laud consistently opposed Roman Catholicism throughout his entire professional career. From the troubled night in 1626 when he dreamt of his own reconciliation with Rome until the day in 1640 when he fell upon his knees and implored the king to persecute the Catholics, Laud attempted to keep Charles free from involvement with Roman Catholics. He knew that he had a difficult task, especially after 1630 when Charles and Henrietta Maria drew closer. The Catholic queen quarrelled continuously with Laud, whom she came to dislike intensely. Shortly after his nomination as archbishop of Canterbury, he twice turned down a cardinal's hat. As he recorded in his diary, he would not accept "till Rome were other than it is."[83] Laud never suggested, as Bishops Goodman and Montagu had done, that the differences between Rome and Canterbury were minimal.

During those days when the pope's emissaries stood so high in the king's esteem, neither Bishop Juxon nor Laud would see Panzani, nor would Laud listen to Conn's proposals to alter the Oath of Allegiance, and the archbishop was very critical of meetings that Conn's successor, Count Carlo Rossetti, held with Roman Catholics in London. Before the Privy Council, which Conn sometimes attended, Laud denounced the growth of the "Roman party," the ease of attending mass in the queen's chapel, and the missionary activities of some Roman Catholics at court. As a result of his charges, a royal proclamation charged that the withdrawal of the king's subjects to "the Roman superstition" and the "resorting to Masses" were contrary to acts of Parliament, royal proclamations, and orders in Privy Council, as well as being a "great scandal of His Majesty's Government in both Church and State." The "severest punishments" were to be applied. Laud was gratified when his godson, Chillingworth, whom the Jesuit John Fisher had converted to Roman Catholicism, announced his apostasy from Rome in 1638. The next year, the archbishop republished his earlier book against Fisher, which deterred Buckingham from conversion to Rome. Laud summarized his fears about Catholics to Viscount Wentworth, who persuaded the Irish Convocation of the Clergy to replace the Irish Articles of 1615 with the Thirty-Nine Articles. "The Papists were the most dangerous Subjects of the Kingdom," wrote Laud, "and that betwixt them and the Puritans, the good Protestants would be ground to powder."[84]

The only aspect of church–state relationships that Archbishop Laud firmly opposed during the period of his hegemony was Charles' rapprochement with Rome. The king's pro-Catholic policy, somewhat similar to that of his father's first decade on the throne, was not an inevitable development of the growth of Arminianism, a movement that James had largely opposed. The pro-Catholic policy and growth of Arminianism were separate phenomena and certainly not compatible in the mind of the archbishop and many of his bishops. Laud was well aware, however, that his Puritan opponents were doing their very best to identify Laudianism with Roman Catholicism publicly. In some respects the archbishop was to become a victim of the same kind of logical oversimplification which he himself had tried to perpetrate upon rigid Calvinist and radical anti-episcopalian Puritans in the 1630s. Unlike Archbishop Whitgift, who successfully split off moderate Puritans from radical Puritans in the 1590s, Laud succeeded in alienating those moderates who, not sharing his vision of the Church, came to the position where they could no longer support him. In their time of crisis, both Laud and Charles fell victim to a public perception that they had perpetrated a double-pronged "popish plot"—the proof of which was both the activity of the pro-Catholic court and that of Laudianism, which John Pym believed was indistinguishable from Catholicism. This public perception of a "popish plot" made it all the more difficult for Laud and Charles to impose a new prayer book on the Scots.[85]

The Scottish Revolution

One of the most important turning points in the fortunes of the Crown and the Church, which culminated in the overthrow of both institutions in the 1640s, was Charles' attempt to bring the Kirk in Scotland into closer accord with the Anglican Church. Earlier in the century, James had hoped to revise the Scottish Book of Common Order (1562) along the lines of the English Book of Common Prayer, but that project died when Scottish opposition arose to the Five Articles of Perth (1615). After Charles came to the throne, a few Scottish bishops, like a few of their counterparts in England, went onto their Privy Council, and John Spottiswood, archbishop of St. Andrews, assumed high civil office. As Bishop Juxon became lord treasurer in England, so Archbishop Spottiswood became lord chancellor of Scotland. The Crown revived the project of Scottish liturgical reform in 1629. Laud would have preferred the imposition of the English Prayer Book without any change, but the Scottish bishops, over whom Laud had no ecclesiastical jurisdiction, insisted upon drawing up their own liturgy based upon the English model but modified for Scottish practice.

In preparation for the new liturgy, the Scottish bishops in 1636 drew up a set of canons for the Church of Scotland—an enterprise which Laud supervised from the start. Issued under the authority of Charles as king of Scotland, the Canons of 1636 dealt at length with presbyters (but made no mention of elders, presbyteries, or general assemblies), incorporated the Five Articles of Perth, and included some Erastian provisions based upon the English Canons of 1604. The Laudian influence appears, for example, in two canons which differed from the Canons of 1604. Canon sixteen called for the communion table to be placed "at the upper end of the chancel or church." Canon eight permitted future innovations, that is, "reformation in doctrine or discipline" of the Church, after a "remonstrance to his majesty" with any decision left to the king. The Canons of 1636 also enjoined obedience to the as yet unfinished liturgy.[86]

James Wedderburn, bishop of Dunblane, an old friend of Laud, sent some suggestions for the new liturgy to Charles, and hence to Laud, for approval. These suggestions included a different phrasing for the administration of the Holy Sacrament. Wedderburn omitted the words of the second line—"Take, eat, in remembrance etc."—on the grounds that they were too Zwinglian in import. As to what remained, he remarked, "There is no more in King Edward VI his first book." After the approval of Wedderburn's suggestions in the final version of the Scottish Book of Common Prayer, Laud was accused of having supported a version which, in effect, justified the corporal presence. This and a few other changes in the direction of the early reformation helped make, if not "Laud's Liturgy," at least a "Laudian liturgy."[87]

The royal proclamation of the new liturgy produced an astonishingly hostile reaction among the Scottish people. It was read for the first time in St. Giles cathedral, Edinburgh, on July 23, 1637. The resulting riot left a picturesque legend of one Jenny Geddes throwing her stool at the bishop. If her arm had not been deflected, the historian Thomas Fuller observed, "the same book had occasioned his death, and prescribed the form of his burial." [88]

The Scottish Presbyterians drew up a band of mutual support in 1638 which came to be called the National Covenant. In the National Covenant, members of all strata of Scottish society, including clergymen, swore to defend the true religion in "Kirk and Kingdom" as it was professed before "Innovations and evils" in the worship of God tended to reestablish "Popish Religion and Tyranny." Not only did the Covenanters band together, but they also sought God's blessing as ones "who have renewed their Covenant with God" as well. In addition, the National Covenant contained the text of an earlier antipapal covenant—the "Negative Confession" of 1581. Despite this precedent for covenanting under James VI, the National Covenant could be regarded as a lay counterpart—a conditional social contract—to covenant theology, even though the National Covenant upheld the authority of the Crown.[89]

In November, 1638 a General Assembly of the Scottish Kirk, under the presidency of Alexander Henderson, the leader of the new generation of Melvilleans, acted decisively against Charles and Laud. This Glasgow Assembly abolished the Five Articles of Perth, the new Canons, the new Prayer Book, the Scottish Court of High Commission, and civil office-holding for all churchmen. With startling speed, the Scottish Presbyterians had wiped out rituals and institutions that in their Anglican forms had been plaguing Puritans for years.

Charles had two courses of action open to him: he could either withdraw the canons and the Prayer Book, or he could raise an army to impose them upon the Scots by force. He did both. The first action, however, was only temporary until the second could take effect. The projected English use at this time, and again the following year, of Catholic troops from the Highlands and Ireland, subsidized by Madrid and Rome, gave some substance to the Puritan fears of a "popish plot." [90] In the spring of 1639, an English army marched north, but the king's limited forces, lacking money and discipline, signed a truce with a sizable army of Covenanters at Berwick. The First Bishops' War had ended with hardly a shot being fired. In the Pacification of Berwick, Charles agreed to call a new General Assembly, which subsequently excluded the bishops from its midst, and a new Scottish Parliament, which subsequently abolished episcopacy.

In order to obtain supplies for a renewed military campaign, Charles summoned his fourth English Parliament into session on April 13, 1640, on the advice of Laud and Wentworth, now Earl of Strafford. Four days later, John Pym's Committee on Grievances, which examined constitutional and financial matters also, looked at the Laudian innovations in religion because he feared that the Canterbury Convocation of the Clergy might enshrine some of them in new canons without the approval of Parliament. Pym's list of Laudian innovations included "universal suspension" of the penal laws against Catholics, popish ceremonies such as bowing to altars, papists appointed to "places of trust" in the Commonwealth, a resident papal nuncio at court, the Book of Sports, the Court of High Commission, its oath ex officio, and episcopacy *jure divino*—all aspects, from Pym's point of view, of a "popish plot." Within three weeks, however, the king dismissed the first Parliament in eleven years—the Short Parliament—when he found out that it preferred discussing grievances to prosecuting a war against the Scots.[91]

Speculation upon the might-have-beens in history, especially on the grand scale, is always a precarious activity. But it seems most unlikely that Charles would have called Parliament into session in 1640 had it not been for the attempt to impose a new Prayer Book upon Scotland. The quarrel with Scotland was a fatal mistake judged from what subsequently happened, but it was also the disastrous culmination of a policy which was attempting to change the whole religious life of the British Isles. It seems most unlikely that the quarrels over Arminianism in Charles' early Parliaments, or the alienation of the Puritan laity over tithes and impropriations, or the persecution of the Puritan proto-martyrs, or the powerful anti-Catholic feeling aroused by the Court and hierarchy in the 1630s would have been enough without the Scottish Revolution to permit the Puritans seriously to challenge the archbishop and the Laudian Church.

The Canons of 1640

While the Short Parliament met, and for some time afterwards, both convocations formulated a new set of canons for the Anglican Church. Designed as an attempt to impose Laudianism formally on the Anglican Church, the canons succeeded only in creating new dissension within the Church. For example, Benjamin Rudyard, writing about the bishops who wrote the canons, said:

> if we shall find among them any Proud *Becket*, or *Wolsey*-Prelates, who stick not to write, *Ego & Rex meus*; or if there shall be found any *Bonners. & c.* such, I profess I would not spare, for they will spare none: but if in the counterbalance there may be found but one good *Cranmer*, or one good *Latimer* or *Ridley*, I would esteem and prize them (as rich as Jewels) fit to be set in the King's own cabinet.

Apparently, there were also some differences of opinion within Convocation itself. The result was, at least partly, an attempt to make the Canons of 1640 more palatable than might otherwise have been the case.[92]

In the royal introduction to the canons, the king denied that "we ourself are perverted, and do worship God in a superstitious way, and that we intend to bring in some alteration of the religion here established." After all, said Charles, his "many public declarations" indicated that. But, continued the king, many religious ceremonies are not uniformly carried throughout all of the churches of the realm. Therefore, in the tradition of Edward VI's and Elizabeth's injunctions, as well as the Canons of 1604 of "our dear father," Charles decided to give his bishops the opportunity in convocation to frame "certain other canons." The king's hope was to return to "the true former splendor of uniformity, devotion, and holy order," which, since the very beginning of the Reformation, had been obscured by the desires of some "ill-affected" men—probably a reference to radical and Separatist Puritans—and by "the inadvertency of some in authority in the Church under us"—probably a reference to Archbishop Abbot. In addition, Charles appeared to be somewhat sensitive to the charge that the rites and ceremonies of the Church were "introductive unto popish superstitions." [93]

Canon three enjoined all ranks of the clergy to use "all possible care and diligence" in holding private conferences with those "who are misled into popish superstition." Only if the conferences failed would the Church "come to her censures." And if neither of these prevailed, resort would be made to the secular power through the justices of the assize. Bishop Goodman, whose sympathies to Roman Catholicism were known to Laud, told the archbishop that "he would be torn with wild horses" before he would subscribe to canon three. Bishops Davenant and Hall tried to persuade Goodman to subscribe to the new Canons, but the Privy Council suspended him for six months from his bishopric and later forced him to subscribe. [94]

Canon seven presumably dealt with "some rites and ceremonies" designed to produce a "uniformity of practice in the outward worship and service of God." Actually, it dealt only with the altar question. Some of its provisions suggested a retreat from the Laudian position. The canon declared, for instance, that the position of "the communion table sideway under the east window of every chancel or chapel" is a thing "indifferent," that the table could be moved for the administration of Holy Communion, and that it was in no sense a true altar where Christ had been sacrificed. But other provisions seriously qualified these apparent concessions. For instance, the canon also declared that according to the law only the bishop could authorize such a move, that the communion table could be called an altar, that it should be railed in to prevent profanation, that all communicants should approach it under the east window unless the bishop dispensed with the rule, and that one should bow to the altar upon entering and leaving the church (not because of any belief in the corporal presence but for "the advancement of God's majesty"). Neither the Elizabethan injunctions nor the Canons of 1604 had included any of these provisions. [95]

But the "etcetera oath" of canon six caused the greatest consternation for the opponents of the Laudian Church. The oath required all who were in holy orders, every Master of Arts except the sons of noblemen, all who had taken a degree in divinity, law, or physics, every registrar, actuary, proctor, and schoolmaster, and all who were incorporated from foreign universities to swear that they approved "the doctrine, and discipline, or government established in the Church of England, as containing all things necessary to salvation" and would never "consent to alter the government of this Church by archbishops, bishops, deans, and archdeacons, &c., as it stands now established." The ambiguous abbreviation, "etcetera," was hastily formulated to stand for Church officials under the rank of archdeacon, but the Puritans regarded the oath as a mask for the introduction of further innovations such as the recognition of the pope or the introduction of the Roman mass. Others felt that the application by the clergy of an oath to laymen (unlike the Canons of 1604) offended the civil power of Parliament. Under pressure, Charles decided to suspend the "etcetera" oath in August of the same year. Once again Laud and Charles had succeeded in alienating important groups within the Anglican Church.[96]

The convocation of the clergy, which Charles converted into a synod, gave the king six subsidies as a benevolence in order to send another army north. The Scots repulsed the English forces in the Second Bishops' War (1640). In the treaty of Ripon, it was agreed that the Scots, who had crossed onto English soil, should receive £850 a day until a permanent settlement could be effected. The ignominy of a foreign army, and a Covenanter one at that, camped on English soil occasioned the meeting on November 3, 1640 of Charles' fifth Parliament—the Long Parliament, which would sit for thirteen years.

The Canons of 1640 were as notable for what they did not state as for what they did state. Although canon one strongly advocated the divine right of monarchy, the canons said nothing about the crucial issue of the divine right of episcopacy. Although the canons called for the suppression of popery, canons four and five confined their criticism of Puritanism largely to Socinians and sectaries, that is, Anabaptists, Brownists, Separatists, and Familists, who did not occupy, at least at this moment, the center stage of the Puritan movement. Although the canons had much to say about the altar controversy—largely repudiating those clauses in the Canons of 1604—all other liturgical matters were neglected. No canon dealt with Arminian theology, possibly suggesting that Arminianism was no longer the burning issue that it had been in the Parliaments of the 1620s or that it was not of critical importance to Laud; or, possibly, but probably because such a canonical forum was not regarded as appropriate, just as the Canons of 1604 had not come to terms with Archbishop Whitgift's Lambeth Articles. The canon that provoked the greatest Puritan opposition, understandably, was the one which appeared to revive Whitgift's subscription oath of Queen Elizabeth's reign. As a comprehensive statement of Laudianism, the Canons of 1640 were woefully inadequate. Still, with all of their limitations, they constituted the grand climax, as well as the last gasp of the Laudian Counter-Reformation.

Despite obvious similarities between the Laudian Counter-Reformation and the reign of Queen Mary—the persecution of the martyrs and the exodus overseas—there is an important difference. The Laudian Counter-Reformation was more eclectic. Whereas Mary simply wanted to return the Church in nearly all of its aspects to where it had been in 1529, the Laudian hierarchy selectively drew from the various religious changes of the Anglican Reformation. First and foremost, Laud and nearly all of the Arminians rejected papal supremacy. From the experience of both Elizabeth and James, Laud had concluded that Catholics were the most dangerous subjects in the kingdom. Second, while Laud appeared to accept royal supremacy in the Church, his notion of episcopacy *jure divino*, set forth earlier by such Jacobean bishops as Bancroft and Andrews, modified the perception of the essentially Erastian relationship. Like Cardinal Wolsey, he wanted to increase the role of the higher clergy in the political life of the nation. Third, though by no means a strong advocate of Arminian theology, Laud undermined the more rigid aspects of Calvinist theology. In this enterprise the Arminians related most closely to the Christian humanists of Henry VIII's reign. Fourth, despite following much of the liturgical ceremonial of the Anglican formularies— what Laud called "the external decent worship of God"[97]—he and the Laudian bishops eliminated most of the Zwinglian elements in the late Edwardian Holy Eucharist as set forth in the Scottish Prayer Book of 1637; and they also resurrected the Henrician use of altars in the Canons of 1640. In doing so, they unraveled the eucharistic settlement in the second Edwardian and Elizabethan Prayer Books, as well as the communion table compromise in the Elizabethan Injunctions of 1559 and the Jacobean Canons of 1604.

Finally, in his effort to resolve the economic problems of the Church, Laud took guidance from late Henrician legislation, but in trying to control the lectures, prophesyings (combination lectures), and prohibitions of the Puritans and their sympathizers, he drew heavily upon the tradition of Archbishop Bancroft. Although there are some notable exceptions—the real presence being the most important—the Anglican Church that Laud wanted to restore was in many ways that of the late Henrician and early Edwardian period. In matters of church and state, he formally advocated the royal supremacy, but he informally related closely to the hierocratic views of the Catholics and to the theocratic views of the Puritans.

Despite their deep differences over sabbatarianism, the role of the altar, and liturgical practices, the Puritans and the Laudians, particularly Archbishop Laud, held some beliefs in common. They shared a hostility toward Rome even though many of the Laudian liturgical ornaments and ceremonies seemed to come very close to those of Catholicism. Theologically, Puritan and Laudian views were both grounded in Calvinist theology, but the Laudians moved from the loose Calvinism of the Thirty-Nine Articles to Arminianism, whereas the Puritans moved from a loose to a rigid Calvinism oftentimes interlaced with some form of covenant theology. Both Puritans and Laudians tried to increase clerical stipends through the return of impropriations from lay to clerical control, but Laud, who wished to increase tithes for the bishops, vigorously opposed the Puritan plan to reestablish feoffees for impropriations. Both groups possessed a vision of a godly society, but the Laudian credal goal of a one-kingdom church and state (national and all-inclusive) embraced a *jure divino* episcopacy, whereas the Puritan experimental goal of two kingdoms (church and state separate but related) stressed particular and sometimes exclusive congregations, some of which called for *jure divino* church government themselves. Laudianism challenged the Erastian state in the early Stuart period mainly through its commitment to "godly rule," but even so that challenge to an Erastian state was not nearly as strong as the challenges of Puritanism and Catholicism had been in the age of Elizabeth.[98]

Conclusion

A church under some degree of state control has been traditional in England ever since the early Norman period, even though the term that has come to characterize it—Erastianism—did not appear until the second half of the sixteenth century. An important exception to this Erastian tradition, however, occurred during the medieval period. A papal hierocracy, foreshadowed by the Gregorian reformers, heightened by the investiture controversy, concentrated against King John by Innocent III, and implemented by papal representatives during the reign of Henry III, ultimately failed. State control over the English Church revived, especially during the fourteenth and fifteenth centuries, through such state actions as the passage of the statutes of Provisors and Praemunire.

When Henry VIII came to the throne in 1509, he could exercise considerable power in many ecclesiastical areas. But one thing almost proved to be an insurmountable obstacle—a divorce from Queen Catherine of Aragon so that he might marry Anne Boleyn. The strong opposition to Henry from the queen herself, Pope Clement VII, Emperor Charles V, most of the English Catholic clergy, and some laity, forced the king to enunciate, with the able assistance of Thomas Cromwell, a new "imperial" theory of church–state relationships. This theory, implemented by the Reformation Parliament, would ultimately justify his efforts to lead England out of the Roman Catholic Church. The royal supremacy replaced the papal supremacy, thereby bringing about the Henrician Schism (chapter 1).

The break with Rome is best called a schism rather than a reformation for a number of reasons. Although England was now a Protestant and no longer a Catholic nation, in many respects, the changes that took place in the 1530s were the logical extension of steps, some large and some small, taken during the middle ages or the period before 1529. Henry took some major steps in addition to assuming the title of "Supreme Head" of the Anglican Church. The dissolution of the monasteries was certainly one such major step, even though the pope controlled only a few of the monasteries. But Henry did not basically change the ecclesiastical organization of the Church through bishops; he did not change the liturgical forms of Church worship; he did not depart significantly from traditional Catholic doctrine, despite the experiments of the Ten Articles and the Bishops' Book; he did not change the canon law or the system of Church courts; he did not finally claim, despite occasional threats to do so, the *potestas ordinis*, the powers of a priest, which might have led to a theocratic monarchy; and he only increased the dependence of the clergy upon the Crown.

Some of those reforms, especially in liturgy and in doctrine, that had not transpired under Henry VIII surfaced with the ascension of Edward VI. Under the influence of continental reformers, Archbishop Thomas Cranmer drafted two versions of an English Prayer Book, participated in a thorough revision of the canon law, chaired a commission that drafted a new Ordinal, and revised a statement of doctrine (the Forty-Two Articles), most of which became the basis for the Elizabethan Settlement. The ecclesiastical organization of the Church did not change—indeed, the Ordinal reaffirmed the structure of bishops, priests, and deacons. Nor did the concept of the royal supremacy change. But that brief period of the Anglican Reformation (chapter 2) under Edward proved to be the most productive period in the history of the Anglican Church. Indeed, church and state—except for Northumberland's rejection of the reformed canon law—worked together as harmoniously as at almost any other time in English history.

The daughter of Catherine of Aragon sought to restore the papal supremacy in England, ironically, by using the authority of the royal supremacy, even after she had abandoned her father's title of "Supreme Head." Acting in two stages, Parliament began a pendulum swing to the right, first by repealing all of the Edwardian ecclesiastical legislation, and second by repealing all of the post-1529 Henrician legislation, except for the dissolution of the monasteries and the restoration of first fruits and tenths. Mary Tudor did not attempt, however, to undo those medieval statutes and customs, including the heresy laws, which had made England essentially an Erastian state by 1529. Mary's persecution of Protestant heretics ultimately forced Archbishop Cranmer to choose between Protestantism, to which he had given his spiritual life, and the royal supremacy, to which he had given his public life. It was a choice between death and the possibility of life. Many of the Marian exiles, who fled to the Protestant lands of western Germany and Switzerland to escape burning at the stake, ultimately returned with one of two ideas. Either they believed in the notion of the monarch's being little more than a "nursing mother" to the Church—a far cry from Henry VIII—or they believed in a theory of active resistance to a tryannical sovereign that did not gain full force until the 1640s.

The daughter of Anne Boleyn reversed the pendulum swing of her half-sister and moved the Anglican Reformation to the left once more (chapter 2). She replaced "Supreme Head" with "Supreme Governor"—an indication that, unlike her father, she would allow the bishops to determine matters of liturgy and doctrine. Her counselor, William Cecil, specifically denied that she had any claim to the powers of a priest (*potestas ordinis*), or even, as

Henry had intimated that he had, any claim to a cure of souls. The Thirty-Nine Articles specifically provided (in article thirty-six) only jurisdictional powers for her in the church (*potestas jurisdictionis*). She strove to bring about a settlement of the Church that represented a compromise—the famous *via media*. It was not a compromise between proto-Puritans and Catholicism, but a compromise between a conservative and a moderate Protestantism that the Marian exiles had found in the Rhineland and Switzerland. In practical terms, the compromise meant the adoption of the Second Edwardian Prayer Book (with modifications from the First) plus the Thirty-Nine Articles. Having made her settlement in the early years of her reign, Elizabeth made no further changes throughout her lifetime. That intransigency gave her settlement all the greater permanency in the history of church and state.

Two strong challenges, however, threatened Elizabeth's *via media* during the remainder of her reign. One of these came from the Puritan community; the other from the Roman Catholic community. Neither of these communities was homogeneous; each was made up of various groups. But in both communities it was the clerics who took the lead in conceptualizing and implementing their views. In both communities the laity exerted the greatest moderating influence, whether a Catholic parish householder, a Puritan member of Parliament, or a Puritan-inclined privy councillor. The more radical groups of both communities opposed the exercise of the royal supremacy. The clerical Catholics wished to replace Elizabeth's supremacy with a reformed papal supremacy, and the radical Puritans wished to reduce the royal supremacy to little more than a "nursing mother" role. Whether the goal of these Elizabethan Challenges (chapter 3) was the old medieval dream of a papal hierocracy or a Reformed version of a Protestant theocracy, the clergy wanted the *potestas jurisdictionis* as well as the *potestas ordinis* in the Church and strong political influence in the state.

The radical Puritans engaged in prophesyings or exercises, but their long-range goal was to set up a Presbyterian system of church government. To implement that system, they developed a classical system on the local level, as at Dedham; on the national level they introduced parliamentary bills, which, however, never passed. Elizabeth's government responded to these moves by bringing Puritans to trial in the prerogative Courts of Star Chamber and High Commission, which often imposed the ex officio oath whereby Puritans would incriminate themselves. As a result, a number of radical Puritans were convicted, and some, including Presbyterians and Separatists, were executed. Such action seriously jeopardized the entire movement and forced it to move underground for the next few years.

The Catholic seminarians tried to convert the English people who had fallen away from the Catholic Church; their long-range goal was to bring England back to the Catholic fold. For assistance, they sought military intervention by foreign powers, most notably Spain. Elizabeth's government, in an effort to extirpate Catholicism, passed harsh legislation, declaring Catholics traitors for a number of religious offenses and, in the case of Catholic priests, for merely living in England irrespective of what they did. In addition,

Elizabeth's government required Catholic priests to answer certain "bloody" questions about their political loyalties, and it executed a good number of the seminarians and Jesuits under the penal statutes. But the biggest blow to the community was not the failure of the Armada and Spain's subsequent military efforts, but rather their virtual abandonment, for the most part, by European Catholics, especially the papacy. The last decade of Elizabeth's reign saw deep division within the ranks of the Catholics over ecclesiastical organization through the archpriest controversy. The decade also brought a Puritan loss of spirit, especially in the House of Commons, coupled with quarrels about the reformulation of Calvinist theology (the Lambeth Articles).

When James VI of Scotland ascended the throne of England, many people hoped that he would be able to reconcile the differences between Puritans and Anglicans, and Catholics and Anglicans, since he had had so much experience with religion as a young man in Scotland. But he was not able to do so. Even before he arrived in England, James was presented with the Puritan Millenary Petition, which led to the Hampton Court Conference. And not long after he arrived, the Catholic Gunpowder Plot led to more repressive legislation, including an Oath of Allegiance.

The only truly significant gain for the moderate Puritans at the Hampton Court Conference was the King James version of the Bible. The king, however, took the occasion to ask the Anglican hierarchy to issue a new set of canons for the Anglican Church. The Canons of 1604 represented a very comprehensive attempt to consolidate the canon law of the Church as it had been expressed in Tudor injunctions and Elizabethan sets of canons. One of the 1604 canons, drawing heavily from the Articles of Archbishop Whitgift and other Elizabethan attempts at ecclesiastical conformity, required clergymen to subscribe to each of the Thirty-Nine Articles, an unrevised Book of Common Prayer, and the royal supremacy. The canons, which affronted the Puritans, are the prime example of James' efforts, unlike Elizabeth's, to be responsive to moderate Puritan criticism and, like Elizabeth's, to stop further Puritan changes in all aspects of the Anglican Church. Those Puritans who did not like James' Church policies often left England, a course of action which created a second generation of covenanted Separatists who found their way to Holland and to America as Jacobean exiles.

The Gunpowder Plot would disgrace Roman Catholicism for decades to come, but more immediately it resulted in James' Oath of Allegiance of 1606. A modification of Elizabeth's Oath of Supremacy of 1559, the Oath of Allegiance represented a continuation of the alleged Elizabethan policy of prosecuting political subversion but not religious heresy. Like most positions or documents James espoused—such as divine right monarchy, the writs of prohibition, which common law judges used against church courts, or the Canons of 1604—the Oath of Allegiance represented a continuation, indeed, a Jacobean Consolidation (chapter 4) of previous Tudor policies regarding the Church. James' reign was the only one between Henry VIII and Queen Anne that did not initiate major changes in church and state.

Like his father, Charles I staunchly defended the Anglican Church; he had little use for the Puritans and almost equally little for the Catholics, although, like his father, he married a Catholic. During the five Parliaments of the 1620s, James and Charles vigorously contended with the Puritans in the House of Commons. Although James went to war with Spain in 1624, and Charles would do so with France in 1628, both had first tried to arrange marriage alliances with these Catholic powers. When Charles married Princess Henrietta Maria of France, putative Catholics began to enter the government. Despite the strong opposition of Archbishop Laud, Charles shared with his father a naive hope for reunion with Rome. England made some rather feeble attempts to bring about such a reconciliation under Charles, but nothing finally came of them.

James and Charles, too, differed seriously with the Puritans, especially those in Parliament who opposed any kind of marriage alliance with Catholic countries. Some of the creative energies of the Puritans had gone into the New England theocracy—the Puritan experiment in the wilderness. At home in Old England, the parliamentary Puritans were contending with the beginning of Arminianism in the upper echelons of the Anglican hierarchy. By accusing the Arminians of being innovators in theology, the parliamentary Puritans claimed that they were defending the Church's traditional positions, particularly its rigid Calvinist theology as expressed in the Lambeth Articles, the Irish Articles, and the conclusions of the Synod of Dort. And when the Laudians came to power in the late twenties and thirties, persecutions of some of the Puritan radicals began again. While the Laudian persecutions of 1630 have some elements in common with the Whitgiftian persecutions of the 1590s, the 1630 Protestant proto-martyrs more closely resemble the Protestant martyrs of the 1550s. In the cases of both the earlier martyrs and the later proto-martyrs, Counter-Reformation forces—Catholic and Laudian, respectively—gave the Protestant Reformers under Elizabeth, and the Puritans under Charles, a new lease on life.

Laudianism, which subsumed Arminianism, formed the third and final challenge to the Erastianism of the English state during the Tudor and early Stuart period. Bishops Richard Bancroft and Lancelot Andrews set forth early aspects of Laudianism, notably the divine right of episcopacy. The Arminian tendency toward universal salvation, which its supporters found more compatible with a national church than Calvin's decrees of election *and* damnation, and the Arminian tendency toward free will and good works, which struck Puritans as a return to Catholicism, had been partially formulated in opposition to those rigid Calvinists at the theological controversy in Cambridge who supported the Lambeth Articles in the 1590s. After the Synod of Dort, where English Calvinists registered their opposition, Arminianism gained momentum when Richard Montagu's *Appello Caesarem* was attacked in the House of Commons and when Charles elevated Arminian bishops to the episcopal bench.

Charles, like Elizabeth, was content to leave the *potestas ordinis* to the clergy, so Laud felt free to reshape Church doctrine and liturgy. And no matter how Laud might try to reconcile divine right episcopacy with the royal supremacy, divine right episcopacy appeared to give both the *potestas ordinis* and the *potestas jurisdictionis* to the Church. Except for the nonrecognition of papal power in England, Laudianism went about as far toward Roman Catholicism as was possible for an Anglican to go—back to where England was in the late Henrician and early Edwardian periods.

The attempt of Charles and Laud to impose their kind of Anglicanism on the Scottish Kirk ultimately proved to be their downfall. Laudianism, then, like Catholicism and Puritanism before it, failed to establish its "godly rule" within the Anglican Church and the Erastian state. When Laudianism and its archbishop went down to ignominious defeat in the first three years of the Long Parliament, Puritanism, whose recent failures had been closely associated with Laudian successes, revived. The persecution of the Puritan martyrs, the alienation of the Puritan laity over tithes and impropriations, and the establishment of Puritan colonies in the New World—all of which added up to a Laudian Counter-Reformation (chapter 5)—gave Puritanism in the early weeks of the Long Parliament a powerful springboard from which to reenter the race for control of the state. Without the Laudians, the Puritans might never have gotten their second chance in the 1640s and 1650s. Unlike the Catholics, who missed their earlier opportunities, the Puritans were determined not to fail again.

Notes

Chapter 1

1. Norman Sykes, *The English Religious Tradition* (London: SCM Press, 1953), p. 10.

2. Norman F. Cantor, *Church, Kingship, and Lay Investiture in England, 1089–1135* (Princeton, New Jersey: Princeton University Press, 1958), p. 259.

3. H. Maynard Smith, *Pre-Reformation England* (London: Macmillan, 1938), p. 25.

4. A. L. Smith, *Church and State in the Middle Ages* (Oxford: Clarendon Press, 1913), p. 104.

5. T. D. Ingram, *England and Rome* (London: Longmans, Green, 1892), p. 123.

6. W. T. Waugh, "The Great Statute of Praemunire," *English Historical Review* 37 (1922): 189.

7. K. B. McFarlane, *John Wycliffe and the Beginnings of English Nonconformity* (London: English Universities Press, 1952), p. 91.

8. Denys Hay, "The Church of England in the Later Middle Ages," *History* 53 (1968): 48.

9. W. A. Pantin, *The English Church in the Fourteenth Century* (Cambridge: Cambridge University Press, 1955), p. 101.

10. A. G. Dickens, *The English Reformation* (London: Batsford, 1964), pp. 91–92; Arthur Ogle, *The Tragedy of the Lollards' Tower* (Oxford: Pen-In-Hand Publishing Company, 1949), p. 83; Richard Marius, *Thomas More, a Biography* (New York: Alfred A. Knopf, 1984), pp. 123–27.

11. Kenneth Pickthorn, *Early Tudor Government, Henry VIII* (Cambridge: Cambridge University Press, 1934), p. 117; for a different view of this quote, see G. R. Elton, *Reform and Reformation, England, 1509–1558* (Cambridge, Massachusetts: Harvard University Press, 1977), p. 56n.

12. *Miscellaneous Writings of Henry the Eighth*, ed. Francis Macnamara (Waltham St. Lawrence: Golden Cockerel Press, 1924), p. 49.

13. William Roper, *The Life of Sir Thomas More*, in *Two Early Tudor Lives*, eds. Richard S. Sylvester and Davis P. Harding (New Haven, Connecticut: Yale University Press, 1962), p. 235.

14. J. J. Scarisbrick, *Henry VIII* (London: Eyre and Spottiswoode, 1968), chap. seven; Henry Ansgar Kelly, *The Matrimonial Trials of Henry VIII* (Stanford, California: Stanford University Press, 1976), introduction and chap. one.

213

15. Kelly, *Matrimonial Trials*, pp. 85–86, 97, 107, 129–30, 204.

16. Kelly, *Matrimonial Trials*, pp. 16–17.

17. G. Constant, *The Reformation in England, the English Schism and Henry VIII, 1509–1547*, trans. R. E. Scantlebury (New York: Sheed and Ward, 1934), p. 70.

18. George Cavendish, *The Life and Death of Cardinal Wolsey*, eds. Richard S. Sylvester and Davis P. Harding, *Two Tudor Lives* (New Haven, Connecticut: Yale University Press, 1962), p. 183.

19. Elton, *Reform and Reformation*, pp. 130–38.

20. Scarisbrick, *Henry VIII*, p. 268.

21. J. A. Guy, "Henry VIII and the *Praemunire* Manoeuvres of 1530–1531," *English Historical Review* 97 (1982): 481–86; G. W. Bernard, "The Pardon of the Clergy Reconsidered," with replies from J. A. Guy and G. W. Bernard, *Journal of Ecclesiastical History* 37 (1986): 284–85; Elton, *Reform and Reformation*, pp. 142–44.

22. Guy, *English Historical Review* 97 (1982): 494–500; Bernard, *Journal of Ecclesiastical History* 37 (1986): 268; Scarisbrick, *Henry VIII*, p. 291.

23. J. J. Scarisbrick, "The Pardon of the Clergy, 1531," *Cambridge Historical Journal* 12 (1956): 34–37; Guy, *English Historical Review* 97 (1982): 497.

24. J. A. Guy, *The Public Career of Sir Thomas More* (New Haven, Connecticut: Yale University Press, 1980), pp. 151–53; G. R. Elton, *Reform and Renewal, Thomas Cromwell and the Commonweal* (Cambridge: Cambridge University Press, 1973), pp. 71–77.

25. Simon Fish, *A Supplication for Beggars*, in *Complaint and Reform in England, 1436–1714*, eds. William Huse Dunham, Jr., and Stanley Pargellis (New York: Oxford University Press, 1938), p. 89.

26. G. R. Elton, "The Commons' Supplication of 1532: Parliamentary Manoeuvres in the Reign of Henry VIII," *English Historical Review* 66 (1951): 507–34; J. P. Cooper, "The Supplication Against the Ordinaries Reconsidered," *English Historical Review* 72 (1957): 616–41; *The Tudor Constitution, Documents and Commentary*, ed. and intro. G. R. Elton, 2nd ed. (Cambridge: Cambridge University Press, 1982), pp. 324–25.

27. Stanford E. Lehmberg, *The Reformation Parliament, 1529–1536* (Cambridge: Cambridge University Press, 1970), p. 150.

28. Michael Kelly, "The Submission of the Clergy," *TRHS*, fifth series, 15 (1965): 103–6, 117–18.

29. Lacey Baldwin Smith, *Henry VIII, the Mask of Royalty* (Boston: Houghton Mifflin, 1971), p. 108.

30. A. F. Pollard, *Factors in Modern History*, 3rd ed. (London: Constable, 1932), pp. 83–85; A. G. Dickens, (*English Reformation*, pp. 107–8), who said "we must avoid the temptation to equate the Henrician Schism with the Protestant Reformation," asked whether the divorce was "anything more than one of the many dangerous reefs which English Catholicism had to circumnavigate?".

31. J. J. Scarisbrick, *The Reformation and the English People* (Oxford: Basil Blackwell, 1984), pp. 56–59. Scarisbrick's examination of wills in the first half of the sixteenth century shows that a very large majority of them still accepted the old religious order, imperfect as it was (pp. 11–12). For the view that anticlericalism was a consequence rather than a cause of the Henrician Schism, see Christopher Haigh, "Anticlericalism and the English Reformation," *History* 68 (1983): 405–6. Haigh demonstrates that numerical indicators that showed approval of the clergy—ordinations and benefactions—increased before the Schism and fell after it, whereas those

that showed conflict—mortuary and tithe litigation—were low before the Schism and increased afterwards.

32. For the development of this statute, I have followed G. R. Elton, "The Evolution of a Reformation Statute," *English Historical Review* 64 (1949): 174–97.

33. This was a far cry from Henry's statement in the *Assertio* against Luther that he received the "crown imperial" from the Holy See.

34. Constant, *The Reformation in England, 1509–1547*, p. 125.

35. Franklin Le Van Baumer, *The Early Tudor Theory of Kingship* (New Haven, Connecticut: Yale University Press, 1940), pp. 78–79.

36. These were technically included within the *potestas jurisdictionis*. See Christopher Morris, *Political Thought in England, Tyndale to Hooker* (London: Oxford University Press, 1953), pp. 51–52.

37. *Obedience in Church and State, Three Political Tracts by Stephen Gardiner*, ed. and intro. Pierre Janelle (Cambridge: Cambridge University Press, 1930), p. 97.

38. *Doctrinal Treatises and Introductions to Different Portions of the Holy Scriptures by William Tyndale*, ed. Henry Walter, The Parker Society (Cambridge: Cambridge University Press, 1848), p. 178.

39. Elton, *The Tudor Constitution*, 2nd ed., pp. 342–43.

40. Guy, *Sir Thomas More*, chaps. 6 and 8.

41. Jasper Ridley, *Statesman and Saint, Cardinal Wolsey, Sir Thomas More, and the Politics of Henry VIII* (New York: The Viking Press, 1983), p. 273.

42. G. R. Elton, *Policy and Police, the Enforcement of the Reformation in the Age of Thomas Cromwell* (Cambridge: Cambridge University Press, 1972), pp. 218–30.

43. Ridley, *Statesman and Saint*, pp. 277–78; More's reply, according to Marius (*More*, p. 497), meant that "the laws of the church were universally binding, but the laws of any separate nation within Christendom were not."

44. Ridley, *Statesman and Saint*, pp. 279–81. According to Rich and the indictment, More said, "a man is not by a law of one realm so bound in his conscience, where there is a law of the whole corps of Christendom to the contrary, in a matter touching belief." Marius, *More*, p. 502.

45. J. Duncan M. Derrett, "The Trial of Sir Thomas More," *English Historical Review* 79 (1964): 471. "Sir Thomas More died for conscience' sake, but not for freedom of conscience, freedom of thought, or tolerance in religion" (Elton, *Policy and Police*, p. 417).

46. For material in this and the two preceding paragraphs, see Stanford E. Lehmberg, "Supremacy and Vicegerency: a Re-examination," *English Historical Review* 81 (1966): 225–35; Elton, *Reform and Renewal*, pp. 134–35; Elton, *Policy and Police*, pp. 247–48; F. G. Emmison, *Tudor Secretary: Sir William Petre at Court and Home* (London: Longmans, Green, 1961), pp. 8–9, 44.

47. J. J. Scarisbrick, "Clerical Taxation in England, 1485 to 1547," *Journal of Ecclesiastical History* 11 (1960): 52.

48. G. W. O. Woodward, *The Dissolution of the Monasteries* (London: Blandford, 1966), p. 122. None of this wealth was held by the Crown at one time, since the disposal of monastic lands began before the acquisition was completed.

49. Dickens, *The English Reformation*, p. 144.

50. C. S. L. Davies, "The Pilgrimage of Grace Reconsidered," *Past and Present* 41 (1968): 54–76; David Knowles, *The Religious Orders in England* (Cambridge: Cambridge University Press, 1959), III, 320–35. For a different view, see A. G.

Dickens, "Secular and Religious Motivation in the Pilgrimage of Grace," *Studies in Church History*, ed. G. J. Cuming (Leiden: Brill, 1967), IV, 39–64.

51. Elton, *Reform and Reformation*, pp. 265–72. Elton has restated his view of the important political role of a hostile court faction, which orchestrated northern social, economic, and religious grievances felt by the regional gentry against a "thrusting and revolutionary court policy" ("Politics and the Pilgrimage of Grace," *After the Reformation, Essays in Honor of J. H. Hexter*, ed. Barbara Malament [Philadelphia: University of Pennsylvania Press, 1980], p. 52), but C. S. L. Davies has responded by contending that Cromwell and his "low-born heretical associates" were the target of a "general opprobrium" against the "destructive spoliation" of an "aggressive state" and an "evangelical protestantism" ("Popular Religion and the Pilgrimage of Grace," *Order and Disorder in Early Modern England*, eds. Anthony Fletcher and John Stevenson [New York: Cambridge University Press, 1985], pp. 73, 76, 87).

52. Dickens, *Studies in Church History*, IV, 49–50; 59–60.

53. Documents Illustrative of English Church History, eds. Henry Gee and William John Hardy (London: Macmillan, 1910), p. 270.

54. Lacey Baldwin Smith, *Tudor Prelates and Politics, 1536–1558* (Princeton, New Jersey: Princeton University Press, 1953), appendix IV.

55. *Formularies of Faith Put Forth by Authority during the Reign of Henry VIII*, ed. Charles Lloyd (Oxford: Clarendon Press, 1825), p. 26.

56. *The Works of Thomas Cranmer*, ed. John Edmund Cox, The Parker Society, 2 vols. (Cambridge: Cambridge University Press, 1844–1846), II, 96–100; E. G. Rupp, *Studies in the Making of the English Protestant Tradition* (Cambridge: Cambridge University Press, 1947, reprinted, 1966), pp. 134–49.

57. Lloyd, *Formularies*, p. 121.

58. Gee and Hardy, *Documents*, pp. 275–81; James K. McConica, *English Humanists and Reformation Politics under Henry VIII and Edward VI* (Oxford: Clarendon Press, 1965), pp. 159–60. Several of the provisions of the second set of Henrician Injunctions were fulfillments of those St. German proposals that had been completed in 1530.

59. Stanford E. Lehmberg, *The Later Parliaments of Henry VIII, 1536–1547* (Cambridge: Cambridge University Press, 1977), pp. 187, 231.

60. *Tudor Royal Proclamations*, eds. Paul Hughes and James F. Larkin, 3 vols. (New Haven, Connecticut: Yale University Press, 1964–1969), I, 270–76.

61. *The Lisle Letters*, ed. Muriel St. Clare Byrne, 6 vols. (Chicago: University of Chicago Press, 1981), V, 542; G. Redworth, "A Study in the Formulation of Policy: the Genesis and Evolution of the Act of Six Articles," *Journal of Ecclesiastical History* 37 (1986): 42–67.

62. G. R. Elton, "Thomas Cromwell's Decline and Fall," *Cambridge Historical Journal* 10 (1951): 165ff. A year earlier, he had written to Lord Lisle as follows: "He that either fears not God nor esteems the King's majesty's injunctions, precepts, ordinances and commandments, is no meet herb to grow in his majesty's most catholic and virtuous garden." *Thomas Cromwell on Church and Commonwealth, Selected Letters, 1523–1540*, ed. and intro. Arthur J. Slavin (New York: Harper and Row, 1969), p. 201.

63. *Letters and Papers, Foreign and Domestic, of the Reign of Henry VIII (1509–1547)*, eds. J. S. Brewer, James Gairdner, and R. H. Brodie, 21 vols. (London, 1862–1910), XV, 484.

64. For material in this and the two succeeding paragraphs, see Cranmer, *Works*, II, 115–17; Scarisbrick, *Henry VIII*, pp. 415–17.

65. Lloyd, *Formularies*, p. 277; Rupp, *Studies*, pp. 149–54.

66. Lloyd, *Formularies*, p. 287, 278–79.

67. I. D. Thornley, "The Destruction of Sanctuary," *Tudor Studies Presented to A. F. Pollard*, ed. R. W. Seton-Watson, new ed. (London: Russell and Russell, 1970), pp. 203–4; G. R. Elton, *Reform and Renewal*, pp. 136–37; Lehmberg, *The Reformation Parliament*, pp. 142, 185, 239.

Chapter 2

1. Lacey Baldwin Smith, "Henry VIII and the Protestant Triumph," *American Historical Review* 71 (1966): 1237–64.

2. G. J. Cuming, *A History of the Anglican Liturgy* (London: MacMillan, 1969), pp. 58–59.

3. *Certain Sermons or Homilies Appointed to Be Read in Churches in the Time of Queen Elizabeth I (1547–1571)*, eds. Mary Ellen Rickey and Thomas B. Stroup, 1623 edition (Gainesville, Florida: Scholars' Facsimiles and Reprints, 1968), I, 72, 74, [75].

4. On the common law and heresy, see William Holdsworth, *A History of the English Law*, 7th ed. (London: Methuen, 1956), I, 618; W. K. Jordan, *Edward VI, the Threshold of Power* (London: George Allen and Unwin, 1970), p. 330.

5. Lloyd, *Formularies*, p. 376.

6. Alan Kreider, *English Chantries, the Road to Destruction* (Cambridge, Massachusetts: Harvard University Press, 1979), p. 175.

7. Jordan, *Edward VI, The Threshold of Power*, chap. 6.

8. Christopher Kitching, "The Disposal of Monastic and Chantry Lands," in Felicity Heal and Rosemary O'Day, eds., *Church and Society in England, Henry VIII to James I* (London: Macmillan Press, 1979), p. 128.

9. In the succeeding paragraphs, I have followed Peter Brooks, *Thomas Cranmer's Doctrine of the Eucharist: an Essay in Historical Development* (New York: Seabury Press, 1965), but also see C. W. Dugmore, *The Mass and the English Reformers* (London: Macmillan, 1958), chap 8; Cyril C. Richardson, *Zwingli and Cranmer on the Eucharist* (Evanston, Illinois: Seabury-Western Theological Seminary, 1949); and Gordon E. Pruett, "Thomas Cranmer's Progress in the Doctrine of the Eucharist, 1535–48," *Historical Magazine of the Protestant Episcopal Church* 45 (1976): 439–58.

10. The manifesto was understandably silent about West Country ability to understand the old mass in Latin.

11. Christopher Hill, *Economic Problems of the Church, from Archbishop Whitgift to the Long Parliament* (Oxford: Clarendon Press, 1956), chap. 5.

12. Paul F. Bradshaw, *The Anglican Ordinal, Its History and Developments from the Reformation to the Present Day*, Alcuin Club Collections, no. 53 (London, S.P.C.K., 1971), pp. 37–38.

13. Horton Davies, *Worship and Theology in England, from Cranmer to Hooker, 1534–1603* (Princeton, New Jersey: Princeton University Press, 1970), pp. 108, 118, 183–84.

14. C. W. Dugmore, "The First Ten Years, 1549–59," *The English Prayer Book, 1549–1662*, Alcuin Club Publication (London: S.P.C.K., 1963), p. 27; Barrett L. Beer, *Northumberland, the Political Career of John Dudley, Earl of Warwick, and Duke of Northumberland* (Kent, Ohio: Kent State University Press, 1973), p. 107.

15. F. Donald Logan, "The Henrician Canons," *Bulletin of the Institute of Historical Research* 47 (1974): 99–103.

16. James C. Spalding, "The Reformatio Legum Ecclesiasticarum of 1552 and the Furthering of Discipline in England," *Church History* 39 (1970): 162–71.

17. Dickens, *The English Reformation*, p. 238.

18. *Synodalia. A Collection of Articles of Religion, Canons, and Proceedings of Convocations in the Province of Canterbury, from the Year 1547 to the Year 1717*, ed. Edward Cardwell, 2 vols. (Oxford: Oxford University Press, 1842; reprinted in Farnborough, England: Gregg Press, 1966), I, 31; for convocations' actions on the two Prayer Books and the Articles of Religion, see Thomas Lathbury, *History of the Convocation of the Church of England from the Earliest Period to the Year 1742*, 2nd ed., (London: J. Leslie, 1853), chap. 6.

19. Hughes and Larkin, *Tudor Royal Proclamations*, II, 5–6.

20. It was an act of the Reformation Parliament that illegitimatized Mary rather than Cranmer's annulment of the marriage between Henry and Catherine because, said the archbishop, according to canon law Mary was still legitimate because her parents were unaware that their marriage was invalid. See Mortimer Levine, "Henry VIII's Use of His Spiritual and Temporal Jurisdictions in His Great Causes of Matrimony, Legitimacy, and Succession," *Historical Journal* 10 (1967): 3–10.

21. Malcolm R. Thorp, however, argues that the leading conspirators were Protestants who had religious concerns that opposed those of the queen. "Religion and the Wyatt Rebellion of 1554," *Church History* 47 (1978): 363–80.

22. D. M. Loades, "The Enforcement of Reaction, 1553–1558," *Journal of Ecclesiastical History* 16 (1965) 56–57.

23. *Foxe's Book of Martyrs*, ed. and abridged by G. A. Williamson (London: Secker and Warburg, 1965), p. 311.

24. Cranmer, *Works*, II, 213.

25. D. M. Loades, *The Oxford Martyrs* (New York: Stein and Day, 1970), p. 226.

26. More to Margaret Roper, April 17, 1534, *The Correspondence of Sir Thomas More*, ed. Elizabeth Frances Rogers (Princeton, New Jersey: Princeton University Press, 1947), p. 505; Edward Allen Whitney, "Erastianism and Divine Right," *The Huntington Library Quarterly* 2 (1939): 392.

27. D. M. Loades, *The Reign of Mary Tudor* (New York: St. Martins Press, 1979), p. 453n.

28. Loades, *Mary Tudor*, pp. 336–37.

29. Rex H. Pogson, "Reginald Pole and the Priorities of Government in Mary Tudor's Church," *Historical Journal* 18 (1975): 3–20.

30. Christina H. Garrett, *The Marian Exiles, a Study in the Origins of Elizabethan Puritanism* (Cambridge: Cambridge University Press, 1938; reprinted, 1966), p. 41.

31. M. M. Knappen, *Tudor Puritanism: a Chapter in the History of Idealism* (Chicago: University of Chicago Press, 1939), p. 148.

32. [Thomas Wood], *A Brief Discourse of the Troubles Begun at Frankfort* (1575), p. cxxx.

33. *The Form of Prayers and Ministration of the Sacraments, &c., Used in the English Congregation at Geneva* (1556), reprinted in *The Works of John Knox*, ed. David Laing (Edinburgh: Ballantyne Club, 1846–1864; reprinted in New York: AMS Press, 1966), IV, 173.

34. Hardin Craig, Jr., "The Geneva Bible as a Political Document," *Pacific Historical Review* 7 (1938): 40–49; Richard L. Greaves, "The Nature and the Intellec-

tual Milieu of the Political Principles in the Geneva Bible Marginalia," *Journal of Church and State* 22 (1980): 233–49.

35. There was a covenant in Calvin's theology, but he thought of it as already fulfilled by God through the incarnation, death, and resurrection of Christ, and the sacraments of baptism and the Lord's Supper were witnesses or testaments of God's fulfillment of the covenant.

36. *The Works of John Milton*, ed. Frank Allen Patterson and others, 20 vols. (New York: Columbia University Press, 1931–1938), V. 52.

37. F. W. Maitland, "Elizabethan Gleanings: I. 'Defender of the Faith, and So Forth,'" *The Collected Papers of Frederic William Maitland*, ed. H. A. L. Fisher, 3 vols. (Cambridge: Cambridge University Press, 1911), III, 157–65; A. F. Pollard, *The History of England from the Accession of Edward VI, to the Death of Elizabeth (1547–1603)* (London: Longmans, Green, 1911), pp. 194–95. In a proclamation of January 15, 1559, Elizabeth styled herself as "defender of the true, ancient, and Catholic faith" without the "etc." (Hughes and Larkin, *Tudor Royal Proclamations*, II, 103).

38. Hughes and Larkin, *Tudor Royal Proclamations*, II, 102–3; Whitney R. D. Jones, *The Mid-Tudor Crisis, 1539–1563* (London: Macmillan, 1973), p. 105.

39. *Calendar of State Papers, Spanish, Elizabeth*, ed. M. A. S. Hume, 4 vols. (London, 1892–1899), I, 37.

40. Winthrop S. Hudson, *The Cambridge Connection and the Elizabethan Settlement of 1559* (Durham, North Carolina: Duke University Press, 1980), chap. 4.

41. Hudson, *The Cambridge Connection*, pp. 110–11.

42. For the "Device" see Henry Gee, *The Elizabethan Prayer-Book and Ornaments* (London: Macmillan, 1902), pp. 195–202. John Strype wrote that Cecil "was a great dealer and director" in the Prayer Book review, "and was very earnest about the book." Strype, *Annals of the Reformation and Establishment of Religion* (Oxford: Clarendon Press, 1824), I, i, 119.

43. Simonds D'Ewes, *A Complete Journal of the Votes, Speeches, and Debates, Both of the House of Lords and House of Commons Throughout the Whole Reign of Queen Elizabeth, of Glorious Memory* (London, 1693, reprinted in Wilmington, Delaware: Scholarly Resources, 1974), pp. 111–12; *Proceedings in the Parliaments of Elizabeth I, 1558–1581*, ed. T. E. Hartley (Wilmington, Delaware: Michael Glazier, 1981), I, 35; Patrick Collinson, "Sir Nicholas Bacon and the Elizabethan *Via Media*," *Historical Journal* 23 (1980): 256–57.

44. *The Zurich Letters, 1558–1579*, ed. Hastings Robinson, The Parker Society, 2 vols. (Cambridge: Cambridge University Press, 1842–1845), I, 10; Wallace MacCaffrey, *The Shaping of the Elizabethan Regime* (Princeton, New Jersey: Princeton University Press, 1968), p. 59.

45. This paragraph and the next two are based in part upon J. E. Neale's reconstruction of events, which first appeared as an article, "The Elizabethan Acts of Supremacy and Uniformity," *English Historical Review* 65 (1950): 304–32, and later in his book *Elizabeth I and Her Parliaments, 1559–1581* (London: Jonathan Cape, 1953), pt. one, chaps. 1 and 3.

46. Neale, who is the advocate of the view that the government did not wish to bring forward a uniformity bill until a later session of Parliament when it could consider a prayer book approved by convocation, maintained that the presence of the communion in both kinds clause in both the first and second supremacy bills was "a sop to the Protestants" (Neale, *English Historical Review* 65 [1950]: 310. C. W. Dugmore, however, challenges the Neale interpretation of alteration in slow stages by

stating that Neale overlooked the *Order of the Communion* of 1548 (and hence a Prayer Book) without which a communion clause in the supremacy bill would have been a "dead letter from the start." *The Mass and the English Reformers*, pp. 209–12. Also see William P. Haugaard, *Elizabeth and the English Reformation, the Struggle for a Stable Settlement of Religion* (Cambridge: Cambridge University Press, 1968), p. 84.

47. Much of Neale's analysis of the Acts of Supremacy and Uniformity of 1559 has been substantially revised by Hudson. *The Cambridge Connection*, and Norman L. Jones, *Faith By Statute, Parliament and the Settlement of Religion, 1559* (London: Royal Historical Society, 1982). Instead of Neale's emphasis on the reforming role of the "Puritan choir" in the House of Commons, Jones has stressed the Catholic opposition in the House of Lords. On the proclamation of March 22, 1559, see Jones, *Faith by Statute*, p. 134.

48. Jones, *Faith by Statute*, pp. 115–20.

49. *Zurich Letters*, I, 11; Jones, *Faith By Statute*, pp. 123–29; 150–51.

50. Maitland, "Elizabethan Gleanings," *Collected Papers*, III, 192; Jones, *Faith by Statute*, pp. 142–43.

51. Henry Norbert Birt, *The Elizabethan Religious Settlement, a Study of Contemporary Documents* (London: George Bell and Sons, 1907), p. 85.

52. Philip Hughes, *The Reformation in England*, 5th, rev. ed., three vols. in one (London: Macmillan, 1963), III, 72.

53. Arnold Oskar Meyer, *England and the Catholic Church under Queen Elizabeth*, trans. J. R. McKee (London: Kegan, Paul, 1916; reprinted in New York: Barnes and Noble, 1967), p. 25.

54. Henry Gee, *The Elizabethan Clergy and the Settlement of Religion, 1558–1564* (Oxford: Clarendon Press, 1898), chap. 13; Birt, *The Elizabethan Religious Settlement*, chaps 4 and 5.

55. The First Prayer Book was authorized by Parliament in the second regnal year of Edward's reign, but technically it was not to have come into use until the third year. John T. Micklethwaite, *The Ornaments of the Rubric*, Alcuin Club Tracts, no. 1 (London: Longmans, Green, 1897), p. 16.

56. Christopher Hill, *Economic Problems of the Church*, chap. 5.

57. Felicity Heal, "The Bishops and the Act of Exchange of 1559," *Historical Journal* 17 (1974): 241, 245; Felicity Heal, *Of Prelates and Princes, a Study of the Economic and Social Position of the Tudor Episcopate* (Cambridge: Cambridge University Press, 1980), chap. 9.

58. Norman L. Jones, "Profiting from Religious Reform: the Land Rush of 1559," *Historical Journal* 22 (1979): 279–94.

59. *Documentary Annals of the Reformed Church of England, Being a Collection of Injunctions, Declarations, Orders, Articles of Inquiry, Etc., from the Year 1546 to the Year 1716.* ed. Edward Cardwell, new edition in two vols. (Oxford: Oxford University Press, 1844; reprinted in Ridgewood, New Jersey: Gregg Press, 1966), I, 232–33.

60. *Zurich Letters*, I, 23.

61. Hudson, *The Cambridge Connection*, pp. 141–42.

62. John Jewel, *An Apology of the Church of England*, ed. J. E. Booty (Ithaca, New York: Cornell University Press, 1963), p. 115.

63. Jewel, *An Apology*, pp. 115, 63. Jewel denied the *potestas ordinis* to kings in his *Defence of the Apology*, in *The Works of John Jewel*, ed. John Ayre, The Parker Society, (Cambridge: Cambridge University Press, 1845–1850), IV, 959.

64. Haugaard, *Elizabeth and the English Reformation*, pp. 30, 277–78.

65. E. J. Bicknell, *A Theological Introduction to the Thirty-Nine Articles of the Church of England*, 2nd. ed., revised by H. J. Carpenter (London: Longmans, Green, 1942), p. 318.

66. Cardwell, *Synodalia*, I, 71.

Chapter 3

1. Joel Hurstfield, "Church and State, 1538–1612: the Task of the Cecils," *Freedom, Corruption, and Government in Elizabethan England*, pp. 79–103 (Cambridge, Massachusetts: Harvard University Press, 1973), p. 103.

2. Paul Christianson, *Reformers and Babylon, English Apocalyptic Visions from the Reformation to the Eve of the Civil War* (Toronto: University of Toronto Press, 1978), chap. 2.

3. Peter Lake, *Moderate Puritans and the Elizabethan Church*, (Cambridge: Cambridge University Press, 1982); A. F. Scott Pearson, *Thomas Cartwright and Elizabethan Puritanism, 1535–1603* (Cambridge: Cambridge University Press, 1925); B. R. White, *The English Separatist Tradition, from the Marian Martyrs to the Pilgrim Fathers* (London: Oxford University Press, 1971); Stephen Brachlow, *The Communion of Saints, Radical Puritan and Separatist Ecclesiology, 1570–1625*, Oxford Theological Monographs (Oxford: Oxford University Press, 1988), Conclusion.

4. John F. H. New (*Anglican and Puritan, the Basis of their Opposition, 1558–1640* [Stanford, California: Stanford University Press, 1964]) sees strong differences between Anglican and Puritans, whereas Charles H. and Katherine George (*The Protestant Mind of the English Reformation, 1570–1640* [Princeton, New Jersey: Princeton University Press, 1961]) see very few differences between them.

5. G. R. Elton, *The Parliament of England, 1559–1581* (Cambridge: Cambridge University Press, 1986), pp. 350–55. Regarding Thomas Norton, M. A. R. Graves states that his parliamentary "record was one of dutiful and energetic collaboration with the council," but that he was "a moderate puritan of the first generation." "Thomas Norton the Parliament Man: an Elizabethan M.P., 1559–1581," *Historical Journal* 23 (1980): 19, 32.

6. *Correspondence of Matthew Parker*, ed. John Bruce, The Parker Society (Cambridge: Cambridge University Press, 1853), pp. 223–27.

7. Parker, *Correspondence*, p. 234.

8. Haugaard, *Elizabeth and the English Reformation*, p. 217.

9. The Zurich Letters, I, 151–55, 345–57, 163–65.

10. Parker, *Correspondence*, pp. 291–92; Elton, *The Parliament of England, 1559–1581*, pp. 200–1.

11. B.I., *The Fortress of Fathers*, 1568, "Certain Conclusions."

12. Neale, *Elizabeth I and Her Parliaments, 1559–1581*, pp. 192–203; Elton, *The Parliament of England, 1559–1581*, pp. 201–10.

13. Even though the Puritans had had eight years to examine the Articles, the curious point is that the significant Puritan differences with the bishops in the 1560s over vestments and ceremonies apparently were not mentioned. J. E. Neale, "Parliament and the Articles of Religion," *English Historical Review* 67 (1952): 510–21; Elton, *The Parliament of England, 1559–1581*, pp. 210–11. Norman L. Jones ("An Elizabethan Bill for the Reformation of the Ecclesiastical Law," *Parliamentary History* 4 [1985]: 171–87) has suggested that Sir Edward Hastings' 1571 bill, recently

discovered at the Huntington Library, called for a thirty-two-member committee, not unlike earlier proposals under Henry and Edward, "for reformation of ecclesiastical laws."

14. Cardwell, *Synodalia*, I, 111–31; Charles Hardwick, *A History of the Articles of Religion* (Cambridge: John Deighton, 1851), pp. 142–54.

15. Neale, *Elizabeth I and Her Parliaments, 1559–1581*, pp. 203–7; Elton, *The Parliament of England, 1559–1581*, pp. 211–13.

16. Hardwick, *A History of the Articles of Religion*, pp. 219, 317; Elton, *The Parliament of England, 1559–81*, p. 213n) has indicated that he could not find one article which did not deal with faith and doctrine, and there would probably be little argument over the first thirty-four. Articles thirty-eight and thirty-nine dealt with Anabaptist "common" goods and oaths, respectively.

17. Hardwick, *A History of the Articles of Religion*, pp. 218–19. The distinction of earlier ecclesiastical historians between "restrictive" and "demonstrative" usage would certainly have been helped if the statute had used a comma between the two adjacent words "Religion" and "which" in the original copy of the statute. Also, see Elton, *The Parliament of England, 1559–1581*, p. 213.

18. *Puritan Manifestoes: a Study of the Origin of the Puritan Revolt*, eds. W. H. Frere and C. E. Douglas, Church Historical Society (London: S.P.C.K., 1907), pp. 21, 18, 30.

19. "Therefore, forasmuch as all things are ordered by the authority of certain chosen men who are chief in the congregation in godliness and virtue, we may call the government of the Church Aristocracy, that is that government and state wherein a few of the best do bear the rule: or rather theocracy, that is the government of god, seeing that they have no authority to do anything but by the word and commandment of god." Walter Travers, *A Full and Plain Declaration of Ecclesiastical Discipline* (1574), p. 177.

20. Collinson, *The Elizabethan Puritan Movement*, p. 107; S. T. Bindoff, *Tudor England* (Hammondsworth, Middlesex: Penguin Books, 1950), pp. 227–28.

21. Patrick Collinson, *A Mirror of Elizabethan Puritanism: the Life and Letters of 'Godly Master Dering'* (London: Dr. Williams' Trust, 1964), pp. 17, 25; Lake, *Moderate Puritans*, p. 21.

22. Conyers Read, *Lord Burghley and Queen Elizabeth* (New York: Alfred Knopf, 1960), p. 117.

23. *The Works of John Whitgift*, ed. John Ayre, The Parker Society, 3 vols. (Cambridge: Cambridge University Press, 1851–1853), III, 160; I, 22. See A. F. Scott Pearson, *Church and State: Political Aspects of Sixteenth Century Puritanism* (Cambridge: Cambridge University Press, 1928).

24. Whitgift, *Works*, III, 189, 191–92, 198. Even the moderate Puritan Whitaker wrote that Cartwright "doth not only think perversely of the authority of Princes in causes ecclesiastical, but also flieth into the papist hold, from whom he would be thought to dissent with a mortal hatred." Lake, *Moderate Puritans*, p. 60.

25. Whitgift, *Works*, I, 273.

26. Claire Cross, *The Royal Supremacy in the Elizabethan Church* (London: George Allen and Unwin, 1969), p. 98. Collinson, *The Elizabethan Puritan Movement*, pp. 168–90; *Elizabethan Puritanism*, ed. Leonard J. Trinterud, A Library of Protestant Thought (New York: Oxford University Press, 1971), pp. 191–99.

27. Parker, *Correspondence*, p. 478.

28. *Proceedings in the Parliaments of Elizabeth I, 1558–1581*, pp. 445–47.

29. W. H. Frere, *The English Church in the Reigns of Elizabeth and James I*, A

History of the English Church (London: Macmillan, 1904), p. 192; Cardwell, *Synodalia*, I, 132–38.

30. Cardwell, *Documentary Annals*, I, 430, 422–24.

31. Trinterud, *Elizabethal Puritanism*, pp. 194–95.

32. Patrick Collinson, *Archbishop Grindal, 1519–1583, the Struggle for a Reformed Church* (Berkeley, California: University of California Press, 1980), p. 242.

33. *The Remains of Edmund Grindal*, ed. William Nicholson, The Parker Society (Cambridge: Cambridge University Press, 1843), p. 389.

34. Edmund Spenser lamented the archbishop's plight through the character of Algrind (Grindal) in the *Shepherd's Calendar*. Wallace T. MacCaffrey, *Queen Elizabeth and the Making of Policy, 1572–1588*. (Princeton, New Jersey: Princeton University Press, 1981), p. 93.

35. Patrick Collinson, "The Downfall of Archbishop Grindal and Its Place in Elizabethan Political and Ecclesiastical History," *The English Commonwealth, 1547–1640: Essays in Politics and Society*, eds. Peter Clark, Alan G. R. Smith, and Nicholas Tyacke (New York: Barnes and Noble, 1979), pp. 39–57.

36. *The Writings of Robert Harrison and Robert Browne*, eds. Albert Peel and Leland H. Carlson, Elizabethan Nonconformist Texts (London: George Allen and Unwin, 1953), pp. 152, 164. Browne's statement denying magistrates the right "to compel religion" is ambiguous, according to Stephen Brachlow, because a few pages earlier he had stated that a magistrate might "force" ministers to make reforms (Brachlow, *The Communion of Saints*, pp. 252–53).

37. Morris, *Political Thought in England*, p. 165.

38. John Bossy, "The Character of Elizabethan Catholicism," *Crisis in Europe, 1560–1660*, ed. Trevor Aston (London: Routledge and Kegan Paul, 1965), pp. 223–46; for a different point of view, see Christopher Haigh, "The Continuity of Catholicism in the English Reformation," *Past and Present* 93 (1981): 37–69; for an evaluation of Bossy and Haigh, see Patrick McGrath, "Elizabethan Catholicism, a Reconsideration," *Journal of Ecclesiastical History* 35 (1984): 414–28.

39. Elizabeth I, *Queen Elizabeth's Defence of Her Proceedings in Church and State*, ed. William E. Collins, The Church Historical Society, vol. 58 (London: S.P.C.K., 1899), pp. 42–43.

40. Rickey and Stroup, *Certain Sermons or Homilies*, II, 277.

41. Meyer, *England and the Catholic Church under Queen Elizabeth*, p. 142.

42. Peter Holmes, *Resistance and Compromise, the Political Thought of the Elizabethan Catholics* (Cambridge: Cambridge University Press, 1982), p. 100 ff.

43. Holmes, *Resistance and Compromise*, p. 142; Neale, *Elizabeth I and Her Parliaments, 1559–1581*, pt. 7. The statute deprived diocesan ecclesiastical commissions from handling recusancy cases. See Roger B. Manning, "The Crisis of Episcopal Authority During the Reign of Elizabeth I," *Journal of British Studies* 11 (November 1971): 22–23.

44. In this, as with all of the Elizabethan Catholic legislation, see Neale, *Elizabeth I and Her Parliaments, 1559–1581*, p. 394.

45. *A Complete Collection of State Trials*, ed. T. B. Howell (London: Longman, 1816), 33 vols., I, 1062–71.

46. William Cecil, *The Execution of Justice in England*, and William Allen, *A True, Sincere, and Modest Defense of English Catholics*, ed. Robert M. Kingdon, Folger Documents of Tudor and Stuart Civilization (Ithaca, New York: Cornell University Press, 1965), pp. 8–9, 20, 46.

47. Cecil, *The Execution of Justice*, pp. 61, 65, 120–21, 155.

48. Garrett Mattingly, "William Allen and Catholic Propaganda in England," *Aspects de la Propagande Religieuse*, ed. G. Berthoud, et al. (Geneva: Droz, 1957), pp. 336–37.

49. For the Bond of Association, see David Cressy, "Binding the Nation: the Bonds of Association, 1584 and 1696," *Tudor Rule and Revolution, Essays for G. R. Elton from his American Friends*, eds. Delloyd J. Guth and John W. McKenna (Cambridge: Cambridge University Press, 1982), pp. 217–34; and Patrick Collinson, "The Monarchical Republic of Queen Elizabeth I," *Bulletin of the John Rylands University Library of Manchester* 69 (1987): 394–424.

50. J. E. Neale, *Elizabeth I and Her Parliaments, 1584–1601* (London: Jonathan Cape, 1957), p. 37.

51. Philip Hughes, *Rome and the Counter-Reformation in England* (London: Burns Oates, 1942), pp. 240–46.

52. Neale, *Elizabeth I and Her Parliaments, 1559–1581*, p. 391.

53. MacCaffrey, *Queen Elizabeth and the Making of Policy*, pp. 140–42.

54. William Allen, *An Admonition to the Nobility and People of England*, in Dunham and Pargellis, *Complaint and Reform*, p. 378.

55. Hughes and Larkin, *Tudor Royal Proclamations*, III, 88.

56. Robert Southwell, *An Humble Supplication to Her Majesty*, 1595, ed. R. C. Bold (Cambridge: Cambridge University Press, 1953), p. 35. John Bossy has discussed the revival of a courtly Catholicism under Elizabeth in *Crisis in Europe, 1550–1650*, pp. 241–42; Thomas H. Clancy, *Papist Pamphleteers, the Allen-Persons Party and the Political Thought of the Counter-Reformation in England, 1572–1615*, Jesuit Studies (Chicago: Loyola University Press, 1964), p. 74.

57. MacCaffrey, *Queen Elizabeth and the Making of Policy*, pp. 143–44. Another clause of the 1593 statute provided that if Jesuits and seminarians, when examined by lawful authority—which presumably included the commissioners of the 1591 proclamation—should refuse to state whether or not they were Jesuits or seminarians, they would be committed to prison.

58. John Bossy, *The English Catholic Community, 1570–1850* (New York: Oxford University Press, 1976), p. 38.

59. Whitgift, *Works*, III, 592.

60. Cardwell, *Synodalia*, I, 140; Collinson, *The Elizabethan Puritan Movement*, pp. 245–47.

61. Peter Lake, on the other hand, believes that instead of splitting moderate from radical Puritans, Whitgift's conformist campaign drove the moderate, William Whitaker, "further into the puritan camp." *Moderate Puritans*, p. 113. Collinson says that four ministers of the Dedham classis asked to subscribe only to the royal supremacy "within the limits of the thirty-seventh Article of Religion" and to "the Articles of Religion themselves, according to the letter and the spirit of the statute of 1571, that is, that it should be confined to matters of doctrine" (*Elizabethan Puritan Movement*, p. 265).

62. Mary Hume Maguire, "Attack of the Common Lawyers on the Oath *Ex Officio* As Administered in the Ecclesiastical Courts in England," *Essays in History and Political Theory in Honor of C. J. McIlwain*, preface, Carl Wittke (Cambridge, Massachusetts: Harvard University Press, 1936), pp. 199–229; see also the early chapters of Leonard W. Levy, *Origins of the Fifth Amendment, the Right Against Self-Incrimination* (London: Oxford University Press, 1968); Cross, *The Royal Supremacy*, pp. 200, 204.

63. Elton, *The Tudor Constitution*, 2nd ed., pp. 231–32.

64. For this, as in some other aspects of Elizabethan Puritanism, I have followed Collinson, *The Elizabethan Puritan Movement*, pt. 6, chap. 1. The Book of Discipline (*De Disciplina Ecclesiae*) of 1586 should not be confused with Travers' *Ecclesiasticae Disciplinae* of 1574. A 1587 version of the Book of Discipline was printed "for the eye of the Westminster Assembly in 1644" (p. 297).

65. Richard Bancroft, *A Survey of the Pretended Holy Discipline* (London, 1593), p. 369.

66. Neale, *Elizabeth I and Her Parliaments, 1584–1601*, p. 149.

67. "Almighty God hath placed the Sovereign magistrate in the highest authority upon earth next under him, within their dominions, over all persons and causes, as well ecclesiastical as civil, to see and command the ordering of them." *Reliquiae Liturgicae, Documents Connected with the Liturgy of the Church of England*, 5 vols., ed. Peter Hall (Bath: Burns and Goodwin, 1847), I, viii, 106.

68. Neale, *Elizabeth I and Her Parliaments, 1584–1601*, p. 163.

69. Neale, *Elizabeth I and Her Parliaments, 1584–1601*, p. 160; Powel Mills Dawley, *John Whitgift and the English Reformation* (New York: Charles Scribner's Sons, 1954), pp. 203–4; Hughes, *The Reformation in England*, III, 146; Hill, *Economic Principles of the Church*, p. 146.

70. Penry is the choice of Donald J. McGinn, *John Penry and the Marprelate Controversy* (New Brunswick, New Jersey: Rutgers University Press, 1966), and Throckmorton is the choice of J. E. Neale, *Elizabeth I and Her Parliaments, 1584–1601*, p. 220. Leland H. Carlson rejects Penry and builds a very strong case for Throckmorton in his "Martin Marprelate: His Identity and His Satire," *English Satire, Papers Read at a Clark Library Seminar, January 15, 1972* (Los Angeles: William Andrews Clark Memorial Library, 1972), and overwhelmingly clinches his argument in his *Martin Marprelate, Gentleman, Master Job Throkmorton Laid Open in His Colors* (San Marino, California: Huntington Library, 1981); Hughes and Larkin, *Tudor Royal Proclamations*, III, 34.

71. Cross, *The Royal Supremacy*, pp. 144–45; Job Throckmorton, *Hay Any Work for Cooper*, [Coventry, 1589], pp. 19–20, contained in *The Marprelate Tracts, [1588–1589]* (Leeds: Scolar Press, 1967).

72. Richard Bancroft, *A Sermon Preached at Paul's Cross* (London, 1589), p. 68; Cross, *The Royal Supremacy*, p. 177. In order to combat Whitgift's alleged views, Knollys, interestingly, whose experience in Parliament went back sixty years or so, proposed the revival of the Henrician concept of a vicegerency. W. D. J. Cargill Thompson, "Sir Francis Knolly's Campaign Against the *Jure Divino* Theory of Episcopacy," *Studies in the Reformation, Luther to Hooker*, eds. C. W. Dugmore and A. G. Dickens (London: Athlone Press, 1980), p. 100. Also see Roger Lockyer, *The Early Stuarts, a Political History of England, 1603–1642* (London: Longman, 1989), p. 95.

73. W. D. J. Cargill Thompson, "Anthony Marten and the Elizabethal Debate on Episcopacy," *Essays in Modern English Church History in Memory of Norman Sykes*, eds. G. V. Bennett and J. D. Walsh (London: Adam and Charles Black, 1966), pp. 51, 58–59. Eventually, the divine right of episcopacy provided the basis for Archbishop Laud's full-blown attempts to free the Church from Erastianism and for the efforts of the Non-Juring supporters of Archbishop Sancroft almost a hundred years later to claim *jure divino* authority when Crown and Parliament tried to deprive him of office. Cargill Thompson, *Studies in the Reformation*, p. 130.

74. For an elucidation of Hooker's seemingly conflicting views, see Peter Lake, *Anglicans and Puritans? Presbyterianism and English Conformist Thought from Whitgift to Hooker* (London: Unwin Hyman, 1988), pp. 197–230; Thomas Fuller,

The Church History of Britain, from the Birth of Jesus Christ until the Year MDCXLVIII, 3rd ed. (London: Thomas Tegg, 1842), III, 128.

75. Richard Hooker, *Hooker's Ecclesiastical Polity, Book VIII*, intro. Raymond Aaron Houk, Columbia University Studies in English and Comparative Literature, no. 102 (New York: Columbia University Press, 1931), pp. 156, 232.

76. Collinson, *The Elizabethan Puritan Movement*, pt. 8, chaps. 1–3.

77. *The Writings of Henry Barrow, 1587–1590*, ed. Leland H. Carlson, Elizabethan Nonconformist Texts (London: George Allen and Unwin, 1962), pp. 206–89.

78. *The Writings of John Greenwood, Together with the Joint Writings of Henry Barrow and John Greenwood, 1587–1590*, ed. Leland H. Carlson, Elizabethan Nonconformist Texts (London: George Allen and Unwin, 1962), pp. 28–29.

79. "Incidentally, it would be accurate enough but not entirely fair to add that Calvinist church courts, where they existed, showed no hesitation in demanding self-incrimination, and it would be hard to imagine how anyone expected to enforce the 'godly discipline' without it." Eliot Rose, *Cases of Conscience, Alternatives Open to Recusants and Puritans under Elizabeth I and James I* (London: Cambridge University Press, 1975), p. 137.

80. Lake, *Anglicans and Puritans?*, p. 59.

Chapter 4

1. Calvin said that Christ died for all and his death is offered to all, yet all do not receive him because of God's predestination, but Beza believed that Christ died for the elect only. See R. T. Kendall, *Calvin and English Calvinism to 1649* (Oxford: Oxford University Press, 1979), pp. 15, 29; Dewey D. Wallace, Jr., *Puritans and Predestination, Grace in English Protestant Theology, 1525–1695* (Chapel Hill, North Carolina: University of North Carolina Press, 1982), pp. 66–69.

2. H. C. Porter, *Reformation and Reaction in Tudor Cambridge* (Cambridge: Cambridge University Press, 1958), chaps. 13–15; Lake, *Moderate Puritans*, pp. 201–18.

3. For the preceding two paragraphs and the following one, see Lake, *Moderate Puritans*, pp. 218–30; Porter, *Reformation and Reaction*, pp. 364–75. Nicholas Tyacke believes that only article four of the Lambeth Articles is open to an anti-Calvinist interpretation. *Anti-Calvinists, the Rise of English Arminianism, c. 1590–1640*, Oxford Historical Monographs (Oxford: Clarendon Press, 1987), p. 31.

4. Peter Lake; "Calvinism and the English Church, 1570–1635," *Past and Present* 114 (1987): 39–47; Peter Lake, "Matthew Hutton: a Puritan Bishop?" *History* 64 (1979): 200–201.

5. Neale, *Elizabeth I and Her Parliaments, 1584–1601*, pp. 356–58; Cardwell, *Synodalia*, I, 147–63.

6. Patrick Collinson, "The Beginnings of English Sabbatarianism," *Studies in Church History*, ed. C. W. Dugmore and Charles Duggan (London: Nelson, 1964), I, 207–21.

7. R. M. Haines, "Some Arguments in Favour of Plurality in the Elizabethan Church," *Studies in Church History*, ed. G. J. Cuming (Leiden: Brill, 1969), V, 166–92.

8. Neale, *Elizabeth I and Her Parliaments, 1584–1601*, pp. 394–410.

9. Bossy, *The English Catholic Community*, chap. 2.

10. Meyer, *England and the Catholic Church*, pp. 420, 424.

11. Meyer, *England and the Catholic Church*, p. 436.

12. Holmes claims that the appellants not only adopted a policy of loyalty and nonresistance to the Crown, but also that they sought religious toleration as they pursued their anti-Jesuit tactics (*Resistance and Compromise*, pp. 186–204).

13. Arnold Pritchard, *Catholic Loyalism in Elizabethan England* (Chapel Hill, North Carolina: University of North Carolina Press, 1979), pp. 128–29.

14. *Scottish Historical Documents*, ed. Gordon Donaldson (Edinburgh: Scottish Academic Press, 1970), p. 145.

15. Robert Ashton, ed., *James I By His Contemporaries*, (London: Hutchinson, 1969), p. 175.

16. *The Political Works of James I*, ed. Charles Howard McIlwain (Cambridge, Massachusetts: Harvard University Press, 1918; reprinted in New York: Russell and Russell, 1965), pp. 54–55.

17. This paragraph and the following one are also based on James I, *Political Works*, pp. 23, 8, 7.

18. Gee and Hardy, *Documents*, p. 508.

19. Gee and Hardy, *Documents*, p. 510; Roland G. Usher, *The Reconstruction of the English Church* (London: Appleton, 1910; reprinted Farnborough, England: Gregg International, 1969), I, 291, 296–97. For the next two paragraphs, see also Gee and Hardy, *Documents*, pp. 508–11.

20. *Stuart Royal Proclamations, Royal Proclamations of James I, 1603–1625*, eds. James F. Larkin and Paul L. Hughes (Oxford: Clarendon Press, 1973), I, 63; Kenneth Fincham and Peter Lake, "The Ecclesiastical Policy of King James I," *Journal of British Studies* 24 (April 1985): 172.

21. Mark H. Curtis, "The Hampton Court Conference and Its Aftermath," *History* 46 (1961): 5–6; Patrick Collinson, "The Jacobean Religious Settlement: the Hampton Court Conference," ed. Howard Tomlinson, *Before the English Civil War* (London: Macmillan, 1981), pp. 33–34; Frederick Shriver, "Hampton Court Revisited: James I and the Puritans," *Journal of Ecclesiastical History* 33 (1982): 53–55. Shriver has argued that the inclusion of the phrase "agreeable to God's word" would have suggested Whitgift's phraseology in the subscription oath, and if so, that would have distressed the radical Puritans, who had been forced to take it, but not the moderates, who had not.

22. *A History of Conferences and Other Proceedings Connected with the Revision of the Book of Common Prayer, from the Year 1558 to the Year 1690*, ed. Edward Cardwell, 3rd ed. (Oxford: Oxford University Press, 1849; reprinted at Ridgewood, New Jersey: Gregg Press, 1966), pp. 170–71.

23. Usher, *Reconstruction*, II, 342. James had said essentially the same thing in his royal proclamation of October 24, delaying the conference from November until January. Larkin and Hughes, *Stuart Royal* Proclamations, I, 62–63.

24. Cardwell, *A History of Conferences*, p. 180.

25. Thomas Sparke, *A Brotherly Persuasion to Unity, and Uniformity in Judgment* (London, 1607), p. 3. According to the account of William Barlow, dean of Chester, the king suggested the addition of the word "often" to the phrase "we may depart from grace given," thereby implying that there could be one or more falls into sin without accepting the possibility of a final or total damnation (Cardwell, *A History of Conferences*, p. 181). And, according to an anonymous account, when John Overall, the dean of St. Paul's, admitted that he had "taught that those that have been received to grace may fall from grace, and if they do not repent they shall perish," the king observed that "the elect indeed might fall, but never finally so that they can perish, for they shall rise again by repentance" (Usher, *Reconstruction*, II, 344–45).

Despite James' basic stance for final and total perseverance, his stress on repentance with Overall indicates that he may not have been quite as close to the rigid Calvinism of the Lambeth Articles on this point as Reynolds would have liked him to be.

26. Mark Curtis has argued that many new preachers wanted to make careers in the ministry, but, because the competition for good livings was so severe, they became frustrated by the limited opportunities, turned into "alienated intellectuals," and as "angry young men," were driven into opposition to the church and state, especially in the 1640s ("The Alienated Intellectuals of Early Stuart England," *Past and Present* [23 (1962: 25–43]). Ian Green, on the contrary, has argued that the many young men who offered themselves for ordination each year under the early Stuarts were not so poor as they have been usually portrayed, shared a rising academic quality and social status, did not necessarily seek their own best financial interest, and were not the leaders of the opposition in the 1640s and 1650s. "Career Prospects and Clerical Conformity in the Early Stuart Church," *Past and Present* 90 (1981): 71–115.

27. Usher, *Reconstruction*, II, 348; Cardwell, *A History of Conferences*, p. 184.

28. Usher, *Reconstruction*, II, 351–52.

29. Shriver, *Journal of Ecclesiastical History* 33 (1982): 60.

30. Cardwell, *A History of Conferences*, p. 206.

31. Cardwell, *A History of Conferences*, pp. 214–16.

32. Usher, *Reconstruction*, II, 353.

33. Larkin and Hughes, *Stuart Royal Proclamations*, I, 74–76.

34. McIlwain, *Political Works of James I*, p. 274.

35. Wallace Notestein, *The House of Commons, 1604–1610* (New Haven, Connecticut: Yale University Press, 1971), p. 43.

36. Constitutional Documents of the Reign of James I, ed. J. R. Tanner (Cambridge: Cambridge University Press, 1930), pp. 226–27.

37. Usher, *Reconstruction*, I, 385–402.

38. Cardwell, *Synodalia*, I, 245–329; Stuart Barton Babbage, *Puritanism and Richard Bancroft* (London: S.P.C.K., 1962), chap. 3.

39. Larkin and Hughes, *Stuart Royal Proclamations*, I, 87–90.

40. Babbage, Puritanism, 217.

41. Michael McGiffert, "Covenant, Crown, and Commons in Elizabethan Puritanism," *Journal of British Studies* 20 (Fall 1980): 32–52.

42. Richard L. Greaves, "The Origins and Early Development of English Covenant Thought," *Historian* 31 (1968): 22–27; John Von Rohr, "Covenant and Assurance in Early English Puritanism," *Church History* 34 (1965): 195–203; Michael McGiffert, "Grace and Works: the Rise and Division of Covenant Divinity in Elizabethan Puritanism," *Harvard Theological Review* 75 (1982): 496–500.

43. William Perkins, *A Golden Chain*, 1592, in *Works*, 3 vols. (Cambridge, 1616–1618), I, 70. John von Rohr believes that the covenant of grace was *both* conditional *and* absolute throughout Puritan theology. See his *The Covenant of Grace in Puritan Thought*, American Academy of Religion Studies in Religion (Atlanta, Georgia: Scholars Press, 1986), pp. 21, 32–33.

44. Michael McGiffert, "God's Controversy with Jacobean England," *American Historical Review* 88 (1983): 1166–67; Greaves, *The Historian* 31 (1968): 29–34.

45. Perry Miller, *Orthodoxy in Massachusetts, 1630–1650: a Genetic Study* (Cambridge, Massachusetts: Harvard University Press, 1933), p. 77.

46. William Bradshaw, *English Puritanism and Other Works*, 1605, intro. R. C. Simmons (reprinted at Farnborough, England: Gregg International, 1972), pp. 6–11, 32–35. Although Bradshaw argued for the election of church officers, among the three

classic forms of political government—monarchy, aristocracy, and democracy—he felt that monarchy was the best (p. 11).

47. William Bradford, *Of Plymouth Plantation, 1620–1647*, ed. Samuel Eliot Morison (New York: Random House, 1967), p. 10.

48. Winthrop K. Jordan, *The Development of Religious Toleration in England: from the Accession of James I to the Convention of the Long Parliament (1603–1640)* (Cambridge, Massachusetts: Harvard University Press, 1936; reprinted Gloucester, Massachusetts: Peter Smith, 1965) pp. 242–43. For a slightly different interpretation, see Timothy George, *John Robinson and the English Separatist Tradition* (Macon, Georgia: Mercer University Press, 1982), pp. 113–14. For the Separatists see White, *The English Separatist Tradition* chaps 6–8. It must be noted that after 1610, Robinson argued that in prayer and in study of the Bible, fellowship between Separatists and those belonging to the Anglican parishes was lawful and did not constitute any breach of Separatist principles.

49. A. C. Underwood, *A History of the English Baptists* (London: Carey Kingsgate Press, 1947), p. 42.

50. *Tracts on Liberty of Conscience and Persecution, 1614–1661*, ed., Edward Bean Underhill (London: Hanserd Knollys Society, 1846), p. 122.

51. David Harris Willson, *King James VI and I* (London: Jonathan Cape, 1956), pp. 219–21; McIlwain, *Political Works of James I*, pp. 274–75.

52. John Bossy, "The English Catholic Community, 1603–1625," *The Reign of James VI and I*, ed. Alan G. R. Smith (London: Macmillan, 1973), p. 95; Joel Hurstfield, "Gunpowder Plot and the Politics of Dissent," *Early Stuart Studies, Essays in Honor of David Harris Wilson*, ed. Howard S. Reinmuth, Jr. (Minneapolis: Min University of Minnesota Press, 1970, pp. 103–11; Jenny Wormald, "Gunpowder, Treason, and Scots," *Journal of British Studies* 24 (April 1985): 141–68.

53. *Political Works of James I*, pp. 281, 285; Tanner, *Constitutional Documents*, p. 86.

54. J. R. Tanner, *Constitutional Documents* p. 91.

55. *Political Works of James I*, pp. 85, 91.

56. The same distinction between the *potestas jurisdictionis* and the *potestas ordinis* was made by other pamphleteers of the time, such as Richard Field and George Carleton (Field, *Of the Church*, London, 1606, Book V, pp. 134–39; Carleton, *Jurisdiction, Regal, Episcopal, Papal*, 1610, "Epistle Dedicatory," pp. 4–10). See also Patrick Collinson, *The Religion of Protestants, the Church in English Society, 1559–1625* (Oxford: Clarendon Press, 1982), chap. 1.

57. On Andrewes' distinction between the *potestas jurisdictionis* and the *potestas ordinis*, see Robert L. Ottley, *Lancelot Andrewes* (London: Methuen, 1894), p. 62; John Donne, *Pseudo-Martyr*, (London, 1610, intro. Francis Jacques Sypher, reprinted in Delmar, New York: Scholars' Facsimilies and Reprints, 1974), p. 347.

58. Cardwell, *Synodalia*, I, 333.

59. John Overall, *Bishop Overall's Convocation-Book*, MDCVI (London, 1690), p. 59.

60. Cardwell, *Synodalia*, I, 334.

61. Cardwell, *Documentary Annals*, II, 135.

62. Edward Coke, *The Second Part of the Institutes of the Laws of England* (London: E. and R. Brooke, 1797), pp. 610–11.

63. Willson, *King James VI and I*, p. 259. Fuller had defended two men who refused to take the oath ex officio and who denied the High Commission's claim to fine and to imprison.

64. *The Stuart Constitution, 1603–1688: Documents and Commentary*, 2nd ed., ed. J. P. Kenyon (Cambridge: Cambridge University Press, 1986), p. 80.

65. *Proceedings in Parliament, 1610*, ed. Elizabeth Read Foster (New Haven, Connecticut: Yale University Press, 1966). II, 294–95; *Select Statutes and Other Constitutional Documents Illustrative of the Reigns of Elizabeth and James I*, ed. G. W. Prothero, 3rd ed. (Oxford: Clarendon Press, 1906), p. 406.

66. John Dykstra Eusden, *Puritans, Lawyers, and Politics in Early Seventeenth-Century England* (New Haven, Connecticut: Yale University Press, 1958), pp. 96–101.

67. John Selden, *The History of Tithes* (1618), preface, pp. xvii, xx. Selden facetiously asked "to whom [does] it belongs more to write the *History of Tithes* than to a Common Lawyer?"

68. The Book of Common Order actually was a recension of the *Form of Prayers*, that directory of church worship drawn up by John Knox and the English exiles at Geneva in 1556.

69. Maurice Lee, Jr., *Government by Pen: Scotland Under James VI and I* (Urbana, Illinois: University of Illinois Press, 1980), pp. 167–68.

70. Ian B. Cowan, "The Five Articles of Perth," *Reformation and Revolution*, ed Duncan Shaw (Edinburgh: Saint Andrew Press, 1967), p. 166.

71. Lee, *Government By Pen*, pp. 179–80.

72. *The Constitutional Documents of the Puritan Revolution, 1625–1660*, ed. Samuel R. Gardiner, 3rd ed. (Oxford: Clarendon Press, 1947), pp. 99–103; James Tait, "The Declaration of Sports for Lancashire (1617)," *English Historical Review* 32 (1917): 561–68. Kenneth Fincham thinks it unlikely that Abbot refused to read *The Declaration of Sports*; see "Prelacy and Politics: Archbishop Abbot's Defense of Protestant Orthodoxy," *Historical Research* 61 (1988); 58.

73. And yet Peter White points out that "the doctrinal revolution" of Arminianism under Charles I actually began with James, who not only advanced Andrewes and Overall to important bishoprics, but also John Buckeridge, John Howson, and, later, William Laud—all of them (if not when appointed, certainly later on) leaders of the Arminian movement in the Church ("The Rise of Arminianism Reconsidered," *Past and Present* 101 [1983]: 40). James did not appoint them to those responsible posts in the Church because of their Arminian theology, but favored them because either they had supported the king in his pamphlet warfare against the papists (Nicholas Tyacke, "Puritanism, Arminianism, and Counter-Revolution," *The Origins of the English Civil War*, Problems in Focus, ed. Conrad Russell [London: Macmillan, 1973], p. 130) or because they were the staunchest upholders of the royal prerogative in both church and state (Wallace, *Puritans and Predestination*, p. 83).

74. Ralph Winwood, *Memorials of Affairs of State in the Reigns of Queen Elizabeth and King James I.*, ed. E. Sawyer, 3 vols. (London, 1725), III, 459; Wallace, *Puritans and Predestination*, p. 80. James was not a thorough-going Beza-type Calvinist: as we shall see shortly, he did not stand "firmly" on the essential doctrinal issues of the Thirty-Nine Articles, as White contends that he did (*Past and Present*, 101 [1983]: 38), because James believed, as we have seen, in *double* predestination (not mentioned in the Thirty-Nine Articles) and took a basic stance that the elect could not finally or totally fall from grace (also not stated in the Thirty-Nine Articles). Fincham and Lake believe that James was a "moderate Calvinist" in theology (*Journal of British Studies*, 24 [April 1985]: 190).

75. Wallace, *Puritans and Predestination*, p. 80; Frederick Shriver, "Orthodoxy and Diplomacy: James I and the Vorstius Affair," *English Historical Review* 85 (1970): 454–55; A. W. Harrison, *Arminianism* (London: Duckworth, 1937), p. 45.

76. Wallace, *Puritans and Predestination*, p. 81; White, *Past and Present*, 101 (1983): 42.

77. John Hales, *Golden Remains* (London, 1659), pp. 2, 5; A. W. Harrison, *The Beginnings of Arminianism to the Synod of Dort* (London: University of London Press, 1926), pp. 336–37; White, *Past and Present* 101 (1983): 43; John Platt, "Eirenical Anglicans at the Synod of Dort," contained in *Reform and the Reformation, England and the Continent, c1500–c1750*, ed. Derek Baker (Oxford: Basil Blackwell, 1979), pp. 238–39; Peter Lake writes, on the basis of the Tanner MS. in the Bodleian Library, that Davenant wrote to Ward that he wished Montagu "had a more modest conceit of himself and a less base opinion of all others who jump not with him in his mongrel opinions." Lake, *Past and Present* 114 (1987): 64.

78. John Selden, *Table Talk*, ed. Samuel Harvey Reynolds (Oxford: Clarendon Press, 1892), p. 71.

79. McIlwain, *Political Works*, p. 322.

Chapter 5

1. Robert Peters, "John Hales and the Synod of Dort," *Studies in Church History*, eds. G. J. Cuming and Derek Baker (Cambridge: Cambridge University Press, 1971), VII, 279; Harrison, *Arminianism*, p. 134; *The Arminian Nunnery*, 1641, p. 10.

2. *Proceedings in Parliament, 1610*, II, 118–19; *Commons Debates, 1621*, eds. Wallace Notestein, Frances Helen Relf, and Hartley Simpson (New Haven, Connecticut: Yale University Press, 1935), IV, 71–72; V, 472.

3. Conrad Russell, "The Parliamentary Career of John Pym, 1621–9," *The English Commonwealth, 1547–1640, Essays in Politics and Society*, eds. Peter Clark, Alan G. R. Smith, and Nicholas Tyacke (New York: Harper and Row, 1979), p. 155.

4. H. R. Trevor-Roper, *Archbishop Laud, 1573–1645*, 2nd ed. (London: Macmillan, 1962), p. 154; Cardwell, *Documentary Annals*, II, 202; Margaret A. Judson, *The Crisis of the Constitution, an Essay in Constitutional and Political Thought in England, 1603–1645* (New Brunswick, New Jersey: Rutgers University Press, 1949), pp. 204–5, 312–13.

5. Cardwell, *Documentary Annals*, II, 198–203; *The Sermons of John Donne*, eds. George R. Potter and Evelyn M. Simpson, 10 vols. (Berkeley and Los Angeles: University of California Press, 1953–1962), IV, 202.

6. Dew Roberts, *Mitre and Musket, John Williams, Lord Keeper, Archbishop of York, 1582–1650* (London: Oxford University Press, 1938), p. 77.

7. Robert E. Ruigh, *The Parliament of 1624, Politics and Foreign Policy* (Cambridge, Massachusetts: Harvard University Press, 1971), p. 240.

8. Ruigh, *The Parliament of 1624*, p. 250.

9. Tyacke, *Anti-Calvinists*, chap. 5.

10. Richard Montagu, *A Gag for the New Gospel? No. A New Gag for an Old Goose* (1624), pp. 109, 148, 164, 177; Hillel Schwartz, "Arminianism and the English Parliament, 1624–1629," *Journal of British Studies* 12 (May 1973): 46; *Debates in the House of Commons in 1625*, ed. Samuel R. Gardiner (Westminster: The Camden Society, 1873), New Series, VI, 46; White, *Past and Present* 101 (1983): 46; Fincham, *Historical Research* 51 (1988): 52–53, 57.

11. Jordan, *The Development of Religious Toleration in England (1603–1640)*, p. 94.

12. Tyacke, *The Origins of the English Civil War*, p. 131. Just before the marriage trip to Spain, Laud had dissuaded Buckingham from conversion to Catholicism urged upon him by a Jesuit priest named Fisher. Timothy H. Wadkins, "The Percy-'Fisher' Controversies and the Ecclesiastical Politics of Jacobean Anti-Catholicism, 1622–1625," *Church History* 57 (1988): 168. Also see Nicholas Tyacke and Peter White, "Debate: the Rise of Arminianism Reconsidered," *Past and Present*, 115 (1987): 211.

13. Gardiner, *Debates in the House of Commons in 1625*, pp. 4, 18–25.

14. *Proceedings in Parliament, 1625*, eds. Maija Jansson and William Bidwell (New Haven, Connecticut: Yale University Press, 1987), pp. 338, 517; Gardiner, *Debates in the House of Commons in 1625*, pp. 48–51.

15. *The Works of . . . William Laud*, eds. W. Scott and J. Bliss (Oxford: John Henry Parker, 1847–1860), VI, 244–46; Davenant to Ward, December 8, 1625, in the Tanner MS. of the Bodleian Library, as quoted in Lake, *Past and Present*, 114 (1987): 64.

16. Nicholas Tyacke, "Arminianism in England, in Religion and Politics, 1604 to 1640," D. Phil. diss., Oxford University, 1968, p. 273.

17. Tyacke, *Anti-Calvinists*, pp. 168–72; James F. Maclear, "Puritan Relations with Buckingham," *Huntington Library Quarterly* 21 (1958): 121; *The Correspondence of John Cosin*, ed. George Ornsby, Publications of the Surtees Society, 2 vols. (Durham: Andrews, 1869–1872), I, xiii.

18. *The Works of . . . John Cosin* [Ed. J. Sansom], 5 vols. (Oxford: John Henry Parker, 1843–1855), II, 57, 59, 63; Tyacke, *Anti-Calvinists*, pp. 172–80; Roger Lockyer, *Buckingham, the Life and Political Career of George Villiers, First Duke of Buckingham, 1592–1628* (London: Longman, 1981), pp. 305–8.

19. Russell, *The English Commonwealth*, p. 160; Laud, *Works*, I, 71; *Debates in the House of Commons in 1625*, pp. 179–81. Actually, Montagu's view of a total, but not final fall from grace was, like Bishop Andrewes' view, halfway between the Calvinist view that the fall was neither total nor final and the Arminian view that it could be both total and final.

20. Laud, *Works*, VI, 249; *Stuart Royal Proclamations*, ed. James F. Larkin (Oxford: Clarendon Press, 1983), II, 92; Peter Heylyn, *Cyprianus Anglicus: Or, the History of the Life and Death, of . . . William . . . Archbishop of Canterbury* (London, 1668), p. 127.

21. Heylyn, *Cyprianus Anglicus*, p. 162; Charles Carlton, *Archbishop William Laud* (London: Routledge and Kegan Paul, 1987), p. 63.

22. Trevor-Roper, *Laud*, p. 79; Robert Sibthorpe, *Apostolike Obedience* (London, 1627), pp. 3, 21; Roger Manwaring, *Religion and Allegiance* (London, 1627), first sermon, pp. 19, 9; Samuel R. Gardiner, *History of England from the Accession of James I to the Outbreak of the Civil War*, 10 vols. (London: Longman, Green, 1883–1884), VI, 209; Tyacke, Oxford D. Phil. diss., p. 186; Richard Cust, *The Forced Loan and English Politics, 1626–1628* (Oxford: Clarendon Press, 1987), pp. 62–63.

23. *Historical Collections*, ed. John Rushworth, 8 vols. (London, 1721), I, 577, 609; *Stuart Royal Proclamations*, II, 197–99.

24. Rushworth, *Historical Collections*, I, 621; *Commons Debates, 1628*, eds. Robert C. Johnson, Mary Frear Keeler, Maija Jansson Cole, and William B. Bidwell, in *Proceedings in Parliament, 1628* (New Haven, Connecticut: Yale University Press, 1977–1978), IV, 313, 309.

25. Johnson, Keeler, Cole, and Bidwell, *Commons Debates, 1628*, III, 515–22.

26. Larkin, *Stuart Royal Proclamations*, II, 219.

27. Gardiner, *Constitutional Documents*, pp. 75–76.

28. *Commons Debates for 1629*, eds. Wallace Notestein and Frances Helen Relf (Minneapolis: University of Minnesota, 1921), p. 127; Laud, *Works*, VI, 67; Hardwick, *Articles of Religion*, p. 140.

29. Notestein and Relf, *Commons Debates for 1629*, pp. 12–13, 24–25, 117–18; Laud, *Works*, VI, 11–12.

30. The Lambeth Articles, the Irish Articles, and the Conclusions of the Synod of Dort, as John Selden pointed out, were not "public acts" of the Church of England. Kenyon, *The Stuart Constitution*, 2nd ed., p. 141; Gardiner, *History of England*, VII, 12; Notestein and Relf, *Commons Debates for 1629*, p. 44; Cosin, *Correspondence*, I, 149.

31. Conrad Russell, *Parliaments and English Politics, 1621–1629*, (Oxford: Clarendon Press, 1979), pp. 29–30. Russell also sees a strong correlation between the anti-Arminians and those who supported the war with Spain. Popery was popery whether in Madrid or Whitehall (p. 429).

32. Tyacke, Oxford D. Phil. diss., p. 167n.

33. Laud, *Works*, III, 159; Notestein and Relf, *Commons Debates for 1629*, p. 27.

34. Hugh Trevor-Roper states that Arminianism was "an intellectual movement which, in England, went back to the time of Erasmus." *Catholics, Anglicans, and Puritans, Seventeenth Century Essays* (Chicago: University of Chicago Press, 1988), p. 114. Margo Todd, however, argues that "Anglicans, especially the Laudian strain, were by the seventeenth century realizing as Catholics had in the sixteenth that Christian humanist social theory was ultimately inimical to the traditional, hierarchical authority structure to which they were committed." *Christian Humanism and the Puritan Social Order*, Ideas in Context (Cambridge: Cambridge University Press, 1987), p. 205.

35. Laud, *Works*, VII, 23; IV, 274; Rushworth, *Historical Collections*, II, 7–9; Heylyn, *Cyprianus Anglicus*, pp. 199–200.

36. William Prynne, *Canterbury's Doom* (London, 1646), pp. 370–71; Julian Edward Davies, "The Growth and Implementation of 'Laudianism' with Special Reference to the Southern Province," Oxford D. Phil. diss., 1987, p. 104.

37. Cardwell, *Documentary Annals*, II, 203; Patrick Collinson, "Lectures by Combination: Structure and Characteristics of Church Life in 17th Century England," *Bulletin of the Institute of Historical Research*, 48 (1975) 182–213.

38. Paul Seaver, *The Puritan Lectureships, the Politics of Religious Dissent, 1560–1662* (Stanford, California: Stanford University Press, 1970), chap. 8.

39. Isabel M. Calder, "A Seventeenth Century Attempt to Purify the Anglican Church," *American Historical Review* 53 (1948): 763; Ethyn W. Kirby, "The Lay Feoffees: a Study in Militant Puritanism," *Journal of Modern History* 14 (1942): 1; Hill, *Economic Problems of the Church*, p. 254.

40. Laud's method of purchasing impropriations, that is, by tapping into the fines of the Court of High Commission, called for the acquisition of a minimum of only two impropriations a year—an appallingly low number, even if it had been successful. Laud, *Works*, IV, 303–4; David D. Hall, *The Faithful Shepherd, a History of the New England Ministry in the Seventeenth Century* (Chapel Hill, North Carolina: University of North Carolina Press, 1972), pp. 47, 72; Raymond Phineas Stearns, *Congregationalism in the Dutch Netherlands, the Rise and Fall of the English*

Congregational Classis, 1621–1635, Studies in Church History (Chicago: American Society of Church History, 1940).

41. Hill, *Economic Problems of the Church*, pp. 321–37.

42. Laud, *Works*, IV, 177; Hill, *Economic Problems of the Church*, pp. 316–17; Felicity Heal, "Archbishop Laud Revisited: Leases and Estate Management at Canterbury and Winchester before the Civil War," *Princes and Paupers in the English Church, 1500–1800*, eds. Rosemary O'Day and Felicity Heal (Totowa, New Jersey: Barnes and Noble, 1981), pp. 129–33.

43. Laud, *Works*, III, 254; Hill, *Economic Problems of the Church*, chap. 12.

44. Hill, *Economic Problems of the Church*, p. 345.

45. Alexander Leighton, *An Appeal to the Parliament, or Sion's Plea Against Prelacy*, 1628, p. 5. "*Arminianism* we know is the very *Elixir* of *Popery* . . . the *mystery* of *Iniquity* . . . the *quintessence* of *Equivocation* . . . the *Cabinet* of the Pope's secret . . . and Spain's *new-found* passage for Britain," (p. 234).

46. Davenant was not charged with violating James' Directions to preachers (1622), which prevented sermons on predestination, because bishops were specifically exempted.

47. Fuller, *Church History*, III, 365; Laud, *Works*, VI, 133. At his trial in 1644 Laud declared, "I have nothing to do to defend Arminianism, no man having yet charged me with abetting any point of it." (*Works*, IV, 267). Kevin Sharpe observes that in his role as chancellor of Oxford University, Laud's statutes and correspondence "are notable for their *silence* on questions of theological controversy" ("Archbishop Laud and the University of Oxford," *History and Imagination, Essays in Honor of H. R. Trevor-Roper*, eds. Hugh Lloyd-Jones, Valerie Pearl, and Blair Worden [New York: Holmes and Meier, 1980], p. 160).

48. Paul Slack, "Religious Protest and Urban Authority: the Case of Henry Sherfield, Iconoclast, 1633," *Studies in Church History*, ed. Derek Baker (Cambridge: Cambridge University Press, 1972), IX, 295–302; Laud, *Works*, IV, 239, 17.

49. Prynne, *Canterbury's Doom*, p. 151; David Underdown, *Revel, Riot, and Rebellion, Popular Politics and Culture in England, 1603–1660* (Oxford: Oxford University Press, 1987), pp. 66–67; Fuller, *Church History*, III, 375–79.

50. Prynne, *Canterbury's Doom*, p. 148; Thomas G. Barnes, "County Politics and a Puritan *cause célèbre*: Somerset Church Ales, 1633," *TRHS*, Fifth series, 9 (1959) 110–11.

51. Cardwell, *Synodalia*, I, 293; Davies, Oxford D. Phil. diss., long abstract, p. 88.

52. W. H. Fryer, "'The High Churchmen' of the Earlier Seventeenth Century," *Renaissance and Modern Studies* 5 (1961): 124–29.

53. William Prynne, *Histrio-mastix* (1633), "Epistle Dedicatory," "To the Christian Reader."

54. *Documents Relating to the Proceedings Against William Prynne in 1634 and 1637*, ed. Samuel R. Gardiner (Westminster: The Camden Society, 1877), New Series, XVIII, 16, 27, 44–45; William M. Lamont, *Marginal Prynne, 1600–1669* (London: Routledge and Kegan Paul, 1963), chap. 1.

55. *News From Ipswich* (Ipswich, 1636), no pagination.

56. Robert Burton, *For God and the King* (1636), pp. 33–34; Richard T. Hughes, "Henry Burton, a Study in Religion and Politics in Seventeenth Century England," Ph.D. diss., University of Iowa, 1972, pp. 127–32. Five years earlier, however, Burton had argued in favor of a "passive obedience" to kings "if they command against God."

Perez Zagorin, *The Court and the Country* (London: Routledge and Kegan Paul, 1969), p. 196.

57. John Bastwick, *The Letany of John Bastwick*, 1637, p. 115. For his role in the overseas publication of *The Letany*, a London apprentice named John Lilburne was sentenced by the Star Chamber to be whipped at the cart's tail from the Fleet Prison to the Old Palace Yard at Westminster.

58. Fuller, *Church History*, III, 386, 388.

59. Laud, *Works*, VI, 37–50.

60. Laud, *Works*, IV, 311; VI, 43; III, 406–7. J. P. Sommerville, "The Royal Supremacy and Episcopacy 'Jure Divino', 1603–1640," *Journal of Ecclesiastical History* 34 (1983): 548–58. William M. Lamont, *Godly Rule, Politics and Religion, 1603–60* (London: Macmillan, 1969), pp. 56–77.

61. Laud, *Works*, VI, 46. However, in a sermon preached before the king more than ten years earlier, Laud had said, "First, the magistrate, and his power and justice. And resist either of these, and ye resist 'the power, and the ordinance of God'" (*Works*, I, 131). For Laud's statement on Juxon, see *Works*, III, 226. Andrew Foster believes that in the 1630s the Laudian bishops "were on the offensive" and that they made "enlarged claims for secular power for the clergy." "Church Policies of the 1630s," *Conflict in Early Stuart England: Studies in Religion and Politics, 1603–1642*, eds. Richard Cust and Ann Hughes (London: Longman, 1989), p. 209.

62. Laud, *Works*, VI, 42; Peter Holmes, "Robert Persons and an Unknown Political Pamphlet of 1593," *Recusant History* 17 (1985): 343. Nicholas Tyacke argues that in 1640 Charles and Laud were the religious innovators (*Origins of the English Civil War*, p. 143). Hugh Trevor-Roper, however, states that the Puritans, not the Arminians, were the innovators, and that "by 1620 their innovations had become quietly established." *Catholics, Anglicans and Puritans*, p. 114.

63. Laud, *Works*, IV, 196.

64. *The Earl of Strafford's Letters and Despatches*, ed. William Knowler (1739), II, 101.

65. Laud observed at his trial that "in Queen Elizabeth's time Penry was hanged, and Udall condemned and died in prison, for less than is contained in Mr. Burton's book." Laud, *Works*, III, 391.

66. Avihu Zakai suggests that in the Boston of John Cotton in Lincolnshire, "'there were scores of pious people in the town, who more exactly formed themselves into an *evangelical Church-State* by entering into *covenant* with God, and with one another, *to follow after the Lord, in the purity of his worship*.'" "The Gospel of Reformation: the Origins of the Great Puritan Reformation," *Journal of Ecclesiastical History* 37 (1986): 589.

67. Edmund S. Morgan, *The Puritan Dilemma, the Story of John Winthrop* (Boston: Little, Brown, 1958), p. 93; T. H. Breen, *The Character of the Good Ruler* (New Haven, Connecticut: Yale University Press, 1970), chap. 2.

68. Edmund S. Morgan, *Visible Saints* (New York: New York University Press, 1963), pp. 100–02; Stephen Foster, *Their Solitary Way, the Puritan Social Ethic in the First Century of Settlement in New England* (New Haven, Connecticut: Yale University Press, 1971), p. 178; Katherine B. Brown, "A Note on the Puritan Concept of Aristocracy," *Mississippi Valley Historical Review* 41 (1954): 105–12.

69. *Letters from New England, the Massachusetts Bay Colony, 1629–1638*, ed. Everett Emerson (Amherst, Massachusetts: University of Massachusetts Press, 1976), p. 191. Four years later, Lord Saye and Sele addressed the same topic in a letter to

Winthrop. According to Saye and Sele, "the church government being wholly spiritual, can consist with any form of outward government good or bad." *Winthrop Papers* (Boston: Massachusetts Historical Society, 1929–1944), IV, 267.

70. Emerson, *Letters from New England*, p. 191. In a letter to Alexander Leighton some ten years earlier, John Davenport had written: "Who can, without sorrow, and fear observe how Atheism, Libertinism, papism, and Arminianism, both at home, and abroad have stolen in, and taken possession of the house, whilst we are at strife about the hangings and paintings of it?" *Letters of John Davenport, Puritan Divine*, ed. Isabel MacBeath Calder (New Haven, Connecticut: Yale University Press, 1937), p. 24, as quoted in Stephen Foster, "English Puritanism and the Progress of New England Insititutions, 1630–1660," *Saints and Revolutionaries, Essays on Early American History*, eds. David D. Hall, John M. Murrin, and Thad W. Tate (New York: W. W. Norton, 1983), p. 15.

71. Morgan, *Visible Saints*, p. 95.

72. Ola E. Winslow, *Master Roger Williams, a Biography* (New York: Macmillan, 1957).

73. John Winthrop, *Journal, 1630–1649*, ed. James K. Hosmer (New York: Charles Scribner's Sons, 1908), I, 209; William K. B. Stoever, *'A Faire and Easie Way to Heaven,' Covenant Theology and Antinomianism in Early Massachusetts* (Middletown, Connecticut: Wesleyan University Press, 1978), pp. 25–27.

74. Emery Battis, *Saints and Sectaries, Anne Hutchinson and the Antinomian Controversy in the Massachusetts Bay Colony* (Chapel Hill, North Carolina: University of North Carolina Press, 1962), p. 146; Philip F. Gura, *A Glimpse of Sion's Glory, Puritan Radicalism in New England, 1620–1660* (Middletown, Connecticut: Wesleyan University Press, 1984), p. 252.

75. *The Antinomian Controversy, 1636–1638, a Documentary History*, ed. David D. Hall (Middletown, Connecticut: Wesleyan University Press, 1968), pp. 401, 405.

76. Hall, *The Antinomian Controversy*, p. 337; Battis, *Saints and Sectaries*, p. 104; Larzer Ziff, *The Career of John Cotton* (Princeton, New Jersey: Princeton University Press, 1962), p. 132.

77. For the text of the *Body of Liberties*, see *Puritan Political Ideas, 1558–1794*, ed. Edmund S. Morgan (Indianapolis, Indiana: Bobbs-Merrill, 1965), pp. 178–203. In 1636, Cotton had drawn up a scriptural law code for the Colony entitled "Moses His Judicials," which the General Court did not adopt, but William Aspinwall, a Boston magistrate, published it in England in 1655 when he was active in the Fifth Monarchy movement. See J. F. Maclear, "New England and the Fifth Monarchy: the Quest for the Millennium in Early American Puritanism," *William and Mary Quarterly* 32 (1975): 223–60; Cotton Mather, *Magnalia Christi Americana, or, the Ecclesiastical History of New-England*, 2 vols. (New York: Russell and Russell, 1852 edition reprinted in 1967), I, 437.

78. *Calendar State Papers, Colonial*, I, 194, as quoted in Perry Miller, *Orthodoxy in Massachusetts, 1630–1650, a Genetic Study* (Cambridge, Massachusetts: Harvard University Press), p. 74. Hugh Peters, who knew Massachusetts well, later referred to the New England Way as a "Tender Presbytery" (*A Dying Father's Last Legacy to an Only Child* [London, 1660], p. 107); Conrad Russell, *The Crisis of Parliaments, English History, 1509–1660* (London: Oxford University Press, 1971), p. 195. Robert F. Scholz points out as well, that William Bradshaw, Henry Jacob, and William Ames, who were most important in helping to develop the New England Way, all

believed in a "presbyterian government independent" as distinguished from a "presbyterian government dependent," which included dependence upon a hierarchy of church courts. "Clerical Consociation in Massachusetts Bay: Reassessing the New England Way and Its Origins," *William and Mary Quarterly* 29 (1972): 398.

79. Lockyer, *The Early Stuarts*, pp. 289–90, 301–2.

80. For much of the material in this and related paragraphs, see Gordon Albion, *Charles I and the Court of Rome, A Study in 17th Century Diplomacy* (London: Burns Oates and Washbourne, 1935); *Stuart Royal Proclamations*, II, 216–18.

81. Arnold Oskar Meyer, "Charles I and Rome," *American Historical Review* 19 (1913): 16–18.

82. Meyer, *American Historical Review* 19 (1913): 20; Gardiner, *History of England*, VIII, 138; Albion, *Charles I and the Court of Rome*, p. 407.

83. Laud, *Works*, III, 219.

84. Larkin, *Stuart Royal Proclamations*, II, 580–82; Albion, *Charles I and the Court of Rome*, 416–18; William Laud, *A Relation of the Conference Between William Laud, Late Lord Archbishop of Canterbury, and Mr. Fisher the Jesuit*, 4th ed., London, 1686; Strafford, *Letters*, I, 426. Strafford got the Irish Convocation of the Clergy to adopt the Thirty-Nine Articles in place of the Irish Articles.

85. Carolyn M. Hibbard, *Charles I and the Popish Plot*, (Chapel Hill, North Carolina: University of North Carolina Press, 1983), pp. 22–24; Robert Ashton, *The English Civil War, Conservatism and Revolution, 1603–1649* (London: Weidenfeld and Nicholson, 1978), p. 124; Robert Clifton ("Fear of Popery," *The Origins of the English Civil War*, ed. Conrad Russell [London: Macmillan, 1973], p. 152) also believes that Catholicism and Laudianism were "distinct," but he feels that the latter "stimulated" the former. Also see Anthony Fletcher, *The Outbreak of the English Civil War* (London: Edward Arnold, 1981), p. xxiv.

86. Laud, *Works*, V, 583–606; Trevor-Roper, *Laud*, 2nd ed., p. 342.

87. Gordon Donaldson, *The Making of the Scottish Prayer Book of 1637* (Edinburgh: Edinburgh University Press, 1954), pp. 56, 81; Cuming, *Anglican Liturgy*, pp. 144–45.

88. Fuller, *Church History*, III, 400.

89. Donaldson, *Scottish Historical Documents*, pp. 200–201.

90. John Morrill, "The Religious Context of the English Civil War," *TRHS*, Fifth series, 34 (1984) 172.

91. Esther S. Cope, "The Short Parliament of 1640 and Convocation," *Journal of Ecclesiastical History* 25 (1974): 167–84; *Proceedings of the Short Parliament of 1640*, eds. Esther S. Cope and Willson H. Coates, Camden Society, Fourth series, vol. 19 (London: Royal Historical Society, 1977), pp. 255–56.

92. Rushworth, *Historical Collection*, IV, 111.

93. Laud, *Works*, V, 610–11.

94. Laud, *Works*, V, 616–20.

95. Laud, *Works*, V, 624–26.

96. Laud, *Works*, V, 623–24.

97. Laud, *Works*, VI, 44.

98. Kevin Sharpe, "Archbishop Laud," *History Today* 33 (1983): 26–30; Lamont, *Godly Rule*, pp. 70–73; Davies, Oxford D. Phil. diss., p. 11. The similarities between Archbishop Laud and a Puritan like Nehemiah Wallington, for example, are most apparent in the continuous self-examination that expressed itself in a strong commit-

ment to proper moral conduct. But beyond that, Laud's diary, which indicated some manifestations of "psychotic" behavior, expressed considerable emotional stress, which, in the journals of Wallington, bordered on "suicidal despair." Carlton, *Archbishop William Laud*, p. 56; Paul Seaver, *Wallington's World, a Puritan Artisan in Seventeenth-Century London* (Stanford, California: Stanford University Press, 1985), pp. 15–16.

Bibliography

Source Materials

Allen, William. *An Admonition to the Nobility and People of England.* In *Complaint and Reform in England, 1436–1714*, eds. William Huse Dunham, Jr. and Stanley Pargellis, pp. 351–81. New York: Oxford University Press, 1938.

Allen, William. *A True, Sincere, and Modest Defense of English Catholics.* See entry under Cecil, William.

Andrewes, Lancelot. [Works]. Eds. J. P. Wilson and J. Bliss. 9 vols. Oxford, 1841–1854.

The Antinomian Controversy, 1636–1638, a Documentary History. Ed. David D. Hall. Middletown, Connecticut: Wesleyan University Press, 1968.

The Arminian Nunnery. 1641.

Ashton, Robert, ed. *James I By His Contemporaries.* London: Hutchinson, 1969.

Bancroft, Richard. *A Sermon Preached at Paul's Cross.* London, 1589.

Bancroft, Richard. *A Survey of the Pretended Holy Discipline.* London, 1593.

Barrow, Henry. *The Writings of Henry Barrow 1587–1590.* Ed. Leland H. Carlson. Elizabethan Nonconformist Texts. London: George Allen and Unwin, 1962.

Bastwick, John. *The Letany of John Bastwick.* 1637.

Bilson, Thomas. *The Perpetual Government of Christ's Church.* 1593.

Bradford, William. *Of Plymouth Plantation, 1620–1647.* Ed. Samuel Eliot Morison. New York: Random House, 1967.

Bradshaw, William. *English Puritanism and Other Works.* 1605. Intro. R. C. Simmons. Reprinted at Farnborough, England: Gregg International, 1972.

Browne, Robert. *The Writings of Robert Harrison and Robert Browne.* Eds. Albert Peel and Leland H. Carlson. Elizabethan Nonconformist Texts. London: George Allen and Unwin, 1953.

Burton, Robert. *For God and the King.* 1636.

Calendar of State Papers, Spanish, Elizabeth. Ed. M. A. S. Hume, 4 vols. London, 1892–1899.

Carleton, George. *Jurisdiction, Regal, Episcopal, Papal.* 1610.

Cavendish, George. *The Life and Death of Cardinal Wolsey.* In *Two Tudor Lives.* Eds. Richard S. Sylvester and Davis P. Harding. New Haven, Connecticut: Yale University Press, 1962.

Cecil, William. *The Execution of Justice in England*, and William Allen, *A True, Sincere, and Modest Defense of English Catholics*. Ed. Robert M. Kingdon. Folger Documents of Tudor and Stuart Civilization. Ithaca, New York: Cornell University Press, 1965.

Certain Sermons or Homilies Appointed to be Read in Churches in the Time of Queen Elizabeth I (1547–1571). Intro. Mary Ellen Rickey and Thomas B. Stroup. 1623 ed., two vols. in one. Gainesville, Florida: Scholars' Facsimiles and Reprints, 1968.

Coke, Edward. *The Second Part of the Institutes of the Laws of England*. London: E. and R. Brooke, 1797.

Commons Debates, 1621. Eds. Wallace Notestein, Frances Helen Relf, and Hartley Simpson. 7 vols. New Haven, Connecticut: Yale University Press, 1935.

Commons Debates, 1628. Eds. Robert C. Johnson, Mary Frear Keeler, Maija Jansson Cole, and William B. Bidwell. Vols. II–IV of *Proceedings in Parliament, 1628*. New Haven, Connecticut: Yale University Press, 1977–1978.

Commons Debates for 1629. Eds. Wallace Notestein and Frances Helen Relf. Minneapolis: University of Minnesota, 1921.

Complaint and Reform in England, 1436–1714. Eds. William Huse Dunham, Jr. and Stanley Pargellis. New York: Oxford University Press, 1938.

A Complete Collection of State Trials. Ed., T. B. Howell, 33 vols. London: Longman, 1816–1826.

A Complete Journal of the Votes, Speeches, and Debates. Both of the House of Lords and House of Commons Throughout the Whole Reign of Queen Elizabeth, of Glorious Memory. Comp. Simonds D'Ewes, London, 1693. Reprinted in Wilmington, Delaware: Scholarly Resources, 1974.

The Constitutional Documents of the Puritan Revolution, 1625–1660. Ed. Samuel R. Gardiner. 3rd ed. Oxford: Clarendon Press, 1947.

Constitutional Documents of the Reign of James I. Ed. J. R. Tanner. Cambridge: Cambridge University Press, 1930.

Cosin, John. *The Correspondence of John Cosin*. Ed. George Ornsby. Publications of the Surtees Society. 2 vols. Durham: Andrews, 1869–1872.

Cosin, John. *The Works of . . . John Cosin*. [Ed. J. Sansom]. 5 vols. Oxford: John Henry Parker, 1843–1855.

Cranmer, Thomas. *The Works of Thomas Cranmer*. Ed. John Edmund Cox. The Parker Society. 2 vols. Cambridge: Cambridge University Press, 1844–1846.

Cromwell, Thomas. *Thomas Cromwell on Church and Commonwealth, Selected Letters, 1523–1540*. Ed. and intro. Arthur J. Slavin, New York: Harper and Row, 1969.

Davenport, John. *Letters of John Davenport, Puritan Divine*. Ed. Isabel MacBeath Calder. New Haven, Connecticut: Yale University Press, 1937.

Debates in the House of Commons in 1625. Ed. Samuel R. Gardiner. New Series, Vol. 6. Westminster: The Camden Society, 1873.

Documentary Annals of the Reformed Church of England, Being a Collection of Injunctions, Declarations, Orders, Articles of Inquiry, Etc. from the Year 1546 to the Year 1716. Ed. Edward Cardwell. New edition in two vols. Oxford: Oxford University Press, 1844. Reprinted in Ridgewood, New Jersey: Gregg Press, 1966.

Documents Illustrative of English Church History. Eds. Henry Gee and William John Hardy. London: Macmillan, 1910.

Documents Relating to the Proceedings Against William Prynne in 1634 and 1637.

Ed. Samuel R. Gardiner. New Series, vol. 18. Westminster: The Camden Society, 1877.

Donne, John. *Pseudo-Martyr*. London, 1610. Intro. Francis Jacques Sypher. Reprinted in Delmar, New York: Scholar's Facsimiles and Reprints, 1974.

Donne, John. *The Sermons of John Donne*. Eds. George R. Potter and Evelyn M. Simpson. 10 vols. Berkeley, California: University of California Press, 1953–1962.

Elizabeth I. *Queen Elizabeth's Defence of Her Proceedings in Church and State*. Ed. William E. Collins. The Church Historical Society, vol. 58. London: S.P.C.K., 1899.

Elizabethan Puritanism. Ed. Leonard J. Trinterud. A Library of Protestant Thought. New York: Oxford University Press, 1971.

Field, Richard. *Of the Church*. London: 1606.

Fish, Simon. *A Supplication for Beggars*. In *Complaint and Reform in England, 1436–1714*, eds. William Huse Dunham, Jr. and Stanley Pargellis, pp. 87–99. New York: Oxford University Press, 1938.

The Form of Prayers and Ministration of the Sacraments, &c., Used in the English Congregation at Geneva. 1556. Reprinted in *The Works of John Knox*. Ed. David Laing. 6 vols. Edinburgh: The Ballantyne Club, 1846–1864. Reprinted in New York: AMS Press, 1966.

Formularies of Faith Put Forth by Authority during the Reign of Henry VIII. Ed. Charles Lloyd. Oxford: Clarendon Press, 1825.

Foxe, John. *Foxe's Book of Martyrs*. Ed. and abridged by G. A. Williamson. London: Secker and Warburg, 1965.

Fuller, Thomas. *The Church History of Britain, from the Birth of Jesus Christ until the Year MDCXLVIII*. 3rd ed., 3 vols. London: Thomas Tegg, 1842.

Gardiner, Stephen. *Obedience in Church and State, Three Political Tracts by Stephen Gardiner*. Ed. and intro. Pierre Janelle. Cambridge: Cambridge University Press, 1930.

Greenwood, John. *The Writings of John Greenwood, Together with the Joint Writings of Henry Barrow and John Greenwood, 1587–1590*. Ed. Leland H. Carlson. Elizabethan Nonconformist Texts. London: George Allen and Unwin, 1962.

Grindal, Edmund. *The Remains of Edmund Grindal*. Ed. William Nicholson. The Parker Society. Cambridge: Cambridge University Press, 1843.

Hacket, John. *Scrinia Reserata*. London, 1693.

Hales, John. *Golden Remains*. London, 1659.

Harrison, Robert. *The Writings of Robert Harrison and Robert Browne*. Eds. Albert Peel and Leland H. Carlson. Elizabethan Nonconformist Texts. London: George Allen and Unwin, 1953.

Henry VIII. *Miscellaneous Writings of Henry the Eighth*. Ed. Francis Macnamara. Waltham St. Lawrence: Golden Cockerel Press, 1924.

Heylyn, Peter. *Cyprianus Anglicus: Or, the History of the Life and Death, of . . . William . . . Archbishop of Canterbury*. London, 1668.

Historical Collections. Ed. John Rushworth, 8 vols. 1721.

A History of Conferences and Other Proceedings Connected with the Revision of the Book of Common Prayer; from the Year 1558 to the Year 1690. Ed. Edward Cardwell. 3rd ed. Oxford: Oxford University Press, 1849. Reprinted at Ridgewood, New Jersey: Gregg Press, 1966.

Hooker, Richard. *Hooker's Ecclesiastical Polity, Book VIII*. Intro. Raymond Aaron

Houk. Columbia University Studies in English and Comparative Literature, no. 102. New York: Columbia University Press, 1931.

I., B. *The Fortress of Fathers*, 1568. "Certain Conclusions."

James I. *The Political Works of James I*. Ed. Charles Howard McIlwain. Cambridge, Massachusetts: Harvard University Press, 1918. Reprinted in New York: Russell and Russell, 1965.

Jewel, John. *An Apology of the Church of England*. Ed. J. E. Booty. Ithaca, New York: Cornell University Press, 1963.

Jewel, John. *The Works of John Jewel*. Ed. John Ayre. The Parker Society. 4 vols. Cambridge: Cambridge University Press, 1845–1850.

Journals of the House of Commons, 1547–1761. 28 vols. 1742–1762.

Knox, John. *The Works of John Knox*. Ed. David Laing, 6 vols. Edinburgh: The Ballantine Club, 1846–1864. Reprinted in New York: AMS Press, 1966.

Laud, William. *A Relation of the Conference Between William Laud, Late Lord Archbishop of Canterbury, and Mr. Fisher the Jesuit*, 4th ed., London, 1686.

Laud, William. *The Works of . . . William Laud*. Eds. W. Scott and J. Bliss. 7 vols. in 9. Oxford: John Henry Parker, 1847–1860.

Leighton, Alexander. *An Appeal to the Parliament, or Sion's Plea Against the Prelacy*. 1628.

Letters from New England, the Massachusetts Bay Colony, 1629–1638. Ed. Everett Emerson. Amherst, Massachusetts: University of Massachusetts Press, 1976.

Letters and Papers, Foreign and Domestic, of the Reign of Henry VIII, 1509–1547. Eds. J. S. Brewer, James Gairdner, and R. H. Brodie, 21 vols. London, 1862–1910.

The Lisle Letters. Ed. Muriel St. Clare Byrne. 6 vols. Chicago: University of Chicago Press, 1981.

Lords Proceedings, 1628. Eds. Mary Frear Keeler, Maija Jansson Cole, and William B. Bidwell. Vol. V. of *Proceedings in Parliament, 1628*. New Haven, Connecticut. Yale University Press, 1983.

Manwaring, Roger. *Religion and Allegiance*. London, 1627.

The Marprelate Tracts, [1588–1589]. Reprinted in Leeds: Scolar Press, 1967.

Mather, Cotton. *Magnalia Christi Americana, or, the Ecclesiastical History of New-England*. 2 vols. New York: Russell and Russell, 1852. Reprinted in 1967.

Milton, John. *Complete Prose Works of John Milton*. Gen. ed. Don M. Wolfe, 8 vols. in 10. New Haven, Connecticut: Yale University Press, 1953–1982.

Milton, John. *The Works of John Milton*. Ed. Frank Allen Patterson and others. 20 vols. New York: Columbia University Press, 1931–1938.

Montagu, Richard. *A Gag for the New Gospel? No. A New Gag for an Old Goose*. 1624.

More, Thomas. *The Correspondence of Sir Thomas More*. Ed. Elizabeth Frances Rogers. Princeton, New Jersey: Princeton University Press, 1947.

News From Ipswich. Ipswich, 1636.

Overall, John. *Bishop Overall's Convocation-Book, MDCVI*. London, 1690.

Parker, Matthew. *Correspondence of Matthew Parker*. Ed. John Bruce. The Parker Society. Cambridge: Cambridge University Press, 1853.

Perkins, William. *A Golden Chain*. 1592. In *Works*. 3 vols. Cambridge: 1616–1618.

Proceedings in the Parliaments of Elizabeth I, 1558–1581. Ed. T. E. Hartley. Wilmington, Delaware: Michael Glazier, 1981.

Proceedings in Parliament, 1610. Ed. Elizabeth Read Foster. 2 vols. New Haven, Connecticut: Yale University Press, 1966.

Proceedings in Parliament, 1625. Eds. Maija Jansson and William Bidwell. New Haven, Connecticut: Yale University Press, 1987.

Proceedings in Parliament, 1628. Eds. Robert C. Johnson, Mary Frear Keeler, Maija Jansson Cole, and William R. Bidwell. 6 vols. *Commons Debates*, Vols. II–IV; *Lords Proceedings*, Vol. V. New Haven, Connecticut: Yale University Press, 1977–1983.

Proceedings of the Short Parliament of 1640. Ed. Esther S. Cope in collaboration with Willson H. Coates. The Camden Society, Fourth Series, vol. 19. London: Royal Historical Society, 1977.

Prynne, William. *Canterbury's Doom.* London, 1646.

Prynne, William. *Histrio-mastix.* 1633.

Puritan Manifestoes, a Study of the Origin of the Puritan Revolt. Eds. W. H. Frere and C. E. Douglas. London: S.P.C.K., 1907.

Puritan Political Ideas, 1558–1794. Ed. Edmund S. Morgan. Indianapolis, Indiana: Bobbs-Merrill, 1965.

Reliquiae Liturgicae, Documents Connected with the Liturgy of the Church of England. Ed. Peter Hall. 5 vols. Bath: Burns and Goodwin, 1847.

Scottish Historical Documents. Ed. Gordon Donaldson. Edinburgh: Scottish Academic Press, 1970.

Selden, John. The History of Tithes. 1618.

Selden, John. *The Table Talk of John Selden.* Ed. Samuel Harvey Reynolds. Oxford: Clarendon Press, 1892.

Select Statutes and Other Constitutional Doucments Illustrative of the Reigns of Elizabeth and James I. Ed. G. W. Prothero. 3rd ed. Oxford: Clarendon Press, 1906.

Sibthorpe, Robert. *Apostolike Obedience.* London, 1627.

Simpson, Martin. "Of the Troubles Begun at Frankfort, A.D. 1554." *Reformation and Revolution.* Ed. Duncan Shaw, pp. 17–33. Edinburgh: Saint Andrew Press, 1967.

Southwell, Robert. *An Humble Supplication to Her Majesty.* 1595. Ed. R. C. Bold. Cambridge: Cambridge University Press, 1953.

Sparke, Thomas. *A Brotherly Persuasion to Unity, and Uniformity in Judgment.* London, 1607.

Strafford, Thomas Wentworth, Earl of. *The Earl of Strafford's Letters and Despatches.* Ed. William Knowler. 2 vols. in one. 1739.

Strype, John. *Annals of the Reformation and Establishment of Religion.* 4 vols. in 7. Oxford: Clarendon Press, 1824.

The Stuart Constitution, 1603–1688, Documents and Commentary. Ed. and intro. J. P. Keynon. 2nd ed. Cambridge: Cambridge University Press, 1986.

Stuart Royal Proclamations. Vol. I. *Royal Proclamations of King James I, 1603–1625.* Eds. James F. Larkin and Paul L. Hughes. Oxford: Clarendon Press, 1973.

Stuart Royal Proclamations. Vol. II. *Royal Proclamations of King Charles I, 1625–1646.* Ed. James F. Larkin. Oxford: Clarendon Press, 1983.

Synodalia. A Collection of Articles of Religion, Canons, and Proceedings of Convocations in the Province of Canterbury, from the Year 1547 to the Year 1717. Ed. Edward Cardwell. 2 vols. Oxford: Oxford University Press, 1842. Reprinted in Farnborough, England: Gregg Press, 1970.

Throckmorton, Job. *Hay Any Work for Cooper.* [Coventry, 1589]. Reprinted in *The Marprelate Tracts, [1588–1589].* Leeds: Scolar Press, 1967.

Tracts on Liberty of Conscience and Persecution, 1614–1661. Ed. Edward Bean Underhill. London: Hanserd Knollys Society, 1846.

Travers, Walter. *A Full and Plain Declaration of Ecclesiastical Discipline.* (Also called *Ecclesiasticae Disciplinae*). 1574.

The Tudor Constitution, Documents and Commentary. Ed. and intro G. R. Elton. 2nd ed. Cambridge: Cambridge University Press, 1982.

Tudor Royal Proclamations. Eds. Paul L. Hughes and James F. Larkin. 3 vols. New Haven, Connecticut: Yale University Press, 1964–1969.

Two Early Tudor Lives: George Cavendish, *The Life and Death of Cardinal Wolsey;* William Roper, *The Life of Sir Thomas More.* Eds. Richard S. Sylvester and Davis P. Harding. New Haven, Connecticut: Yale University Press, 1962.

Tyndale, William. *Doctrinal Treatises and Introductions to Different Portions of the Holy Scriptures by William Tyndale.* The Parker Society. Ed. Henry Walter. Cambridge: Cambridge University Press, 1848.

Whitgift, John. *The Works of John Whitgift.* Ed. John Ayre. The Parker Society. 3 vols. Cambridge: Cambridge University Press, 1851–1853.

Winthrop, John. *Journal, 1630–1649.* Ed. James K. Hosmer. 2 vols. New York: Charles Scribner's Sons, 1908.

Winthrop, John. *Winthrop Papers.* 4 vols. Boston: Massachusetts Historical Society, 1929–1944.

Winwood, Ralph. *Memorials of Affairs of State in the Reigns of Queen Elizabeth and King James I.* Ed. E. Sawyer. 3 vols. London, 1725.

[Wood, Thomas]. *A Brief Discourse of the Troubles Begun at Frankfort.* 1575.

Wood, Thomas. *Letters of Thomas Wood, Puritan, 1566–1577.* Ed. Patrick Collinson. London: The Athlone Press, 1960.

The Zurich Letters, 1558–1579. Ed. Hastings Robinson. The Parker Society. 2 vols. Cambridge: Cambridge University Press, 1842–1845.

Books and Articles

Acton, Lord John. *Essays on Church and State.* Ed. and intro. Douglas Woodruff. London: Hollis and Carter, 1952.

Albion, Gordon. *Charles I and the Court of Rome, a Study in 17th Century Diplomacy.* London: Burns Oates and Washbourne, 1935.

Alexander, Michael Van Cleave. *Charles I's Lord Treasurer, Sir Richard Weston, Earl of Portland (1577–1635).* London: Macmillan, 1975.

Ashton, Robert. *The English Civil War, Conservatism and Revolution, 1603–1649.* London: Weidenfeld and Nicholson, 1978.

Atkins, Jonathan M. "Calvinist Bishops, Church Unity, and the Rise of Arminianism." *Albion* 18 (1986): 411–27.

Babbage, Stuart Barton. *Puritanism and Richard Bancroft.* London: S.P.C.K., 1962.

Baker, Derek, ed. *Reform and Reformation, England and the Continent, c1500–c1750.* Oxford: Basil Blackwell, 1979.

Bangs, Carl. "'All the Best Bishoprics and Deaneries,' the Enigma of Arminian Politics." *Church History* 42 (1973): 5–16.

Barnes, Thomas G. "County Politics and a Puritan *cause célèbre*: Somerset Church Ales, 1633." *TRHS* 9 (1959): 103–22.

Battis, Emery. Saints and Sectaries, Anne Hutchinson and the Antinomian Controversy in the Massachusetts Bay Colony. Chapel Hill, North Carolina: University of North Carolina Press, 1962.

Baumer, Franklin Le Van. "Christopher St. German." *American Historical Review* 42 (1937): 631–51.

Baumer, Franklin Le Van. *The Early Tudor Theory of Kingship*. New Haven, Connecticut: Yale University Press, 1940.

Beales, Derek, and Best, Geoffrey, eds. *History, Society and the Churches, Essays in Honour of Owen Chadwick*. Cambridge: Cambridge University Press, 1985.

Beer, Barrett L. *Northumberland, the Political Career of John Dudley, Earl of Warwick, and Duke of Northumberland*. Kent, Ohio: Kent State University, 1973.

Bennett, G. V., and Walsh, J. D., eds. *Essays in Modern English Church History in Memory of Norman Sykes*. London: Adam and Charles Black, 1966.

Bernard, G. W. "The Pardon of the Clergy Reconsidered." With replies from J. A. Guy and G. W. Bernard. *Journal of Ecclesiastical History* 37 (1986): 258–87.

Berthoud, G. et al. *Aspects de la Propaganda Religieuse*. Geneva: Droz, 1957.

Bicknell, E. J. *A Theological Introduction to the Thirty-Nine Articles of the Church of England*. 2nd ed. revised by H. J. Carpenter. London: Longmans, Green, 1942.

Bindoff, S. T. *Tudor England*. Hammondsworth, Middlesex: Penguin Books, 1950.

Birt, Henry Norbert. *The Elizabethan Religious Settlement, a Study of Contemporary Documents*. London: George Bell and Sons, 1907.

Blethen, H. T. "Bishop Williams, the Altar Controversy, and the Royal Supremacy, 1627–41." *The Welsh History Review* 9 (1978–1979): 142–54.

Booty, John E. *John Jewel As Apologist of the Church of England*. London: S.P.C.K., 1963.

Bossy, John. "The Character of Elizabethan Catholicism." *Crisis in Europe, 1550–1660*, ed. Trevor Aston, pp. 223–46. London: Routledge and Kegan Paul, 1965.

Bossy, John. *The English Catholic Community, 1570–1850*. New York: Oxford University Press, 1976.

Bossy, John. "The English Catholic Community, 1603–1625." *The Reign of James VI and I*. Ed. Alan G. R. Smith. London: Macmillan, 1973.

Bourne, E. C. E. *The Anglicanism of William Laud*. London: S.P.C.K., 1947.

Bowker, Margaret. "The Commons Supplication Against the Ordinaries in the Light of Some Archdiaconal Acta." *Transactions, Royal Historical Society* 21 (1971): 61–77.

Brachlow, Stephen. *The Communion of Saints, Radical Puritan and Separatist Ecclesiology, 1570–1625*. Oxford Theological Monographs. Oxford: Oxford University Press, 1988.

Bradshaw, Paul F. *The Anglican Ordinal, Its History and Development from the Reformation to the Present Day*. Alcuin Club Collections, no. 53. London: S.P.C.K., 1971.

Breen, T. H. *The Character of the Good Ruler*. New Haven, Connecticut: Yale University Press, 1970.

Brett, M. *The English Church under Henry I*. Oxford: Oxford University Press, 1975.

Brook, V. J. K. *A Life of Archbishop Parker*. Oxford: Clarendon Press, 1962.

Brook, V. J. K. *Whitgift and the English Church*. London: English Universities Press, 1957.

Brooke, Z. N. *The English Church and the Papacy from the Conquest to the Reign of John*. Cambridge: Cambridge University Press, 1952.

Brooks, Peter. *Thomas Cranmer's Doctrine of the Eucharist, an Essay in Historical Development*. New York: Seabury Press, 1965.

Brown, Katherine B. "A Note on the Puritan Concept of Aristocracy." *Mississippi Valley Historical Review* 41 (1954): 105–12.

Burrage, Champlin. *The Early English Dissenters in the Light of Recent Research (1550–1641)*. 2 vols. London: Cambridge University Press, 1912.

Burrell, Sidney A. "The Apocalyptic Vision of the Early Covenanters." *Scottish Historical Review* 43 (1964): 1–24.

Calder, Isabel M. "A Seventeenth Century Attempt to Purify the Anglican Church." *American Historical Review* 53 (1948): 760–75.

Caldwell, Patricia. *The Puritan Conversion Narrative, the Beginnings of American Expression*. Cambridge: Cambridge University Press, 1983.

Cantor, Norman F. *Church, Kingship, and Lay Investiture in England, 1089–1135*. Princeton, New Jersey: Princeton University Press, 1958.

Cargill Thompson, W. D. J. "Anthony Marten and the Elizabethan Debate on Episcopacy." *Essays in Modern English Church History in Memory of Norman Sykes*. Eds. G. V. Bennett and J. D. Walsh, pp. 44–75. London: Adam and Charles Black, 1965.

Cargill Thompson, W. D. J. "The Philosopher of the 'Politic Society': Richard Hooker as a Political Thinker." *Studies in Richard Hooker, Essays Preliminary to an Edition of His Works*. Ed. W. Speed Hill, pp. 3–76. Cleveland, Ohio: The Press of Case Western Reserve University, 1972.

Cargill Thompson, W. D. J. "Richard Bancroft's Paul's Cross Sermon." *Journal of Ecclesiastical History* 20 (1969): 253–66.

Cargill Thompson, W. D. J. "Sir Francis Knollys's Campaign Against the *Jure Divino* Theory of Episcopacy." *Studies in the Reformation: Luther to Hooker*. Eds. C. W. Dugmore and A. G. Dickens. London: Athlone Press, 1980.

Carlson, A. J. "The Puritans and Convocation of 1563." *Action and Conviction in Early Modern Europe, Essays in Memory of E. H. Harbison*. Eds. Theodore K. Rabb and Jerrold E. Siegel, pp. 133–53. Princeton, New Jersey: Princeton University Press, 1969.

Carlson, Leland H. *Martin Marprelate, Gentleman, Master Job Throkmorton Laid Open in His Colors*. San Marino, California: Huntington Library, 1981.

Carlson, Leland H. "Martin Marprelate: His Identity and His Satire." *English Satire, Papers Read at a Clark Library Seminar, January 15, 1972*. Los Angeles: William Andrews Clark Memorial Library, 1972.

Carlton, Charles. *Archbishop William Laud*. London: Routledge and Kegan Paul, 1987.

Cheney, C. R. *From Becket to Langton, English Church Government, 1170–1213*. Manchester: Manchester University Press, 1956.

Child, Gilbert W. *Church and State under the Tudors*. London: Longmans, Green, 1890.

Christianson, Paul. *Reformers and Babylon, English Apocalyptic Visions from the Reformation to the Eve of the Civil War*. Toronto: University of Toronto Press, 1978.

Clancy, Thomas H. *Papist Pamphleteers, the Allen-Persons Party and the Political Thought of the Counter-Reformation in England, 1572–1615*. Jesuit Studies. Chicago: Loyola University Press, 1964.

Clark, Peter, Smith, Alan G. R., and Tyacke, Nicholas, eds. *The English Commonwealth, 1547–1640, Essays in Politics and Society*. New York: Barnes and Noble, 1979.

Clebsch, William A. *England's Earliest Protestants, 1520–1535*. New Haven, Connecticut: Yale University Press, 1965.

Clifton, Robert. "Fear of Popery." *The Origins of the English Civil War*. Ed. Conrad Russell, pp. 144–67. London: Macmillan, 1973.

Cohen, Charles Lloyd. *God's Caress, the Psychology of Puritan Religious Experience*. New York: Oxford University Press, 1966.

Collinson, Patrick. *Archbishop Grindal, 1519–1583, the Struggle for a Reformed Church*. Berkeley, California: University of California Press, 1980.

Collinson, Patrick. "The Beginnings of English Sabbatarianism." *Studies in Church History*. Eds. C. W. Dugmore and Charles Duggan, I, 207–21. London: Nelson, 1964.

Collinson, Patrick. "The Downfall of Archbishop Grindal and Its Place in Elizabethan Political and Ecclesiastical History." *The English Commonwealth, 1547–1640, Essays in Politics and Society*. Eds. Peter Clark, Alan G. R. Smith, and Nicholas Tyacke, pp. 39–57. New York: Barnes and Noble, 1979.

Collinson, Patrick. "The Elizabethan Church and the New Religion." *The Reign of Elizabeth I*. Problems in Focus. Ed. Christopher Haigh, pp. 169–94. London: Macmillan, 1984.

Collinson, Patrick. *English Puritanism*. General series 106. London: The Historical Association, 1983.

Collinson, Patrick. *The Elizabethan Puritan Movement*. London: Jonathan Cape, 1967.

Collinson, Patrick. "The Jacobean Religious Settlement: the Hampton Court Conference." *Before the English Civil War*. Ed. Howard Tomlinson, pp. 27–51. London: Macmillan Press, 1983.

Collinson, Patrick. "John Field and Elizabethan Puritanism." *Elizabethan Government and Society, Essays Presented to Sir John Neale*. Eds. S. T. Bindoff, J. Hurstfield, and C. H. Williams, pp. 127–62. London: Athlone Press, 1961.

Collinson, Patrick. "Lectures by Combination: Structure and Characteristics of Church Life in 17th Century England." *Bulletin of the Institute of Historical Research* 48 (1975): 182–213.

Collinson, Patrick. *A Mirror of Elizabethan Puritanism: the Life and Letters of 'Godly Master Dering.'* London: Dr. William's Trust, 1964.

Collinson, Patrick. "The Monarchical Republic of Queen Elizabeth I." *Bulletin of the John Rylands University Library of Manchester* 69 (1987): 394–424.

Collinson, Patrick. *The Religion of Protestants, the Church in English Society 1559–1625*. Oxford: Clarendon Press, 1982.

Collinson, Patrick. "Sir Nicholas Bacon and the Elizabethan *Via Media*." *The Historical Journal* 23 (1980): 255–73.

Constant, G. *The Reformation in England, the English Schism, and Henry VIII, 1509–1547*. Trans. R. E. Scantlebury. New York: Sheed and Ward, 1934.

Constant, G. *The Reformation in England, Introduction of the Reformation into England, Edward VI, (1547–1553)*. Trans. E. I. Watkin. London: Sheed & Ward, 1942.

Coolidge, John S. *The Pauline Renaissance in England, Puritanism and the Bible*. Oxford: Clarendon Press, 1970.

Cooper, J. P. "The Supplication Against the Ordinaries Reconsidered." *English Historical Review* 72 (1957): 616–41.

Cope, Esther S. *Politics Without Parliaments, 1629–1640*. London: Allen and Unwin, 1987.

Cope, Esther S. "The Short Parliament of 1640 and Convocation." *Journal of Ecclesiastical History* 25 (1974): 167–84.

Cowan, Ian B. "The Five Articles of Perth." *Reformation and Revolution*. Ed. Duncan Shaw, pp. 160–77. Edinburgh: Saint Andrew Press, 1967.

Coward, Barry. "Was There an English Revolution in the Middle of the Seventeenth Century?" *Politics and People in Revolutionary England, Essays in Honour of Ivan Roots*. Eds. Colin Jones, Malyn Newitt, and Stephen Roberts, pp. 9–39. Oxford: Basil Blackwell, 1986.

Craig, Jr., Hardin. "The Geneva Bible as a Political Document." *Pacific Historical Review* 7 (1938): 40–49.

Cressy, David. "Binding the Nation: The Bonds of Association, 1584 and 1696." *Tudor Rule and Revolution, Essays for G. R. Elton from his American Friends*. Eds. Delloyd J. Guth and John W. McKenna, pp. 217–34. Cambridge: Cambridge University Press, 1982.

Cross, Claire. *Church and People, 1450–1660, the Triumph of the Laity in the English Church*. Fontana Library of English History. Glasgow: William Collins Sons, 1976.

Cross, Claire. "Churchmen and the Royal Supremacy." *Church and Society in England: Henry VIII to James I*. Eds. Felicity Heal and Rosemary O'Day, pp. 15–34. London: Macmillan, 1977.

Cross, Claire. *The Royal Supremacy in the Elizabethan Church*. London: George Allen and Unwin, 1969.

Cuming, G. J. *A History of the Anglican Liturgy*. London: Macmillan, 1969.

Curtis, Mark H. "The Alienated Intellectuals of Early Stuart England." *Past and Present* 23 (1962): 25–43.

Curtis, Mark H. "The Hampton Court Conference and Its Aftermath." *History* 46 (1961): 1–16.

Cust, Richard. *The Forced Loan and English Politics, 1626–1628*. Oxford: Clarendon Press, 1987.

Cust, Richard, and Hughes, Ann, eds. *Conflict in Early Stuart England: Studies in Religion and Politics, 1603–1642*. London: Longman, 1989.

Danner, Dan G. "Christopher Goodman and the English Protestant Tradition of Civil Disobedience." *Sixteenth Century Journal* 8 (1977): 61–73.

Davies, C. S. L. "The Pilgrimage of Grace Reconsidered." *Past and Present* 41 (1968): 54–76.

Davies, C. S. L. "Popular Religion and the Pilgrimage of Grace." *Order and Disorder in Early Modern England*. Eds. Anthony Fletcher and John Stevenson, pp. 58–91. Cambridge: Cambridge University Press, 1985.

Davies, E. T. *Episcopacy and the Royal Supremacy in the Church of England in the XVI Century*. Oxford: Basil Blackwell, 1950.

Davies, Godfrey. "Arminian versus Puritan in England *ca.* 1620–1640." *Huntington Library Bulletin* 5 (1934): 157–79.

Davies, Horton. *Worship and Theology in England, from Andrewes to Baxter and Fox, 1603–1690*. Princeton, New Jersey: Princeton University Press, 1975.

Davies, Horton. *Worship and Theology in England, from Cranmer to Hooker, 1534–1603*. Princeton, New Jersey: Princeton University Press, 1970.

Davies, Julian Edward. "The Growth and Implementation of 'Laudianism' with Special Reference to the Southern Province." Oxford D. Phil. diss., 1987.

Dawley, Powel Mills. *John Whitgift and the English Reformation*. New York: Charles Scribner's Sons, 1954.

Dent, C. M. *Protestant Reformers in Elizabethan Oxford*. Oxford: Oxford University Press, 1983.

Derrett, J. D. M. "The Trial of Sir Thomas More." *English Historical Review* 79 (1964): 449–77.

Dickens, A. G. *The English Reformation*. London: Batsford, 1964.

Dickens, A. G. "Secular and Religious Motivation in the Pilgrimage of Grace." *Studies in Church History*. Ed. G. J. Cuming, IV, 39–64. Leiden: Brill, 1967.

Dix, Gregory. *The Shape of the Liturgy*. London: Dacre Press, 1945.

Donaldson, Gordon. *The Making of the Scottish Prayer Book of 1637*. Edinburgh: Edinburgh University Press, 1954.

Donaldson, Gordon. *Scotland, Church and Nation Through Sixteen Centuries*. London: SCM Press, 1960.

Donaldson, Gordon. *The Scottish Reformation*. Cambridge: Cambridge University Press, 1960.

Dugmore, C. W. "The First Ten Years, 1549–59." *The English Prayer Book, 1549–1662*. Alcuin Club Publication. London: S.P.C.K., 1963.

Dugmore, C. W. *The Mass and The English Reformers*. London: Macmillan, 1958.

Dugmore, C. W., and Dickens, A. G., eds. *Studies in the Reformation, Luther to Hooker*. London: Athlone Press, 1980.

Elton, G. R. "The Commons' Supplication of 1532: Parliamentary Manoeuvres in the Reign of Henry VIII." *English Historical Review* 66 (1951): 507–34.

Elton, G. R. "The Evolution of a Reformation Statute." *English Historical Review* 6 (1949): 174–97.

Elton, G. R. "Parliament." *The Reign of Elizabeth I*. Problems in Focus. Ed. Christopher Haigh, pp. 79–100. London: Macmillan, 1984.

Elton, G. R. *The Parliament of England, 1559–1581*. Cambridge: Cambridge University Press, 1986.

Elton, G. R. *Policy and Police, the Enforcement of the Reformation in the Age of Thomas Cromwell*. Cambridge: Cambridge University Press, 1972.

Elton, G. R. "Politics and the Pilgrimage of Grace." *After the Reformation, Essays in Honour of J. H. Hexter*. Ed. Barbara Malament, pp. 25–56. Philadelphia, Pennsylvania: University of Pennsylvania Press, 1980.

Elton, G. R. "The Real Thomas More?" *Reformation Principle and Practice, Essays in Honour of Arthur Geoffrey Dickens*. Ed. Peter Newman Brooks, pp. 21–31. London: Scolar Press, 1980.

Elton, G. R. *Reform and Reformation, England, 1509–1585*. Cambridge, Massachusetts: Harvard University Press, 1977.

Elton, G. R. *Reform and Renewal, Thomas Cromwell and the Commonweal*. Cambridge: Cambridge University Press, 1973.

Elton, G. R. "Thomas Cromwell's Decline and Fall." *Cambridge Historical Journal* 10 (1951): 150–85.

Elton, G. R. "Thomas Cromwell Redivivus." *Archiv für Reformationgeschichte* 68 (1977): 192–208.

Emerson, Everett H. "Calvin and Covenant Theology." *Church History* 25 (1956): 136–44.

Emmison, F. G. *Tudor Secretary, Sir William Petre at Court and Home*. London: Longmans, Green, 1961.

Essays in Honor of C. J. McIlwain. Preface, Carl Wittke. Cambridge, Massachusetts: Harvard University Press, 1936.

Eusden, John Dykstra. *Puritans, Lawyers, and Politics in Early Seventeenth-Century England*. New Haven, Connecticut: Yale University Press, 1958.

Fincham, Kenneth. "Prelacy and Politics: Archbishop Abbot's Defense of Protestant Orthodoxy." *Historical Research* 61 (1988): 36–64.

Fincham, Kenneth, and Lake, Peter. "The Ecclesiastical Policy of King James I." *Journal of British Studies* 24 (April 1985): 169–207.

Finlayson, Michael G. *Historians, Puritanism, and the English Revolution, the Religious Factor in English Politics before and after the Interregnum.* Toronto: University of Toronto Press, 1983.

Fletcher, Anthony. "Factionalism in Town and Countryside: The Significance of Puritanism and Arminianism." *Studies in Church History* 16 (1979): 291–300.

Fletcher, Anthony. *The Outbreak of the English Civil War.* London: Edward Arnold, 1981.

Fletcher, Anthony, and Stevenson, John, eds. *Order and Disorder in Early Modern England.* New York: Cambridge University Press, 1985.

Foster, Andrew. "Church Politics of the 1630s." *Conflict in Early Stuart England: Studies in Religion and Politics, 1603–1642.* Eds. Richard Cust and Ann Hughes, pp. 193–223. London: Longman, 1989.

Foster, Stephen. "English Puritanism and the Progress of New England Institutions, 1630–1660." *Saints and Revolutionaries, Essays on Early American History.* Eds. David D. Hall, John M. Murrin, and Thad W. Tate, pp. 3–37. New York: W. W. Norton, 1983.

Foster, Stephen. *Their Solitary Way, the Puritan Social Ethic in the First Century of Settlement in New England.* New Haven, Connecticut: Yale University Press, 1971.

Foster, Walter Roland. *The Church before the Covenants, the Church of Scotland, 1596–1638.* Edinburgh: Scottish Academic Press, 1976.

Fox, Alastair. *Thomas More, History and Providence.* New Haven, Connecticut: Yale University Press, 1982.

Fox, Alistair, and Guy, John, eds. *Reassessing the Henrician Age, Humanism, Politics and Reform, 1500–1530.* Oxford: Basil Blackwell, 1986.

Frere, W. H. *The English Church in the Reigns of Elizabeth and James I.* A History of the English Church. London: Macmillan, 1904.

Fryer, W. H. "The High Churchmen of the Earlier Seventeenth Century." *Renaissance and Modern Studies* 5 (1961): 106–78.

Gairdner, James. *The English Church in the Sixteenth Century from the Accession of Henry VIII to the Death of Mary.* A History of the English Church. London: Macmillan, 1904.

Garbett, Cyril. *Church and State in England.* London: Hodder and Stoughton, 1950.

Gardiner, Samuel R. *History of England from the Accession of James I to the Outbreak of the Civil War.* 10 vols. London: Longmans, Green, 1883–1884.

Garrett, Christina H. *The Marian Exiles, a Study in the Origins of Elizabethan Puritanism.* Cambridge: Cambridge University Press, 1938; reprinted, 1966.

Gasquet, Francis, and Bishop, Edmund. *Edward VI and the Book of Common Prayer.* 2nd ed. London: John Hodges, 1891.

Gee, Henry. *The Elizabethan Clergy and the Settlement of Religion, 1558–1564.* Oxford: Clarendon Press, 1898.

Gee, Henry. *The Elizabethan Prayer-Book and Ornaments.* London: Macmillan, 1902.

George, Charles H., and George, Katherine. *The Protestant Mind of the English Reformation, 1570–1640.* Princeton, New Jersey: Princeton University Press, 1961.

George, Timothy. *John Robinson and the English Separatist Tradition*. Macon, Georgia: Mercer University Press, 1982.

Graves, M. A. R. "Thomas Norton the Parliament Man: an Elizabethan M. P., 1559–1581." *Historical Journal* 23 (1980): 17–35.

Gray, Stanley. "The Political Thought of John Winthrop." *New England Quarterly* 3 (1930): 681–705.

Greaves, Richard L. "John Knox, the Reformed Tradition, and the Development of Resistance Theory." *Journal of Modern History* 48 (1976): On-Demand Supplement.

Greaves, Richard L. "The Nature and Intellectual Milieu of the Political Principles in the Geneva Bible Marginalia." *Journal of Church and State* 22 (1980): 233–49.

Greaves, Richard L. "The Origins and Early Development of English Covenant Thought." *Historian* 31 (1968): 21–35.

Greaves, Richard L. "The Puritan-Nonconformist Tradition in England, 1560–1700, Historiographical Reflections." *Albion* 17 (1985): 449–86.

Greaves, Richard L. *Society and Religion in Elizabethan England*. Minneapolis, Minnesota: University of Minnesota Press, 1981.

Green, Ian. "Career Prospects and Clerical Conformity in the Early Stuart Church." *Past and Present* 90 (1981): 71–115.

Gura, Philip F. *A Glimpse of Sion's Glory, Puritan Radicalism in New England, 1620–1660*. Middletown, Connecticut: Wesleyan University Press, 1984.

Guth, Delloyd, and McKenna, John W., eds. *Tudor Rule and Revolution, Essays for G. R. Elton from his American Friends*. Cambridge: Cambridge University Press, 1982.

Guy, J. A. "Henry VIII and the *Praemunire* Manoeuvres of 1530–1531." *English Historical Review* 97 (1982): 481–503.

Guy, J. A. *The Public Career of Sir Thomas More*. New Haven, Connecticut: Yale University Press, 1980.

Gwatkin, H. M. *Church and State in England to the Death of Queen Anne*. London: Longmans, 1917.

Haigh, Christopher. "Anticlericalism and the English Reformation." *History* 68 (1983): 391–407.

Haigh, Christopher. "The Church of England, the Catholics and the People." *The Reign of Elizabeth I*, Problems in Focus. Ed. Christopher Haigh, pp. 195–29. London: Macmillan, 1984.

Haigh, Christopher. "The Continuity of Catholicism in the English Reformation." *Past and Present* 93 (1981): 37–69.

Haigh, Christopher, ed. "Introduction." *The English Reformation Revised*. Cambridge: Cambridge University Press, 1987.

Haigh, Christopher, ed. *The Reign of Elizabeth I*, Problems in Focus. London: Macmillan, 1984.

Haines, R. M. "Some Arguments in Favour of Plurality in the Elizabethan Church." *Studies in Church History*. Ed. G. J. Cuming, V, 166–92. Leiden: Brill, 1969.

Hall, David D. *The Faithful Shepherd, a History of the New England Ministry in the Seventeenth Century*. Chapel Hill, North Carolina: University of North Carolina Press, 1972.

Haller, William. *Foxe's Book of Martyrs and the Elect Nation*. London: Jonathan Cape, 1963.

Haller, William. *The Rise of Puritanism*. New York: Columbia University Press, 1938.

Hambrick-Stowe, Charles. *The Practice of Piety, Puritan Devotional Disciplines in*

Seventeenth-Century New England. Chapel Hill, North Carolina: University of North Carolina Press, 1982.

Hardwick, Charles. *A History of the Articles of Religion*. Cambridge: John Deighton, 1851.

Harrison, A. W. *Arminianism*. London: Duckworth, 1937.

Harrison, A. W. *The Beginnings of Arminianism to the Synod of Dort*. London: University of London Press, 1926.

Haugaard, William P. *Elizabeth and the English Reformation, the Struggle for a Stable Settlement of Religion*. Cambridge: Cambridge University Press, 1968.

Havran, Martin J. *Caroline Courtier, the Life of Lord Cottington*. London: Macmillan, 1973.

Havran, Martin J. *The Catholics in Caroline England*. Stanford, California: Stanford University Press, 1962.

Hay, Denys. "The Church of England in the Later Middle Ages." *History* 53 (1968): 35–50.

Heal, Felicity. "Archbishop Laud Revisited: Leases and Estate Management at Canterbury and Winchester before the Civil War." *Princes and Paupers in the English Church 1500–1800*. Eds. Rosemary O'Day and Felicity Heal, pp. 129–51. Totowa, New Jersey: Barnes and Noble, 1981.

Heal, Felicity. "The Bishops and the Act of Exchange of 1559." *Historical Journal* 17 (1974): 227–46.

Heal, Felicity. *Of Prelates and Princes, a Study of the Economic and Social Position of the Tudor Episcopate*. Cambridge: Cambridge University Press, 1980.

Heal, Felicity, and O'Day, Rosemary, eds. *Church and Society in England, Henry VIII to James I*. Problems in Focus. London: Macmillan Press, 1979.

Heath, Peter. *Church and Realm, 1272–1461, Conflict and Collaboration in an Age of Crisis*, Fontana History of England. London: Fontana Press, 1988.

Heath, Peter. *The English Parish Clergy on the Eve of the Reformation*. London: Routledge and Kegan Paul, 1969.

Henson, Herbert H. *Church and State in England*. London: S.P.C.K., 1930.

Hibbard, Carolyn M. *Charles I and the Popish Plot*. Chapel Hill, North Carolina: University of North Carolina Press, 1983.

Hill, Christopher. *Economic Problems of the Church, from Archbishop Whitgift to the Long Parliament*. Oxford: Clarendon Press, 1956.

Hill, Christopher. *Society and Puritanism in Pre-Revolutionary England*. New York: Shocken Books, 1964.

Hill, W. Speed, ed. *Studies in Richard Hooker, Essays Preliminary to an Edition of His Works*. Cleveland, Ohio: The Press of Case Western Reserve University, 1972.

Hirst, Derek. *Authority and Conflict, England, 1603–1658*. A New History of England. Cambridge, Massachusetts: Harvard University Press, 1986.

Holdsworth, William. *A History of English Law*. 7th ed., 14 vols. London: Methuen, 1956.

Holifield, E. Brooks. *The Covenant Sealed, the Development of Puritan Sacramental Theology in Old and New England, 1570–1720*. New Haven, Connecticut: Yale University Press, 1974.

Holland, S. M. "George Abbot: the Wanted Archbishop." *Church History* 56 (1987): 172–87.

Holmes, Peter. *Resistance and Compromise, the Political Thought of the Elizabethan Catholics*. Cambridge: Cambridge University Press, 1982.

Holmes, Peter J. "Robert Persons and an Unknown Political Pamphlet of 1593." *Recusant History* 17 (1985): 341–47.

Hopf, Constantin. *Martin Bucer and the English Reformation.* Oxford: Basil Blackwell, 1946.

Hudson, Winthrop S. *The Cambridge Connection and the Elizabethan Settlement of 1559.* Durham, North Carolina: Duke University Press, 1980.

Hudson, Winthrop S. *John Ponet (1516?–1556), Advocate of Limited Monarchy.* Chicago: University of Chicago Press, 1942.

Hughes, Philip. *The Reformation in England.* 5th, rev. ed., three vols. in one. London: Macmillan, 1963.

Hughes, Philip. *Rome and the Counter-Reformation in England.* London: Burns Oates, 1942.

Hughes, Richard T. "Henry Burton: The Making of a Puritan Revolutionary." *Journal of Church and State* 16 (1974): 421–34.

Hughes, Richard T. "Henry Burton, a Study in Religion and Politics in Seventeenth Century England," Ph.D. diss., University of Iowa, 1972.

Hurstfield, Joel. "Church and State, 1538–1612: the Task of the Cecils." *Freedom, Corruption, and Government in Elizabethan England.* Pp. 79–103. Cambridge, Massachusetts: Harvard University Press, 1973.

Hurstfield, Joel. "Gunpowder Plot and the Politics of Dissent." *Early Stuart Studies, Essays in Honor of David Harris Willson.* Ed. Howard S. Reinmuth, Jr., pp. 95–121. Minneapolis, Minnesota: University of Minnesota Press, 1970.

Ingram, T. D. *England and Rome.* London: Longmans, Green, 1892.

Jones, J. A. P. *King John and Magna Charta*, Seminar Studies in History. London: Longman, 1971.

Jones, Norman L. "An Elizabethan Bill for the Reformation of the Ecclesiastical Law." *Parliamentary History* 4 (1985): 171–87.

Jones, Norman L. *Faith by Statute, Parliament and the Settlement of Religion, 1559.* London: Royal Historical Society, 1982.

Jones, Norman L. "Profiting from Religious Reform, the Land Rush of 1559." *Historical Journal* 22 (1979): 279–94.

Jones, Whitney R. D. *The Mid-Tudor Crisis, 1539–1563.* London: Macmillan, 1973.

Jordan, W. K. *The Development of Religious Toleration in England from the Accession of James I to the Convention of the Long Parliament (1603–1640).* Cambridge, Massachusetts: Harvard University Press, 1936. Reprinted in Gloucester, Massachusetts: Peter Smith, 1965.

Jordan, W. K. *Edward VI, the Threshold of Power.* London: George Allen and Unwin, 1970.

Jordan, W. K. *Edward VI, the Young King, the Protectorship of the Duke of Somerset.* Cambridge, Massachusetts: Harvard University Press, 1968.

Judson, Margaret Atwood. *The Crisis of the Constitution, an Essay in Constitutional and Political Thought in England, 1603–1645.* New Brunswick, New Jersey: Rutgers University Press, 1949.

Kaufman, Peter Iver. *The "Polytyke Churche," Religion and Early Tudor Political Culture, 1485–1516.* Macon, Georgia: Mercer University Press, 1986.

Kautz, Arthur P. "The Selection of Jacobean Bishops." *Early Stuart Studies, Essays in Honor of David Harris Willson.* Ed. by Howard S. Reinmuth, Jr., pp. 152–79. Minneapolis, Minnesota: University of Minnesota Press, 1970.

Kelly, Henry Ansgar. *The Matrimonial Trials of Henry VIII.* Stanford, California: Stanford University Press, 1976.

Kelly, Michael. "The Submission of the Clergy." *TRHS*, fifth Series. 15 (1965): 97–119.

Kendall, R. T. *Calvin and English Calvinism to 1649*. Oxford: Oxford University Press, 1979.

Kirby, Ethyn W. "The Lay Feoffees: a Study in Militant Puritanism." *Journal of Modern History* 14 (1942): 1–25.

Kitching, Christopher. "The Disposal of Monastic and Chantry Lands." *Church and Society in England, Henry VIII to James I*. Eds. Felicity Heal and Rosemary O'Day, pp. 119–36. London: Macmillan Press, 1979.

Knappen, Marshall M. *Tudor Puritanism, a Chapter in the History of Idealism*. Chicago: University of Chicago Press, 1939.

Knowles, David. *The Religious Orders in England*. 3 vols. Cambridge: Cambridge University Press, 1959.

Knox, S. J. *Walter Travers, Paragon of Elizabethan Puritanism*. London: Methuen, 1962.

Kreider, Alan. *English Chantries, the Road to Destruction*. Cambridge, Massachusetts: Harvard University Press, 1979.

Lake, Peter. *Anglicans and Puritans? Presbyterianism and English Conformist Thought from Whitgift to Hooker*. London: Unwin Hyman, 1988.

Lake, Peter. "Calvinism and the English Church, 1570–1635." *Past and Present* 114 (1987): 32–76.

Lake, Peter. "Matthew Hutton: a Puritan Bishop?" *History* 64 (1979): 182–204.

Lake, Peter. *Moderate Puritans and the Elizabethan Church*. Cambridge: Cambridge University Press, 1982.

Lake, Peter. "Presbyterianism, the Idea of a National Church and the Argument from Divine Right." *Protestantism and the National Church in Sixteenth Century England*. Eds. Peter Lake and Maria Dowling, pp. 193–224. London: Croom Helm, 1987.

Lamont, William M. *Godly Rule, Politics and Religion, 1603–60*. London: Macmillan, 1969.

Lamont, William M. *Marginal Prynne, 1600–1669*. London: Routledge and Kegan Paul, 1963.

Lathbury, Thomas. *History of the Convocation of the Church of England from the Earliest Period to the Year 1742*. 2nd ed. London: J. Leslie, 1853.

Lee, Jr., Maurice. *Government by Pen: Scotland under James VI and I*. Urbana, Illinois: University of Illinois Press, 1980.

Lee, Jr., Maurice. *The Road to Revolution, Scotland under Charles I, 1625–37*. Urbana, Illinois: University of Illinois Press, 1985.

Lehmberg, Stanford E. "Archbishop Grindal and the Prophesyings." *The Historical Magazine of the Protestant Episcopal Church* 39 (1965): 87–145.

Lehmberg, Stanford E. *The Later Parliaments of Henry VIII, 1536–1547*. Cambridge: Cambridge University Press, 1977.

Lehmberg, Stanford E. *The Reformation Parliament, 1529–1536*. Cambridge: Cambridge University Press, 1970.

Lehmberg, Stanford E. "Supremacy and Vicegerency: a Re-Examination." *English Historical Review* 81 (1966): 225–35.

Levine, Mortimer. "Henry VIII's Use of His Spiritual and Temporal Jurisdictions in His Great Causes of Matrimony, Legitimacy, and Succession." *Historical Journal* 10 (1967): 3–10.

Levy, Leonard W. *Origins of the Fifth Amendment, the Right Against Self-Incrimina-tion.* London: Oxford University Press, 1968.

Lindley, K. J. "Lay Catholics of England in the Reign of Charles I." *Journal of Ecclesiastical History* 22 (1971): 192–221.

Little, David. *Religion, Order, and Law, a Study in Pre-Revolutionary England.* New York: Harper and Row, 1969.

Loach, Jennifer. "Conservatism and Consent in Parliament, 1547–59." *The Mid-Tudor Polity c. 1540–1560.* Eds. Robert Tittler and Jennifer Loach, pp. 9–28. Totowa, New Jersey: Rowman and Littlefield, 1980.

Loades, D. M. "The Enforcement of Reaction, 1553–1558." *Journal of Ecclesiastical History* 16 (1965): 54–66.

Loades, D. M. *The Oxford Martyrs.* New York: Stein and Day, 1970.

Loades, D. M. *The Reign of Mary Tudor.* New York: St. Martin's Press, 1979.

Lockyer, Roger. *Buckingham, the Life and Political Career of George Villiers, First Duke of Buckingham, 1592–1628.* London: Longman, 1981.

Lockyer, Roger. *The Early Stuarts, a Political History of England, 1603–1642.* London: Longman, 1989.

Logan, F. Donald. "The Henrician Canons." *Bulletin of the Institute of Historical Research* 47 (1974): 99–103.

MacCaffrey, Wallace T. *Queen Elizabeth and the Making of Policy, 1572–1588.* Princeton, New Jersey: Princeton University Press, 1981.

MacCaffrey, Wallace. *The Shaping of the Elizabethan Regime.* Princeton, New Jersey: Princeton University Press, 1968.

McConica, James Kesley. *English Humanists and Reformation Politics under Henry VIII and Edward VI.* Oxford: Clarendon Press, 1965.

McFarlane, K. B. *John Wycliffe and the Beginnings of English Nonconformity.* London: English Universities Press, 1952.

McGee, J. Sears. *The Godly Man in Stuart England, Anglicans, Puritans, and the Two Tables, 1620–1670.* New Haven, Connecticut: Yale University Press, 1976.

McGiffert, Michael. "Covenant, Crown, and Commons in Elizabethan Puritanism." *Journal of British Studies* 20 (Fall 1981): 32–52.

McGiffert, Michael. "God's Controversy with Jacobean England." *American Historical Review* 88 (1983): 1151–1174.

McGiffert, Michael. "Grace and Works: the Rise and Division of Covenant Divinity in Elizabethan Puritanism." *Harvard Theological Review* 75 (1982): 463–502.

McGinn, Donald J. *The Admonition Controversy.* New Brunswick, New Jersey: Rutgers University Press, 1949.

McGinn, Donald J. *John Penry and the Marprelate Controversy.* New Brunswick, New Jersey: Rutgers University Press, 1966.

McGrath, Patrick. "Elizabethan Catholicism: a Reconsideration." *Journal of Ecclesiastical History* 35 (1984): 414–28.

McGrath, Patrick. *Papists and Puritans under Elizabeth I.* London: Blandford Press, 1967.

Maclear, J. F. "New England and the Fifth Monarchy: the Quest for the Millennium in Early American Puritanism." *William and Mary Quarterly* 32 (1975): 223–60.

Maclear, James F. "Puritan Relations with Buckingham." *Huntington Library Quarterly* 21 (1958): 111–32.

McNeill, John T. *The History and Character of Calvinism.* New York: Oxford University Press, 1954.

Maguire, Mary Hume. "Attack of the Common Lawyers on the Oath *Ex Officio* As Administered in the Ecclesiastical Courts in England." *Essays in History and Political Theory in Honor of C. J. McIlwain*, Carl Witte, preface, pp. 199–229. Cambridge, Massachusetts: Harvard University Press, 1936.

Maitland, F. W. "Elizabethan Gleanings: I. 'Defender of the Faith, and So Forth.'" *The Collected Papers of Frederic William Maitland*. Ed. H. A. L. Fisher. 3 vols. Cambridge: Cambridge University Press, 1911.

Malament, Barbara, ed. *After the Reformation, Essays in Honor of J. H. Hexter*. Philadelphia: University of Pennsylvania Press, 1980.

Manning, Roger B. "The Crisis of Episcopal Authority During the Reign of Elizabeth I." *Journal of British Studies* 11 (November 1971): 1–25.

Marius, Richard. *Thomas More, a Biography*. New York: Alfred A. Knopf, 1984.

Mason, Thomas A. *Serving God and Mammon, William Juxon, 1582–1663, Bishop of London, Lord High Treasurer of England, and Archbishop of Canterbury*. Newark, New Jersey: University of Delaware Press, 1985.

Mattingly, Garrett. "William Allen and Catholic Propaganda in England." *Aspects de la Propaganda Religieuse*. Ed. G. Berthoud, *et. al.*, pp. 325–39. Geneva: Droz, 1957.

Meyer, Arnold Oskar. "Charles I and Rome." *American Historical Review*. 19 (1913): 13–26.

Meyer, Arnold Oskar. *England and the Catholic Church under Queen Elizabeth*. Trans. J. R. McKee. London: Kegan, Paul, 1916. Reprinted in New York: Barnes and Noble, 1967.

Meyer, Carl S. *Elizabeth I and the Religious Settlement of 1559*. Saint Louis, Missouri: Concordia Publishing House, 1960.

Micklethwaite, John T. *The Ornaments of the Rubric*. Alcuin Club Tracts, no. 1. London: Longmans, Green, 1897.

Miller, Perry. "The Marrow of Puritan Divinity." *Publications of the Colonial Society of Massachusetts*, vol. 32, *Transactions*, 1933–1937, pp. 247–300. Boston, Massachusetts: Colonial Society of Massachusetts, 1937.

Miller, Perry. *Orthodoxy in Massachusetts, 1630–1650, a Genetic Study*. Cambridge, Massachusetts: Harvard University Press, 1933.

Milsom, S. F. C. "Richard Hunne's 'Praemunire.'" *English Historical Review* 76 (1961): 80–82.

Milward, Peter. *Religious Controversies of the Elizabethan Age, a Survey of Printed Sources*. Lincoln, Nebraska: University of Nebraska Press, 1977.

Milward, Peter. *Religious Controversies of the Jacobean Age, a Survey of Printed Sources*. Lincoln, Nebraska: University of Nebraska Press, 1978.

Møller, Jens G. "The Beginnings of Puritan Covenant Theology." *Journal of Ecclesiastical History* 14 (1963): 46–67.

Morgan, Edmund S. *The Puritan Dilemma, the Story of John Winthrop*. Boston: Little, Brown, 1958.

Morgan, Edmund S. *Visible Saints*. New York: New York University Press, 1963.

Morgan, John. *Godly Learning, Puritan Attitudes Towards Reason, Learning, and Education, 1560–1640*. Cambridge: Cambridge University Press, 1986.

Morrill, John, "The Attack on the Church of England in the Long Parliament, 1640–1642." *History, Society and Churches, Essays in Honour of Owen Chadwick*. Eds. Derek Beales and Geoffrey Best, pp. 105–24. Cambridge: Cambridge University Press, 1985.

Morrill, John, ed. "Introduction." *Reactions to the English Civil War, 1642–1649. Problems in Focus.* London: Macmillan, 1982.

Morrill, John. "The Religious Context of the English Civil War." *TRHS*, fifth series. 34 (1984): 155–78.

Morris, Christopher. *Political Thought in England, Tyndale to Hooker.* London: Oxford University Press, 1953.

Murray, John Courtney. "Bellarmine on the Indirect Power." *Theological Studies* 9 (1948): 491–535.

Neale, J. E. *Elizabeth I and Her Parliaments, 1559–1581.* London: Jonathan Cape, 1953.

Neale, J. E. *Elizabeth I and Her Parliaments, 1584–1601.* London: Jonathan Cape, 1957.

Neale, John. "The Elizabethan Acts of Supremacy and Uniformity." *English Historical Review* 65 (1950): 304–332.

Neale, J. E. "Parliament and the Articles of Religion." *English Historical Review* 67 (1952): 510–21.

New, John F. H. *Anglican and Puritan, the Basis of Their Opposition, 1558–1640.* Stanford, California: Stanford University Press, 1964.

Nicholson, Graham. "The Act of Appeals and the English Reformation." *Law and Government under the Tudors, Essays Presented to Sir Geoffrey Elton, Regius Professor of Modern History in the University of Cambridge, on the Occasion of His Retirement.* Eds. Claire Cross, David Loades, and J. J. Scarisbrick, pp. 19–30. Cambridge: Cambridge University Press, 1988.

Notestein, Wallace. *The House of Commons, 1604–1610.* New Haven, Connecticut: Yale University Press, 1971.

O'Day, Rosemary. *The English Clergy, the Emergence and Consolidation of a Profession, 1558–1642.* Leicester: Leicester University Press, 1979.

O'Day, Rosemary, and Heal, Felicity, eds. *Princes and Paupers in the English Church, 1500–1800.* Totowa, New Jersey: Barnes and Noble, 1981.

Ogle, Arthur. *The Tragedy of the Lollard's Tower.* Oxford: Pen-In-Hand Publishing Company, 1949.

Olsen, V. Norskov. *John Foxe and the Elizabethan Church.* Berkeley, California: University of California Press, 1973.

Ottley, Robert L. *Lancelot Andrewes.* London: Methuen, 1894.

Pantin, W. A. *The English Church in the Fourteenth Century.* Cambridge: Cambridge University Press, 1955.

Parker, T. M. "Arminianism and Laudianism in Seventeenth-Century England." *Studies in Church History.* Eds. C. W. Dugmore and Charles Duggan, I, 20–34. London: Nelson, 1964.

Parmiter, Geoffrey de C. *The King's Great Matter, a Study of Anglo-Papal Relations, 1527–1534.* London: Longmans, 1967.

Patterson, W. B. "King James I's Call for an Ecumenical Council." *Studies in Church History.* Eds. G. J. Cuming and Derek Baker, VII, 267–75. Cambridge: Cambridge University Press, 1971.

Pauck, Wilhelm. "Martin Bucer's Conception of a Christian State." *Princeton Theological Review* 36 (1928): 80–88.

Pearson, A. F. Scott. *Church and State, Political Aspects of Sixteenth Century Puritanism.* Cambridge: Cambridge University Press, 1928.

Pearson, A. F. Scott. *Thomas Cartwright and Elizabethan Puritanism, 1535–1603.* Cambridge: Cambridge University Press, 1925.

Peters, Robert. "John Hales and the Synod of Dort." *Studies in Church History.* Eds.
    G. J. Cuming and Derek Baker, VII, 277–88. Cambridge: Cambridge Univer-
    sity Press, 1971.
Pickthorn, Kenneth. *Early Tudor Government, Henry VIII.* Cambridge: Cambridge
    University Press, 1934.
Pierce, William. *An Historical Introduction to the Marprelate Tracts, a Chapter in the
    Evolution of Religion and Civil Liberty in England.* London: Archibald Con-
    stable, 1908.
Platt, John. "Eirenical Anglicans at the Synod of Dort." *Reform and the Reforma-
    tion: England and the Continent, c1500–c1750.* Ed. Derek Baker, pp. 221–44.
    Oxford: Basil Blackwell, 1979.
Pogson, Rex H. "The Legacy of the Schism: Confusion, Continuity, and Change in the
    Marian Clergy." *The Mid-Tudor Polity, c. 1540–1560.* Eds. Robert Tittler and
    Jennifer Loach, pp. 116–36. Totowa, New Jersey: Rowman and Littlefield, 1980.
Pogson, Rex H. "Reginald Pole and the Priorities of Government in Mary Tudor's
    Church." *Historical Journal* 18 (1975): 3–20.
Pogson, R. H. "Revival and Reform in Mary Tudor's Church: a Question of Money."
    Journal of Ecclesiastical History 25 (1974): 249–65.
Pollard, A. F. *Factors in Modern History.* 3rd ed. London: Constable, 1932.
Pollard, A. F. *The History of England from the Accession of Edward VI, to the Death
    of Elizabeth (1547–1603).* London: Longmans, Green, 1911.
Pollen, J. H. *The English Catholics in the Reign of Queen Elizabeth.* London, 1920.
    Reprinted in New York: Burt Franklin, 1971.
Porter, H. C. *Reformation and Reaction in Tudor Cambridge.* Cambridge: Cam-
    bridge University Press, 1958.
Pritchard, Arnold. *Catholic Loyalism in Elizabethan England.* Chapel Hill, North
    Carolina: University of North Carolina Press, 1979.
Pruett, Gordon E. "Thomas Cranmer's Progress in the Doctrine of the Eucharist,
    1535–48." *Historical Magazine of the Protestant Episcopal Church* 45 (1976):
    439–58.
Ratcliff, E. C. "The Liturgical Work of Archbishop Cranmer." *Journal of Ecclesiasti-
    cal History* 7 (1956): 189–203.
Read, Conyers. *Lord Burghley and Queen Elizabeth.* New York: Alfred Knopf, 1960.
Read, Conyers. *Mr. Secretary Cecil and Queen Elizabeth.* New York: Alfred Knopf,
    1961.
Redworth, G. "A Study in the Formulation of Policy: the Genesis and Evolution of the
    Act of Six Articles." *Journal of Ecclesiastical History* 37 (1986): 42–67.
Reinmuth, Howard, ed. *Early Stuart Studies, Essays in Honor of David Harris
    Willson.* Minneapolis, Minnesota: University of Minnesota Press, 1970.
Richardson, Cyril C. *Zwingli and Cranmer on the Eucharist.* Evanston, Illinois:
    Seabury-Western Theological Seminary, 1949.
Ridley, Jasper. *The Life and Times of Mary Tudor.* London: Weidenfeld and Nichol-
    son, 1973.
Ridley, Jasper. *Statesman and Saint, Cardinal Wolsey, Sir Thomas More, and the
    Politics of Henry VIII.* New York: Viking Press, 1983.
Roberts, B. Dew. *Mitre and Musket, John Williams, Lord Keeper, Archbishop of
    York, 1582–1650.* London: Oxford University Press, 1938.
Roper, William. *The Life of Sir Thomas More.* In *Two Tudor Lives.* Richard S.
    Sylvester and Davis P. Harding. New Haven, Connecticut: Yale University
    Press, 1962.

Rose, Eliot. *Cases of Conscience, Alternatives Open to Recusants and Puritans under Elizabeth I and James I.* London: Cambridge University Press, 1975.

Ruigh, Robert E. *The Parliament of 1624, Politics and Foreign Policy.* Cambridge, Massachusetts: Harvard University Press, 1971.

Rupp, E. G. *Studies in the Making of the English Protestant Tradition.* Cambridge: Cambridge University Press, 1947, reprinted 1966.

Russell, Conrad. *The Crisis of Parliaments, English History, 1509–1660.* London: Oxford University Press, 1971.

Russell, Conrad, ed. *The Origins of the English Civil War.* Problems in Focus. London: Macmillan, 1973.

Russell, Conrad. "The Parliamentary Career of John Pym, 1621–9." *The English Commonwealth, 1547–1640, Essays in Politics and Society.* Eds. Peter Clark, Alan G. R. Smith, and Nicholas Tyacke, pp. 147–65. New York: Harper and Row, 1979.

Russell, Conrad. *Parliaments and English Politics, 1621–1629.* Oxford: Clarendon Press, 1979.

Scarisbrick, J. J. "Clerical Taxation in England, 1485 to 1547." *Journal of Ecclesiastical History* 11 (1960): 41–54.

Scarisbrick, J. J. *Henry VIII.* London: Eyre and Spottiswoode, 1968.

Scarisbrick, J. J. "The Pardon of the Clergy, 1531." *Cambridge Historical Journal* 12 (1956): 22–39.

Scarisbrick, J. J. *The Reformation and the English People.* Oxford: Basil Blackwell, 1984.

Scholz, Robert F. "Clerical Consociation in Massachusetts Bay: Reassessing the New England Way and Its Origins." *William and Mary Quarterly* 29 (1972): 391–414.

Schwartz, Hillel. "Arminianism and the English Parliament, 1624–1629." *Journal of British Studies* 12 (May 1973): 41–68.

Seaver, Paul S. *The Puritan Lectureships, the Politics of Religious Dissent, 1560–1662.* Stanford, California: Stanford University Press, 1970.

Seaver, Paul. *Wallington's World, a Puritan Artisan in Seventeenth-Century London.* Stanford, California: Stanford University Press, 1985.

Seidman, Aaron B. "Church and State in the Early Years of the Massachusetts Bay Colony." *New England Quarterly* 18 (1945): 211–33.

Seton-Watson, R. W., ed. *Tudor Studies Presented to A. F. Pollard.* New ed. London: Russell and Russell, 1970.

Sharpe, Kevin. "Archbishop Laud." *History Today* 33 (August, 1983): 26–30.

Sharpe, Kevin. "Archbishop Laud and the University of Oxford." *History and Imagination, Essays in Honor of H. R. Trevor-Roper.* Eds. Hugh Lloyd-Jones, Valerie Pearl, and Blair Worden, pp. 146–64. New York: Holmes and Meier, 1982.

Shaw, Duncan, ed. *Reformation and Revolution.* Edinburgh: Saint Andrew Press, 1967.

Shriver, Frederick. "Hampton Court Re-visited: James I and the Puritans." *Journal of Ecclesiastical History* 33 (1982): 48–71.

Shriver, Frederick. "Orthodoxy and Diplomacy: James I and the Vorstius Affair." *English Historical Review* 85 (1970): 449–74.

Simpson, Richard. *Edmund Campion, Jesuit Protomartyr of England.* London: Burns and Oates, 1907.

Skinner, Quentin. *The Foundations of Modern Political Thought, Volume Two, The Age of Reformation.* Cambridge: Cambridge University Press, 1978.

Slack, Paul. "Religious Protest and Urban Authority: the Case of Henry Sherfield, Iconoclast, 1633." *Studies in Church History*. Ed. Derek Baker, IX, 295–302. Cambridge: Cambridge University Press, 1972.

Smith, A. L. *Church and State in the Middle Ages*. Oxford: Clarendon Press, 1913.

Smith, H. Maynard. *Pre-Reformation England*. London: Macmillan, 1938.

Smith, Lacey Baldwin. "Henry VIII and the Protestant Triumph." *American Historical Review* 71 (1966): 1237–1264.

Smith, Lacey Baldwin. *Henry VIII, the Mask of Royalty*. Boston, Massachusetts: Houghton Mifflin, 1971.

Smith, Lacey Baldwin. *Tudor Prelates and Politics, 1536–1558*. Princeton, New Jersey: Princeton University Press, 1953.

Solt, Leo F., et al. "The Bishops," Appendix G. *Complete Prose Works of John Milton*. Vol. 1. New Haven, Connecticut: Yale University Press, 1953.

Sommerville, J. P. *Politics and Ideology in England, 1603–1640*. New York: Longman, 1986.

Sommerville, J. P. "The Royal Supremacy and Episcopacy 'Jure Divino', 1603–1640." *Journal of Ecclesiastical History* 34 (1983): 548–58.

Southgate, W. M. *John Jewel and the Problem of Doctrinal Authority*. Cambridge, Massachusetts: Harvard University Press, 1962.

Southgate, William. "The Marian Exiles and the Influence of John Calvin." *History* 27 (1942): 148–52.

Spalding, James C. "The Reformatio Legum Ecclesiasticarum of 1552 and the Furthering of Discipline in England." *Church History* 39 (1970): 162–71.

Starkey, David. *The Reign of Henry VIII, Personalities and Politics*. London: George Philip, 1985.

Stearns, Raymond Phineas. *Congregationalism in the Dutch Netherlands, the Rise and Fall of the English Congregational Classis, 1621–1635*. Studies in Church History. Chicago: American Society of Church History, 1940.

Stevenson, David. *The Scottish Revolution, 1637–1644, the Triumph of the Covenanters*. Newton Abbot: David and Charles, 1973.

Stoever, William K. B. *'A Fair and Easie Way to Heaven,' Covenant Theology and Antinomianism in Early Massachusetts*. Middletown, Connecticut: Wesleyan University Press, 1978.

Sykes, Norman. *The English Religious Tradition*. London: SCM Press, 1953.

Tait, James. "The Declaration of Sports for Lancashire (1617)." *English Historical Review* 32 (1917): 561–68.

Thompson, J. V. P. *Supreme Governor, a Study of Elizabethan Ecclesiastical Policy and Circumstance*. London: S.P.C.K., 1940.

Thornley, I. D. "The Destruction of Sanctuary." *Tudor Studies Presented to A. F. Pollard*. Ed. R. W. Seton-Watson, new ed., pp. 182–207. London: Russell and Russell, 1970.

Thorp, Malcolm R. "Religion and the Wyatt Rebellion of 1554." *Church History* 47 (1978): 363–80.

Tittler, Robert, and Loach, Jennifer, eds. *The Mid-Tudor Polity, c. 1540–1560*. Totowa, New Jersey: Rowman and Littlefield, 1980.

Todd, Margo. *Christian Humanism and the Puritan Social Order*, Ideas in Context. Cambridge: Cambridge University Press, 1987.

Tomlinson, Howard, ed. *Before the English Civil War*. London: Macmillan, 1983.

Trevor-Roper, H. R. *Archbishop Laud, 1573–1645*. 2nd ed. London: Macmillan, 1962.

Trevor-Roper, H. R. *Catholics, Anglicans, and Puritans, Seventeenth Century Essays*. Chicago: University of Chicago Press, 1988.

Trimble, William. *The Catholic Laity in Elizabethan England, 1558–1603*. Cambridge, Massachusetts: Harvard University Press, 1964.

Trinterud, Leonard J. "The Origins of Puritanism." *Church History* 20 (1951): 37–57.

Tyacke, Nicholas. *Anti-Calvinists, the Rise of English Arminianism, c. 1590–1640*. Oxford Historical Monographs. Oxford: Clarendon Press, 1987.

Tyacke, Nicholas. "Arminianism in England, in Religion and Politics, 1604 to 1640." D. Phil. diss., Oxford, 1968.

Tyacke, Nicholas, and White, Peter. "Debate: The Rise of Arminianism Reconsidered." *Past and Present* 115 (1987): 201–29.

Tyacke, Nicholas. "Puritanism, Arminianism, and Counter-Revolution." *The Origins of the English Civil War*. Ed. Conrad Russell, pp. 119–43. London: Macmillan, 1973.

Underdown, David. *Revel, Riot, and Rebellion, Popular Politics and Culture in England, 1603–1660*. Oxford: Oxford University Press, 1987.

Underwood, A. C. *A History of the English Baptists*. London: Carey Kingsgate Press, 1947.

Usher, Roland G. *The Reconstruction of the English Church*. 2 vols. London: Appleton, 1910. Reprinted in Farnborough, England: Gregg International, 1969.

Usher, Roland G. *The Rise and Fall of the High Commission*. Oxford: Clarendon Press, 1913, reprinted in 1968.

von Rohr, John. "Covenant and Assurance in Early English Puritanism." *Church History* 34 (1965): 195–203.

von Rohr, John. *The Covenant of Grace in Puritan Thought*, American Academy of Religion Studies in Religion. Atlanta, Georgia: Scholars Press, 1986.

Wadkins, Timothy H. "The Percy-'Fisher' Controversies and the Ecclesiastical Politics of Jacobean Anti-Catholicism, 1622–1625." *Church History* 57 (1988): 153–69.

Wallace, Jr., Dewey D. *Puritans and Predestination, Grace in English Protestant Theology, 1525–1695*. Chapel Hill, North Carolina: University of North Carolina Press, 1982.

Walzer, Michael. *The Revolution of the Saints*. Cambridge, Massachusetts: Harvard University Press, 1965.

Watkins, Owen C. *The Puritan Experience*. London: Routledge and Kegan Paul, 1972.

Watts, Michael R. *The Dissenters, from the Reformation to the French Revolution*. Oxford: Clarendon Press, 1978.

Waugh, W. T. "The Great Statute of Praemunire." *English Historical Review* 37 (1922): 173–205.

Welsby, Paul A. *George Abbot, the Unwanted Archbishop, 1562–1633*. London: S.P.C.K., 1962.

White, B. R. *The English Separatist Tradition from the Marian Martyrs to the Pilgrim Fathers*. London: Oxford University Press, 1971.

White, Peter. "The Rise of Arminianism Reconsidered." *Past and Present* 101 (1983): 34–54.

Whitney, Edward Allen. "Erastianism and Divine Right." *Huntington Library Quarterly* 2 (1939): 373–98.

Willson, David Harris. *King James VI and I*. London: Jonathan Cape, 1956.

Winslow, Ola E. *Master Roger Williams, a Biography*. New York: Macmillan, 1957.

Woodward, G. W. O. *The Dissolution of the Monasteries*. London: Blandford, 1966.

Wormald, Jenny. "Gunpowder, Treason, and Scots." *Journal of British Studies* 24 (May 1985): 141–68.

Wunderli, Richard. "Pre-Reformation London Summoners and the Murder of Richard Hunne." *Journal of Ecclesiastical History* 33 (1982): 209–24.

Zagorin, Perez. *The Court and the Country*. London: Routledge and Kegan Paul, 1969.

Zakai, Avihu. "The Gospel of Reformation: the Origins of the Great Puritan Reformation." *Journal of Ecclesiastical History* 37 (1986): 504–602.

Zaller, Robert. *The Parliament of 1621, a Study in Constitutional Conflict*. Berkeley, California: University of California Press, 1971.

Ziff, Larzer. *The Career of John Cotton*. Princeton, New Jersey: Princeton University Press, 1962.

Index